BOOKS BY ADAM SMITH

The Money Game

Supermoney

Powers of Mind

POWERS OF MIND

POWERS

OF MIND

ADAM
SMITH

RANDOM HOUSE
NEW YORK

Library of Congress Cataloging in Publication
Data
Goodman, George J. W.
Powers of mind.
Bibliography: p.
1. Psychology. I. Title.
BF121.G65   150   75-10310
ISBN 0-394-49832-1
Manufactured in the United States of America
9 8 7 6 5 4 3 2
First Edition

Grateful acknowledgment is made to the following for permission to reprint previously published song lyrics:

C'Est Music/Quakenbush Music Ltd.: For the
lyrics from the second verse of "Haven't Got
Time for the Pain" by Carly Simon and Jacob
Brackman (page 47). Copyright © 1974 by C'Est
Music and Maya Productions Ltd. All Rights
Reserved. Used by permission.

Bob Dylan and Warner Bros. Music: For the
selected lyrics from "Mr. Tambourine Man,"
music and words by Bob Dylan (page 47). Copyright © 1964 M. Witmark & Sons. All Rights
Reserved. Used by permission.

Contents

[v i i]

CONTENTS

Contents

[ix]

Contents

[x i]

I:

This Side of Paradigm

MYSTERY: TIME, SPACE, INFINITY, STATISTICAL ABERRATION

Nel mezzo del cammin di nostra vita
Mi ritrovai per una selva oscura . . .

O N the first day of Christmas, my alleged true love gave to me a silver pillbox. Infuriating. It was true, of course, that gentlemen of finance consumed pain-easing pills, traveled with them, and even offered them to each other, but then, there was a lot of pain around. Fund managers chewed absently on antacids, wondering where the last hundred million went to so quickly. When you met them, they might offer you one, as if proffering a cigarette or a Life Saver. A high-risk, high-stress profession, wrote one psychologist in a paper. The University of San Francisco offered a course for clergymen, a Laboratory in Pastoral Ministries, Course #261, to "communicate with persons with unusual needs . . . such as the sick, the aging, broken families, alcoholics, ethnic minorities, homosexuals, stockbrokers." No wonder drug companies had such nice profit margins, and sold at such high premiums.

Two gallants of my acquaintance wrote one of the best short reports I have ever read. The university portfolio they managed was down by a little over two hundred million dollars. (Do you know how long it takes to *raise* two hundred million dollars?) They remained fully invested, they said, because things were so bad they thought they could get no worse. "The light we saw at the end of the tunnel," they said, "was a freight train coming the other way."

Some people disappeared from the money business, and some disappeared right off the planet, ahead of schedule. If somebody had a heart attack, we said, oh, sorry, when will he be back in the office? It was certainly a statistical aberration when I lost my panel, the investment strategy panel I moderated at the annual convention. My panelists were in their thirties and forties and not fat and they liked their work, so statistically they should not have exited with one heart attack, one ulcer attack, and one something I forget. We recruited another panel without even a moment of silence for our fallen comrades. Very cool, very macho, the show must go on.

I think what I had in mind when I began my research was that I would do some research on health. I would leave my nine-foot teak desk, my phone with all its buttons lit up, and my totally filled in Month at a Glance calendar, go find some answers, and be welcomed back to the business community, like the first Arapaho that came back to his horseless tribe with a Pawnee pinto. Look, fellas, now we can go twice as fast. I thought this might take a couple of months but well worth it, very important. (I could return the silver pillbox with the appropriate insult.) There was something else, misty, unarticulated, in this program. One of my convention panelists had told me what his plans were, just as soon as he had enough time and enough money. He certainly had enough money, but he had had time back when he thought he didn't, and then he didn't.

The first physicians I consulted in this venture had all the same symptoms as my compatriots. We have to take it easier, they said wisely. Then they would answer the phone, rub their eyes, and say, yes, they would cover for their buddy till midnight. And then they would say, what's happening, my Gawd, my stocks are down 40 percent, we may have to sell our ski condominium unless we raise our fees.

I would not have believed, at the outset, that I would be spending any time with exotics like Tibetan lamas and witch doctors and gentlemen who had beards and wore funny clothes. I did not have a beard and I did not own any funny clothes. I

[4]

would not have believed that I would ever sit in a room chanting a Sanskrit syllable, or drawing a lotus in the air with a $1.98 G. Schirmer recorder.

Minds. The trouble is minds, not organic medicine, not some germ that comes flying through the air looking for a home. This is Dr. Hans Selye, sixty-eight years old, the distinguished dean of stress medicine. Stress is "a physiologic response inappropriate to the situation." Misfired signals between mind and body. The physiologic response is the caveman's response when the shadow of a pterodactyl falls over him. Adrenal secretions increase and muscles tense and the coagulation chemistry gets ready to resist wounds. Fight or flight. But what pterodactyl is this? They tell you: the market is down twenty points, or, the vice-president wants to see you, or, this whole operation is going to be shut down and moved to Chicago. Blam, pterodactyl time. Gives you, says Dr. Selye, headaches, insomnia, high blood pressure, sinus, ulcers, rheumatism, cardiovascular and kidney disease. And more. One from Column A, one from Column B. Some people have a pterodactyl every day. Why? An imbalance, says Dr. Selye, an imbalance. In what? In living. Western medicine doesn't extend its authority there, except to say take it easy, take off some weight, watch your diet.

So: lots of explorers have headed west by going east, saying, there must be a better way, and that was how this venture in—what? It's hard to define, some sort of psychology or awareness, maybe. That was how it began. Nonexistent pterodactyls flapping their great wings over fallen security analysts.

Some of my opening questions were:

Could we really learn to control our internal processes with our heads instead of with pills? (If true, I made a note, sell drug companies.)

Could we learn to pop ourself into an alpha state? What is an alpha state? What happens if we succeed?

If someone can't hear and they have one session with a psychologist and fifteen minutes' worth of hypnotic induction, and suddenly they say, "I can hear!" what just happened in their brains?

What about all these claims for meditation? What do they mean by meditation? (I had just read an article in a technical journal.)

Is it true that a Sanskrit sound has a different effect on your head than one in English? (I don't know where I got that one.)

The field was not well marked. For example, in the great pharmacology textbook *The Pharmacological Basis of Therapeutics*, Goodman and Gilman—it has the same lock on its field that Samuelson does in economics—three phrases begin to recur when you get to the effects of mind, or the interaction of some substance and the mind. *The etiology is unknown.* We don't know the cause. *The site is unknown.* We don't know exactly where it happens. *The mechanism is unknown.* We're not exactly sure how it happens.

Unknown, unknown, pictures of elephants and white space in the middle of the old maps of Africa.

At one juncture I sent a careful letter to an official in the National Institute of Mental Health in suburban Washington. I wanted to know, in this instance, about placebos—sugar pills —and I detailed all my references and the work done so far, and asked: where can I go to find more? Who is doing the work in this field?

"*You* are," the answer came. "The field is open. Please let us hear from you when you finish."

In an unmarked field, it is easy to wander. Why on earth would I ever have read six years' worth of a British medical journal called *Brain*? Sheer inertia. I looked up one article on consciousness and then—look, the editor of *Brain* is Lord Brain. If you sent him a post card, addressed only "Brain, *Brain*, London," would it get there? Was his name Brain already, or did he take "Lord Brain" as a title because he was the editor of *Brain*? Let's see what goes on here in Brain's *Brain*. (You do not have to turn to the back for the answer. The distinguished neurophysiologist Lord Brain, now deceased, was born Russell Brain, and the post card "Brain, *Brain,* London" would have reached him, but faster if you added "Harley Street" and the zip code.)

It occurred to me that all the answers were not in *Brain* or even in medicine as we know it, fabulous as it is. There is a case in one of the journals about a Nigerian princeling in London who got sick and depressed, about two generations ago. He sent home for the witch doctor, since the Harley Street crowd couldn't do much for him. The witch doctor chanted whatever witch doctors chant, gave him a magic extract of a plant, and the Nigerian recovered. The magic extract came from a plant called *Rauwolfia serpentina,* named by a French botanist.

A generation went by, and Western medicine sought to control high blood pressure and to calm people with tranquilizers. The detail salesmen from the big drug companies, CIBA and Riker and Squibb, fanned out to doctors and hospitals with their great new drugs, and one of the great new drugs was reserpine, called Serpasil or Rauwiloid or Raudixin, depending on the drug company. And what did reserpine come from? Of course, *Rauwolfia serpentina.* The drug companies found it and wrote it up in learned journals and analyzed it; the witch doctor didn't have any journals, he got it from his daddy, who got it from *his* daddy, who was one hundred years ahead of CIBA and Riker and Squibb, and he was late because Ayurvedic medicine in India knew *Rauwolfia* when the ancestors of the Harley Street crowd were staining themselves blue.

I had to go back to school. I brought certain abilities as a student and the willingness to be an utter fool, to make up for a native skepticism. Some of the customs had changed. I knew the dorms were coed, but when did they make the bathrooms coed?

One evening in a movie theater near the University of California campus in Berkeley, the following conversation took place in the seats behind me:

She: Say, I dig George.

He: Mmmmmmmmm.

She: I mean, I really dig George's bod.

He: *(a grunt)*
She: Why don't we have a threesome or a fivesome sometime?
He: Okay.

Often I felt a stranger in a strange land, or an anthropologist with a new tribe. What happened to the *even* numbers?

Strange schools, sometimes. Some trips, you go to Abercrombie & Fitch to get your mountaineering boots or your fishing vest. I had to buy tie-dyed jeans, because my new classmates were staring at my suit and tie.

I followed where the trail led. I met more Nobel Prize winners than I knew there were. I met biofeedback technicians who said people could train control of their heartbeats. I met meditators who said meditation was more restorative than sleep.

And: an astronaut who had a mystic experience on the way back from the moon. A pro quarterback who could send signals to his wide receiver by telepathy, or something like telepathy. A blue-eyed British witch doctor, apprenticed in Lesotho or Botswana, who could track lions by scent; Manhattan traffic gave him a tic, I had to help him across the street.

And: masters of martial arts, aikido and kung fu, who said those arts repatterned brains. Bushels of psychiatrists and pecks of gurus. A gentleman who could push a knitting needle through his arm, command the blood to stop, and it would. Another gentleman who could smoke a cigar and send his mind to Jupiter and Mercury, simply by having it clear.

Some of it gets very far out. That was a phrase I learned from my new classmates. Far out.

There is a peculiar characteristic to this field. It is never easy to explain, and it is impossible to photograph.

THREE STORIES
IN WHICH SOMETHING
IS GOING ON WHICH
IS VERY HARD TO
PHOTOGRAPH

TWO of these stories have a personal element and one is from a journal. They are here to show an odd power—even mysterious—which is present but not articulated, in the relationship of mind and body.

Stewart Alsop Doesn't Get Off the Train in Baltimore

Stewart Alsop was a tough-minded, brilliant reporter, a well-known correspondent from the wars and from Washington. He wrote a weekly essay on the last text page of *Newsweek* that was as tightly constructed as a sonnet. We exchanged literary references and had lunch perhaps once a year. Then he got leukemia. He wrote about the experience in his weekly essay: most of us, he said, spend our lives behind a "thick carapace," where we live, from fear, emotions unexposed, defended, not totally alive. His essays under this "sentence of execution," as he called it, were the best pieces of writing he had ever done.

I met him for lunch at the Metropolitan Club in Washington. He looked surprisingly fit. I knew he had been in and out of the hospital; he had skipped a number of columns. He had this one with him that day.

> I woke up suddenly, feeling very wide awake, pulled the light cord, and sat straight up in bed.
>
> "We'll be stopping in Baltimore," I announced loudly, in an authoritative voice. I looked around me. A private car, evidently. Good of the railroad people to supply those fruits, and all those flowers. The furniture looked a bit shoddy, but what can one expect these days? I got up to explore.
>
> The car was swaying heavily—the roadbed must be a disgrace. I supported myself on a table, and then a desk. Then there was a space of empty floor. I was halfway across it when the car gave a lurch, and I fell down. I sat on the floor for a bit, getting my bearings, then scrambled to my feet again, and opened a narrow green door. A locker, with my own clothes in it. I opened another door —a small bathroom.
>
> Then I came to a much bigger door, and opened it, and leaned against the doorjamb. The swaying had stopped—the train, apparently, had halted. Outside was what I assumed was the Baltimore station—wide platform, dim lights, green tile. A whimpering noise, then silence, and no one to be seen. There was something hellishly grim about the place. Suddenly I was quite sure I didn't want to stop in Baltimore.
>
> "We won't stop here," I said, again in a firm, authoritative voice. "Start up the train, and carry on."
>
> I turned back toward my bed, and the big door closed behind me. I fell down twice on the way back—the crew must be pouring on the power, I thought—and getting into bed was like mounting a bucking horse. Safe in bed, I turned off the light, and was asleep in an instant.

Alsop had not been, he wrote, in a railroad car; he had been in the solid tumor ward of the National Institutes of Health, but his bruises from falling down were real. He had had pneumonia, a lung clot, three operations, and the lethal "infiltrate" was spreading across his lungs; the prognosis was "grim."

The day after he had "not stopped in Baltimore," the x-rays of his lungs looked a bit better. The infiltrate was receding. Some days later, they were close to normal. He resumed his column.

And in the Metropolitan Club, sipping a martini, pink-cheeked, he looked very well indeed. Was he really recovered?

"Well, I can't really play tennis, and if you wake up early, it's hard to go back to sleep if you're afraid. But the protective mechanism takes over. God tempers the wind to the shorn lamb."

And why the reprieve from the illness? That was in the column:

> Why? . . . the doctors say frankly they don't know, though they all have a favorite guess. I have a favorite guess, too. My guess is that my decision not to stop at Baltimore had something to do with it. In a kind of fuzzy, hallucinated way, I knew when I announced the decision that it was a decision not to die.
>
> Perhaps my decision not to stop in Baltimore had nothing to do with my astonishing recovery. But there are mysteries, above all the mystery of the relationship of mind and body, that will never be explained, not by the most brilliant doctors, the wisest of scientists or philosophers.

But, some time later, his reprieve was over. The deadly infiltrate came back, and, three years or so after his cancer had first been diagnosed, he died. But I was not in touch with him closely then, so I never knew whether there was a chapter after the Baltimore station.

Norman Cousins Laughs Himself Back

The end of Norman Cousins' Russian trip was not particularly pleasant. Cousins was—and is—the editor of *Saturday Review*. He publishes a lot of people, and he sits on a lot of committees, and in addition the magazine business is never without problems. Now Cousins was in Moscow, on his way to an important intercultural dinner set for 7:30 P.M., and he was late. The dinner was somewhere on the outskirts of Moscow, and the driver assigned to him by the Russians couldn't find it. While Cousins fumed in the car, the driver wandered endlessly around Moscow, looking for the site of the dinner. When they finally arrived, it was after nine. The hours from seven to nine were full of outrage: Cousins was an honored guest, and the dinner had been set up for a long time. After the embarrassment of being an hour and a half late to dinner, Cousins went back to his hotel, but he did not sleep well. The windows were open, he was on the second floor, and heavy diesel trucks roared by all night on the way to a construction site.

During his return trip to the U.S., Cousins had a headache on the plane, and noticed some heaviness in his legs and back. By the time he landed, he had a fever of 104°. After two days in bed, his doctor put him into the hospital. The heaviness in his legs and back was becoming paralysis. The least movement brought excruciating pain. Tests did not show what might have been the first guess—heavy metal poisoning, perhaps from breathing in the fumes from the trucks. But one of the tests was alarming. The sedimentation rate of his blood—the rate at which blood precipitates solids—was high. If normal is 12 to 20 mm per hour, 80 would represent danger. Cousins' rate was 85. Perhaps, said his physicians, it was a collagen disease, a disintegration of the connective tissue between the cells. But they weren't sure. They gave him two dozen aspirin a day, sleeping pills to sleep, and drugs for the pain. With the drugs, his disabilities intensified. "I wasn't hurting any more, but I wasn't moving, either," he says.

For more than two weeks, in the hospital, Cousins got quietly worse. He could not move his neck—then he could only move his jaws with difficulty.

"I was very scared," he says. "My doctors said something had happened. Maybe an allergy had lowered the normal protection. My physician was trying to get me to put my affairs in order." One of the doctors left a note for another doctor. When no one was in the room, Cousins read it. "I'm afraid," said the physician, "we may be losing Norman."

Cousins thought back over his trip and over the previous six months. It had been a very stressful time. He sent his wife out for books on stress, Cannon and Selye. "If negative emotions produce negative chemical changes, then positive emotions could produce positive changes."

Cousins announced he was taking the responsibility for himself. He checked out of the hospital and into a hotel room. He went off all the drugs. The pain was intense. "To move your thumbs was like walking on your eyeballs," he said. "But what I needed was laughter."

He sent out for Marx Brothers movies. A projector was set up in the hotel room. "I watched *A Night at the Opera* twice. It's still funny. I watched *Animal Crackers*. I sent out for segments of old *Candid Camera* shows. You know, *Candid Camera?*"

When I was taping these accounts, Cousins was harried and behind schedule. He had to be two places simultaneously, fifteen minutes ago. But as he told this part, his face began to change. The lines went out of it.

"Do you remember," Cousins said, "the *Candid Camera* where they put a speaker in one of those big street mailboxes? The guy is walking by, and the mailbox says, excuse me, sir, do you have a minute? And the guy stares. And the mailbox says, could you open the lid, there? The guy opens the lid, and the mailbox says, ah, that air feels good. Finally the voice in the mailbox says that it's fallen into the mailbox, could the passer-by go get a cop? And the passer-by brings back this cop, explaining there's somebody in the mailbox, and as the passer-by and the cop peer into the mailbox, there's no sound at all."

Harried, and fifteen minutes behind schedule twice, Cousins was breaking up just telling the *Candid Camera* mailbox story. Then he looked at his watch and began dictating crisply.

"Ten minutes of belly laughter gave me an hour of pain-free sleep. My sedimentation rate dropped from 115 to 109 the first morning. I was caught up in something exciting. The body writes prescriptions for itself I knew I needed adrenalin, or nor-adrenalin, and I knew Linus Pauling, who experimented with vitamin C and I knew vitamin C was related to collagen problems, so I took massive doses of vitamin C intravenously, slowly, so the acid wouldn't burn my veins out. The sedimentation rate began to come down ten points at a time.

"And every day I watched the Marx Brothers and segments of

Candid Camera, and the hours that were pain-free got longer and longer, and the more I laughed, the better I got."

"Under this treatment," wrote Cousins' physician, "his sedimentation gradually became normal. Since then he has never regained the slightest vestige of the syndrome. Was it a streptococcus contracted in Russia? There was also a diagnosis of severe, possibly irreversible, ankylosing spondylitis of the rheumatoid type."

Cousins' doctor went on: "The relationship of Mr. Cousins' treatment to his recovery was not clearly understood nor adequately explained, and was initiated at the specific insistence of Mr. Cousins. To date, I have not clearly established a rational cause, nor how Mr. Cousins cured himself via his own hand and mind."

A Case of Stigmata

A ten-year-old girl began bleeding, without any pain, from her left palm one day in school, several years ago. It was two weeks before Easter. A couple of days later she bled from her right palm, then later from the upper part of her left foot, upper right foot, right chest, and, by the fourteenth day, from the middle of her forehead. On Good Friday she bled from all six areas. Then the bleeding stopped, and never came back again.

About a week before the bleeding began, Miss X had read a religious book about the crucifixion, and a few days later she had watched a television movie on the same subject, and had had a vivid dream that night. She liked Bible stories, particularly the life of Christ, and could quote Bible verses. She said she also heard voices during her bedtime prayers a few days before the bleeding began, the voices being a few simple phrases such as "Your prayers will be answered."

Miss X continued to go to school while her two weeks of bleeding went on; she didn't want to miss playing the clarinet in the school band.

One can speculate on what might have happened had Miss X lived a while back in Spain or France or Italy.

But Miss X is black, a Baptist, and lives in Oakland, California.

She had never heard of stigmata, or of St. Francis of Assisi. The school nurse took the dressing off her right palm one day so she could play the clarinet in the school band. There were a couple of drops of blood on her palm, and no lesions. The pediatrician who examined her said there was no skin damage, even when the skin was looked at under a magnifying glass.

Miss X was cheerful and in no pain throughout. On Good Friday she said, "It's over now," and presumably took the dressing off so she could handle the clarinet better.

The pediatrician was joined by a psychiatrist who had written previously on psychogenic bleeding, and who was coordinator of psychiatry in various capacities at the University of California at Berkeley. They wrote it up in the *Archives of General Psychiatry*, Volume 30, February 1974, which is where I found it.

The possibility of fakery was almost nil, they said. They referred to other cases of strange spontaneous hemorrhages which did not result from physical injury "in people of strong hysterical dispositions." "One can no longer dispute the power of mental and emotional forces to control such [bleeding]," they wrote. "By analogy we need not doubt that profound, intense, religious and emotional forces, conscious and unconscious, could cause stigmatic bleeding."

I showed these cases—and some others—to the physicians who were kind enough to help me with research. This was their reaction:

Of Stewart Alsop, they said, "Well, in cancer there are many cases of unexplained remissions. Surgeons open up a patient, shake their heads, sew him back up, and write him off. Five years later the patient turns up on a visit, feeling very chipper." Did the unexplained remissions have anything in common? Nobody knew. Could mental states have an influence? The physicians passed on some reprints of an oncologist in Texas who was treating cancer with radiation and with certain mental exercises; the results so far were sketchy.

Of Norman Cousins they said, "He probably would have gotten better anyway." And, "He was aware of the stress he'd originally imposed on himself, and he found a way to un-stress himself."

Of Miss X, they said, "The case is interesting, but the article is right, intense emotional forces can cause bleeding, and curiously, even stigmatic bleeding."

All of these cases seem to suggest that our minds affect processes at the level of our cells. That isn't such a radical notion—psychosomatic medicine is defined on such cases. But could we get into the act, consciously, with our word-using, symbol-using consciousness?

PLACEBOS AND RUMPELSTILTSKIN

PLACEBOS also show us how our minds affect our bodies. Placebo is *I shall be pleasing* in Latin, and nothing at all in pharmacology. It's a fake. Sugar and water. It's there to fool the mind. Of course, you have to believe the placebo is real, and clever psychologists have even tested what is most real in this nothing pill. If you can taste it, it should taste slightly bitter. It works best when it's either large and purple or brown, or small and bright red or bright yellow.

The clever psychologists compared placebos and pain relievers, in a double blind, where neither the experimenter nor pill taker knew what was what, and the placebos were 50-something percent as effective as partically everything: 54 percent as aspirin, 54 percent as Darvon (a tranquilizer), 56 percent as effective as morphine. Two placebo pills work better than one. Placebo injections are more powerful than placebo pills. Placebos work better when they aren't given by doctors, because doctors like to give real medicine, not sugar pills, and the patient gets the unverbalized message from the doctor's face and tone: the vibes give it away.

When the actor in the white coat on the TV commercial holds up the bottle of pills and says, you'll be better by morning, the odds are with the company sponsoring him, because almost everything is better by morning.

When a drug company wants to test a new pill at a certain stage, it uses a double-blind procedure, new drug vs. placebo. Confusing, because sometimes the placebo group improves, too.

A team of researchers working on high blood pressure ran into this. They tested the medication and placebos with four groups of subjects; down went the blood pressure in all four groups. Placebos even work specifically. When asthma sufferers were given a new drug, their bronchial dilation—their ease of breathing—was twice as great when they were told that the pill would open them up as when they were told the opposite.

Another experimenter gave his subjects a stomach pill. There wasn't anything in it except something magnetic to help the measurement. The stomach activity of the subjects increased when they were told that's what it did, decreased when they were told that's what it did, and stayed the same when they were told it had no effect.

Not all symptoms are mental, and placebos don't work better than drugs, but how can a placebo work at all? This is a mind-body debate that goes back a long way. Franz Anton Mesmer—from whom comes our word "mesmerized"—was an eighteenth-century physician who used to cure with techniques we now call hypnotic induction. He named his technique "animal magnetism" because he used magnets in his first experiments. Louis XVI was so interested he appointed a Royal Commission to investigate, headed by the astronomer Bailly. It also included Lavoisier, the chemist, Dr. Guillotin and Benjamin Franklin. The Bailly Commission decided that mesmerism worked due not to magnetism but to imagination. "Imagination without magnetism can produce convulsions," said the Bailly Report. "Magnetism without imagination has no effect at all." (This is from *Rapport des Commissaires par le Roi de l'Examen du Magnétisme Animal*, J. A. Bailly, Imprimerie Royale, 1784.)

A young physician who is both psychiatrist and anthropologist, Fuller Torrey, wrote a comparison between witch doctors and psychiatrists. People who went to see each felt better immediately because of the certainty exuded by the authority figure, the diploma on the wall, or the proper headdress, bones and rattles, and, finally, because the authority in each case gave the condition a name. You have a curse from your dead-mother-in-law, or you have a bug that's been going around. Torrey called it the Rumpelstiltskin effect. Rumpelstiltskin, you remember, was the dwarf who helped the miller's daughter weave the flax into gold and claimed her first-born child after she was queen. The miller's daughter wanted to renege, and the dwarf said, you don't even know my name. If she could learn his name by midnight of the third day, she could keep the kid. At midnight the third day there is a scene where the queen says archly, "Is your name Michael? John? Rumpelstiltskin?" And poor Rumpelstiltskin goes POP! Vaporizes. Disappears. If you can give it a name, it will disappear.

Harvard psychologists tested people at a clinic. The people felt much better after they'd been to the clinic. More tests—the people in the waiting room. They felt better, too. Finally, the people who hadn't even come to the clinic yet, but had made an appointment. They felt better already.

No one doubts the effect of mind on body to some extent, and the extent varies with the believer. George Bernard Shaw said he considered Lourdes a blasphemous place because they kept there all the crutches and wheelchairs of the people who walked away, but among these items was not one wooden leg, one glass eye, or one toupee.

Stewart Alsop said, "There are mysteries, above all the mystery of the relationship of mind and body, that will never be explained, not by the most brilliant doctors, the wisest of scientists or philosophers."

There is a reason we are so sketchy on minds, and that is that we perceive the world through whatever paradigm we live in, and our present paradigm is sketchy when it comes to "mind." The design of this book is to begin well within the paradigm, with the familiar, work up to the edges, and then go beyond, and since "paradigm" is so important we had better have a brief look at what it is.

PARADIGMS

THE dictionary says a paradigm—pronounced *para-dime*—is a model or a pattern. This usage of "paradigm" goes beyond that. A paradigm is a shared set of assumptions. The paradigm is the way we perceive the world, water to the fish. The paradigm explains the world to us and helps us to predict its behavior. When we are in the middle of the paradigm, it is hard to imagine any other paradigm.

For this use of the word I have to do some hat-tipping. Many years ago James Bryant Conant, the president of Harvard and a distinguished scientist and educator, taught a course in science for nonscientists. Conant called the paradigm a "conceptual scheme." Science was not merely the careful and accurate observation of facts, biologists classifying worms and physicists reading instruments. A concept tied those observations together—then there were more observations and experiments—and new concepts rose from those, and the concepts led to still further observations and experiments. Conant wrote a little book on conceptual schemes, called *On Understanding Science*. (At the end of the year, when we got to ask sassy questions, I asked Dr. Conant why our busy president would take the time to teach us clunks, who could barely light a Bunsen burner, and he said it was important for citizens to understand the nature of science, and if we could grow up and keep the basic idea in later years, his efforts would have been worthwhile.)

An instructor in the course was Thomas Kuhn, a physicist who became a well-known professor of the history of science. Kuhn extended the "conceptual scheme" still further into "paradigm" in a seminal book, *The Structure of Scientific Revolutions*.

A famous historical paradigm is the Ptolemaic view of the world. Here's the earth in the middle of the universe, for as any fool can plainly see, the sun comes up in the east, moves overhead, and sets in the west, and the stars move around in very predictable courses. Ptolemy's science won out in its day because it explained the world better than its competitors.

Astronomers using Ptolemy found discrepancies, and tried to solve them. The discrepancies just moved to another place in the scheme. By the sixteenth century the advanced astronomers were saying that no system so cumbersome and complicated could be true to nature. The paradigm, said Copernicus, though he didn't call it that, was a monster, and he began to look for a new one. The earth, said Copernicus, moves around the sun.

Paradigms do not change easily. Copernicus was cautious. Galileo considered himself cautious; he was genuinely surprised when he was called to Rome before the cardinals. He had engineered new telescopes, unfolded new areas of the heavens, scientists everywhere made their way to see him, but he had written that perhaps the earth was *not* the center of the universe. In Rome, they took him downstairs and showed him the thumbscrews and the rack. Galileo was seventy and he recanted. The Establishment was so eager to silence him it introduced a forgery into his prosecution. Galileo spent the rest of his life under house arrest, and the official Church view continued: the sun moves around the earth.

The Establishment is always invested in the old paradigm. So the new paradigm does not get adopted just because it is neater and works better than the old one. The old crowd wins the first few battles, and in fact the paradigm doesn't change until the old crowd dies and the new young crowd grows up and rewrites the textbooks and becomes the Establishment itself.

"Paradigm" in this book is extended from *The Structure of Scientific Revolutions*. The grand paradigm in which we live is basically rational and scientific. Scientists measure a phenomenon, and try to set up an experiment that can be repeated by other scientists. What is measurable and repeatable becomes "true."

All of us, scientists or not, share the assumptions of the paradigm. If something comes along that doesn't fit the paradigm, it makes us feel uncomfortable, and it sounds bizarre and kooky. We assume, for example, that for an effect there must be a cause. What if the connection between cause and effect is just something we made up, a cumbersome system that sometimes works, just as Ptolemaic astronomy sometimes worked? What if there is no objective connection between cause and effect, but just something we supply from our perception? That gets to be very confusing. In our paradigm, we assume that causes produce effects.

Obviously, paradigms have great utility. They provide us a ground for communication, so we don't have to start over each time, and they make the world seem continuous and stable and somewhat predictable. But they also limit us, especially when we forget that we made up the paradigm in the first place.

Now let's say we want to explore the powers of mind, from the safest part of the paradigm to the thin air outside the paradigm.

We could begin with brains. Surgeons, paradigmatic gentlemen always, will give us a Latin or Greek name for every last ratchet and gear in the brain. The surgeons can even tell us what parts do what: see, this is sight, and this is sound, and this little ratchet controls the little finger, and here we come to the Fissure of Roland, and here we come to the Fissure of Sylvius. Memory's in here somewhere, but we haven't found it yet.

Then there are experimental psychologists. They can't work with human brains very well, so they use rats and cats, and leave us the hint that if that's the way a cat's brain is, maybe so is ours. They run rats through mazes, keep the cats up all night, and teach monkeys to communicate by hitting colored buttons hooked to a computer. The physiologically oriented psychologists peer into the brains of beautiful fluffy white New Zealand bunnies, big as cats, the bunny with his nose in a nozzle of anesthetic and his brains all hooked up—look, the bunny learns at the end of the sixth cranial nerve, implications for science and medicine.

Now we know the names of all the parts of the brain, and what they do, and we know about cats and monkeys, and we have a lot of very accurate measurements published in technical journals.

Along come the social scientists. They ask people: What's on your mind? Then they tabulate the results, using more and more complex statistics. The results may or may not be what's on people's minds. Sometimes the pollees lie, sometimes they can't quite articulate what's on their minds, sometimes they don't know, but the statistics have a kind of symmetry after a while, like a wasp's nest.

Then come the psychiatrists. They too are trying to find out why we behave as we do, so they say, tell me your dreams. Or, let's talk. Or, scream a little and see what happens. Up to this point, we have been very safely within the paradigm, because everything has been so accurately measured. But dreams are not so easily measured. We can tell when they occur, from the sleeper's rapid eye movements, but the meaning of the dream is an old human mystery. That makes psychiatry more art than science. Or, as defined by Eric Berne, the transactional analyst who wrote *Games People Play,* a science about the level of science in sixteenth-century Paris.

Could you get a message from your grandmother across the country, no telephone, straight ESP? Not in our paradigm. Of course, if you and your grandmother can repeat the experiment on command, and you can analyze the technique for us, and then other people can do it, we will adopt the paradigm to incorporate your achievement, and you can be just like Copernicus and Lavoisier and Newton. Or we will get a new paradigm. Sometimes the paradigm bends, and sometimes it falls apart and gets replaced.

Is there any way we can know the future? No so far, in our paradigm. Crazy Horse, the Sioux chief, would get, so he said, symbolic messages that told him the future—even as to who would kill him—but Crazy Horse did not have very accurate measurements and the experiments were not repeatable.

Our scientific paradigm has produced the absolute and splendid technological achievements of Western man. But it leaves us with a problem, and that is that we have an unconscious tendency to consider as "real" that which can be easily measured, and less real, or unreal, that which can't. What cannot be mathematically or empirically manipulated is "irrational" or "subjective."

The danger is that we consider what can be measured easily as more important than what can't, or to ignore what can't.

With the advent of the computer, social scientists have joined the physical scientists in quantifying everything within reach, and even English scholars are quantifying the lines of seventeenth-century sonnets.

But quantification has not noticeably increased our understanding of dreams or feelings, and some observers think we exclude those of our perceptions that don't match the paradigm because that's what we're trained to do. To give an exaggerated example, the child says, oh look, Mommy, a purple cow, and the mother says, there is no such thing as a purple cow, sweetheart, and so the kid stops reporting purple cows, and gradually as he gets older the visual messages processed by his brain are modified and translated in terms of Mommy's world until he can't remember seeing a purple cow. (The purple cows then walk around with impunity, unseen by anyone.)

A team of Stanford psychologists raised batches of kittens, some of whom were brought up seeing only vertical stripes and some of whom were brought up in a horizontally striped world. Even after they grew up to be smart Stanford laboratory cats, with the ability to move anywhere, the vertical-stripers thought the world was vertical and the horizontal-stripers thought the world was horizontal, both groups behaved that way, and it wasn't just belief, their brains actually recorded the impressions that way. The horizontal-stripers could not see the vertical world, and vice versa. In their technical language the psychologists wrote: "Functional neural connections can be selectively and predictably modified by environmental stimulation." In other words, even physiologically *our experience shapes our perception*.

We know that our perception does not tell us the world the way it "really" is. Otherwise, the railroad tracks really would meet at a point on the horizon. When we look out the window as the plane banks to land, we can see little toy cars on the road, but we know that when we land, the little toy cars will have grown to full size. So we test our perception against what we know, and we have a model of reality that provides day-to-day continuity. We learn from our parents and our society and our language to construct categories that help us maintain that day-to-day continuity, Rumpelstiltskin Rumpelstiltskin, and we all agree on the categories. If somebody "sees" something that the rest of us do not see—seeing being a certain excitation of the central nervous system, to which the eyes contribute—we say he is dreaming or crazy or out of touch with reality, because reality is the model, the consensus, the paradigm. Our experience shapes our perception, yet our experiences are different. So what is it that's real out there? Does the world have vertical stripes or horizontal stripes? It depends on the paradigm, and paradigms are not only belief systems, they can be innate.

All of this is to show that there are paradigms we are not aware of, because our daily assumptions aren't articulated. We have a hard time quantifying "mind," but our big rational and scientific paradigm insists that what is real is measurable and predictable, and sometimes all we know of "mind" is the size of its footprints in the snow the next morning. "Mind" becomes real as it is quantified, because that's the name of our particular game.

We can start with mind as a subject for quantification. Mind plus placebo equals new drug, and since placebo is nothing, we have a quantity for mind, in one context. We can keep thinking up contexts to give us a quantity, what can we do, what can we measure. But if we keep going long enough, the outlines of the paradigm in which we operate appear, and then the question becomes "What is it that is really real?"

THE ASTRONAUTS OF
INNER SPACE

A tenet of psychiatry is that unconscious memories affect present behavior. The dead hand of the past is irrationally alive. But no one ever located these memories in a specific spot in the brain. There was a flurry of excitement two decades ago when a Canadian neurosurgeon, Wilder Penfield, seemed to have found physical locations for repressed feelings and repressed memories; the touch of an electrode would bring them out.

For medical reasons, Penfield had to perform more than a thousand brain operations with local anesthesia. The housewife who had grown up in Holland was on the operating table, conscious, her skull open, Penfield's electrode probing, and: "That song," she said, "it's Christmas Eve, in Amsterdam, in 1945 . . . the choir is so beautiful." "The stimulation," Penfield wrote, "activates a neuron sequence that constitutes the record of the stream of consciousness . . . a selected past is made available—selected by some event in the present."

The recall was so clear that the smallest details could be identified, though they had been out of present, conscious mind for years. "A strip of time seems to run forward again at time's own normal pace," Penfield wrote, "and the individual is aware of the things he selected for his attention then. All of the available sensory information that he had ignored is absent. If he was frightened by the experience, he is frightened again. If he thought the music was beautiful, he thinks so again."

That was exciting—a physical location to hidden feelings and forgotten experiences! If you could find them, maybe you could let them out, and be at least conscious of the hand of the past! But no one, to date, has been able to find memory in a specific spot in the brain; it seems to be all through it.

About fifteen years ago I was in a psychology experiment at UCLA which produced with pharmacology the same result Penfield had found with an electrode: detailed recall of something out of conscious mind.

The experiment did more than that: it also showed, firsthand, how strong are the unquantified feelings which guide so much of our behavior from subterranean locations, and the visual symbols these feelings sometimes wear. The experiment was billed as exploration.

"You are the astronauts of inner space," said the project director. "You are going deeper into the mind than anyone has gone so far, and you will come back to tell us what you found."

That made me a bit nervous, astronaut of inner space. So did one of the astronauts who had returned.

"You get to know your own mind," she said. "You will be amazed at what's in there." I wasn't sure I wanted to know. "All the pill does is to make the unconscious conscious. Like a dream, only in a dream, you're dreaming, but with this, you're right there."

Mission Control, in the form of a graduate student, could sometimes provoke suggestions and feelings that weren't always pleasant. "For example, I saw this giant spider, maybe thirty feet tall. You just don't know how terrifying that is. I was terrified the spider was going to eat me, and my guide said, tell me about the spider, and describe it, and when it got closer, the spider was my mother, it had her face and it was just about to eat me —let it, said my guide—and zoop, it disappeared, and I had this incredible flow of feelings, I guess they had been locked in there for years, and I wept, and now I can talk to her all the time, where before I never even returned her phone calls."

I was uneasy. What were we astronauts to do if we met *two* thirty-foot spiders? Or a hundred-foot gnat?

There was a magazine lying around with a story by James Thurber. I began to read it, casually.

I swallowed my blue pill with a glass of water and sat down to read the magazine. Nothing happened. My guide from Mission Control was checking one-two-three-four into the tape recorder. Something in the Thurber made me giggle. It was hard to read further. I was getting gangrene in my left hand from this iron vise around the wrist. I took off my watch. That made my arm feel wonderful. A hot, leaden weight in the back of my pants threatened to drag me through the floor. I took my wallet out and hurled it across the room. That made me about six thousand pounds lighter.

The guide—they called them "baby-sitters" in that lab—made some notes on the pad. Probably time and money.

"What's so funny?" she said.

I was not about to answer. First of all, I didn't want any intrusions. And second, everything was moving much faster than the words we invent to describe them. There weren't, in fact, any words.

There still aren't. Compared to the gradations of experience, words are leaden, clumsy, two-left-footed things. The blanket won't cover the bed. Mystics shrug and say the experience is ineffable, and the venerable *Tao* from China said, first line, "The way that can be described is not the Way." Physicists are glad they can talk to each other in mathematics because the concepts beyond everyday reality can't quite be expressed in language. But until you get one foot out of everyday reality, you don't know there's another kind.

Part of me was scampering like a puppy that feels green grass instead of floor under its feet, and has wriggled from its leash, and part of me was following with the leash, saying, here boy, here boy. What's so funny, the baby-sitter had said. There did indeed seem to be somebody laughing—no, that's not it, the laughter was laughing somebody. The part of me panting along with the leash thought, it's not *that* funny, thinking that it was some line of James Thurber causing the disturbance. The part with the leash tried to tell the baby-sitter why this serious job was not going to be accomplished on schedule—"No . . . words . . ." it gasped, already feeling guilty—we would have to get a sound movie camera inside the head somehow—and then it was swept away and was not heard from for several hours, the first time it had been silent since the age of probably one and a half.

Now then, on the other side of this breath-taking display of kaleidoscopic colors was a purple universe, a very profound discovery, which was the true universe, and if you just let go you would fall in; it was always there, but we held ourselves away from it; it vibrated at a certain frequency, and so did you, and that frequency was the frequency of laughter. The frequency of laughter extends from the limits of the galaxy to the other limits, and there's nothing to do, you don't even have to go ha-ha, you just float.

And there was this clock on the wall with Roman numerals and some spots of sunlight on it, the details very clear, the hands snapping with a loud click from 3:28 to 3:30 and then to 3:31, a soaring free feeling simultaneously.

I could see the basic molecules of the universe, too bad there weren't any words because there they were, all the component parts, little building blocks of DNA.

Out of control, I wrote in my report later. That feeling is quite frightening, but there was the baby-sitter, and all the other astronauts had come back, and the purple universe vibrating at the frequency of laughter seemed more wonderful and more human than the dreary ordinary one.

Other people's trips can be very boring—somewhat like other people's dreams—so I hesitate to extend the description. When I listened to the tape later, I realized I had never heard such gut-laughter coming from myself, or at least very rarely.

The molecule of DNA I drew was not DNA, alas. It was du Pont plastic, patented, called Delrin. That was just as mysterious as DNA; I am no chemist, and do not really know one chemical from another, especially at the molecular level, how come I could draw a du Pont plastic monomer? The clock with the Roman numerals indeed did face the western sun, it was on the wall facing the west windows of Miss Pannell's fourth grade, somebody had watched the hands of that clock a lot as they clicked ever so slowly toward 3:30 and the end of school. Who would have thought that old clock would still be there in the memory bank after so many years? And the feelings, the impatience and boredom and restlessness at 3:28, and the exhilaration at 3:30, those feelings were so clear, was it like that at first? And was it now 3:28 too much of the time, and 3:31 too seldom?

"That's some pill," I said the next day. I felt very good.

"There's nothing in the pill per se," said Mission Control. "It's a trigger. You provide all the comedy and all the drama. The first session is usually good."

I signed up to do more guinea-pigging. No more than once a month; this really was no search for highs. There was great excitement about the explorations, and that excitement was contagious. Frontiers of mind, astronauts of inner space.

The report of this astronaut sometimes sounded a bit bizarre. Second session, listening to Bach, I announced, "Bach wrote his music in the shape of a three-dimensional cross, the same architecture as a cathedral." You could walk inside the music. Stone columns of music, arches and naves and flying buttresses. Another session: real estate. Real estate? Sure, looking up from the middle of the earth, real estate becomes very comic if you see some tiny figure the size of a mayfly going into City Hall with a tiny paper clutched in his hand, saying he owns some bit of the earth's surface and everything under it all the way down to the middle. The earth is ignorant of the piece of paper. How can anybody own the earth?

As a guinea pig with credentials, when on the East Coast I reported in to an experiment there. Different chemical. Primordial big cobra, sun symbol, you could sit in front of it and get a sunburn. Did I really get a sunburn? It certainly looked like a sunburn, and felt like a sunburn. Package that snake and we can really cut into the sunlamp market.

. . .

[3 0]

The experiments opened an interest for me in altered states, as it did for many people who went through some similar experience. I began to read the technical literature.

"Did you see the weird things the yogis can do?" said somebody. "It's in *The Journal of Electroencephalography and Clinical Neurophysiology.*" I read the article. Only the first three sentences and the last three were in English, the rest was in some tortured form of noncommunication designed to show the methods, but after a while I got the hang of it. As an astronaut I was only a weekend warrior, a part-time guinea pig, since I was running a mutual fund portfolio the rest of the time. Reading the journals was a bit like reading *Motor Trend* and *Hot Rod* without owning a car, but among other things I was looking for the experiments in which I was a subject. If you come in second in the potato sack race at the school picnic, you might very well look in the weekly paper for the results of the potato-sack races, to see if they spelled your name right.

Alas, the closest we came to publication was in a footnote on page 282 of a book called *Altered States of Consciousness,* and the group in the footnote wasn't even mine.

It is nineteenth-century psychology, this business of exploring the mind with chemicals and reporting back. (Chemicals are chemicals and minds are chemicals and they react on each other.) At the beginning of the twentieth century, a psychologist called John Watson turned the whole field away from this sort of thing, toward behaviorism and harder science and the more accurate measurement of rats.

One curious sidelight is that so many subjects made profound discoveries which were comically trivial later. Dr. Oliver Wendell Holmes sniffed ether and reported of the universe: "The whole is pervaded with the smell of turpentine." William James tried nitrous oxide, wrote down his cosmic discovery, and found the next day that the cosmic discovery was "higamous, hogamus, woman's monogamous, hogamus, higamus, man is polygamous." A contemporary psychologist perceived the absolute secret of the universe: "Please flush after using."

Naturally, physicians checked out the chemical effects. If you were in medical school, this is what you would find in your pharmacology course, in Goodman and Gilman, *The Pharmacological Basis of Therapeutics*: The agents act upon the central nervous system, causing the pupil of the eye to dilate, though not by direct application to the eye. Muscular weakness also results. But what distinguishes these agents, says the text, "is their capacity to induce or compel states of altered perception, thought and feeling that are not (or cannot be) experienced except in dreams or at times of religious exaltation." Interesting language for a cautious medical school text. It goes on: "Frequently there is a feeling that one part of the self seems to be a passive observer (a 'spectator ego') rather than an active organizing and directing force, while another part of the self participates and receives the vivid and unusual experiences. The environment may be perceived as novel, often beautiful, and harmonious. The attention of the user is turned inward, pre-empted by the seeming clarity and portentous quality of his own thinking processes. In this state the slightest sensation may take on profound meaning. Indeed, 'meaningfulness' seems more important than what is meant, and the 'sense of truth' more magnificent than what is true. Commonly, there is a diminished capacity to differentiate the boundaries of one object from another and of the self from the environment. Associated with the loss of boundaries there may be a sense of union with 'mankind' or with the 'cosmos.' To the extent that these drugs reveal this innate capacity of the mind to see more than it can tell and to experience and believe more than it can explain, the term *mind expanding* is not entirely appropriate."

An "innate capacity of the mind to see more than it can tell" is like the first line of the *Tao*, the way that can be described is not the Way. That's nice stuff for the medical students. And loss of boundaries, union with the cosmos—that's a description of a mystical experience. A chemical mystical experience. Eventually there grew up an argument as to whether chemical mystical experiences counted as mystical experiences, but then, in those days, serious intellectual theologians like Father John Courtenay Murray were participating. A Harvard divinity school student did a Ph.D. thesis: as an experiment, he recruited twenty divinity school students and, in a double-blind procedure, gave placebos to some and psychedelics to others. Deliberately he chose Good Friday. He sent the future theologians off to church. The placebo-taking students said, "I think I'm dizzy," or, "I feel funny." The other students wandered out, crying, "I see God! I see God!" The Divinity School student wrote up his results very soberly.

The chemical that produced the snake that produced a sunburn was mescaline, and the blue pill taken by the astronauts of inner space was lysergic acid diethylamide. It is hard to believe now that lysergic acid, or LSD, was around for twenty years as a neutral and interesting chemical agent, because in the Sixties it became a symbol of sensuality and witchcraft and decadence and terror. Our attitudes and assumptions are part of our paradigm, so it is useful to have a brief excursion into some of these attitudes, to see what happened to the tools.

A VERY SHORT
HISTORY OF SOME
AMERICAN DRUGS
FAMILIAR TO
EVERYBODY

OUR attitude toward the word "drug" depends on whether we are talking about penicillin or heroin or something in-between. The unabridged three-volume Webster's says a drug is "a chemical substance administered to prevent or cure disease or enhance physical and mental welfare" or "a substance affecting the structure or function of the body." Webster's should have added "mind," but they probably thought that was part of the body. Some substances that aren't drugs, like placebos, affect "the structure or function of the body," but they work because we *think* they're drugs.

We are a drug-using society. We take, for example, twenty thousand tons of aspirin a day, almost one aspirin per person in the whole country. Aspirin is a familiar drug from a family called salicylates, specifically, acetylsalicylic acid. It lowers body temperature, alleviates some types of pain, and stimulates respiration.

Nicotine is a familiar and widely recognized drug, a stimulant to the central nervous system. It is addictive. The toxic effects of nicotine have been detailed at great length by the Surgeon General. Americans smoke 600 billion cigarettes a year.

Alcohol is also a widely recognized drug. In the United States

70 million users spend $10 billion a year. Five million of the 70 million alcohol users are said to be addicts, that is, they have a physical dependence on the drug. Alcohol is unique, says the pharmacology textbook, because it is "the only potent pharmacological agent with which self-induced intoxication is socially acceptable." Alcohol is so much a part of everyday life we do not think of it, on the rocks or straight up, as a drug or a potent pharmacological agent.

Then there is the family of drugs called the xanthines. Americans take xanthines at the rate of 100 *billion* doses per year. Xanthines are alkaloids which stimulate portions of the cerebral cortex. They give you "a more rapid and clearer flow of thought, allay drowsiness. . . . motor activity is increased. There is a keener appreciation of sensory stimuli, and reaction time to them is diminished." This description, again from the pharmacology textbook, is similar to descriptions of cocaine and amphetamine. Of course, the xanthine addict pays a price. He is, says Sir Clifford Allbutt, Regius Professor of Medicine at Cambridge, "subject to fits of agitation and depression; he loses color and has a haggard appearance. The appetite falls off; the heart suffers; it palpitates, or it intermits. As with other such agents, a renewed dose of the poison gives temporary relief, but at the cost of the misery."

Xanthines are generally taken orally through "aqueous extracts" of the plants that produce these alkaloids, either in seeds or leaves. In the United States the three most common methylated xanthines taken are called caffeine, theophylline and theobromine. The seeds of *Coffea arabica* contain caffeine, the leaves of *Thea sinensis* contain caffeine and theophylline, and the seeds of *Theobroma cacao* contain caffeine and theobromine. In America the three are known as "coffee," "tea" and "cocoa," and they are consumed daily, at the rate of billions of pounds a year. They are generally drunk as hot drinks, but Americans also drink cold drinks containing caffeine from the nuts of the tree *Cola acuminata*. The original drinks ended in the word "cola," but now there are many "colas" which do not bear that name in the title. The early ads for Coca-Cola said it gave you a lift.

Coffee, tea, cocoa and cola drinks are all drugs. Caffeine is a central nervous system stimulant, theophylline less so, and theobromine hardly at all. All xanthines increase the production of urine. Xanthines act on smooth muscles—relaxing, for example, especially in the case of theophylline, bronchi that may have been constricted. Like the salicylates—aspirin—xanthines can cause stomach irritation. Caffeine can cause sleeplessness, and researchers have found that it causes chromosome breaks.

Maxwell House, meet the Regius Professor of Medicine. Is the stuff good to the last drop, or another dose of the poison? Is it a food, to be sold in supermarkets, or a stimulant to the central nervous system like the amphetamines? "The popularity of the xanthine beverages depends on their stimulant action, although most people are unaware of any stimulation," says the giant pharmacology text.

It is suprising to find substances we think of so cheerfully, perkin' in the pot, listed as drugs. That's the point. In our society, there are some drugs we think of as okay drugs, and other drugs make us gasp. A coffee drinker who drinks coffee all day and cannot function without it is just a heavy coffee drinker, but someone using a non-okay drug is a "drug user" or an "addict."

Consumer Reports asked: how did drugs with such potential hazard spread without arousing the legal repression and social condemnation aroused by other drugs? They were domesticated, it said. There was no illegal black market, the dosages were relatively small, and some people buffered the drug effect with cream and sugar.

The worst of what our society thinks of as "hard drugs" comes from the unripe capsule of the opium poppy. In the nineteenth-century United States, you could buy opiates at grocery stores and drugstores, and by mail. Godfrey's Cordial—a molasses, sassafras and opium combination—was especially popular. Genteel Southern ladies in lace and ruffles, smelling of verbena and other sweet things, sounding like Scarlett O'Hara, were slugging down daily a combination of opium and alcohol called laudanum. The first surveys of narcotics showed that women outnumbered men three to one, because "the husbands drank alcohol at the saloon, and the wives took opium at home."

The point of this capsule history is not to warn people from the perilous xanthines. (I drink them all, *Coffea arabica* and *Thea sinensis*, sweetened, no cream, please, and *Theobroma cacao* on cold winter days, and *Cola acuminata* on warm summer ones, and I have to be paying attention to be aware of the stimulant action.)

Nor is it to diminish the danger of illegal narcotics. (Legal narcotics are part of legitimate medicine). There is no comparison between legal, domesticated, mild, buffered drugs and illegal and undomesticated ones, but it is society that has produced the legalities and the domestication. Illegal narcotics, producing huge profits and employing the worst criminal elements, are merchandised to the least stable elements of society, producing tremendous social problems.

A Coke at snack time, a drink before dinner, a cup of coffee after dinner, a cigarette with the coffee—very relaxing. Four shots of drugs. Domesticated ones. It would be rather comic to have addicts sneaking down dark alleys for a shot of coffee, but nicotine is so strong that when currencies fail—Germany right after World War II, for example—cigarettes become currency.

In some Muslim countries, you can sit and smoke hashish all day at a café, but possession of alcohol will land you in jail; in the United States you can sit in a saloon ingesting alcohol all day, but possession of hashish will land you in jail.

The drug taken by the astronauts of inner space was, at that time, legal. It was also nonnarcotic and nonaddictive. It crops up in the story not only because it was used in the exploration of the mind, but because so many explorers in meditation, biofeedback and other disciplines went through a stage with it.

Lysergic acid diethylamide was invented by the Swiss. Curious to think of the Swiss, the symbol of sobriety and industry, watch-making and cuckoo clocks, as having invented LSD, Librium and Valium, psychedelics and tranquilizers, the turn-ons and the turn-offs, but then the Swiss have been in the drug business since Paracelsus of Basle, roughly a contemporary of Columbus.

THE WORLD'S FIRST
ACID TRIP, AND
SUBSEQUENT
HAPPENINGS

O N April 16, 1943, Dr. Albert Hofmann, a chemist, was working in his lab at Sandoz, a pharmaceutical firm in Basel, Switzerland. He was working with the derivatives of ergot, a fungus that grows on grains. Sandoz had successfully marketed ergot derivative for use in obstetrics and in treating migraine headaches. Midway through Friday afternoon Hofmann decided to go home. He felt restless and dizzy. At home, "I lay down and immediately fell into a peculiar state similar to a drunkenness, characterized by an exaggerated imagination. With my eyes closed, fantastic pictures of extraordinary plasticity and intensive color seemed to surge towards me. After about two hours this condition disappeared." Hofmann had just taken the first acid trip.

He had been working with three chemicals. The effects of the first two were well known, so he must have unwittingly ingested the third. He and an associate had discovered it five years before, but when preliminary tests on animals revealed nothing of interest they put it aside. Since it was the twenty-fifth compound in the lysergic acid series, it had been named d-lysergic acid diethylamide, or LSD-25.

Hofmann went back to the lab the next week and took what

he thought was a very small amount of his new chemical. He began taking notes: "mild dizziness . . . inability to concentrate . . . uncontrollable laughter." Because of the war there were no cars, so Hofmann got on his bicycle to ride the four miles home, probably the last time anybody has tried to ride a bicycle four miles on LSD. "My field of vision swayed before me and was distorted like the reflections in an amusement park mirror. The faces of those around me appeared as grotesque, colored masks; marked motoric unrest." He also had "a clear recognition of my condition, in which state I sometimes observed, in the manner of an independent, neutral observer, that I shouted half insanely or babbled incoherent words. Occasionally I felt as if I were out of my body. Sounds were transposed into visual sensations so that from each tone or noise a comparable colored picture was evoked, changing in form and color kaleidoscopically." That was the second acid trip. Sandoz sent the new drug off to the University of Zurich, and Hofmann's associate, W. A. Stoll, wrote up the results of the testing. LSD was not toxic and was not addicting, but an extremely small dosage had profound results. Most drugs are measured in milligrams, or thousandths of a gram; LSD was measured in micrograms, or millionths of a gram. Five grains, an aspirin-sized tablet, could produce effects in 3,000 people.

The United States Army began to stockpile LSD. Therapists around the world began to use it with patients. It allowed, they said, repressed memories to come forth, and the material that came up could be better understood because it took the form of visual symbols. Yet, with all the imagery, the patient kept a state of awareness, and retained his insights after the experience. Originally, LSD was called a hallucinogen, that is, an agent that causes hallucination. But the LSD ingester was not quite like, for example, an alcoholic with delirium tremens, who sees snakes and green elephants. The alcoholic thinks the snakes and green elephants are real; the LSD subject "does not ordinarily accept them as real. He remains aware that what he is experiencing is a drug-induced phenomenon." So LSD was not a hallucinogen. Dr. Humphrey Osmond, one of the first psychiatrists to use the drug, called it psychedelic, mind-manifesting or mind-expanding.

Osmond is an Englishman of diverse enthusiasms whose speech comes in a torrent; he had sat up all night with Indians in peyote ceremonies, and he hoped LSD would be an aid to curing schizophrenia in his Saskatchewan hospital.

An American authority on LSD amassed some statistics: after the first seventeen years of LSD usage, it had been tried thousands of times, with medical supervision. Fifteen hundred papers had been written on it, and it was a promising research drug, suitable for the volunteers, the astronauts of inner space.

The Maryland Psychiatric Research Center reported great success in curing alcoholics. Researchers there and at the Cook County Hospital in Chicago and the Sinai Hospital in Baltimore tried LSD on terminal cancer patients in great pain. They reported that the pain diminished more than with opiates, that the pain no longer seemed important, and that the outlook under these grim sentences of death became more serene. They did caution that the results did not come from the psychedelics only; an experienced researcher or therapist came along with it.

No one ever said that the agents were not powerful, or that they were to be treated lightly, or that the experiences were all pleasant, or for entertainment. There were adverse psychological reactions possible in unstable people, but a review of the literature said "no instance of serious, prolonged physical side effects was found" in the use of psychedelics. One hospital team reported four such instances in 6,522 supervised sessions. The long-range effects had not been tested.

Then it all changed.

The Sixties took over, the psychedelics became a subcult, the partisans said it brought Utopia, the antagonists said it brought the plague; LSD became a terror symbol, which made it attractive to children whose bones had not fused and whose minds had not matured but who knew that the Establishment and the law and their parents were all lying. "The anti-LSD publicity, the scare campaigns, and the laws," said *Consumer Reports*, "helped to convert what had been [for twenty years] a relatively unknown and innocuous drug into a quite damaging one."

Sandoz Pharmaceutical stopped making LSD. It had been only an experimental drug, not the source of any real revenues, and

Sandoz did not want to jeopardize its legitimate drugs. Restrictive laws were passed. The legitimate researchers turned in their drugs, sorrowfully. They were worried about black market LSD. One noted that all the statistics showing safety had come from clinicians and supervised surroundings. Another used the analogy of x-rays: they were an incredible boon to medicine, but if untrained people shot x-rays in all directions, there might be some damage. All the researchers worried that historic opportunity for exploration would be lost in all the sensationalism; it had taken hypnotism a hundred years to recover from "animal magnetism."

The laws were passed, the police were alerted, raids began, the generation gap widened, and the epidemic spread.

AND A SHORT
CHRONICLE OF
THE MADNESS

THE research in psychedelics now stands as a discrete unit in time, with finite boundaries, twenty years or so and a few thousand papers. We will come back to what was learned in a moment.

It would take an acute social historian to chronicle the epidemic, the children, the hippies, the parents, the law, the police, the media. LSD was colorless, odorless, not too expensive to produce, and a very small amount went a very long way. The markup from LSD to "street acid" was 1,000 percent to 3,000 percent. Two million people took what they thought was LSD, but except for brief periods (1965–66) almost all of it was bulked out with other active chemicals. A team of researchers reported in *Science*, from nationwide samples, that the "so-called LSD" was in many cases not LSD at all, but anything ranging from arsenic to rat poison. They said, uniformly, the drugs were not advertised, and "very frequently they contain only inert substances and/or dangerous drugs." Professor Charles Tart reported that many people who believe they had the experience never had any LSD."

Alas, the efforts of the entrepreneurs extended even to the organic items from woodland and forest, the psilocybin mushroom. Wide profit margins invite such activity. The mushrooms sold, reported another authority, were not directly from woodland and forest. They were from cans in the grocery store. Then they would be soaked in phencyclidine (PCP), a veterinary anesthetic that causes an alcohol-like intoxication and makes muscles feel rubbery. Frozen and packaged in plastic bags, the mushrooms were sold up and down the West Coast, "very trippy."

The consumers were not suspicious enough. They said: my LSD is pure, it's made by this graduate student in chemistry who wants to earn a little extra money, he just turns out enough for his friends. Or: "This is the real Owsley." For a while, it looked as though Owsley was going to have his name become part of the language, like Captain Boycott and Samuel Maverick and Mr. Booze of Glassboro, who stamped his names on the glass bottles used for spirits.

The acute social historian could chronicle Owsley, August Owsley Stanley III, grandson of a governor of Kentucky, sound man for the Grateful Dead, acid entrepreneur. Owsley's chemists in their hideaway lab in northern California took lysergic acid and ergotamine tartrate and produced a million tabs of Orange Sunshine, but Owsley was no Sandoz: like a crazed Julia Childs, he salted and peppered the Orange Sunshine with strychnine and amphetamines, trying recipes; he wanted to see what would sell best. A million tabs—that was just Orange Sunshine, the statistics on Clear-Lite and Window Pane and Purple Pie and Yellow Smash are uncertain, but all of them outsold Sandoz' all-time output.

When the children took the strychnine, or the arsenic, or the atropine, or the Methedrine, or even LSD—sometimes there really was a college chemist just cooking for his friends—they sometimes had adverse reactions, whereupon their friends dumped them into the emergency room of a hospital, an environment that can produce a bad trip in people who are stone cold sober and just passing through. Imagine being in the waiting room stoned and watching the bloody accident victims come in. It took years for the word to filter down: do not take the people on bummers to the hospital, or the doctor, doctors don't know. (Indeed, they did not know; harried interns and busy doctors do not read technical papers in experimental psychology, which would have been useful.)

The acute social historian would have to spend some time on Timothy Leary, handsome, charming, charismatic, the guru of the Brotherhood of Eternal Love, a non-profit California corporation, itself merged into the League for Spiritual Discovery, patron saint of Orange Sunshine. Leary was a military child, the son of Eisenhower's dentist. He went to Holy Cross. Is he remembered in the alumni bulletin? He went to West Point for a year and a half. Are there generals at the outskirts of empire who recall him? He went to the University of Alabama. Did he watch the Crimson Tide roll?

As a young psychology instructor, Leary was thrown out of Harvard for his LSD experiments, together with his sidekick, Richard Alpert. Post expulsion, they landed in a fifty-five-room mansion in Millbrook, New York, owned by a Mellon heir, Billy Hitchcock, with the local cops peering through the bushes. The local cops were led by G. Gordon Liddy, later known as a Watergate burglar. Small world.

"Turn on, tune in, drop out," said the Pied Piper of psychedelics, and a lot of children did. The story is not over, but the social historian will be able to chronicle a fascinating tale: G. Gordon Liddy went to prison for burglarizing the Watergate, and Leary went to prison for possessing a fingernail's worth of marijuana, and Owsley went to prison and paid $142,276 in taxes, plus penalties, taxes due on unreported income from Orange Sunshine, and Richard Alpert went to India and became Baba Ram Dass, the very symbol of the seeker.

Aldous Huxley, the novelist, had written of psychedelics in *Heaven and Hell* and in *The Doors of Perception*, which described his own experience in the early 1950's with mescaline. Huxley brought great cultural depth to the experience, and Leary went to see him, since Huxley was the Respectable Intellectual of the Further Reaches. Leary's visit in 1962 brought forebodings to Huxley. "He talked such nonsense," Huxley wrote to Humphrey Osmond. ". . . this nonsense-talking is just another device for annoying people in authority, the reaction of a mischievous Irish boy to the headmaster of the school. One of these days the headmaster will lose patience—and then good-bye to the research. I am fond of [him], but why, oh why, does he *have* to be such an ass? I have told him repeatedly that the only attitude for a researcher in this ticklish field is that of an anthropologist living in the midst of a tribe of potentially dangerous savages. Go about your business quietly, don't break the taboos or criticize the locally accepted dogmas. Be polite and friendly— and get on with the job. If you leave them alone, they will probably leave you alone."

But Leary thought he was on the edge of a revolution, and did not heed the advice. "You are never the same after you've had that one flash glimpse down the cellular time tunnel," he said. "Turn on." The savages did not like having their customs taunted, and they put the anthropologist into a big iron pot and boiled him for supper.

An Evelyn Waugh guerrilla warfare broke out. One Briton traveled the fruit stalls of London, injecting the apples and oranges with LSD; another spiked the punch at a party given by Queen Juliana of the Netherlands, and made his escape in a stolen limousine. The savages stoked the fires higher.

Poor Dr. Hofmann of Basel, his name was not to be one with Pasteur and Salk and Fleming. Fifteen years after his LSD bicycle ride, in another burst of brilliance, he synthesized psilocybin, the element in the "magic mushrooms" used by Indian cultures for the ceremonial altering of consciousness. The Nobel prize committee looked the other way. He was not even getting royalties on LSD. The U.S. Patent Office supplied the formula for LSD for fifty cents.

For twenty years, from 1943 to 1963, the dissolving boundaries and unleashed memories and flowing feelings produced by the interaction of Dr. Hofmann's chemicals and minds brought no talk of revolution. The subjects and the therapists both had short hair, and society paid them no attention. Of the loves and fears that burbled beneath the surface with such intensity the researchers said, ve-r-y interesting. The Freudians found Freudian symbols. The Jungians found Jungian archetypes and the collective unconscious, the Rankians found separation anxiety, the

Sullivanians found oral dynamism. In short, everybody found something, and they used their own language to describe it.

Much of the early work involved patients in therapy, but anthropologists and artists and social scientists were also beginning to show interest.

Then came: Free Speech, birth control pills, long hair, brotherly love, Flower Children, predators on the Flower Children, cops, narcotics, speed, laws, judges, politicians campaigning, busts, riots, Vietnam, war resisters, the Mafia, Richard Nixon, Woodstock. Confrontation.

Psychedelics were no longer experimental substances used by researchers to peel back the layers of the mind, they were a social issue—and a divisive one at that. LSD ADDICTS STARE AT SUN, the the newspapers reported; no point in detailing the hoax, newspapers print what they believe sells. Someone at *The Saturday Evening Post* must have known that picture was thalidomide babies, not "LSD babies," but they gave it the LSD caption; more proof that the Establishment lies, said the counter-culture. Were there some chromosome breaks in the lab experiments? Why was that front-page, said the counter-culture, when the same breaks for caffeine and aspirin go unreported? Could it be because coffee and tea and aspirin are major advertisers?

The research was over. Just before it ended, the researchers were detailing several stages of the psychedelic trip. On the surface, there were all those distorted images, the fireworks, the color displays. That was not from "seeing"; it by-passed the optic system; blind people had the same displays. And then there were the images, winged beasts, mythic animals, everything eating everything; the perspectives and the colors and the images went into the art and the music. College bookstores sold posters by Magritte and Dali and Man Ray—and M. C. Escher; the perspectives suddenly looked familiar. The underwater figures in *The Yellow Submarine* swallowed everything; Sergeant Pepper's Lonely Hearts Club Band played psychedelic imagery—if you missed it, the initials of "Lucy in the Sky with Diamonds" spelled it out.

The imagery appeared long before the research died out. "I want to play you something," said our friend in the record business, in a house over the Pacific surf. At that moment, the rumblings of confrontation were still in the future. The record producer was one of the explorers. A nasal, reedy voice came on, with this crazy harmonica—*he-y-y, Mis-ter Tam-bourine Man, play a song for me, take me on a trip upon your magic swirling ship, my senses have been stripped, my hands can't feel to grip— take me disappearing through the smoke rings of my mind, down the foggy ruins of time, far past the frozen leaves, the haunted, frightened trees, out to the windy beach, far from the twisted reach of crazy sorrow, to dance beneath the diamond sky with one hand waving free, let me forget about today until tomorrow . . .*

"Who is that guy?" I said.

The Tibetan *Book of the Dead* no longer seemed quite so exotic; in fact, it seemed quite familiar. Same old winged beasts, same old time tunnel. The Egyptian *Book of the Dead*, too. A new burst of interest in anthropology, a new burst of interest in Oriental religions. Richard Alpert's guru, in India, said of the psychedelics, "Well, America is a materialistic country, it is natural that it should find consciousness through a material."

A decade later, the tambourine man leading through the smoke rings of the mind was a golden oldie, and a Carly Simon song went:

> *You showed me how, how to leave myself behind*
> *How to turn down the noise in my mind*
>
> *Now I haven't got time for the pain*
> *I haven't got room for the pain*
> *I haven't the need for the pain*
>
> *Not since I've known you . . .*

a love song, one would think, but, as it turns out, about meditation, and a meditation teacher.

The children's epidemic that shut down the research seemed very remote to me at the time. I was at work on other things, and the confrontations came thorugh like the dull thump of unseen artillery over the horizon. My guinea-pigging was long over, and the journals did not seem as interesting once the high excitement of being on the frontiers of mind faded. It was easy to let subscriptions lapse, because the next issue was unlikely to bring a paradigm-busting discovery.

WHAT DID WE
LEARN?

THE research in psychedelics, seen from here, is just sitting there in midair, suspended and frozen, overtaken by events like a potter working at his wheel in Pompeii when the lava flowed past and preserved him. It is interesting to know that psychedelics expand the pupil of the eye, letting in more light, disorganizing the perception. But not very, unless you are working with schizophrenics and noticing some similarities in eye muscles. It is interesting to note the visual displays that by-pass the optic system so the even blind people see wild dancing colors. But most of the research was either sponsored by the government for somewhat ill-defined purposes, or concerned with abnormal people. Out of thousands of papers, surprisingly few were for sheer exploration. But some of those had some fascinating observations.

The depths of the memory bank were stunning. Never mind the molecular diagram of the du Pont plastic; there were subjects who knew no physics and came up with physics, and subjects who knew no foreign languages and yet could speak them.

Dr. Jean Houston is a tall, attractive woman of enormous energy and exotic vocabulary who did a lot of research not only with psychedelics but with other consciousness-altering devices.

(She constructed, for example, a "witches' cradle" that would swing the subject around, disorienting him and producing parallel effects to some psychedelics, much as the medieval "witches' cradles" would do.)

Jean Houston had a subject in an LSD experiment who was walking on the waterfront in ancient Athens with Socrates. That is, he was lying on a sofa with a mask on and a calibrated amount of blue Sandoz, and he said he was in Greece, walking around with Socrates.

"What does Socrates have to say?" asked Jean Houston.

"I don't know," said the subject, "he's talking in Greek, and I don't understand Greek."

"Well, I do," said Ms. Houston. "I took six years of Greek in school. Just repeat the words."

The time traveler reported the conversation, which was indeed *in classic Greek, which he did not understand*!

Remember the Denver housewife who, under hypnosis, could come up with the details of "a previous life" in Ireland, where she had lived as "Bridie Murphy"? She knew all the details of Bridie Murphy's neighborhood, in a country she had never visited.

There are other examples—the uneducated cleaning lady who could speak cultured German under hypnosis, and so on.

Surprising, but all this is well within the paradigm. The rational hypothesis runs: *we perceive more than we are aware of, and on some level we remember what we perceive.*

The brain is more complex than a computer; it is as if somebody pressed a button—RECORD—when we start life, and it is never turned off, though sometimes the amplification varies. All the sights and sounds and feelings are recorded.

The Denver housewife had a maid, or a nurse, as a little girl, who told her about Ireland, though she did not consciously remember the details. (That explanation isn't totally accepted by Bridie Murphy enthusiasts.) The cleaning lady cleaned for a German professor and overheard him talking. One day I was reading a magazine and I read the caption under the molecular model of Delrin, and hurriedly turned the page.

The recall mechanism doesn't necessarily do the job right.

For example, I really do not care about Delrin, I wanted to express some feeling about the building blocks of existence. There was no DNA model filed in the memory bank, so the memory bank coughed up Delrin instead.

Jean Houston had other subjects who reported back from ancient Egypt and medieval Europe. Previous lives? "The details," she says, "are a tribute to television and the news magazines and schools. So much information pours into us—and goes right through us—but some of it sticks, and we carry it around."

Ordinarily, of course, we get no exposure to the depths of the memory bank. It takes a jolt that disorganizes our everyday perception, extreme stress ("My life flashed before me") or a drug that scrambles the familiar neuronal pathways in the brain. Consciously, we find it easier to remember words that we can associate with images, that are meaningful, than words that don't have meaning. Scrambling or stressing can bring up feelings tied to old images, or images not there but assembled for the purpose of illustrating a feeling, or images recorded but not comprehended.

Think of all the books in school, and all the voices of different teachers, and all the movies, and the clock on the wall of your own schoolroom, and thousands of TV programs—and then think of that RECORD button being on all the time. Could you sing a Czech drinking song? No? Are you sure that in all the choral music you've heard, and in all the segments of *Foreign Intrigue* on TV, and in all the movies, there was no Czech song?

If there wasn't, the retrieval system will come up with something it considers close enough. Maybe it will play back a bit of Swedish from some Ingmar Bergman movie.

Out of conscious mind and willful memory things pass very quickly; we have statistics by experimental psychologists on how rapidly we forget. And yet there is all that stuff sitting sullen in the memory bank. Wilder Penfield, the neurosurgeon, reported that what came up with the touch of the electrode was, for the most part, trivia. Why on earth was that time traveler carrying ten sentences of classic Greek, and why on earth would I squirrel away a molecular diagram?

I began to see the retrieval system as a surly messenger boy with untied gym shoes and a scruffy jacket that says *Roosevelt High* across the back. You need to know somebody's name—his face is right there before you, saying hello—or your sister's phone number, and you hit RETRIEVE, and the kid ties his gym shoes, goes back to the stacks, gets a Pepsi-Cola from the vending machine, smokes a cigarette, and comes back with the line-up of the 1956 New York Giants or the lyrics to "Blue Suede Shoes."

Feelings came up as symbols. That was something else the researchers found; words being a bit leaden, people came up with symbols, clocks and beasts and dark woods. And then: there was a commonality to the symbols.

I went by a dark woods in one session. It was really rather frightening, and it took some urging from Mission Control to get me to go in. My voice on the tape says: "Well, okay, but I'm going to hang this tape recorder on this tree, and if I don't come back, first person to see this tape recorder, come in and get me." (There was no tree, and there was a tape recorder, but they seemed equally real at the time, as real as the fear of not finding the way back.)

But it wasn't just me. Everybody had a dark woods in the middle of their head, and sooner or later they got around to it. So when Bob Dylan sang about the foggy ruins of time, past the frozen leaves, the haunted, frightened trees, he touched a universal of sorts.

Why did so many normal, integrated psychedelic subjects come up with the symbol of the dark woods? (There were a number of papers by psychologists on The Meaning of the Forest.) One answer could come from the extent of the retrieval system. You are in a disorienting situation, sensitive to the least suggestion, open to a flow of emotions greater than usual, and this recalls a childhood situation when emotions flow stronger, a Disney movie with dark woods, the illustration in a Grimms' fairy tale. The dark woods is a pervasive symbol in all of Western civilization. The prescript for the first chapter of this book is from the *Divine Comedy*: "In the middle of the journey of our life, I found myself in a dark wood." (What about other civilizations? The research never got intercultural enough before it stopped.) But the retrieval system answer didn't seem complete enough.

Symbols, of course, are old stuff to psychiatric theory. Some people don't like elevators, and some people have dreams about taking exams, and some people are afraid of flying. They know the elevator is okay and the plane isn't going to crash and the exam was years ago, but still they wake up in a sweat because the exam in French 203 is tomorrow and they haven't done the work, or they drive a thousand miles rather than fly because they can't help it, the symbol is attached to a feeling and the feeling is still there.

That people are walking around with a woods in their head is taken for granted by some psychologists, but they have their own favorite symbols. One friend of mine leads transactional marathons. That's where everybody arrives Friday night and stays up, slogging, and by about four o'clock Sunday morning people say some interesting things. My friend's symbol was the Judge. Everybody had the Judge in their heads, and their actions and behavior would be shaped to what the Judge said. My psychologist would tape these encounters, and he would keep spinning the tape recorder like some electronic surveillance expert, and sure enough there would be sentences in there that belonged to the Judge and not to the people who said them. The eerie part was that between FORWARD and REWIND, as the recorder closed in on the phrases, the voices would actually change; the Judge had a different from the speaker's, like the demon in *The Exorcist*. My psychologist, index fingers on FORWARD and REWIND like a true virtuoso, would say, "Whose voice is that?" The voice would be something out of the past, a parent or teacher, or perhaps not even a real parent or teacher but a child's idea of those people, still alive in mid-age and mid-voice.

The psychedelic researchers were well enough versed. Jean Houston and her husband, R. E. L. Masters (no relation to Masters and Johnson), declared four stages in *The Varieties of Psychedelic Experience*. First there was the sensory stage, the geometry of the room changing, the light displays, the crossing of sound and vision, called synesthesia. That was almost universal. Then some subjects went on to a second stage, called recollective-analytical by Houston and Masters. This is the extended memory bank. Still fewer subjects went on to a third stage, the symbolic or mythic. And a very few went on to a fourth stage, integral, or mystic.

In the third stage—the Meaning of the Forest and all that— the subject in the experiment would go through, present tense, something that we would recognize as a myth: a sacred quest, a child hero, paradise and fall, eternal return, polarity (light and darkness, order and chaos). The subject, lying there with the mask and the blue Sandoz, would be the character in the myth. The thesis of Houston and Masters was that these turned up because "our society offers so little in the way of the important rites of passage and initiation provided by other civilizations."

If we never saw a Disney movie or read a Grimms' fairy tale, how do we get a dark woods in the middle of the head?

We inherit it, some people speculate. We know, for example, that if you pass a V-shaped shadow sideways or backwards over a baby chick in a lab, nothing happens. But if you move the same shadow forward, the baby chick goes into a panic. He has inherited the genetic message—*hawk, danger*—for a certain-shaped shadow, even though he is only a couple of days old and has not talked to his mother and may never see a hawk. Children from five to ten are afraid of the dark, and the animals they see in the dark—animals we know aren't there—are the same across the lines of cultural childhood. There was a time when humanity slept by the fire and the predators really were there in the dark. One cell carries the instructions on how to make a whole new person: let's see, make the eyes brown, make the ears thus, make the nose thus, let's set the trigger for adolescent growth at 12.2 years, and oh, yes, let's throw in the message about the bears, predators by the fire, for ages five to nine.

Stanislas Grof led a research team in Czechoslovakia. (Later, he came to the United States.) Grof ran more than 2,600 LSD sessions. Behind the thick carapace of daily life were violent emotions, devils and angels, love, hate, murder, jealousy. The dominant myth in Grof's accounts was death and rebirth. When the subjects were reborn, they went down the birth canal, twisting and grimacing, and exploded into the world again. On the mythic level, they identified with the death and resurrection of

Christ. Alcoholics were not just drinking; they were trying hard to get to a space called DIE.

Grof is a Freudian psychoanalyst. But no existing theoretical system covered, for him, the phenomena that were coming up: "Freudian analysis barely scratches the surface," he said. "The model of personality and image of man emerging from LSD research is much closer to Hindu philosophy than to the Freudian concepts widely accepted by Western science and philosophy . . . [that is,] the human mind as a multilayered dynamic structure with elements of the individual and collective unconscious, as well as karmic and evolutionary memories buried in its depths."

Really? Could the disorganized Hindus have even a vague concept more complete at some level than ours?

R. Gordon Wasson is a businessman turned world's greatest mushroom expert. He has chewed with shamans from Siberia to Guatemala. The Hindu Vedas had referred to a godly substance, soma. In 1971 Wasson identified soma as a hallucinogenic mushroom, *Amanita muscaria*. The layers of the mind, as spun by *Amanita muscaria*, had already been cataloged for thousands of years, but not in the nice, neat way we like it—all analyzed with cause and effect. Much of it, in fact, was incomprehensible, all wound up with legends and myths. Did the legends and myths produce the layers of the mind, or the layers of the mind produce the legends and myths?

And what of the fourth stage, the integral or mystic experience? This is the most lightly researched of all, for no one knows exactly how to define a mystic experience.*

Trying to chart the mystic aspects, or perhaps playing turn on the clergy, Timothy Leary gave LSD to seventy certified pastors and priests. The religious myths and symbols were rampant in

---

* Two sociologists, Andrew Greeley and William McCready, gave it the following attempt: "They are episodes of intense and immediate cognition in which the total personality of a person is absorbed in an intimate though transient relationship with the basic forces, cycles and mechanisms at work in the universe and in his own psychosomatic composite—gravity, cosmic rays, light, heat, electromagnetism, cycles of breathing, circulation, digestion, day, year, life, death."

their minds, much as they had been for the divinity school student doing his Good Friday experiment. A Hasidic rabbi went outside into the garden about four o'clock in the morning. The trees, he said, had faces and arms which were threatening but which became friendly if you said, "Nice trees." "Sha, sha, trees," said the rabbi, "next time I will be a tree, and you will be a human being."

Later the rabbi wrestled with the experience: was it a genuine *aliyath han'shamah*, an ascent of the soul as described by the founding rabbi of the Hasidic sect, the great Baal Shem-Tov? It certainly was something extraordinary. Did it turn plain folks into saints? He didn't think so. It upset him a bit, and left him with more questions than answers.

Aldous Huxley had suggested, in *The Doors of Perception*, that certain experiences, usually considered religious, which came from severe fasting and chanting, might also be available from vegetables, such as mushrooms. Were the experiences the same? A genteel and scholarly debate went on, intellectual Jesuits, theology professors, Oxford dons—were the experiences a "gratuitous grace"?

These shadings were lost in the roar of the Sixties. Jean Houston wrote, "It is frequent and funny, if also unfortunate, to encounter young members of the Drug Movement who claim to have achieved a personal apotheosis when, in fact, their experience appears to have consisted mainly of depersonalization, disassociation, and similar phenoma." But when the psychedelics were merchandised, IT—the Experience—became part of the commercial, along with peer pressure and curiosity.

It should be noted for the record that Albert Hofmann did not have a mystic experience in the lab at Sandoz. He felt dizzy and saw all those crazy colors, and the geometry of the room changed, and he went home and called a doctor. And for many years afterward, the experiences produced by the psychedelics were, for some reason, not thought of as "mystic."

We have been folding and unfolding some of the old maps, the stories of old expeditions. The stories are fascinating, but we cannot linger too long.

William James, resplendent in Victorian beard, Professor of

Psychology at Harvard when there was almost no psychology, himself went on just such map-making expeditions. In contemporary psychology, James is barely looked on as a psychologist. He did not put knife to brain of rat. He did not set up experiments with controls, plain cats vs. dizzy cats. He did not take any polls. He never gave children funny-shaped blocks and clocked them. How could he be a psychologist? Maybe he belongs to philosophy; in psychology now we find him archaic and a bit speculative.

There were no synthetic chemicals for William James. He tried mushrooms. They made him violently ill, and gave him a monumental hangover, and once was enough. "I will take the visions on trust," said William James to Henry James. But after his experiment with nitrous oxide James wrote a paper, and then later he wrote an essay on the dimensions in life. In the essay was a paragraph which gets quoted over and over and over in the more speculative, non rat parts of mind exploration. And this is it:

"One conclusion was forced upon my mind at that time, and my impression of its truth has ever since remained unshaken. It is that our normal waking consciousness, rational consciousness as we call it, is but one special type of consciousness, whilst all about it, parted from it by the filmiest of screens, there lie potential forms of consciousness entirely different. We may go through life without suspecting their existence; but apply the requisite stimulus, and at a touch they are there in all their completeness, definite types of mentality which probably somewhere have their field of application and adaptation. No account of the universe in its totality can be final which leaves these other forms of consciousness quite disregarded. How to regard them is the question —for they are discontinuous with ordinary consciousness. Yet they may determine attitudes though they cannot furnish formulas, and open a region though they fail to give a map. At any rate, they forbid a premature closing of our accounts with reality."

". . . they may determine attitudes though they cannot furnish formulas," said James, seeming to anticipate Freud, "and open a region though they fail to give a map."

And that is still where we are.

II: | Hemispheres

LEFT SIDE,
RIGHT SIDE,
WHY RALPH NADER
CAN'T DANCE

IT is amusing to think that we could all have buried, in the depths of memory, some damn Czech drinking song. It is amusing, because we are not children any more, to think that the little beggars are afraid of bears in the dark when we know there aren't any bears. It is not so amusing to think that we have these symbols influencing our behavior, exams from long ago still there, and cops finding us naked on the streets at midnight. And for everybody to have some symbol in common, the dark woods in the middle of the head, gets a bit discomforting.

But neurophysiology and the skills of surgery have not found, in the brain, at any given location, a Czech drinking song, or a bear, or an exam, or a dark woods. Yet there is, in the structure of the brain, a division of function which affects our individual and social behavior. Not only that, it gives us a metaphor for a whole area of psychology that is not traditionally even in psychology.

The research in this area is called split-brain research, or lateral specialization, getting more attention now. It says that we have a mute self, and we don't usually know it's there because it can't talk, and the only way we know something is there is if it makes more noise than we do when we talk to ourselves. The mute self is at least potentially a dancer, an athlete, a sculptor—maybe screaming to get out, but not knowing the words.

Brains are divided into left and right. More specifically, a part of the brain most important for thought, called the cerebral cortex, is divided into left and right. A hundred years or so ago, the surgeons would notice that a damaged left half stopped speech, and a damaged right half stopped spatial recognition. Expression on the left side, recognition on the right, said the neurologist Hughlings Jackson, 1864. In the last few years, the research has accelerated.

The left brain controls the right side of the body, the right hand. And, cross-court again, the right brain controls the left side of the body. The left side is verbal, rational, functioning and practical. Left hemisphere, right-handed. The right side of the brain, intuitive, spatial, is the artist and dreamer.

Every culture in the world, with or without physiology, has picked this up, usually in terms of left-handed and right-handed. *The Left Hand Is the Dreamer*, novel title. Law and order in French is *le droit*, the right; an illegitimate descendant is *à main gauche*, on the left hand. The Australian aborigines hold a "male" stick in the right hand, and a "female" stick in the left hand. The Mohave, the Bedouin and the Bantu all have the concept that the right side is the father, the left, maternal and passive. "We listen for the heart on the left," wrote psychologist Jerome Bruner, in *On Knowing; Essays for the Left Hand,* "though it is virtually in the center of the thoracic cavity. Sentiment, intuition, bastardy."

Up to the ages of six to ten or so, both halves of the brain operate. After that, speech becomes specialized in the left side of the brain. If a small child suffers brain damage on the left side, the right side will take over language functions. But the same damage in adults leaves them mute. Damage to the right side, in an adult, interferes with musical ability, spatial ability, recognition of people, body awareness. (This is necessarily over-simplified, and is based on right-handers. Left-handers also speak with the left side of the cortex, but some are bilateral and a few are reversed.)

The captain of left-right research is a graying Cal Tech professor, Roger Sperry. It was his contribution to show that both halves of the brain operate independently. In fact, sometimes the left half doesn't know what the right half is doing.

Sperry's team worked on epileptics whose left and right halves had been disconnected from each other in order to stop their seizures. "What is experienced in the right hemisphere seems to be entirely outside the realm of awareness in the left hemisphere," Sperry wrote.

For example: a subject would be blindfolded, and a familiar object—a comb, let's say—would be placed in the subject's left hand. Left hand, right brain. And the subject wouldn't be able to say, "That's a comb." The subject could *demonstrate* using a comb, and he could pick a comb from a whole pile of objects, so the right hemisphere indeed *knew* what a comb was, it just couldn't get out the word "comb."

The patient is still blindfolded. Now they let the left brain work—the right hand creeps over, feels the comb, and immediately, the subject says, "Comb."

Did the two halves of the brain get in each other's way? Wouldn't they get into conflict? Something like that, Sperry reported. "The left hand, after just helping to tie the belt of the patient's robe, might go ahead on its own to untie the completed knot, whereupon the right hand would have to supervene again to retie it. The patient and his wife used to refer to the 'sinister left hand' that sometimes tried to push the wife away aggressively at the same time that the hemisphere of the right hand was trying to get her to come and help."

As good as it was at knot-tying, the right hemisphere was hopeless at math. It couldn't even double the number four.

Furthermore, the left brain wouldn't trust its twin. It knew the left hand belonged to the right brain. So, in the split-brain patients, the left brain wouldn't believe that the left hand could retrieve the comb out of the bag, as if to say, that dummy can't do anything without me. When they were asked to reach with the left hand, patients would say the left hand was numb, or just didn't work. If the left hand did the job, the patient would say, "I was just guessing."

Sperry felt the right half was badly underrated in our society. Some of his papers read as if he is about to call the Civil Liberties Union and demand a better break for the Right Brains. "Excellence in one hemisphere tends to interfere with top-level performance in the other," Sperry said. If that's true, then Ralph Nader and and superrational lawyers and great mathematicians should make lousy dancers. (If any of them show up in a corps de ballet, their courtroom skills or their calculations should suffer. On the other hand—a figure of speech well ingrained— right-sided activities should be a nice vacation for verbal, rational people. Smart old Winston Churchill. Between volumes, writing the life of his ancestor, the Duke of Marlborough, or between speeches, he would daub away in the meadow, or build a brick wall.)

So: we experience outside of language—right-brained—but we can't communicate that experience in words without running it through the left brain. To be "knowledge," to live beyond the moment, it has to be communicated or articulated. "A thought comes," said Einstein, "and I may try to express it in words later."

The experimenters got to work. If you balanced something on each index finger, and timed it, and then repeated the balancing, this time talking while you balanced, would the time be the same? No: talking cut the balancing time. One activity inhibits the other.

If you were looking at a friend, and you asked which way George Washington faces on a quarter, would his eyes go left or right while he thought? Which way would they go if you asked, what is one hundred minus seven times two?

(Some of my friends, curve-busters to the end, shut their eyes, or rolled them straight up.)

"We added emotion to the lateral eye movements," said Harvard's Gary Schwartz. "Emotion is nonverbal, so it's right-brained. We would ask, what's the difference between 'thought' and 'rational' and track the eyes. Then we would ask, which do you feel more often, tearful or angry? The abstract questions led the eyes right, the emotional ones left."

Two researchers at the University of California Medical Center, David Galin and Robert Ornstein, asked: do the hemispheres work continuously in parallel and alternate body control, or do they share? In most activities, they concluded, we pick one and inhibit the other. Who could learn to ride a bicycle from purely verbal instruction?

Ornstein went further in his books *On the Psychology of Meditation* and *The Psychology of Consciousness*. The opposites had long been known: rational and emotional, Dionysius and Apollo, intellectual and intuitive. "Argument and experience are the two modes of knowing," said Roger Bacon. The complementarity had been known, and the left-right distinction in physiology had been known. The Italian psychiatrist Roberto Assagioli had noted how gingerly intellectuals treated intuition. Roger Sperry pointed out how our whole society was built on the left-sided presumptions of the verbal and rational. Robert Ornstein made a kind of metaphor of the right brain. To the unexplored right side, he said, belonged the "esoteric psychologies" of Sufism and yoga, dervish dancing and chanting, mantra and "magic words," meditation—all unexplored territory, from the left-sided, Western point of view.

To think of Oriental religions as Eastern psychologies, right-brained and left-handed, gave a new perspective. They would seem strange to us because we are left-brained, verbal and rational: they wouldn't make any "sense."

The *I Ching*, that venerable Chinese document, expressed the left-right complementarity by dividing the world into light and dark, creative and receptive. The *I Ching* itself is a right-brained document.

There was a time, in this research, when the *I Ching* appeared simultaneously in the worlds I was shuttling between: psychology and finance. Psychology, well, yes, right-brained Eastern esoterica, but the *I Ching* and the stock market?

THE *I CHING*
COMES TO WALL
STREET

THERE are no coincidences, said Carl Gustav Jung, the great Swiss psychiatrist. We think they're coincidences because our model of the world doesn't account for them. We're tied up in cause and effect.

The adventure of the *I Ching* on Wall Street began with one day's mail. At the time, I was out in "experiential" courses of some sort, right-brained, left-handed stuff, and the journals would pile up on my desk. Psychology journals and financial journals. The psychology journals I thought of as The Adventures of Freddie the Rat, In Which Our Investigators Reveal Some New and Dramatic Clockings.

And amidst The Adventures of Freddie the Rat, mixed in, were the economic journals, in this case a whole batch from the Wharton School of the University of Pennsylvania. Nice white plastic covers. Somebody had written, "The Association Between a Market Determined Measure of Risk and Alternative Measures of Risk." Somebody else had written, "The Error Learning Hypothesis and the Term Structure of Interest Rates in Eurodollars."

I know about the term structure of interest rates. It is full of equations that will bite you, and little Greek letters lying on their sides.

Someone at the Wharton School had added a title in ink at the bottom of the mimeographed list of published titles, maybe just for me. This paper was in the series but it hadn't been published. It was: "Can the *I Ching* predict the stock market?"

The *I Ching* and the stock market! Far out!

The *I Ching*, pronounced "E Ching," not "eye Ching," is an ancient Chinese book of wisdom used to tell you what course of action to take and what the future may bring. It has sold one million copies in the last five years. You toss three coins or forty-nine yarrow stalks—most Americans throw three coins—and from the results of the tosses you create a hexagram, and then you look up the hexagram in the *I Ching*. I was learning not to scoff at such right-brained activities, since the left brain is the scoffer, but even not scoffing the *I Ching* sometimes seemed like a bag of fortune cookie slips from a Chinese bakery. "Youthful folly has success," said the *I Ching*. "The maiden is powerful. One should not marry such a maiden. It furthers one to undertake something."

Still, this was not some lunatic fringe, this was the Wharton School of Business and Finance, and there was the *I Ching*, right under the term structure of interest rates in Eurodollars.

I bought a $7.50 Bollingen edition of the *I Ching* and hastened to Philadelphia. On the train I noticed that the title of a best seller on the Vietnam war was taken from Hexagram #49: "FIRE IN THE LAKE. The image of REVOLUTION . . . starting brings misfortune. Perseverance brings danger. Changing the form of government brings good fortune."

The *I Ching* paper, it turned out, had been done by a student of a young, mustachioed professor, Dan Rie. Rie is a mathematical economist, into random walks and such, teaching security analysis. What do I spy on his shelves? *The Power of Witchcraft, The Magic Power of Your Mind* and a button that says REALITY IS A CRUTCH. I am on the right track.

"I had a student," said Rie, "who was into the Guru Maharaj Ji. He was a good student, but he said he wasn't interested in writing a thesis on capital asset pricing or income velocity, the only thing that interested him was the *I Ching*. Every day when he got up he would throw the *I Ching*, and he would follow its dictates. Other than the *I Ching*, he was into the stock market. So I said he could do his thesis on the *I Ching* and the stock market."

Wharton is a business school, and finance deals in precision, however artificial. Onto the computer went the *I Ching*. The heads-tails construction is a binary form anyway, and then the student assigned a range of numerical values for the hexagrams, started with A on the stock market page, and asked the *I Ching* about the first eighty stocks. "Whereas Aristotelian logic attempts to find causes, and on that basis make projections, the *I Ching* prefers to find patterns," said the thesis. "The potential of the moment is the future. The future however is to an extent dependent on the past. The basic circular nature of the *I Ching* patterns is now seen. Circles seldom have reasons."

"In his first sample," Rie said, "the *I Ching* significantly outperformed all the random portfolios. The department got quite interested."

I bet they did. I could see them, teacups trembling in the faculty common room—maybe they've tapped an ancient power, like atomic energy, Keynes after all endowed his Cambridge college by stock market speculations, what if the thing works? It's academically unrespectable, they would have to do it quietly, maybe hit the computer at night when nobody was around—

"So we ran the *I Ching* on two hundred and forty stocks. This time it did significantly less well."

I asked what time period the *I Ching* was being asked to predict. Eighty days, Rie said. That seemed like a short time for so venerable an instrument.

"When the *I Ching* didn't do as well the second time, the department cooled off," Rie said. "We're still working on it. Now we have the Fu Shi Circle on the computer, as well as the binary values and the subjective assignments." The Fu Shi Circle is a further refinement of the *I Ching*.

"So you really believe it works?" I asked.

Rie was cautious. "There is a mode of causality outside what we perceive," he said. "I collect these things but I don't have great faith in any one of them. The *I Ching*, you see, gives you the answer you *need* rather than the one that is 'correct.' It works in your long-run best interest, maybe longer than a single lifetime. To the *I Ching*, this lifetime is a minor manifestation of something bigger."

I said I would like to concentrate on stocks for this lifetime—in fact, for the immediate future.

"Even if it works, I doubt if the *I Ching* will be used in security analysis," Rie said. "If the AT&T pension fund was run according to the *I Ching*, the managers just wouldn't be able to conform to it. They wouldn't be able to keep heir hands off."

We got out the coins and the *I Ching* and the handy computer reference, and tried on a couple of stocks for size.

"Okay, *I Ching*," I said. "IBM."

IBM came up *Shih,* Hexagram #7. K'un, the Receptive, over K'an, the Abysmal.

"The superior man increases his masses," Rie said.

"I guess they'll throw out the antitrust suit," I said. "IBM will increase its share of the market."

We gave IBM a bullish reading.

I tried American Can.

"Enthusiasm," said the *I Ching*. "It furthers one to install helpers and to set armies marching."

"Gee, that's good," I said. "I wonder if they know how good business is going to be. I hope they're ready to put on the second and third shifts. Maybe they should build a new plant. Looks real good for American Can," I said. "Let's try Leasco."

"If someone is not as he should be, he has misfortune," the *I Ching* said.

"Well, they shouldn't have tried to raid the Chemical Bank, that was hubris, they're still trying to shake off that reputation," I said. Leasco had an unstable line in its hexagram: If you really get into the *I Ching*, you learn about unstable lines. The unstable line converts to another hexagram, which we looked up, for Leasco. It came out Work On What Has Been Spoiled.

"They'll be okay," I interpreted, "if they clean up their accounting procedures and keep their nose clean."

When asked about the market, the *I Ching* hedged. At first it said, "Strength with elegance . . . leads to great wealth," and then it converted sourly, a black cloud over the sun, "Undertakings bring misfortune."

"I think one uses the *I Ching* to support what he already thinks," I said. "I've seen this with the people that consult the computer about the stock market."

"It works better when you're really sincere," Rie said. "When the second batch of stocks didn't come through, we asked the *I Ching* why our method wasn't working. The *I Ching* said, 'Even the best of hunters finds no game in an empty field.' "

To Jung, the *I Ching* was no bag of fortune cookie slips. He studied it for thirty years and wrote the preface to the Bollingen *I Ching*. He warned that the *I Ching* was not for "the frivolous minded and immature, nor is it for intellectualists and rationalists." He was impatient with "the heavy-handed pedagogic approach that attempts to fit irrational phenomena into a preconceived rational pattern."

The great attraction to Jung was that the *I Ching* presented a way to explore the unconscious. "If the *I Ching* is not accepted by the conscious, at least the unconscious meets it halfway, and the *I Ching* is more closely connected with the unconscious than with the rational attitude of consciousness."

In the West, cause and effect are assumed in the paradigm. The *I Ching* blithely ignores cause and effect; it is concerned with the quality of the exact moment the coins are thrown. Our Western axioms of causality are "merely statistical truths and thus must allow for exceptions," Jung wrote, "every process is partially or totally interfered with by *chance*," and it was this chance which the Chinese mind was concerned with. The yarrow stalks thrown to the floor formed the pattern characteristic of the moment, but that only meant something when you added the observer's knowledge. The Chinese, in other words, had skipped Aristotle and Newton and gone right to the probabilities of quantum mechanics, in which the observer had to be part of the process.

If you know any of Jung, you can see why he was attracted to the *I Ching*. Here is his theory of the collective unconscious, and here are the archetypes that are the same for everybody in the unconscious, the Wise Old Man and the Dark Woods and the Earth Mother and so on. And then here is this ancient Chinese document, which operates with archetypes, heaven and lake, prince and maiden, fire and earth. Further, Jung coined the term "synchronicity," which he opposed to causality. Causality was just a working hypothesis of how events evolve out of each other; synchronicity took the coincidence of events in space and time as more than chance, an interdependence of the event and the psychic state of the observer.

I got myself an *I Ching* teacher. My *I Ching* teacher did not have a long white goatee and speak in the fortune cookie talk of *Kung Fu.* He had two Ph.D.'s, one in economics, one in psychology, and he had read every word Jung had ever written, which is why my reading of the *I Ching* has such a Swiss accent. "Think of the *I Ching* as decision theory," said my teacher the economist. "What is your decision—consult the *I Ching*—see if you change the decision the *I Ching* is information input, how beneficial is the additional information—utility maximization, cost benefit analysis." "The *I Ching* can free your intuition," said my teacher the psychologist. "You project your own unrealized thoughts onto its symbolism, just like Jung said in the foreword."

I asked the *I Ching* whether the study of it was a proper use of my energy. "The Clinging, Fire," said my teacher. "Your own idea implies that time and energy are finite. You are going to cram in as much as you can as fast as you can, or bewail and discard it. Time brings illumination, without the polarity you project."

That made me a bit dizzy, but I kept on practicing. One realization grew on me: the Wharton School had the *I Ching* pointed in the wrong direction, like using a microscope to view the stars, or a telescope to look at cells. The *I Ching,* Jung had said, was like having an old and courteous friend—I supposed a Ben Franklin, who would talk to you in axioms. Asked about the stock market, the old and courteous friend got vague and could not find his glasses. The *I Ching* should not be pointed at an *object,* such as a list of stocks, but at the *mind* of the questioner.

That is the only Western use of the *I Ching*: to tell you what you already know in your own mind, but may not be listening to because of old habit patterns, or other voices in your head.

I wrote a respectful letter to the Wharton School on the subject of the *I Ching*, recommending that they unhook it from the computer and turn it around. If random-walk theoreticians asked the *I Ching* about the stock market, what they were going to get back would be a random walk.

I suspect the Wharton School was turning back to income velocity. In the next list of papers, there was no *I Ching*; in fact, Dan Die was there with "Security Analysis in Efficiency Markets."

Then I went to Wall Street with the *I Ching* under my arm.

I would sit in the conference room of the firms I called on, and one by one the partners would come in and ask the *I Ching* a question.

Why did they put up with this? The moment is important, as the *I Ching* says. They were confused. Five years previous, they would not have taken the time, and their assumptions were that since they were smart, they put information together and evaluated it in such a way that they made a lot of money. But now everybody who was in the market at all was losing money—indeed, all this professional management was doing worse than the random averages. (In one investment partnership, my partners put out a monthly memo in which, month after month, they explained this performance with carefully rational reasons, saying they were right and the market was wrong. The next month again they would say they were right and the market was wrong because their reasons were right. If you're stubborn, you can lose a fortune with causality and plain logic.)

I explained that the *I Ching* was not about to predict the market, but maybe it would bring something up out of their minds, and they should pay attention to that something. They would throw the coins and I would simply read the hexagram and its interpretation and ask them what it meant.

Dick threw Work On What Has Been Spoiled, Keeping Still, Mountain, over The Gentle, Wind. He had asked about his view of the market. "That's very good," he said. "Very good. It means pay attention, and don't get sucked into the rallies. See, it says, 'Setting right what has been spoiled by the father.' Well, that means that the last guy to run this portfolio missed the market completely. We need a new tack. Intellectually is not the way to make money."

The hexagram had an unstable line, which converted to #46, Pushing Upward.

"You see that? You see that?" Dick said. "Encounters no obstruction! That confirms my technical position! When there are spikes off the bottom on the chart, we hit the supply!'

Dick was so turned on by the *I Ching*'s confirmation of his technical position that he wanted another turn, but Chuck was waiting at the door to the conference room.

"I only have a couple of minutes," Chuck said. "I got a big European bank coming in here. I want to know: should I play my logic against other people's emotions, which is the way that's always worked for me?"

"*Shih Ho*, Biting Through," I read. I handed him the interpretation.

He nodded as he read. "Okay, this means Do you have the guts to do it? Go ahead. See—'Traitor': 'Traitor' is those who act emotionally. I've been feeling wishy-washy and giving decisions to Jack. I should make the decisions because I'm gentler. And when the lightning comes, there's a storm ahead, lightning clears the air. Once people see that the storm has cleared the air, rationality will prevail. So you buy at sensible prices and forget the storm. Thanks, my big bank is here."

"Splitting Apart," the *I Ching* said to Al. "It does not further one to go anywhere."

"That's easy," Al said. "You remain quiet. Nothing to do about the accounts, they will go through their stages. Wait till things get right. Let's see, 'Steep and narrow must topple over.' That means the growth stocks are going to get killed. 'Favor comes through the court ladies'—what the hell does that mean, date the secretaries? 'A large fruit still uneaten' means money in undervalued situations."

Does the *I Ching* really work?

There are all those people who swear by it, skiers who leave home on a warm ground-bare day, and when they get to the mountains there's the snow. If the *I Ching* says, "It does not further one to go anywhere," and you leave your house and get into a big traffic jam, you say, 'Well, the *I Ching* said so," and if you don't know the *I Ching* that morning, it's just another traffic jam. In order to have predictive power, the *I Ching* would have to be operating in some system of time other than the one we have in our paradigm.

But as a symbol around which unconscious thoughts can be projected—well, that is the area Jung thought so promising, and one which we use so little that anything we do seems like progress.

I did not keep up with my *I Ching* lessons, nor did I check to see how the *I Ching* had done in the stock market. It could not possibly have done worse than most of the professionals I knew. Using it for the market seemed almost a little profane for one of the world's great documents. Something must have worked, though, because a couple of months later I got a phone call from a busy trading room, with shouts of numbers in the background.

"Hey, where you been?" said the voice. "What the hell are you doing these days? Nobody ever sees you."

There was something in the caller's voice that made me ask what was on his mind.

"You know that Chinese book you had? I got a question for it. I already threw the coins, to save time. First line, two heads and a tail. Second line, one head, two tails."

I interrupted to ask: what was the question?

"Ask that book if my wife knows about my girl friend."

"The *I Ching* does not take calls over the phone," I said. "The best of hunters finds no game in an empty field," I added.

There is one more point. To pay profound attention, really profound attention, to the exact pattern made by forty-nine yarrow stalks in a moment requires a meditative state, almost a trance, and the serious users of the *I Ching* in the era of King W'en, like the oracles at Delphi, were most likely in some altered state of consciousness. I doubt that the subliminal and ethereal powers of mind have much chance to work in the five minutes before the man from the big bank arrives, or in a quick toss of the coins before breakfast. If we pull the *I Ching* into the rational, analytic, left-brained world we live in, we get fortune cookie stories and reruns of *Kung Fu* from this old and revered gentleman. Maybe the people who swear it works take the time, maybe they trance easily, and maybe the old gentleman is laughing up his flowered sleeve.

ON THE LEFT HAND (RIGHT BRAIN), AMERICA'S LEADING ASHRAM

THE *I Ching* is one monument to the right cerebral hemisphere. A couple hundred yards over the Pacific surf, in the timeless misty Big Sur range of the California coast, is another: Esalen, not as old as the *I Ching,* but certainly as well publicized. It was not the publicized group encounter techniques of the Sixties that made Esalen important as a right-brained citadel. Esalen was the counter-culture's university, where the right-brained techniques could surface, and the right-brained ideas could find articulation.

"Our primary concern," wrote Mike Murphy, its founder, "is the affective domain—the senses and feelings, though we're interested in the cognitive, too." So, on the Esalen grounds, you might see a blindfolded person being led, to "restore the sense of touch and the experience of dependency." Or you could see people "conversing" with their eyes alone, or their hands alone, "cutting through society's excessive verbalism to authentic feelings."

Ah, those authentic feelings. What an effort to get to them, encountering and gestalting and confronting—the authentic feeling made king. There were the far-out therapists paying attention to the sound of the participants' voices, their breathing and posture.

You could take belly dancing at Esalen, and movement, and sensory awareness, or you could sit on the lawn and eat a single grape very slowly. Or you could find six or eight people rolling over and over each other in a sandwich, like kids do: it's all right to do that as a kid in our society, but not as an adult. It's all right to touch, said Esalen. It does your head good.

So you could go from the baths to your massage class and get sort of stoned amidst the sheer tactility of sunlight and oils and touch, and all the bodies would begin to look good, not only the light and tanned ones, but the flabby ones as well: all human, all together. A cheering experience.

"We shape our houses and then they shape us," Churchill said. Esalen was a small place, ninety acres or so, a hundred people at most there, more now, but it became a symbol. Let the mute right side speak!

Had Esalen not been so beautiful, it might have folded when the Sixties ran out, like all the other growth centers. Dr. Patrick Murphy had bought it for its beauty and its natural sulfur springs in 1910, when there was no road. The Esalen Indians had used the springs. Dr. Murphy intended to make it a spa for patients, but never did. It slumbered in the Pacific fogs. The state road pushed through. The Pentecostal Church rented it.

Dr. Murphy practiced in Salinas, John Steinbeck's hometown. The Cain and Abel of *East of Eden,* it was said, were Dr. Murphy's grandsons, Dennis and Michael. Dennis would get stabbed in the chest in a barroom brawl and blow cigarette smoke through the stab wounds: Michael was high school class president and gave speeches to the local Rotary Club—Why I Am Proud to Be an American. Michael got turned on by a course in Oriental religions at Stanford and went off to the Sri Aurobindo ashram in India. When he got back, he was a bellboy at the Del Monte Golf Club. His Stanford classmates, clambering up the financial ladder, in white oxford button-downs and narrow ties, would do a double take on their way to the golf course.

To restore dance and touch and the other right-brained activities, Murphy had to retrieve the place from his grandmother and her tenants, the Pentecostal Church. (Murphy was not thinking in terms of brain hemispheres, only in terms of an institute of human potential, of nonverbal humanities.) The site had be-come—unbeknownst to the church—a homosexual hangout. Hunter Thompson, later of *Fear and Loathing* books, was hired as caretaker. "Hunter brought a lot of guns," said Murphy, "and he almost got himself killed because he would sit in the care-taker's shack firing away at the homosexuals who climbed the fence, and one night the window was blasted away." Thompson escaped. The church left. The institute was founded.

No television, no newspapers, only one phone, outdoors. The noise of the outside world quickly dropped away in the mists of the mountains. For the education of the nonverbal mode, it was a particularly sensual place. To sit in the hot sulfur baths was an agreeable communal experience. The nudity became natural. Esalen evolved its own massage techniques and even-tually published them. It was said that if everybody gave a mas-sage every day and received one there would be less violence and fewer wars.

And along came a neuropsychologist to say the same thing. If you don't touch enough, your brain dries up; societies that don't touch become aggressive. Witness, said Dr. James Prescott of the National Institutes of Health, infants separated from their par-ents can develop mental retardation, they sit and rock for hours, like monkeys reared in isolation. "If the deprivation is extreme," said Dr. Prescott, "you get actual structural damage to the brain —the brain cells don't have as many dendritic branches, so the cells don't make contact with as many other cells." We're miss-ing body pleasure, so we have visual substitutes like pornog-raphy; the Judeo-Christian belief had set up that body pleasure is evil. "Somatosensory deprivation" creates an environment that produces an aggressive species. The stakes were high: "If vio-lence becomes fixed genetically, the species will no longer be capable of expressing affectionate, peaceful behavior. Mankind will be able to express only physically violent behavior. Mankind will self-destruct."

Make love, not war. If we could only get the Russians and the Chinese and the Arabs and everybody all together, and break out the massage oils—see, it sounds funny already, the way things sound from beyond the paradigm, like surrealist art can

[78]

seem funny. But figure: the cost of one guided-missile submarine would keep the world in massage oil for years. A trillion and a half for arms, back and forth across the world: in massage oils, that would last forever.

Everything that surfaced in humanistic psychology checked in at Murphy's ashram. But the seekers perhaps no longer believe that the world is about to change so quickly. Alas.

Now you can stay at Esalen on an American Express card. It has become its own monument. College students take courses there for credit. Corporations send management teams for short sessions.

At the great outpost of nonverbal learning, you cannot buy an Esalen sweat shirt, or a candy bar, or a pencil, or in fact anything at all. Except books. You can buy books. Books written by the people who lecture or lead groups at Esalen. Every man jack of *them* has written a book or is writing one and has contracts for three more. The courses people sign up for are by the people they've read. Those are the "stars." Everything else is just the daily operation.

So: nice, linear, book-reading people come to Esalen, and they do their nonlinear, nonreading, touching, feeling workshop, and then they go to the bookstore and buy a linear, verbal book about the nonlinear, feeling experience they just had, and they take it home and read it. And the book said: get out of your head, you stupid, the head is not where it's at. The body is where it's at

The body never lies.

THE GRANDMA
AND GRANDPA OF
GRAVITY

IT was at Esalen that the right-brained body activities surfaced, and it was Esalen, or Esalaneers, who found Ida Rolf and Moshe Feldenkrais, or at least brought them to the attention of those interested in releasing their inhibitions and developing their personalities through new bodies and thence new minds.

The body never lies. So say the people who say the body never lies. I am not quite sure what it means, even after all this time. I understand part of the message: you have a lot of irrelevant stuff in your head and your head is not your friend, you are watching television and your body is reasonably happy, purring away, and the TV commercial says, we've come to a break in the action, folks, why don't you go get another beer. And you do it. Your body doesn't want the beer, in fact you had to wake it up with associations and images, and you sell it to yourself. You also sell yourself another ten pounds.

Or: you are playing something, something physical, and you want to win. Your body doesn't give a damn, it's right-brained, it can't even count beyond four so it certainly doesn't care who gets the highest number of whatever. But you do, so you give a little extra lunge, and there goes your back or your knee or your shoulder or your neck. If you and your body were grooving together, say the body people, you wouldn't have a bad back and a tennis elbow and a bursitic shoulder, and you wouldn't put on weight when you don't want to.

Well, okay. I have trouble squaring body-never-lies with my textbooks in physiological psychology, and in perception, which say the body lies all the time, or, if it doesn't lie, at least it doesn't tell the truth because it doesn't know. It will tell you things are out there that aren't there, optical illusions, and it will give you false signals on how hot is hot and how full is full, and which is red and which is black in certain trick patterns. That may not be lying, but you wouldn't trust it, either.

The body-never-lies people say body and mind are all the same, in spite of the division made in Platonic and Christian and Cartesian theory, and if you get the body integrated and aligned, you get the mind integrated and aligned, too.

Ida Rolf's theory is based on your relationship to gravity. There is a right way for you to be in relation to gravity, to sit, stand, walk, and if you're out of line, so is your mind. Ida called her technique Structural Integration. Therapy by body manipulation, get yourself back in line with gravity and you will see life steadily and see it whole.

Practically nobody is in line correctly with gravity. When you were a kid, you fell off your bike, and some muscles went into trauma and they released only partially, and ever since, your right shoulder is a little higher than your left. Or you fell on the ice, or you were in a car accident, and you don't even remember these things but your body does, it's holding a little knot there in trauma and you don't even know it. Some of the knots aren't in trauma, and Rolfing is not only for the accident-stricken.

If this were only an extension of Swedish massage, or chiropracting, it would hardly belong among the powers of mind, but the mind-traumas are there, too; the insult that made you tense your shoulder, fight-or-flight, or the feeling that you had about your father is translated into stomach tension and is still there. (Followers of the character-armor theories of Wilhelm Reich like this part, since it was influenced by Reich.)

Nor does the insult or injury stay just where it was; in order to compensate, the body shifts, changing the pattern of carrying weight. Sometimes the temporary solution becomes permanent. The muscles thicken, and then the droopy shoulders or the sunken chest become familiar and comfortable. And, in this body-mind continuum, emotions thicken and grow inelastic as well.

Ida Rolf got a doctorate in biochemistry and physiology in 1920, worked as a biochemist for a dozen years, and spent the next forty on this physiological technique. Around the muscle groups are myofasciae—tissues that envelop and support them. The fasciae have a certain plasticity—they can be molded and moved, to a degree. Rolfing involves manipulating the fasciae, and detaching fibrils between muscles, and repositioning muscles and ligaments. To this end the Rolfer uses his fingers, his elbow, his fist, his hand, and pretty nearly all of his weight.

The result is a massage given by Thomas Torquemada. (Torquemada was the bishop in Spain, during the Inquisition, who loved your soul so dearly that to save it he would tear your tongue out by the roots.)

But how much can it hurt? I met a psychologist who had a peak experience with his first Rolfing. His chest released and he breathed for the first time in his life and his shoulders undrooped and his works, his written work, started to flow. Sam Keen, a writer for *Psychology Today,* sang the Body Electric and said the memory of an old conflict had been encysted, and came out with pressure on the shoulder, and he warmed to new people and new events.

I signed up for Rolfing.

That buried feelings influence current action is, of course, an axiom in Freudian analysis. Bring it up and it isn't buried, and then you can at least have the option of whether you want it to be of influence or not. If the distorting influence could be brought up by an elbow into the belly, that might be quite interesting, except that most Rolfers aren't analysts.

A trauma-free body-mind! I lay down upon the Rolfing table with some apprehension. Who knew what knots were in there?

"Standard fucked-up American male body," said the Rolfer.

"I can do seventy-five push-ups," I said, defensively.

"That's just the trouble," said the Rolfer. "All that armor. No movement. No feeling. Thick muscles. No fluidity. American games are terrible for you. You need to dance."

"The games I play are all inside rectangles," I volunteered, "and come to think of it, so are the ones I watch. The playing fields are rectangles, never circles or ovals. Maybe those geometric shapes have a psychic dimension."

The Rolfer wasn't interested in my quite profound comparison between geometry and psychic space, he had his elbow in my chest and was pressing with all his weight.

"Hey," I said. "That hurts."

He continued to press, outlining some muscle all the way into the armpit.

"That hurts even more," I said.

Have you ever had the Novocaine wear off in the dentist's office, or had a tooth filled without it, and there's pain, and the dentist says just a minute, he doesn't want to stop right then, and you think it can't get more painful but it does?

"I am not making the pain, you are making the pain," said the Rolfer.

"I felt fine when I came in here," I said.

"Stop resisting. Relax. Breathe."

"How can I relax with your elbow in my armpit? I never knew armpits were so sensitive."

The Rolfer continued to press, push, twist.

"You enjoy this work?" I grunted.

A hot red sear of pain went around the left side of my chest. I decided to let my mind go elsewhere. Where did my mind want to go?

"Ve haff vays to make you talk. Schwein! Vere vill de invasion come?"

"Name, rank and serial number is all you get from me."

"So far ve haff been chentle. Vun more time—vich place do de shtupid Amerikaners land?"

"Name, rank and serial number . . ."

"You're not participating," the Rolfer said. "Stay with it. Stay here."

"I don't like it here," I said.

After the session, the Rolfer said: some people after they are Rolfed grow an inch or two. Their shoe sizes increase. It's a trip. At some point you have a *gestalt,* a breakthrough, and you're changed. "When I was Rolfed," he said, "I felt like I was sixteen again."

I did feel better after the session, but I wrote in my notes that I thought I felt better because it was over.

"Americans, Westerners in general, have lost the balance in their bodies," said the Rolfer, warming up his knuckles for the next session. "They develop the big muscles, the ego-controlled muscles, and the smaller muscles behind those atrophy. Calisthenics only stretch the muscles temporarily, games traumatize them, even jogging isn't good."

It was very difficult, upon feeling a painful pressure, not to want the painful pressure to go away, not to resist. Resistance makes tension, tension makes pain, how come I couldn't get the message? Some sessions were easier than others. I thought I was improving when all the pressure on the backs of the legs didn't make me try to wriggle off the table. But then we hit the insides of the thighs. Who would think that moving all the muscles a couple of inches would cause such objections in the head?

The Rolfer had his elbow on the inside of my thigh, and he had so much weight on it he was perspiring. I looked at the ceiling: *Name, rank and serial number . . .*

"All men are sensitive here," he said, slightly out of breath. "Their mind fears the mutilation of the genitals. That's why African tribes have the mutilation of the genitals as an initiation ceremony—you have to go through the fear to the other side, to gain the use of your legs. Otherwise you don't have the full use of them. The tribe is interdependent, if you're an integral part of it they must have confidence in you, in your legs. Zulus can run fifty miles a day. If your survival depended on running down an antelope—"

"Absolutely—no—call—for—antelope—meat—in—my—family," I gasped.

The Rolfer pulled my feet together, halfway through the session. "There," he said, with some satisfaction. "See, one of your legs is an inch longer than the other."

"Match them up again, for God's sake," I said.

And so we proceeded. Did I stand a bit straighter? Was there more bounce in my step? Did I feel lighter? Maybe—but I was probably not a good Rolfee. (In every culture, the patient's failure is the patient's fault. You didn't work hard enough with the psychiatrist, or you quit, or you didn't bring the right chicken bones to the witch doctor and the old curse is still on.) About a month later, three of us Rolfees were comparing notes at dinner, and when we went out onto the street, there was our Rolfer walking along. Spontaneously the cry arose, *git im*. The Rolfer ducked into a doorway, went into a crouch, covered his head with his hands. I thought I saw terror in his eyes and a lack of confidence in his craft. (In fairness, the middle one of the three of us bearing down the street shouting *git im* was a former pro basketball player who was a shade over seven feet tall.)

A goodly year after the Rolfing, I talked to Ida Rolf, the inventor. She is said to be a very scary old lady. I found her snappish and curt. Yes, to be under elbow there would be scary.

"Your joints," she said, "are lifeless."

"But I've been Rolfed!" I protested.

"Who did it?" she asked.

I told her.

"Oh, well, him," she said, with a wave of her hand. "There are hacks everywhere. He shouldn't be Rolfing. Most Rolfers shouldn't be Rolfing."

"They come here and train," said Ida's son, who was also present, "and then we don't have their allegiance once they leave, and they start to do other things as well."

"There's no other profession," Ida said darkly, "where you can take six months' training and make twenty-five dollars an hour. I know why they come, most of them."

I asked how many hours of Rolfing one needed. Maybe I hadn't, with my lifeless joints, had enough; Dick Price, the co-chairman of Esalen, had had three hundred hours. "Ten hours is the course," Ida said. "Dick Price," she snorted. "Who Rolfed Dick Price?"

"Who are the good Rolfers?" I asked.

"There's me, and there's my son here," Ida said.

Then there was a silence.

"That's a very tight guild," I said.

"He was the only Rolfer for ten years other than me," Ida said. "Why should I train others? It's a damn hard job and there's no money in it."

"But there are others."

"A few. There are a few."

"Who would you like to have as trainees? Doctors? Psychologists?"

"Psychologists don't know bodies," Ida said.

"Doctors' minds are already set," her son said.

"Maybe if it were taught in medical school—"

"Not while I'm alive," Ida said. "I know them. They'll put it in a corner."

I began to have the feeling that Rolfing was not going to sweep the country.

"I don't like osteopaths and chiropractors, either," Ida said.

Who would they like to have as subjects? There must be, for example, athletes who have gotten themselves out of line—

"Athletes are too hard," Ida said. "I don't want to take on those oversized hard bodies."

"They take too much time, too," her son said.

I got the glimmer of a *gestalt,* a whole new thing. I had arriver at Madame Rolf's feeling slightly guilty about my Rolfing —was I a bad Rolfee? How come people swore by it? How come Sam Keen could sing the Body Electric and get a whole new self and lose his childhood body-traumas and I was still walking around scrunched up from when my bicycle ran into the guardrail? When I left Madame Rolf's, I felt freer and better, just for talking to her, without having had an elbow laid on me. The glimmer that hit me was from W. C. Fields or somebody like that: if at first you don't succeed, quit.

Ida Rolf is the grandma of the gravity and structure cult; Moshe Feldenkrais is the grandpa, but that is figurative, since they scarcely know each other. In person, Ida makes you feel like you have just farted in church; Feldenkrais is Grandpa-come-to-Sunday-dinner, making rabbit ears out of the handkerchief corners for you, telling terrible jokes and dramatic long stories. Feldenkrais is an Israeli, round, short, with twin crests of white hair like David Ben-Gurion used to have—and that accent! Lovable, but what is it? Feldenkrais surveys the American scene, *tranzen trichten meshugas blichten,* he says; those are nonsense words designed for flavor, since I couldn't catch the ones he did say, though I asked him twice; the only real word, as far as I know, is meshuga, crazy. "I said, Americans pay people to make them crazy."

No wrenching of myofasciae with Feldenkrais. They are all slow, deliberate, mild exercises, based on the "reversibility relationship" of the muscular and nervous system. Our patterns, and muscle movements of which we are all unaware, are brought into awareness by a reversed pattern. Most of the lessons are lying down, to help break the habitual motion of the muscle in gravity. Lying flat on the floor, wanting to get up, do we jerk ourselves up using our stomach muscles? What if we rolled over and pressed ourselves up, and put our feet slowly under our bodies? The Feldenkrais exercises are exercises in sensing. What does the motion feel like? Slowly, no strain, no push, stop whenever you feel a strain—"In the end one should improve to the point," says a Feldenkrais paper, "where one feels that one's body is hanging lightly from the head, so that the body glides when moving."

So we are all on the floor, a whole class worth of psychologists and dance people and so on—Feldenkrais has lectured to the company of director Peter Brook on movement—and Feldenkrais himself is sitting in a director's chair facing us, a lavaliere microphone around his neck, telling us motion by motion, watching—

"—now, slowly, move your hands away—fust row, second man, move your hands away, you're afraid somebody would steal them? hands away, and now, slowly, no strain, find the right knee and move back—back—where is back, dollink? redhead, in third row, where is back? good, back, and now, slowly, sit back, sit back, left knee behind right—

"OY! Who said to take the hands from the floor! OY! Clumsy oxes! You need a discipline!"

The voice becomes soothing again—

"—nicely, nicely, slowly, roll to center position, good, with the right hand take the laft foot, LAFT FOOT which is laft you in first row, good, notice breathing, notice which way the knee turns, notice which way the shoulders go—the right path is the one the skeleton would move in as if it had no muscles, body must be organized so it will follow the shortest path, no strain, no effort, the bones will follow a path of the skeleton pulled by its head—"

Sometimes we do exercises on one side and then visualize them on the other side before doing them, and the other side has learned more quickly through the visualization. One Feldenkrais warmer-upper is to lie with the back on the floor, arms over the head in line with the legs, and scan the body for the contact points with the floor. Are all the vertebrae on the floor? If they aren't, what muscles are working to hold them off? It probably takes a conscious effort to press the spine to the floor, and as soon as that stops, the original pattern comes back. With a shoulder movement, raise the right upper arm until there is an infinitely small space between the back of the hand and the floor, then let the arm drop back again. Rest, and repeat, twenty times. Is the back of the hand beginning to creep along the floor as the arm stretches before it's raised? Is the breathing beginning to match the exercise, with the exhale as the arm stretches? Slowly, slowly bring the arms back to the sides, draw up the knees, and rest. Scan the body. Is there a difference between right and left sides?

Something is going on: we come into the class and hold up our arm and turn in an arc and it goes to *there,* and then, after the reversal exercise, we try it again and it will go all the way to *there,* thirty degrees further—

It's easy to do this in a class, with a voice telling you, but it would be harder alone, because we are so used to gross, major movements, and these movements are so quiet, so small, so subtle—

And this is going to help our heads too?

"Certainly," says Feldenkrais. "We have a self-image in the

motor cortex of the brain. We learn just enough to get by with that self-image. It limits our capacity. We maybe use five percent of ourselves, maybe ten percent. A man who has mastered several languages makes use of more combinations of cells than someone with one language, more neuronal pathways. If we say, 'I will never understand mathematics,' or 'I cannot dance well,' that limits us."

But we get to this expanded potential through movement?

"Certainly," says Feldenkrais. "We only know what is happening through muscle movement. We know it is laughter or fear or anxiety through the heart or the eye muscles or the lungs. Sometimes something happens within us and we don't know what it is until we interpret the new pattern of organization. These exercises attack at the hinge of habit. A change in the motor integration leaves thought and feeling without the usual anchorage, and open to change. If somebody can do something in half an hour that he thought he could never do, that changes his image of himself."

Feldenkrais is Dr. Feldenkrais, just as Ida Rolf is Dr. Rolf, but neither is a doctor of medicine. Feldenkrais' doctorate is in physics. He also taught judo for thirty years. An Israeli black-belt judo-expert physicist with a muscle-pattern system to change body-minds.

"I warn you, my life is complicated," Feldenkrais says. "I got interested in movement because of my own knees. I was a football player for years—soccer football, you call it. I was a left back. And when I began to have a lot of trouble, the surgeons wanted to operate—"

"This was in Israel?"

"No, in Scotland, the surgeons wanted to operate, and I didn't like the sound of the chances, so I started studying anatomy and physiology and biochemistry, and I didn't have the operation. Without knowing it, the judo had matured some ideas in my mind—"

"Judo in Scotland?"

"No, in Paris, the judo had matured some ideas in my mind, and after the war I put them down, in the evening—"

"In Paris?"

"No, in London, you know, you're still hung up in cause and effect. When will you learn cause and effect are not what you think?"

Feldenkrais' soccer days were in Israel, or rather, in British Palestine, and as a member of a touring club. He was also a member of the Haganah, the Jewish self-defense force under the British mandate in Palestine, and he wrote a booklet on jujitsu. "We had some Jews who had been on the Berlin police force, who taught jujutsu." When he went to Paris to study physics, he joined a judo club, and in fact became the chief disciple of an expert he calls Professor Kano, who had been impressed with his exposition in the jujitsu booklet, and felt that Feldenkrais could be a good teacher of judo. "It was not just judo Professor Kano taught, it was the way of teaching. He was a great man, more than a great man. The Japanese ambassador in Paris called him his father. When he died, six million people in Japan practiced judo in his honor on one day." Feldenkrais did his physics work with Joliot-Curie, the Nobel prizewinning physicist, in Paris, on ultra-high tension, and went, in World War II, to Fairlie, Scotland, to work as a scientist on submarine detection and antisubmarine warfare. He organized a judo club in Fairlie, and had trouble with his soccer injuries.

"I was thinking, I told you, how does a person ruin his knees? I mean, exactly what is it that happens when he ruins the knees? And then, from the judo, I was thinking, why is it some people can't learn to fall? Why can an intelligent man who understands the concept perfectly not perform a clean fall for years? Some people can do it in one day. What is anxiety in falling? Why do neurotic people have poor balance? What is the connection of structure and function in the body? I had in my own experience elements I didn't understand myself. My own accident with the knees became clear, a joke. I was a highly neurotic type and fought like an idiot during a game. So I had matured in my head without knowing it."

Feldenkrais presented his ideas in papers before his fellow scientific workers in Fairlie. After World War II, he went to work in an acoustical laboratory in London as a research scientist, and spent a lot of time, it seems, with the Japanese and the Indians.

"I did Zen, I did yoga, I met Kazuma and Suzuki, I spent six weeks with Suzuki, sometimes I would be up till three in the morning." Feldenkrais' papers on his body work were reworked and published in 1949 as *Body and Mature Behavior*. It is heavy in physiology, and has formulas from physics to demonstrate the body's movement in space. It was soberly reviewed in *The New England Journal of Medicine* and the *Quarterly Review of Biology*. It brought a trickle of interested people to see him—but Feldenkrais considered himself an amateur. "I was not confident," he said, "because it contradicted other books I had read, and I said to myself, you're an amateur, you said what you said, now go back to work."

Feldenkrais became a chief scientist with the Israeli Army, and on the side he began to treat people with his body theories.

"For the first three years, I wouldn't take any money, if you give me a ride in your car should I pay you like a taxi? And then after that I thought, I spent seven years in the British Admiralty on top-secret work, and three years in the Israeli Army on secret work, and no one knows what I have done, not even scientists. I am not even a scientist, I am more like a government official. And scientists made very little in the Israeli Army; it was not long before the body work promised to pay more."

"So we have a compendium of exercises," I said, "some of them never repeated even once in a course, from an Israeli physicist. But it looks to me like the grandfather of your thought is Japanese."

"No."

"No?"

"Japanese in Japan are like Englishmen in London now, or New Yorkers in New York. Not Japanese that way. But Japanese like Professor Kano, you could say that."

"Is this like a martial art, then, like judo and aikido and kung fu?"

"Like some maybe in a little technique, but martial arts are learned by doing, not understanding. My exercises the person understands and feels the first day."

"And doing the exercises makes a change in mental attitude, or habit patterns?"

"It's *how* you do the exercises," Feldenkrais said. "It's the learning that changes your attitude. It's not what, it's how, everybody painted apples, but Cézanne painted Cézanne apples. You only need to understand one exercise. What is awareness? What is consciousness? That's all. Waghhhhh."

Feldenkrais heaved a sigh, I suppose with the effort of getting through to so dense a pupil.

"America," he sighed. "Such a poverty of spirit. Books—how to fight with your wife, how to fuck, how not to kick yourself in the morning. Ask: What is awareness? You enlarge your ability to perceive in your own way, not what somebody said, it's a change in the mobilization of yourself, what do you need, what is the best way? Who is holding the body in such a way?"

"You've worked out thousands of these exercises. Do you do them yourself?"

Feldenkrais looked out with some amusement.

"Wagghhh, eh, I did them enough."

"You started to become known in your middle sixties, or late sixties—where do you want to go with this system? What do you want?"

"What do I want? I would like to have a clinic, if somebody would give the money, and what do I want right now is maybe a sandwich and a cream soda, let's go." And he began to tell a story, about a man who had come to see him, who had been a footballer, who had a bad shoulder, who was a pilot, who was having trouble piloting, who was not helped by orthopedics, and who then, one day—and off we went, to get a cream soda.

The surgeon's probing electrode in a brain brings up a choir in Amsterdam on Christmas Eve. Chemical agents that disorient the perception also reveal engrams of memory beyond normal recall, and elements of symbolic language. The engrams, or bits, of memory have an influence over present-day behavior, and even over physiology and posture.

To run through that sequence you don't have to push the paradigm very hard. We are still within it. (That doesn't mean all the sentences are "true"; to be "true," you need a predictive hypothesis, repeatable experiments and independent verification.)

The psychologist whose chest muscles released, and whose breathing and work then flowed, was a sophisticated fellow, but he did not think this technique so extraordinary that he began to proselytize for it. If aerobics, or oxygenation, can affect one's daily outlook, why not an elbow in the myofasciae? But maybe I am a bit biased. It seemed like science from sixteenth-century Paris, pressing an elbow into the armpit to line up the body and clear the mind. Besides, the accustomed posture of the Rolfees would soon bring their frames out of line, and they would have to be "done" again. Whether their heads, or minds, also slipped a bit is not quite clear.

The Chinese of the *I Ching* certainly lived with kinds of attention which we do not grant ourselves, bizarre old right-brained stuff. They also developed patterns of ritualized body motion, some of which was called *t'ai chi,* variously described as a moving meditation or shadowboxing, which had its influence when the Japanese imbibed Chinese culture. Then the Jews on the Berlin police force learned one descendant, jujitsu, and took it to British Palestine, and foxy Grandpa wrote his pamphlet and became the student of Professor Kano in judo, and applied his understanding of physics to physiology, so these right-brained movements have a long lineage.

I met one other practitioner of this study of bodies, who made no claims for its influence upon the mind. He was a trainer, an athletic trainer on a university medical staff, working under a physician. It was said he could pick a broken quarterback up from the field in the second quarter and have him back in the third without any drugs or injections. I watched him with the most violent wrenches intercollegiate competition supplies to young male bodies—football, wrestling and hockey. Some required traditional athletic medicine. But he had also improvised his own exercises, somewhat like the reversibility relationship in Feldenkrais, and they were so small, the movements were so small, to perform them would drive you crazy. Until you changed your set of mind, and then the traumatized muscles began to release, with so little damage it was astonishing.

But these are all individual artisans, working pragmatically, like the metallurgists who used oxygen before oxygen was discovered. Only after Priestley discovered oxygen and Lavoisier quantified the results did the metallurgists have some glimmer of the conceptual scheme in which their craft functioned.

These unarticulated impulses of mind do get quantified in the next section, and because they are quantified and repeated, the paradigm bends to accommodate them.

BIOFEEDBACK: WHO'S AT HOME HERE?

BIOFEEDBACK *sounds* so respectable. That Greek root "bio," as in biochemistry or biology, and "feedback" from the crisp, quantified world of engineering, from servomechanisms: "A method of controlling a system by reinserting into it the results of its past performance." Definition by Norbert Wiener. Your room thermostat turns the heat on when it senses that the room has gotten too cold. Biofeedback gives you a reading on something going on within your body, just as a thermometer does. But just knowing your temperature doesn't let you affect your temperature. Or does it?

Biofeedback machines monitor some function of the body and give you a continuous visual or aural report. And then— this is the part that got everybody so excited—you learn to change the signal, to alter the dynamics of that part of the body. But nobody knows how it's done. It seems to happen outside of the rational, language-using part of the mind. You can raise your arm if somebody tells you to raise your arm. But could you raise or lower your blood pressure, or your heartbeat, just by *thinking* about it? (Not *thinking*, precisely, because thinking implies the verbal and rational. Better say, putting your mind to it.) No Westerner believed it until recently; those functions belonged to the autonomic nervous system, over which we have no control. Or thought we had no control. The big outlines of the paradigm don't have to change, but they have to give in one sector.

The implications were terrific. If people could really control their own autonomic functions, they could bring down their blood pressure, relax, get to sleep, unlearn bad habits such as smoking and drinking, and do away with some of their daily drugs.

Unfortunately, biofeedback went through a fad stage where it was advertised as Electric Zen, where gushy reporters described it as the greatest advance since Copernicus. (The popular press was no more accurate on biofeedback than on drugs.) The Magic of Alpha.

I signed up for a biofeedback course.

"Put your fingers in these little loops here," Josh said. I was sitting in an easy chair in a darkened room at Josh's Institute. "Okay, make that tone go down." The machine was giving an annoying whine.

"We are measuring GSR, galvanic skin response," Josh said. "Tension shows up as increased moisture on your fingers, and this picks up even a minute amount."

The whine on the machine rose. "I am not tense, you sonofabitch," I said to the machine. I glared at it.

Josh said, "Don't try," and then left us alone. Don't try?

The machine began to descend in tone. "That's better," I said. It whined up again. "You do that again, I'll kick you," I warned it. It whined higher. I decided to ignore it. It stayed on its high whine, just to let me know, and then grudgingly began to drop. Finally it dropped to a low growl, and I began to get a bit bored. The growl went lower. Josh opened the door. The whine went up a bit.

"How you doin," he said.

"Just keep it chained up, it bites," I said. The machine growled higher in response. I took my fingers out of the loops.

We moved on to the big stuff, the electrodes pasted on the head, EEG, electroencephalogram wired for sound. I was sitting in a big easy chair, with the machines on a table at one side.

Josh fiddled the dials like a hi-fi mechanic, and plugged it in. The machine went beep boop beep boop.

The beep is alpha and the boop is beta," Josh said.

"Hot dog, alpha already," I said.

"Most people have some alpha all the time," Josh said, "and some beta too."

Josh turned one of the dials. The boop went away and the machine went beep beep beep, pause, beep, pause pause beep.

"That's alpha," Josh said.

"So what's all the fuss about getting into alpha?"

"You want a nice, consistent alpha. See if you can lose the beta and make the alpha tone nice and steady, get some nice smooth waves going."

"How do I do that?"

"Don't figure it out, just let yourself respond. I'll leave you alone with the machines and you play around."

The alpha-beta terminology came from a German psychiatrist and researcher, Hans Berger, who first put electrodes to scalp in the 1920's. Berger found two distinct patterns; one he called alpha, at roughly eight to thirteen cycles per second, and the other beta, at fourteen and up. The beta state seemed to be associated with mental activity, and the alpha with drowsiness and relaxation. Years later, the machines got much more sensitive with transistorization, and filters for extraneous noise made the signals clearer. Theta, four to seven cycles, and delta, four down to a half cycle, got added to the list.

In 1958, a husky, pleasant Nisei psychologist, Joe Kamiya, was looking at EEG patterns as part of a sleep project, and wondered whether there was a connection between what a person's brain was doing—as reported by the EEG machine—and what he reported verbally himself. He had his subjects sit in a darkened room wired up to the EEG, and asked them to guess what state they were in: A or B, alpha or not alpha. By the third hour, many of the subjects were guessing right three times out of four. Given a soft beep tone for alpha waves, the subjects learned to sustain the alpha, to turn it off and on, and—some of them—to control the wave amplitude. Yet none of them

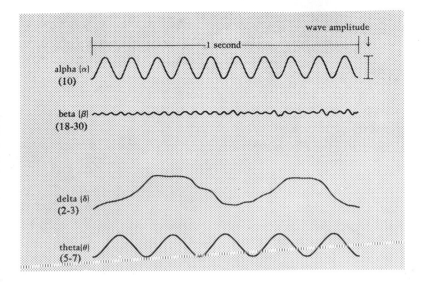

could describe, in English, what was going on. The internal cues were far more subtle than the vocabulary available to describe them. "The ineffability of the meditative state," wrote Kamiya, "so often stressed in mystical writings is similar to statements many of my subjects make, for example, '... I can't describe ... this state ... it has a certain feel about it.'" Kamiya found that people who were at home with images and feelings, and those who did, however loosely, some sort of meditation, made the best subjects.

The vocabulary never did get a whole lot better, but the enthusiasm increased. "I feel calm." "I feel sort of stoned." "I feel like I'm floating off the chair." Stoned! Floating off the chair! The biofeedback boom was off and running. Engineers working on hi-fi amplifiers switched to making biofeedback equipment, and ads began to appear in all sorts of papers and magazines: TURN ON WITH ALPHA. I clipped an ad out of the paper announcing A SPECIAL SEMINAR ON ALPHA WAVES AND ESP and I went to the special seminar. It was a come-on for Silva Mind Control, which does not use biofeedback equipment, and which is largely autohypnosis. Alpha, like energy, became a hot word in the counter-culture. ALPHA MACHINES, $199.50. THINK AWAY YOUR

HEADACHES. ACHIEVE SELF-CONTROL. Tune into your own special genius. Electric Zen! Drugless high!

For a young profession insecure about its place in science, the biofeedback boom was a great embarrassment. "It was awful," said Joe Kamiya. "The hucksters got it, and the acid-heads, and all those cats who believe in magic. It didn't help me at all. And grants aren't easy to get anyway. I'd like to try it in education, let the kids play with it, no grades, no competition, just see what they can control with it." I told Kamiya about a short biofeedback course I'd just been to, where the wife came back from the machines and said to her husband, whadja get, and upon hearing his score, said, I did better. "That's it," Kamiya said. "Even the yogis are competitive, first they wouldn't do it, and then they all wanted to show they could do the best yoga. Competition doesn't do it."

Some of the biofeedback machines during the boom were so crude they would register all kinds of twitches. And, in fact, at one time my instructor, Josh, had gotten a tic in his eye because the out-of-kilter machine was giving him feedback for a twitch. It kept rewarding him with beeps for the eye twitch, like an FM tuner on the wrong station, and then he couldn't stop.

Going through journal literature and transcripts for TV shows and meetings on biofeedback, I found some weird ideas amongst the public questioners. There were those who thought —machine-worshiping culture—that the machine put the alpha waves into people's heads, like radiation. There were those who thought if they could just borrow a machine—same principle— they could go zap somebody's brains with it.

Back in my darkened room at the Institute, in the easy chair, my machines were going beep boop beep boop. I could get many more beta boops simply by thinking of telephone calls I had to make, and I could get the machine to go beeeeeep pause beeeeeep by doing as little as possible and watching my breath go in and out and not even having a flicker of telephone calls.

Josh came in.

"Listen to this," I said. I wanted him to hear the alpha tone.

The minute I said, listen to this, the capricious little bastard started to go boop.

"Go out and come in again," I said. It took a while to get back to beep pause beep, and there were always boops cropping up, like crab grass in the lawn.

"Okay," Josh said, once I had the beep going, "what's a hundred minus seven minus eight minus seven?"

Boop boop boop boop went the machine, even before I could begin to think.

"Now, wait a minute," I said. "I hadn't even started when it started its damn booping."

"Who's I?" Josh said. "The machine's just a machine."

"Well, it's ahead of me," I said, "and that's a little eerie. I don't like its knowing what I'm thinking before I know myself."

A psychologist who was very good at amplifying the twitches from the base of people's thumbs once wired some up and then played soothing music. Into the soothing music, periodically, would come a loud, jarring, grating sound, and then it would cease, and the music would come back on. The subjects were wired up at a number of places, and they weren't told that a twitch at the base of the thumb would cut off the grating sound. Wouldn't you know it, the thumb twitch soon learned it could cut off the grating sound and get back to the pretty music. Now, obviously it took ears to register both the music and the harsh sound, and the interpretative cortex in the brain to distinguish them, but the people didn't know they were cutting the time of the grating sound down, and they wouldn't believe it when they were told it after the experiment. Who did that? Your thumb twitch, and it got better and better, you have a smart thumb twitch. How come I didn't know about it, then? Why doesn't anybody tell me anything? they would, in effect, say.

And here I am at the Institute, in this semi-darkened room, alone with this machine that has switched from beep pause beep to boop boop before I have switched myself. Who's at home here, anyhow?

My biofeedback course was in the summer, and I turned from a star performer into a very middling one because of the outside environment. The machines were in an air-conditioned room, and I would come up from the hot sidewalks into this nice easy chair in this darkened room and go: telephone calls to make, beta, boop boop, no telephone calls, white space, watch breath go in and out, don't try, alpha, beeeep pause beeeep, and then I would go boop beep zonk, right down through theta to delta and a wonderful nap.

"I can go from beta to delta in one minute flat," I said, when I woke up. "Express. No stops, not even alpha and theta."

"So can every exhausted commuter," Josh said. "Let's see you go from beta to delta and come back again."

Given those instructions, I couldn't even get out of beta.

At another session, my machine was going beeeeep pause beeeeep in a nice alpha and Josh did the number bit, what's fifty-six times seven hundred forty-eight. Have you ever had somebody try to wake you when the sleep you were sleeping was just going to keep right on going? The alpha beeeep kept right on, even though I heard the question, and "I" was quite willing to try for the answer, but the relaxation had cast molasses over everything. "In a minute," I said.

"Right now," Josh said, "fifty-six times seven hundred forty-eight."

The alpha tone went beeeep pause beeeep and the molasses felt very comfortable indeed.

"Go away," I said to Josh.

"You come up here every afternoon and go from beta straight down to delta and then you can't get back again until you've had your nap, and now you can't get out of alpha when you want to, that's not control," Josh said.

"I don't want to, I like it here," I said.

"Okay, stay there," Josh said. "Say, what happened in the stock market today? I heard on the radio it was down thirty-five points at noon."

Boop boop boop boop boop boop boop.

"Was it really?" I said.

"No," Josh said, "but now you're in beta and you didn't put yourself there. You have a way to go. A Zen monk in alpha wouldn't have been bothered."

"A Zen monk wouldn't be in the stock market," I said.

As far as alpha is concerned, you can see that alpha describes a brain state more relaxed than beta, and that you need beta to solve problems. Sometimes creativity is associated with alpha, for people who are creative while relaxed, but getting your head to fire at eight to thirteen cycles per second isn't going to make you Picasso unless you're already Picasso. And while some researchers associate alpha with creativity, some, like Barbara Brown, believe that "people who have a lot of alpha in their EEGs are dull, uninteresting, unimaginative, hard-working, plugging-along, ordinary people." Alpha is easier to produce with your eyes closed, because focusing your eyes is a beta activity. Beta would seem to be a more left-brained rhythm, but all the rhythms occur in both hemispheres of the brain. So: eyes open, it is easier to produce alpha at the beach or in the mountains, because your eyes can be on the horizon, unfixated.

Alpha training does sensitize people to internal cues. No one yet knows the connection between various brain wave patterns and behavior traits, but there are lots of interesting theories.

The breakthrough was to show that some control of the autonomic nervous system was possible.

RESPECTABILITY, CONFIRMATION AND THE MYSTERY OF THE REBELLING RATS

SOMEHOW, the dancers and psychologists who learned the quiet exercises of Feldenkrais used their minds to release their muscles. Or vice versa. And the biofeedback subjects used some unfamiliar part of their minds, or neurophysiological systems, to control autonomic functions, when nobody had been able to do that before. "Biofeedback" refers to the mechanical system; what the subjects were doing has been called "visceral learning." That is, crudely, learning from the gut, without the head. Controlling the involuntary with the assist of instruments.

They said it couldn't be done, and Neal Miller took his fellow behavioral scientists to task. Miller is an absolute duke of rat psychology, past president of the American Psychological Association. He has been teaching animals to learn for more than forty years, first at Yale, then at Rockefeller University—a hatchery for Nobel prizewinners along the East River in New York. Rockefeller University is a research place, no undergraduates. Miller is a burly, square-jawed man, bald except for a white fringe, who would look at home in a lumberjack plaid. There are, said Miller, general laws governing all learning, and visceral learning is similar to ordinary learning. "It's a common assumption," Miller said, "that the visceral system is stupider than the consciously-controlled system, but the evidence doesn't show that."

To have Miller and the Rockefeller University crew publishing in this area gave it respectability. What Miller and his collaborators did—we need repeatable experiments and common denominators, remember—was to teach rats visceral control. These rats were not just finding their way through mazes and pressing little levers, no sir. They were speeding up and slowing down their heartbeats, raising and lowering their blood pressure, and controlling their intestinal contractions.

That took the whole biofeedback and visceral learning business away from the kooks, and created a stir in the scientific community. At first Miller and one graduate student rewarded thirsty dogs for salivating. But they weren't sure that the dogs didn't produce some skeletal response, unobserved, that affected the result.

It was important for Miller to account for all the variables. To see if the heart was genuinely learning, for example, you would have to blank out all the other possibilities, immobilize the conscious, skeletal control, and yet leave the heart free to function. Could you paralyze an animal, and then teach his heart to control itself?

The Miller team used a drug, d-tubocurarine, derived from curare, the nerve poison that South American Indians boil up from jungle plants to dip their darts in. Curare paralyzes the end plates of those motor nerves connected to skeletal muscles, including those used in breathing, so if you got hit with a curare dart you would stop breathing very soon. Miller's rats, however, could be kept alive by a mechanical breathing machine, and though they couldn't move a muscle, everything else would be intact.

There isn't much you can do by way of rewarding a paralyzed rat, but the Miller people thought of hitting the pleasure center in the rat's brain with an electric jolt. (In the original pleasure-center experiments done by James Olds and Peter Milner at McGill, the rats would ignore food and water and go on hitting the bar that delivered the pleasure jolt to their brain until they were exhausted.) And that worked. The rats not only learned to control their heartbeats and their intestinal contractions on demand, but some of them learned to blush in one ear and not the other, and a couple of smart little fellows learned to control the rate of urine formation in their kidneys. To show that the visceral learning could be done without the electric jolt to the pleasure center, the Miller people fixed up a more standard experimental technique of escaping a painful stimulus, and that worked too.

If people could do what rats could do, then they could learn to control high blood pressure, spastic colon, irregular heartbeats, and other ailments without drugs or therapy or surgery. Out from the Miller group went a spate of papers, the results were duplicated in other labs, and worldwide attention in this particular branch of science focused on Miller.

People, of course, are more complex than rats, so there would be much greater flexibility. The response could be modified before it actually occurred—we do that through social attitudes and symbols anyway. Urination and defecation are visceral functions brought under voluntary and conscious control quite routinely; maybe we just hadn't gotten around to anything else. It's a tough job to teach a two-year-old the concept of blowing his nose, and maybe we are pre-two in some other areas. "This may be oversimplified," said Miller, "but perhaps we can say that the average person does not have any specificity of feelings from the viscera because he hasn't learned the right labels for them, and perhaps he doesn't have the right labels because most visceral functions aren't normally observed by other people, and so are not normally brought under social control. It may be that we are not conscious of these sensations only because we have not been trained to label them."

If visceral learning was possible without the usual ego-controlled muscles getting into the act, then a specific learning situation can produce a specific response. "This means," Miller wrote in his contribution to a textbook on psychiatry, "that psychosomatic symptoms can be reinforced by the full range of rewards, including escape from aversive stimulation." If a kid finds that he can escape going to school by having some stomach distress, he may learn the stomach symptoms as a response to stress. The stomach symptom has been learned by reinforcement, a direct relationship between mama and kid's stomach, while the kid walks around inventorying his bubble gum cards. The kid doesn't even know it; the contract is between his stomach and his mother. Presumably you could design a program to get the kid's stomach to unlearn its successful symptoms.

Some interesting hypotheses came up in the wake of the Miller work. One of Miller's associates, Barry Dworkin, speculated that some individuals learn high blood pressure because they have both the physiology and the unconscious tendency to regulate their cardiovascular reflexes. A sudden rise in blood pressure produces a decrease in general alertness, just as barbiturates do. Maybe these people learned early in life, unconsciously, that they could tune out a disturbing stimulus by raising their blood pressure; the stimulus could be noise or light or internal in origin, some sort of tension or conflict, and the awareness of it wouldn't come through to the cerebral cortex, or brain center, quite as strongly while the blood pressure was rising. Even a brief reduction in the unpleasantness would act as a reward that would keep the habit going, so, ironically, the person with this attribute would calm himself down unknowingly by boosting his blood pressure.

I asked Miller whether he thought too much conscious control of visceral areas could cross all the signals.

"Oh, I doubt it," he said. "When you're learning, you can't talk and ride a bike at the same time. You have to give all your attention to it. After you've learned, you can talk and ride a bike with ease."

The advancement of biofeedback and learning theory seemed well off the ground when it hit an air pocket, one of those most curious events that happen in science but are largely unreported because, as both George Orwell and Thomas Kuhn said, history is written by the winners.

Miller's rats stopped learning. And then the rats in the other laboratories stopped learning. Check the machines, check the rats, check the curare, the beasts would not perform, a rat conspiracy. The rat learning curve continued to decline. "The unexplained difference between earlier repeated success and present repeated failure is an extraordinarily perplexing dilemma," Miller wrote. It could have been that the companies breeding the white rats were changing their product slightly, in an effort to improve it; or that the respirator wasn't as accurate; or that the curare wasn't consistent (curare is a natural product, and d-tubocurarine batches can vary in make-up); or maybe, says Miller, it was mass hallucination, except that other labs did duplicate the results. The rat problems were ironic, because Miller's successes had inspired some of the successful clinical work with people.

"I am less encouraged than I was at the start," Miller said of biofeedback in general. Miller's group went back to work, doing the experiments from scratch, concentrating on the breathing apparatus for the paralyzed rats.

The original reports of changes in autonomic functions were greeted with a lot of skepticism. The changes were quite small, and the critics said these changes could have been produced by something extraneous that didn't have any lasting medical significance. But when Miller's rat studies made biofeedback research with people a bit more respectable, some clinicians tried experimenting. Barnard Engel and Theodore Weiss in Baltimore were rigging devices even before the Miller work gained circulation. One device had red, yellow and green lights for people with irregular heart rhythms—premature ventricular contraction. The light cues indicated when a premature ventricular contraction occurred, and sensitized the patients to the sensation of the irregular beat, since most people with these PVC's don't even know they have them. The training sessions were long—eighty minutes a shot, three times a day—but a couple of patients not only learned to speed up and slow down their hearts, but got weaned eventually from the machine with a regular heartbeat and took the ability away with them.

"How do you do it?" Engel asked his patients. "None of them could tell me," he said, "and after years I realized it was a silly question. I can't tell you how I hit a golf ball."

There were other scattered successes. Some people get headaches because they have tensed the forehead muscle, the frontalis, and they get so used to the sensation they don't even realize they've tensed it. Using the EMG—the machine that picks up the electrical activity from skeletal muscles—two of the biofeedback pioneers devised a chattering of clicks that corresponded to the tension in the muscle. By slowing down the clicks, the patients were able to relax the muscle, and cut down their headache medication. Still another psychologist was able to use the EEG with lights, bells and pictures to cut down epileptic seizures.

There were also flops. Neal Miller tried getting a group to control its blood pressure and labeled the results disappointing, and undoubtedly there were others; people are slower to write up their marginal failures than their marginal successes. Miller's associate, Dworkin, said: "In biofeedback, success seems to be inversely proportional to the competence of the investigator, and directly proportional to the subjectivity of the symptom. It works best on capricious psychosomatic disorders, and is going to be more promising for research than for physicians."

So far we have looked at two types of biofeedback. In one, people responded to a signal; in the other, animals responded to rewards. In the first, nobody much asked the subjects themselves what they were doing to make the light go on, and anyway the subjects didn't have a great vocabulary to describe the process, since it went on outside the language department in their heads. In the second, no rat, of course, fills out a questionnaire, and the experimenters saw themselves as extending existing principles of conditioning.

Now let us introduce another element: what the subject, all wired up, is doing with his own head. One more step. For example, in the "straight" biofeedback, if the clicks were showing you that your forehead muscle was tense, you would not consciously do anything except to try to make the clicks slow down. Some part of you would learn that something—ineffable—made the clicks slow down and something else made them speed up, and that the learning process could go on without running through language in your head. In the next biofeedback step, you can help to trigger this by thinking with your conscious, language-using mind.

The use of a formula by the language-using mind is hardly a new technique. It was blended with biofeedback by Menninger Clinic researchers Elmer and Alyce Green and Dale Walters. The technique used by the Menninger researchers was called autogenic, or self-generated, training. It has its roots in both hypnosis and yoga, and has been more widely used in Europe than here. Dr. Johannes Schultz published his first paper on autogenic training in 1905. One should not, says the Autogenic Training text, combat stress with stress—"master distressful situations by will power." So autogenic training uses muscular relaxation, increase (warmth) or decrease (coolness) in circulation, and "the trainee's passive and casual attitude."

Schultz advised his German readers: "The system works automatically, you do not do it. Become more negligent. Do not please the therapist with notes." Tough stuff for energetic Germans, become negligent, stop taking notes!

And then you lie down, relax, mouth slightly open, and think, "My forehead is cool," and then, "Heartbeat calm and regular," and then, "My breathing is calm," or "It breathes me." ("It breathes me" sounds less awkward in German.) The phrases go on: "I feel quite quiet, my neck and shoulders are warm and heavy, warm and heavy," and so on, like hypnotic induction.

Autogenic training, said its author and his followers, produced relaxation, and cured insomnia, tension, and drug addiction. To get to sleep: "Waking does not matter, it sleeps me, warmth makes me sleepy." The abstinence formula, for cutting something out: "I know that I avoid." "I know that I avoid a single cigarette, at any time under any circumstances, in any mood; others smoke, but for me cigarettes do not matter."

At the Menninger Clinic, the Greens had combined the autogenic my-hands-are-warm with biofeedback, and were testing a group of volunteers. The slightest increase in hand-warming would give the volunteers a signal. By chance, one of the volunteers was a Kansas housewife who had migraine headaches, and she began to have one during her training session. She was allowed to sit quietly in a darkened room, still hooked up to the equipment, and the Greens were surprised to see the hand-temperature indicators pop ten degrees. The housewife said that when her hands warmed with a surge of blood, the headache vanished. The Greens leapt upon this and launched an experiment with migraine sufferers, more than two-thirds of whom ended up with warmer hands and fewer headaches.

During a migraine attack, the blood vessels in the head dilate, and while no one has matched this up or knows exactly why, the blood vessels in the hand contract. The migraine sufferers were given portable temperature meters to practice with at home. Normal hand temperature is about 90°; migraine sufferers may have hand temperatures as low as 70°. Those who could send their hand temperatures up—and some could by fifteen to twenty degrees—had fewer and less intense headaches.

Why not just plant your hands on the stove, then? Well, that doesn't help much, because this isn't really a hand exercise, it's a head exercise. The Greens and their colleagues postulated that a part of the brain—we'll call it the emotional brain, for the moment—responds to stress by triggering the sympathetic nervous system, the one that increases the heart rate and blood flow and screams fight or flight. In the case of the successful migraine feedback, the migraine subjects learned not to redistribute the blood through various parts of the body, but to turn off the excess juice in the sympathetic system.

The Greens expanded the migraine workshops, and found that some people had no success at all—these were "skeptical of the training, or suspicious that hypnosis was being used, or very self-determined." People who *tried*, like the conscientious Germans, also flopped; in fact, the physiological changes were the opposite, the stress on stress made the hands get colder and the headaches worse. Passive volition and a casual attitude, like the good German doctors said, were necessary. Another researcher reported that people who picked up the internal cues could head off the headache; one woman would "focus on serenity and say to the blood in her head, go back down, blood, and continue her activities without concern." The Greens released some of their volunteers from the exact autogenic formula, my-hands-are-warm, and let them visualize whatever they wanted that would get them warm, lying on the beach and so on, and that individual tailoring improved the results.

The number of people who have actually learned a visceral response with biofeedback is still very small, and the results are not consistent. (Still, it took only two of James Lind's sailors, sucking on limes, to produce the breakthrough with what turned out to be vitamin C in curing scurvy.) Volunteers may well get hyped up for an experiment, and perform in a lab, which is a kind of theater, with an audience. It is harder without the theater and the audience. Taking a pill is a lot easier than learning a new skill, and even so, more than 20 percent of patients on medication don't take their medication. If Neal Miller is right, of course, the skill, once learned, would be like swimming or riding a bicycle: you would know it, safely, and wouldn't have to learn it again each time.

The relief from headache pains is so obvious that headache sufferers will pay for biofeedback sessions, but the results from controlling blood pressure take years to show up, so that the researchers in controlling blood pressure have to pay their subject. One such subject in a Harvard experiment would lower his blood pressure each week, get paid, and arrive the following Monday with the blood pressure back up again, because he took his biofeedback pay to the track and blew not only the money but his blood pressure.

In general, the patterns of reaction that people have to their environments are not easy to unlearn. People will change their bodies before they will change their environments. It's one thing to sit in a lab and be rewarded with pleasant slides for lowering your blood pressure. It's another to go back to the plant or the office or the house and *still* keep your head relaxed or your blood pressure down. The biofeedback devices have gotten more sophisticated, but they are still not totally portable, continuous and dynamic; if and when they are, somebody with high blood pressure, for example, might walk around wearing one, and when the device started to go boop boop boop he could add years to his life by walking out of that place, shutting his eyes, and saying, I am lying on a bowl of lime jello, I am lying in a bowl of lime jello, or whatever else works.

We have been looking at the first tottering steps taken in the area of visceral learning, which nobody believed possible only a few years ago. We are not used to producing change by "a passive and casual attitude." We think we have to control with our language-using, ego mind. (It should be noted that the passive and casual attitude was for states of relaxation, lowering metabolism. To increase the heartbeat required a more active, if still unarticulated, effort.)

There are, of course, people from outside our paradigm of Western science who never knew it wasn't possible, so they amazed us with their feats, because the feats just weren't part of the logic of our system. Those were the practitioners from the East. If Kansas housewives could calm their heads by warming their hands on the first try, what could someone do who had real experience in tuning internal controls?

WIRING UP
THE YOGIS

FOR two hundred years the British in India had been reporting that yogis could do odd things; in fact, there is a classic, recognizable scene in Victorian adventure literature. Everybody else is off pig-sticking on Saturday afternoon, and the curious, pipe-smoking Regimental Surgeon is wandering around the countryside, and there is this yogi being buried alive, or stopping his heart, or walking on coals. The regimental Surgeon comes back to the mess, mmmmm, most curious thing I saw this afternoon, mmmm, and between sounds of their smashing glasses in the fireplace the pig-stickers say, sure, sure, Reggie. You really believe that? No, I don't believe it, says Reggie, but I saw it. And then, later, Reggie gets an invitation: the old yogi announces that on Thursday at noon he is going to leave his body, and he invites all his friends, Reggie too, and everybody gathers around and there is a nice ceremony and the yogi sits and crosses his legs and precisely at noon he isn't there any more, that is, his body is, but there's nobody in it any more. The CO says later: damn good surgeon, Reggie, but he was getting a bit too thick with the natives. Began staying out to all hours at strange ceremonies, staying in his room alone humming some damn wog tune, well, it doesn't do, you know. He'll be all right once he's been back in England six months.

Turns out Reggie was really on to something. For even before Miller's rats were developing their subtle shades of kidney functioning, the physiologists were fanning out across India with their portable EEG equipment, hunting for yogis. The yogi is sitting in his cave and suddenly a shadow falls outside the cave, and a voice calls in, "Excuse me, but we're conducting a little experiment . . ."

The yogis, of course, were not doing biofeedback, they were doing their meditating and ignoring the plates on their skulls and the wires leading to the machines. It wasn't that easy to get the yogis to cooperate at first, since the inward, meditative experience of yoga didn't have much to do with keeping score. The yogis sat in lotus position, eyes closed, for up to two and a half hours, and the GSR, the skin test, showed high resistance, meaning they were very relaxed. The EEG, brain waves, showed a strong alpha rhythm, and no evidence of drowsiness or sleep. Most people go through alpha on the way to sleep, but the yogis went to alpha and stayed there; that is, they were in a state of deep relaxation physiologically and they were wide awake. Normally, the alpha pattern is broken up, or blocked, when the brain has to process some information—visual, aural, or simply a hundred minus seven minus seven. In some yogis, outside stimuli—noises, lights—didn't show up on the machines; the alpha continued.

Most of the four hundred-odd yogis who were tested by the Physiology Department of the All-India Institute of Medical Sciences didn't show unusual abilities. The stopping-the-heart exercise, as it turned out, wasn't actually a heart-stopper, it was a combination of breathing and skeletal muscle contractions that shut off the veins bringing blood to the heart. With no blood to pump, the usual heart sounds—budd bump, budd bump—couldn't be heard even with a stethoscope, yet the EKG showed that the hearts went right on pumping. But if you didn't have an EKG machine, you'd certainly have thought there was no heartbeat.

One yogi could drop his heartbeat to half the normal rate by increasing the firing rate of the vagus nerve, the one that conducts impulses from the abdominal and chest cavities to the brain. The vagus nerve can inhibit the heart rhythm, and that, speculated the Chairman of the Physiology Department, is what would happen when the old yogi would have his going-away ceremony and leave his body. He would have such interior control that he could inhibit his heart rhythm.

I called up my consulting team of physicians. Could somebody sit down, cross his legs, and die, on command? No, absolutely not.

I gave them a little Rumpelstiltskin, names for the process. What if the subject could sit down, increase the firing rate in his vagus nerve, and block the action of the sinoatrial node?

Well, if somebody could increase the firing rate in his vagus nerve —and almost nobody can do that consciously—and could block the action of the sinoatrial node, and that led to something else, then sometimes, sometimes but probably not every time, it would work.

So there you are. Increase the vagus nerve firing, block the action of the cardiac pacemaker, the sinoatrial node, and you have a religious suicide and one hell of an example of internal control.

And buried alive? Well, consider "Studies on Shri Ramanand Yogi During His Stay in an Air Tight Box," which the good Chairman of Physiology, Dr. B. K. Anand, and his colleagues wrote up in the *Indian Journal of Medical Research*. Into the box, metal and glass, with electric leads for the information, went the yogi, and he stayed there until the oxygen got dangerously low. And what the experienced yogi did was to drop his body metabolism down to half its normal rate. In a normal person, body metabolism even in deep sleep never drops more than 10 to 12 percent. So a yogi in an Indian village could spend a good long time in a freshly dug grave, since fresh earth wouldn't be as airtight as a metal and glass box.

In Japan, the physiologists went knocking on the doors of the Zen monasteries. Sure enough, the Zen monks could go right to alpha, relaxed but alert, and the alpha amplitudes got bigger and slower as the meditation went on. A control group sitting in the same position but not meditating stayed in beta. One difference between the yogis and the Zen monks was in the reaction to an outside disturbance. The yogis simply shut it out, and after the experiment they weren't aware that there had been any noises or lights. The outside world is phenomena, illusion, anyway, and they were transcending it according to their philosophy. The Zen monks, present here and now, registered each of a series of clicks, and the alpha went right on. Normal people —the control group—register the first click the most, and then —ah, that's a click, that's another click—each click is registered *less* as they get used to it. After the fourth click they aren't startled. But the Zen monks perceived each click afresh. Said Drs. Kasamatsu and Hirai: "The Zen masters reported to us that they had more clearly perceived each stimulus than in their ordinary waking state. In this state of mind, one cannot be affected by either external or internal stimulus, nevertheless he is able to respond to it. He perceives the object, responds to it, and yet is never disturbed by it. Each stimulus is accepted as stimulus itself and treated as such." One Zen master described such a state of mind as that of noticing every person one sees on the street but of not looking back with emotional curiosity. Not only did the Zen masters stay in alpha, some of them produced the long theta waves that most people generate only when falling asleep. This, said the authors, reflected concentration without tension. Zen meditation, they concluded, "influences not only the mind but the body as a whole organism," and "is the method through which we can communicate with the unconscious." Not Freud's unconscious, they added quickly, but more closely "that of Jung, C. G., or Fromm, E., what Dr. Suzuki called 'the Cosmic unconscious.' "

By the early 70's, the Menninger Clinic had gotten some big hitters wired up to its machines. There was, for example, Swami Rama, who looked, said one observer, more like an Italian nobleman than a swami, dressed in his turtleneck and Nehru jacket. The swami, in his mid-forties and trained in yoga since four, had been told by his own teacher to go to the West and show the lesser folk without the law what could be done. On the first try, the swami made two spots on his right palm differ by ten degrees: the left side turned red as if it had been spanked and the right side turned gray. "He did this," wrote the Greens, "by apparently controlling the flow of blood in the large radial and ulnar arteries of the wrist. Without moving or using muscle tension, he 'turned on' one of them and 'turned off' the other." But how did he learn that control?

Well, the swami had put in his time meditating in a cave. He called the first step "even breathing"; he had practiced breathing slower and slower until he was able to take as few as one or two breaths per minute, which is below the threshold where an involuntary breathing reflex is triggered, forcing air into the lungs. The swami had approached the border between voluntary and involuntary very cautiously, sort of tiptoeing across, and once he could do that he could go on to other things.

How long could he stop his heart? Oh, three or four minutes, said the swami. The Greens got a bit nervous; this would give him indigestion, at least, since he hadn't fasted properly, so they settled for a ten-second heart stop. Elmer Green stood with him and a group of technicians sat in the control room. The swami took a couple of dry runs and then freaked out the machines. From a steady seventy beats per minute, he jumped, in the space of one beat, to three hundred beats a minute. "When you stop the heart like this, it trembles," he said, fluttering his hands. What the swami had produced was an atrial flutter, a condition in which the heart vibrates so fast the blood doesn't fill the chambers, the valves don't work, and no blood is pumped. The swami had no pulse for seventeen seconds; an atrial flutter can produce unconsciousness; the swami went off to give a lecture.

The second big hitter at Menninger was Jack Schwarz, a Dutchman now in his fifties who emigrated to the United States in 1957. Schwarz's thing is to show he feels no pain: he can push a knitting needle all the way through his arm. Which is what, all wired up, he did. "Will it bleed?" asked Elmer Green, and it bled for about fifteen seconds. "Now it stops," said Schwarz, and it stopped. The holes that were visible during the bleeding closed up. On the second try there was no bleeding at all. The skin monitors showed no stress, and the EEG showed that before Schwarz began, he was emitting the usual beta waves of activity, but when the needle entered his arm, he slowed right into alpha.

There is, of course, a condition called hypalgesia, in which the person is impervious to pain. Usually he doesn't survive, because nothing tells him to take his hand from the stove. And the perception of pain varies from culture to culture: witness the reports of cheerful Gurkha recruits bringing chopped-off thumbs to the sergeant to be sewn back on. Schwarz has done his demonstration now for innumerable medical groups, and apparently doesn't come off as hypalgesic. Not only does Schwarz pierce his arms and cheeks with needles, he presses cigarettes to his skin, and nothing burns. "Pain," he says, "is an alarm clock that wakes you when something goes wrong, but if you're doing something of your own free will, something that you know is not going to hurt you, then there's no reason for the alarm, right?"

Schwarz has been into metaphysics and Oriental religions since he was twelve, and he says that he noticed the pain-blocking when he was sixteen and working in a clothing store, with needles in the lapel of his suit. One of the shopgirls slapped him playfully and, when the needles went into his skin, he noticed he could turn off the pain. He pulled the needles out, stuck them back in again, and went out to show everybody in the store. Then he went home and had a carpenter friend build a bed of nails.

A McGill psychologist, Ronald Melzack, posited that there were gates all along the axis of the central nervous system which either let the pain through or turned it back. Some people can learn to work the volume controls and the on-off switches.

Schwarz, of course, did not know from internuncial neurons or the reticular activating system. "I do it by changing a single word," he said. "I don't stick a needle through my arm, I stick it through *an* arm, I move outside my body and look at the arm from a distance; with that detachment it becomes an object, like the arm of a chair. My friend Swami Rama says, 'All of the body is in the mind, but not all of the mind is in the body.'"

Schwarz was careful, says Elmer Green, to get "cooperation

from his subconscious. He does not force the phenomena to take place, but asks his subconscious if it is willing." When he was asked to repeat his demonstration, there was a pause before Schwarz agreed. "When we asked why he had paused, he said, 'I had to ask the subconscious if it was willing to do it again. When it said yes, I said okay.' "

Green was impressed by the possibilities for education: "If every young student knew, by the time he finished his first biology class, that the body . . . responds to self-generated inputs . . . it would change prevailing ideas about both physical and mental health. We are individually responsible to a large extent for our state of health or disease. Perhaps then people would begin to realize it is not life that kills us but rather it is our reaction to it, and this reaction can be to a significant extent self-chosen."

Pragmatic experimental psychologists were eager to demystify the yogic tricks and the needle performance of Jack Schwarz. Non-yogis, too, could vary their skin temperatures, they reported, by imaging warmth or cold, and they hypothesized it might work this way: If you imagine your arm or hand is cold, you may tense the muscles, and that cuts the flow of blood, and that drops the temperature. Or, if you imagine it warm, that produces a relaxation which increases the flow of blood, which actually does warm the limb. As for the needles, we overestimate how much of our body is susceptible to pain. While the skin certainly signals pain, much of the interior of the body is relatively insensitive, which accounts for surgical incisions in which hypnotism or acupuncture is used, the first creating a state of relaxation, and the second, a state of distraction.

I have little interest in sticking needles through my arm, although certainly the state of mind that permits that degree of control is fascinating. And if I were to give a goodbye party Thursday at noon, and leave my body, I would probably give a big grunt, botch up the vagus nerve firing rate, and tell everybody to have another drink.

The researchers with the monitoring equipment noticed that subjects who practiced meditation had easier control of the involuntary systems. The yogis and Jack Schwarz were all heavily into meditation. (Jack Schwarz said the meditation so rested him that he slept only two or three hours a night.) But the meditation they used is not our usually defined meditation. Here again we have a problem with our language, which is primitive for feelings and extensive for things. The dictionary definition says, of *meditate*: "to consider as something to be done or effected . . . purpose." That's almost the opposite of Eastern meditation. As, "to meditate revenge." Certainly not. Of *meditation*: . . . "thought or contemplation"—certainly not thought. too linear and left-brained, maybe more like contemplation, but the verbs go: contemplate, plan, devise, contrive, ponder, muse, ruminate, cogitate, study, think.

You can see what the problem is. The activity described by our noun "meditation" is an activity which has to be controlled by the ego-mind. Even the Bible suggests this—happy is the man who meditates in the law of the Lord.

So we need another word for "meditation." The performer of this "meditation" is the self within you that can turn off the jarring sound when your thumb is wired up, without your participation. Or it can talk to the biofeedback machine before you know there is any conversation going on. The proponents of meditation say that if you turn the job of meditating over to this person, who lives in there with you, a lot of the *have to*'s in your make-up drop away like yellow leaves, and then you're more there than you were.

"Meditation"—we will drop the quotes now, but we mean Meditation II, the new definition—is not easy to read about because it is too easy. We read left-sided and cognitively, and the words have to have a rhythm, boomalaka boomalaka boom boom boom. To be really important, it has to be hard. It isn't the cognitive part that's hard, it's the understanding, from the old German doctors, of "It sleeps me," or, in this case, "It meditates me."

How do we get into this? Many of the Indian techniques use a sound, such as *hum* or *buz*—

And now we're suspicious. This suspicion is at least a thousand years old and certainly not indigenous to the United

States. Here is a play first performed at the Globe in London in 1610, Ben Johnson's satire, *The Alchemist*. The master of the house goes away, and various dupes come to see the Alchemist, who is a servant with a hustle going. Some of the dupes want gold, and some want success, and power, and knowledge, and how to win friends and influence people, and how to find a nice mate, and how to achieve poise and fight moral decay. Same old stuff, things don't change that quickly. Everybody gets gulled by what they want most. Here, the Alchemist announces a prescription:

> *Sir, against one o'clock, prepare yourself.*
> *Til when you must be fasting; only, take*
> *Three drops of vinegar, in, at your nose;*
> *Two at your mouth; and one, at either ear;*
> *Then, bathe your fingers' ends; and wash your eyes;*
> *To sharpen your five senses; and, cry* hum
> *Thrice, and then* buz, *as often . . .*

Too easy, three drops of vinegar and cry *hum,* look at the dupes go for it.

So we are prepared when a guy wearing a wrinkled bed sheet gets off an Air India flight and starts telling us what we need to know. How can anything good come out of a country as screwed up as India? Sixty-two different languages and cows in the streets and starving since anybody can remember—how can they really know something if they're starving? So assume we want all this interior control, and serenity, and how to find a nice mate— we're already slipping into the roles in *The Alchemist*—what do we do?

Well, says the guy in the wrinkled bed sheet, you fast, or you stop eating meat, or you watch the tip of your nose, and you say Om. Or Hum.

Hum? What about the three drops of vinegar, Jack? And which way to the Egress? We've seen this play, rewritten for each generation. That's the majority reaction.

There is a minority that thinks nothing good can come from the United States—rampantly materialistic, insensitive—and all good things come from where incense is burned and customs are more exotic. But the minority are setups. Witness:

Two friends of mine promoted the visit of a swami. I will give the friends the fictitious names of Michael Murphy and Robert Ornstein. The swami was the Swami Suchabanana, that's right, Suchabanana, and was said by some to look very much like Ornstein, who has a beard anyway.

The faithful of Los Angeles filed in, and "Murphy" introduced the swami. "Murphy," the audience knew, was very well qualified to introduce swamis, being an alumnus of the Sri Aurobindo ashram, and able to give long raps on the Atman and the Brahman and Consciousness. The swami was in his swami robes and his swami turban, and he had that singsong Indian accent—

"Now the mantram that I use is bah, nah, nah, say it, please, bah—"

"Bah" said the audience.

"Nah," chanted the swami.

"Nah," chanted the audience.

"Nah," chanted the swami.

"Nah," chanted the audience.

"Very good, bah-nah-nah," said the swami. "Very holy word, bah-nah-nah."

Bah-nah-nah? Bah-nah-nah? A couple of skeptics in the audience are beginning to eye each other. Bah-nah-nah? You know what that sounds like?

Murphy and Ornstein are still alive today, so it could not have been they. The two hoaxers were stoned to death.

But there's nothing wrong with bah-nah-nah, as we will see.

III: | Meditations

Redefining meditation is a beginning. Meditation—that is, Meditation II—is not part of the fabric of our culture. It has been introduced, or reintroduced, in a very American way, not as part of religion, but as a process that will do you some good. The aspect of it that will do you some good is relaxation, but curiously, where Meditation II comes from, that aspect is almost trivial.

It may be that the importers know this, that they are selling what is easiest to sell, and they figure the other benefits will just creep up on their clients.

YOU DESERVE
A BREAK TODAY

TRANSCENDENTAL Meditation is the McDonald's of the meditation business. Or maybe the Howard Johnson's. Whatever suggests: a relatively low fixed price, a standard item, and increasing numbers of franchises, or outlets. Like McDonald's, TM suggests, "You deserve a break today," in fact, you deserve two, twenty minutes in the morning and twenty minutes in the evening. TM has processed somewhere between 400,000 and 500,000 Americans, most of them in the last four or five years, and that gives it respectable size among service organizations.

In one sense, TM is a pioneer. Indians have been bringing the vedanta, or Hindu scriptures, here for almost a hundred years, but TM made a meditation technique work with an audience that didn't want to hear any Hindi. And for de-Hindizing the technique, TM deserves its success, which has been spectacular. It took the strangeness—and the threat—from the second definition of meditation, and once the threat was gone, even the Rotary Club and the Illinois State Legislature took to it.

Transcendental Meditation comes from a gentleman called Maharishi Mahesh Yogi—born Mahesh Prasad Varma in 1918 in the Central Provinces, father forest ranger, degree in physics from Allahabad University in 1942, says the official biography. (Maharishi, or Maharaj Ji, appears as a title before a number of figures from the East, since it means Sage, or Wise One, and if you mix among the followers of several of them it can get confusing. There is Maharishi the TM leader, and Maharaj Ji the sixteen-year-old guru, and Maharishi the late guru of Baba Ram Dass. I once had file folders organized by my favorite technique among all the Maharishis, e.g., Maharishi—Sound, Maharishi—Light, Maharishi—Reads Minds.) Maharishi was on his way to become, like the members of his caste, a merchant or a clerk, and to have a marriage arranged for him, when he met one of the major religious leaders of India: Swami Brahmanada Saraswati, the Jadgadguru Bhagwan Shankaracharya, and he became a disciple and spent thirteen and a half years with him. His assignment, given when it became time for the master to leave his body, was to find a simple form of meditation for everyone to practice. Maharishi spent two years in a cave in the Himalayas and emerged with TM. (Two years in a cave, for a religious Indian, is like two years at the Harvard Business School for a commercial banker.)

Maharishi seems to have started his efforts quite innocently, without any great world plan, talking to Indian businessmen. His instincts steered him in the direction of acceleration; things moved faster in the West, so by 1960 he was setting up the International Meditation Society in London. Being pragmatic in nature, he was not afraid to use radio, television and public relations—an approach that, needless to say, did not go down well with the gurus left in India. By the late 1960's he had, as followers, the Beatles and Mia Farrow; John Lennon, a former Beatle, once spent eight hours a day meditating with the Maharishi in the Himalayas. The bearded, giggly presence of the Maharishi became familiar on the talk shows: there was Maharishi on Johnny Carson.

And that crested and passed. John Lennon said that the gurus of India were like rock stars in the West, if you couldn't be Mick Jagger you could be a maharishi. The Maharishi went on a nationwide tour with the Beach Boys, another rock group, and nobody came. The tour had to be canceled, and it looked like TM was another one of those Sixties Things, fading with the natural rhythms of time. Within a couple of years, the Maharishi was to say he had failed in his mission, and yet even as he spoke another wave was beginning to curl.

Before we complete that story, it might be useful to see what this is all about. When I signed up for TM, I had already been through a year of other trips that involved meditations, and my attitude was more that of an engineer taking part somebody else's widget—well, let's see how *they* do it. Unlike most of my TM classmates, I did not have a friend who had just done it, and also unlike my TM classmates, I had been through much of the literature of meditation.

I happened to do this at a university, so our first lecture was in a university building. On the table in our room were glossy reprints of articles telling us how TM would fix us up, color charts in them of stress relief. Not only was there TM's own literature, but also reprints from *Scientific American* and *The Wall Street Journal*. Our instructor was a clean-cut junior called Buzz, who wore a sport jacket and loafers, and who smiled a lot. The audience was naturally mostly students, but with a sprinkling of older people, for the TM lectures were advertised— mostly in diners and on tree trunks, it seemed to me—over a wide area.

"Anybody can do this," Buzz said, "no matter how old or how smart. As we meditate we become clearer, you can do more, students get better grades, the mind doesn't wander. TM rest is deeper than sleep. It gets rid of really deep stresses. It helps your relationship with other people. You will get along better with your roommates."

What we would do, if we wanted to sign up, was to come to two lectures, and then be initiated on the weekend, and then one more lecture and one more weekend—that's all there was.

"Previously, we had three states of consciousness," Buzz said. "Waking, sleeping and dreaming. This is the fourth state, cosmic and all-inclusive. The mind is evolutionary, a blessing of the Creator, approaching the Infinite One"—Buzz giggled a bit, and the audience got restless—"but there's nothing to believe in TM. You don't have to believe in anything. And nothing to give up."

"Is this the same as yoga?" somebody wanted to know.

"No, all you do in TM is sit still," Buzz said. "Yoga will give you a charley horse. Zen monks meditate for twenty-five years to get the same result TM will give you in two weeks. It's different from concentration, and from contemplation."

TM, said Buzz, used a sound. Different sounds match different people—you and your roommate might not like the same music. A sound in the Vedic tradition is a mantram. Each of us would get his own mantram. Were all the mantrams really individual? They were, though there were far more people than mantrams, since 20,000 people a month were signing up for TM. How do the instructors match the mantram to the individual? I wanted to know. Buzz said you went to a teacher training course—ten or twelve weeks—and learned how to do this, but it was privileged information how it was done. We would fill out a questionnaire, have an interview, and get your mantram.

"Never," Buzz said, "tell anybody your mantram. That will ruin the whole effect." How come? "We have found that through experience. Your mantram is secret. Every once in a while somebody goes through TM, and then a friend gets interested, and they tell the friend the mantram, just to save the initiation fee. It doesn't work. There was a guy in Rhode Island who used somebody else's mantram and he got edgy and irritable and lost energy. It's worth the fee." The fee was $45 for students and $75 for adults. The fee for adults is now up to $125.

All kinds of medical tests had showed that TM relieved stress, Buzz said. The body was carrying stress, the imprint of the daily activities, but sleep didn't relieve all the stress. Every mental condition has a corresponding physical one: the release of stress—Buzz drew bubbles rising on the blackboard—is an activity, maybe a chemical change, and that activity creates a mental activity, a thought.

If we got so relaxed, how would we ever get around to do anything?

The mind is spontaneously capable, said Buzz. When anxiety is down, capabilities develop. It doesn't lead to inertia. Just twenty minutes, twice a day, would leave us refreshed.

If meditation was so good, why only twenty minutes?

So you can adjust to the change, Buzz said. You have to have a balance of meditation and activity.

We filled out questionnaires, rather brief questionnaires, age, occupation, and so on. The only unusual question was: had we used any drugs?

We made appointments for Saturday.

"Bring six to twelve fresh flowers, two to three sweet fresh whole fruit, and a clean white handkerchief. And the fee for the course," Buzz said. "Don't eat a lot. And we ask that you not use any recreational chemicals while you are learning TM. Give it a chance to work. We find that many people cut down on their recreational chemicals after learning meditation."

Hands went up in the audience. What kind of fruit? What kind of flowers? They wanted to be told exactly. *All* recreational chemicals?

On Saturday I reported with one apple, one orange, one white handkerchief, and a bouquet from the florist. We were in the basement of a university building. No English 212 today. One at a time, we went into the initiation room (English 212). Candles, incense, bowls of fruit, lots of flowers, very pretty.

It was so dark in the room I could barely see the pictures scotch-taped on the wall: Maharishi, I supposed, and Guru Dev, his teacher. The offerings, said Buzz, were symbolic, flower of life, fruit the seed of life, and the handkerchief, the cleansing of the spirit. We were both in our socks. Buzz went through a ten-minute ceremony, all by himself and all in Sanskrit, with rice, salt and sandalwood.

"What was that?" I said when he stopped.

"That's the ceremony, initiation," Buzz said. "Some of it is the names of the masters who preserved the technique. We're grateful to the Vedic tradition for having preserved it, it's as applicable today as thousands of years ago. Okay, I'm going to give you your mantram. The mantram is meaningless, a sound whose effect is known. Your mantram is *Shiam*."

"*Shiam*?" I said. "*Shiam*? You sure *Shiam* is mine?"

Buzz looked stunned. What's the matter with Shiam? And I was thinking: You sure it's Shiam and not Shiom? And I had been looking for some basic Sanskrit sound, Hum or Aum or Hrim or Bam, I didn't exactly remember Shiam. And I was also remembering an unpublished article on the "rise times" of sounds in physiological psychology, how mantra were always soft and mellifluous, never any k's, nothing sharp, lots of soft mmm's and o's, see, Campbell's Soup is secretly conditioning you, they have you going mmm-mmm good.

"Shiam," Buzz said. "Let's say it." We said it. "Okay, just keep it going, to yourself, and if thoughts come let them come, and don't try." We closed our eyes. I could see the letters: SHIAM. Then I thought, I bet these guys screwed up my mantram, that one doesn't sound quite right, there's no quality these days, car mechanics fake repairs; plumbers, no craftsmen left; but at the same time I knew I just as many mantrams as Buzz, so I thought, well, what the hell, they all work, and I kept it going. It was very quiet. Toward the end of the twenty-minute period I peeked a couple of times. Buzz had his eyes shut and was breathing evenly. I tried it a couple of different speeds. S h i a m, slow, and Shiam Shiam Shiam, fast. It doesn't have to stay consistent. "Very slowly, open your eyes," Buzz said. "Take a couple of minutes to come out." Was it easy? Yes, Was it pleasant? Yes. Did the mantram change, get faster or slower or disappear? Yes. Did thoughts come? Yes. "Good," said Buzz.

Some people have reported dizziness and nausea and all sorts of wild things. I guess all that is possible, magnetism without imagination is nothing, imagination without magnetism can produce convulsions, as they told Louis XVI, but it's not my experience.

Buzz said I could have my handkerchief and flowers and fruit back. I took the handkerchief, I ate the apple, and I left the orange and the flowers.

In our midweek sessions, we discussed our experiences and asked questions. Did anybody forget their mantram? Some people had. Okay, don't worry about it, if it doesn't come back in a couple of days, call your instructor. Did the mantram show up sometimes when it wasn't TM time? Tell it cheerfully to go away, like a friend who has dropped in when you're working.

Did people fall asleep while meditating? That's okay, that's a good meditation, wake up and finish. Did a lot of thoughts come? That's okay, just notice the thoughts and go back to the mantram. Why weren't we getting progressively better? Because there's always the release of stress, until the very last stress is relieved, and that's pure consciousness. When you're in pure consciousness, do you know it? No, you know it later. Does the appearance of the thought correspond in intensity to the stress released? No. A lot of people hadn't noticed any change in themselves. You won't notice the change, it's like staring at a rosebud all night, by morning it's bloomed, but it's hard to notice the changes.

I asked Buzz, after class, "Is this a good job? Part-time?"

"For me, you mean?" Buzz said. "Well, you make a little, but you could certainly make more doing something else in the same time."

There seemed to be a fair dropout rate between the first and second weekends. We went to get our meditations checked. Close your eyes, open your eyes, close them again. Do your meditation. Take a couple of minutes to come out when you're through. Was it easy? Was it pleasant? Good.

The girl who was doing my checking sounded like a recording. Did thoughts come? Yes. Good, the mantram should come as easily and effortlessly as the thoughts. We do not concentrate, we do not try. Any questions? Yes, do a lot of people think this is a waste of time? Yes, but the effects are going on whether you think they are or not, just keep going. Did a lot of people think they were doing it wrong? Yes, just keep going, there is no wrong way if you know there is no wrong way, we do not concentrate, we do not try ("Be relaxed," said the German doctors, "und stop taking notes!") Well, I get the meditation part, but where is the transcendental? We are transcending thought when the mantram becomes so refined that it disappears, then the mind transcends everyday awareness and experiences pure awareness, or cosmic consciousness.

"That name puts people off," said one of the TM hierarchy. "We shouldn't say transcendental, we should say approaching transcendental, I wish Maharishi had called it creative intelligence. (The Science of Creative Intelligence is the name of a course within TM.)

But is it really different from sitting with your eyes shut, or taking a nap?

The Maharishi may have thought he had failed, at one point, but events were running independent of him. Actually, while TM faded from the newspapers, and the Maharishi faded from the talk shows, the word-of-mouth on TM continued, so that the numbers of people who signed up for the course didn't diminish. But the candidates were to change character; TM was to shift slowly from the exotic, Beatles-gone-to-Himalayas Sixties thing to the more traditional Ben Franklin, early-to-bed, Dale Carnegie self-help American procedure. At the pivot point of this turn was a slight, blond student in Los Angeles, Robert Keith Wallace. Wallace had begun TM as an undergraduate at UCLA, and he was a friend of Jerry Jarvis, who had been one of the protagonists in starting the Students' International Meditation Society. Wallace proposed a Ph.D. thesis in physiology at UCLA.

"Maharishi had been free to go out with a simple technique, because he wasn't part of a religious hierarchy, and I was free to try something in physiology that nobody with an established reputation would want to risk," Wallace said. Maharishi liked the idea. Nobody had done anything objective, the West was objective, Maharishi said. In India, people went uncritically from master to master, without distinguishing techniques.

For his thesis experiment, Wallace wired up twenty-seven meditators. Each subject would sit connected to instruments that would record continuously. Each subject had a catheter in one artery in the arm; the arm would be poked through a hole in a curtain so the subject wouldn't see the instruments and the blood, should they peek during meditation, because most people do not find the sight of their blood gurgling into instruments conducive to serenity. The wires were on for blood pressure, heart rate, rectal temperature, skin resistance and EEG. The subjects sat quietly for thirty minutes, then did twenty to thirty minutes of meditation, and then sat again quietly for another thirty minutes.

That must have been some group of meditators. I gave them points just for sitting still with all those wires and with a catheter in the arm.

In the middle period, the meditation period, the oxygen consumption on inhaling, and the carbon dioxide on exhaling, went way down. A 20 percent drop like that really should indicate a lower metabolism. The EEG showed nice alpha patterns. The heart rates slowed by an average of three beats per minute. Resistance of the skin to an electrical current went up fourfold— this is the GSR from biofeedback vocabulary, the higher the skin resistance, the greater the degree of relaxation. Blood pressure went down before meditation, and stayed low. The lactate concentrations in the blood took a steep dive. At the end of the meditation period, the lactate concentration rose a bit but stayed well under their premeditation period.

Lactate comes from the skeletal muscle tissue, and increases during any kind of stress. Exercise will bring it up, and so will the telephone call about losing all your money and your house burning down. Not only do you find lactate concentrations in people who are anxious, you can *make* people anxious, perfectly happy people, by giving them a shot of lactate. (You would only do that if you were researching lactate, naturally. The correlation between lactate and anxiety is controversial.)

And how did this differ from a good nap? Well, it does. Oxygen consumption starts to drop right away with meditation, and it takes a couple of hours to start tapering off during sleep. Skin resistance increases during sleep, but not as much as while meditating. (The carbon dioxide in the blood increases during sleep. There are, of course, different stages of sleep and different patterns within those stages.)

And how did TM compare to subjects who were hypnotized? Interesting: hypnosis has no particular physiology. The brain-wave and visceral readings for a hypnotic subject will be those of the state he is in; if he is super-relaxed, they may come up like meditation; otherwise they will be normal.

In short, the relaxation Wallace reported was, indeed, deeper than sleep, or than some stages of sleep. In fact, he said, the state produced by transcendental meditation was different from waking, dreaming and sleeping. It was a fourth state of consciousness.

Wallace's thesis, "The Physiological Effects of Transcendental Meditation," was not in the nature of the paradigm-busting papers of the *Annalen der Physik,* when Einstein and the other fellas used to publish in that journal; it was a descriptive proof of one technique where none had been done. But it was for Wallace the hat trick in this whole field.

Wallace's thesis went off to the prestigious journal *Science.* And with Herbert Benson, a cardiologist and assistant professor of medicine at the Harvard Medical School, the physiological changes of transcendental meditation appeared not only there, but in the *American Journal of Physiology, Scientific American* and *New England Journal of Medicine,* all very heavy, *Scientific American* as usual with nice graphs. Hat trick. That's not even counting *Connecticut Medicine, Science Digest* and the Proceedings of the American Societies for Experimental Biology.

Benson had been in public health service in Puerto Rico, working on blood pressure. Why did the Puerto Ricans have fewer cardiac ailments than the mainlanders?

"I give up, why," I said.

"Because of their attitude," Benson said. *"Mañana.* We need some of that if everybody doesn't want to keep dying so young, a different attitude."

Benson was working on primates at the Harvard Medical School, training them to control their blood pressure, when the meditators presented themselves. Wallace and Benson combined on a couple of experiments, and now the results went out with the prestige of a Harvard Medical School by-line. "Mental states can markedly alter physiologic function," wrote Benson and Wallace, as if nobody had ever reported to Louis XVI. They called the meditation state "a wakeful hypometabolic physiologic state," a phrase that went ringing through the journals. "Wakeful," because the subjects were awake and you would think they would have to be asleep to get those numbers; "hypometabolic," well, remember *hypo* is "under," Greek, and *hyper* is "over," excess. A hyp*er*metabolic state—excess, over—accompanies "anticipated stressful situations"; a hy*po*metabolic state "may accompany meditational states." What an anomaly, a waking state with such low metabolism!

Benson was enthused. One-third of all the adults in this country suffered from definite or borderline hypertension, high blood pressure. By meditating, he said, "we may be able to prevent and even treat it." And, at the same time, Benson said of TM: "It appears that . . . TM is the fastest and easiest way of doing so at this time."

The partnership of Benson and Wallace was not to last. Wallace was quiet, sincere, soft-spoken, but you sense somehow the steel spring of the divinity student, the true believer. Wallace was, first and foremost, a meditator, a disciple of the Maharishi; Benson was a physician, a cautious medical researcher who had never meditated and didn't intend to. Benson winced when his enthusiasm turned up in sleek reprints at all the TM lectures, Herbert Benson, M.D., Harvard Medical School.

By the time I got to Benson and Wallace they were polite but not really speaking to each other. Wallace became the charter president of Maharishi International University near Santa Barbara (now in Fairfield, Iowa); when you call, the switchboard says, "M-I-U." Every course includes "the Science of Creative Intelligence" in its title, from astronomy on. Benson was back in the lab, so cautious it took him six months to send me his first paper, so cautious he wouldn't even let his students know what he was about to publish in some journal, lest somebody leak it to TM and have it turn up in the press or in a glossy reprint at the TM introductory lecture. For ten months, tracking research, I would be calling them alternately, trying to pin down points: "But Benson says . . ." "But Wallace says . . ." Benson said he had a new blood pressure study, it was going to come out in *The Lancet,* the distinguished British medical journal, *and it didn't use TM.* Could I see it? No, not now. "Herb," I said, "it takes three years to do a book like mine, *The Lancet* will have hit the stands and have been gobbled up long before." Nope. Three weeks after *The Lancet* hit the stands I had my copy from Herb, for which I thanked him, except that my interest had been so whetted that by that time I already had my copy from *The Lancet.*

The research rolled on. My favorite head-bump phrenology journal, *The Journal of Electroencephalography and Clinical Neurophysiology,* reported that not only did meditators have those dollops of alpha, and different thetas than sleep has, but the brain-wave rhythms were synchronized, and beta spikes were appearing from deep meditation. "That's when you're touching consciousness, the beta spike," said the TM physiology people. A California researcher reported that TM reduced the symptoms of asthma. Poor damn asthmatics, first they got cured by placebo pills and then by TM, absolutely nobody will believe the trouble is in their chests.

By now, researching TM was replacing the sit-in in the dean's office of a few years back. In my own TM class, two students handed out questionnaires. (What they were researching had already been done—they didn't seem to know it, but what the hell.) And the TM people were hitting research like a fixed slot machine, and printing it with pretty charts on sleek paper. FASTER REACTION TIME, said the poster, showing a quarterback with his arm cocked, linemen descending upon him.

The State Legislature of Illinois endorsed TM. So did General Davis of the Army War College. Joe Namath was into it, and Bill Walton the basketball pro, and "there are a couple of strong contenders for the Presidency—very strong—who practice TM," said the Research Coordinator.

TM put out a booklet for businessmen, *Creative Intelligence in Business,* which said that research showed that TM improved behavioral stability, lessened susceptibility to psychosomatic disease, reduced nervousness, aggression, depression and irritability, increased the clarity of perception, improved learning ability, speeded comprehension, produced better memory and faster absorption of difficult material—and that's only part of it.

Plainly, TM was the greatest thing since peach ice cream.

And all this from sitting still twice a day, closing the eyes, and going "Hrim, hrim," or "Shiam, shiam"?

Well, yes. "Sometimes," said Wallace, "people make things more difficult than they are."

There are critics. Some of the critics called up the local TM chapter and said send over some meditators, we want to test them. The local TM chapter seemingly always obliges. And then the critics found, well, in one instance the skin temperature didn't go up sharply at all, and in several others there was a lot of flak about TM promoting "creativity and intelligence." What's creativity and intelligence, anyway? The testers rolled out the Barron-Welsh Art Scale and the Wallace-Kogan Test and the TM people didn't do any better than anybody else, some things better, some things worse. Then Gary Schwartz, Harvard, noticed: the TM testees did better on right-sided activities, associations, twilight visions, and worse on the left-sided, cognitive, problem-solving activities. That would be consistent with left-side, right-side, but you need both sides, perspiration as well as inspiration. If you need a little less tension to be intelligent, okay; some people need a little more.

(I always get suspicious of the promises to help creativity and intelligence, because they make it sound like a twist of the key makes you a genius. Silva Mind Control says, "The difference between genius mentality and lay mentality is that the genius uses more of his mind and uses it in a different way." Other than being very close to meaningless—and Silva is full of meaningless phrases—that seems to promise if you can learn the different way in some two-weekend course you can be a genius. It's like: ah, tap that right side, the old subconscious, and there is genius. Well, maybe, if you've been working at something eighteen hours a day. Why don't people remember that James Joyce learned Norwegian just so he could read Ibsen, and Edmund Wilson learned Hungarian just so he could read Molnar, and there were lots of translations in both cases, and for all his exquisite right-sidedness, Einstein carefully figured out he could wear the same jacket all week and not have to spend thirty seconds thinking on clothes, so he could spend eighteen hours thinking about geometrodynamics, space and time. Not much time goofing off for those fellas.)

And some critics said that the TM research was all a series of one-shots, though TM was starting longer-range longitudinal studies.

And other critics said, what is all that mumbo jumbo with the handkerchief and the flowers, what is this secret mantram business, some sort of gnosticism? And some critics said that TM sets up experiments, pops the results, and has them out in a sleek, glossy booklet before they can be critiqued. FASTER REACTION TIME, they said, was based on an unpublished experiment with eight undergraduates and uncritiqued statistics. And some critics said that people who had previously reported psychosomatic ailments such as ulcers and headaches, but had them under control now, didn't have them under control.

And some critics said TM was getting as metallic as the phone company, the checkers sound like telephone company recordings, nyeyun, fiyuv, threeyuh, that is not a working number. Of course they sound that way, they have memorized a thirty-point program, just like a computer:

> It is better to refrain from using "you," "your," or "I." Whenever possible, use "we" or "our."
>
> Say: (1) "Let's close our eyes." (Ten seconds).

There are choices along the way, just like a computer program:

> (14) "Did you have any thoughts?" If the answer is yes, go to (15); if no, go to (12).

Not much room for heresy in that program. With a university and a bureaucracy and secretaries who don't meditate, and gaining all the time on McDonald's, naturally TM is a target. But in one instance they have been discreet; they do not promote it as an alternative religion. You do not have to go to the Vedanta Society on Sunday morning instead of to church. The emphasis is on the technique, and not on the antecedents. If the technique is all you want, you take it and go away. Otherwise, you stick around and do Advanced Meditation, still twenty minutes a time, and learn more of the Vedas and Upanishads and Bhagavad-Gita as taught by the Maharishi. General Davis is probably not in it for the Bliss Consciousness; publicly, he says his blood pressure went down ten points.

This is not the first time Transcendental has come wafting across our shores, if you remember your American literary history, for there was good old Emerson telling his fellow Americans that there was something more than hard work and prosperity, there was the Oversoul, a good, natural, optimistic philosophy, a little short of Bliss Consciousness, but Emerson had been into "translations from the Hindoo" and German metaphysicians and he must have known his audience. Meditation: you can do it twice a day like brushing your teeth, and you can be sitting in a car or a plane or a train. It's almost—not quite—American and respectable, but here's *The New Yorker* with a cartoon in which the imperious chicken-chested four-star general is saying to his orderly, I missed the prayer breakfast, Smedley, book me into the Meditation Room just before lunch.

As for me, I practiced my TM faithfully, well, almost faithfully, once a day if not twice a day, and I went to my checking sessions—was it easy? was it pleasant? did thoughts come? we do not try, remember, we do not try. Some of the time I was so nudgy I couldn't wait for the twenty minutes to be up, and spent them thinking of things to do, simultaneously mantraming away. But some of the time, once you get used to it, it is like a combination lock. You go nine right, twenty-five left, twelve right, and as you turn it close to twelve it just falls open. You don't even have to pull. Sometimes, planes, trains, ka-zonk, just like an awake nap, though sometimes at minute #14 you want to read the paper.

(Charlie Tart, of *Altered States,* wrote a journal article in response to TM. He said what he seemed to do was to churn through the undigested stuff of the day, images, thoughts, much as the dream mechanism is said to do. The dream mechanism, it is said, runs all that stuff through the brain that has been run through during the day, trying to get it organized on all levels, emotional as well as rational. The longer Tart did it, he wrote, the more all that churning calmed down, leaving him finally calmer, short of bliss, and with an aversion to alcohol. He went on to more complex disciplines, where alcohol is considered pretty gross anyway.)

My instructor Buzz was wrong literally but answered the question correctly when he was asked is this like yoga. The questioner meant hatha yoga, the quest for unified consciousness through physical means, breathing and postures; that is what yoga is to most people. But of course there are a lot of other yogas, of which TM is but part of one. The TM enthusiasts sometimes put down the other techniques, but then so do many religions and religious techniques.

I don't know when Joe Namath and Bill Walton do their meditating, but I found it hard to do anything competitive afterward, for an hour or two. You just watch whatever ball it is go by and say, oh, nice shot. It's okay with you, like you've had two beers.

For some of the people, some of the time, TM works.

There, I said it. That is, it teaches a technique of meditation that produces relaxation, and relaxation has some beneficial effects. It may produce even more than relaxation. *Meditation works.* Funny phrase, yet there it is. But before you put me in the newest TM booklet as an endorser saying "TM works"— which it does—you have to finish the story.

Benson, half of the great research team, was back in the lab at the Harvard Medical School, without Wallace. Now he emerged from the laboratory firing salvos into the medical journals. (The mysterious *Lancet* article was one.) Benson had analyzed, dissected and reassembled the whole mantram business, and TM had no monopoly.

No? What else works?

Some secular techniques, autogenic training, progressive relaxation—and some religious techniques—

Well, some forms of Christianity, some forms of Judaism, some forms of Islam, just possibly Subud (that's Indonesian), Hichiren Sho Shu, Hare Krishna, Meher Baba—

Everything works?

No, not at all, it's just that certain techniques can produce an altered state of consciousness, and some altered states of consciousness produce a response of relaxation. In fact, that's what we're calling it, "the Relaxation Response."

The *Lancet* article said Benson and his team had reduced the blood pressure in the experimental subjects without TM and without anything fancy and, in fact, just by a very ordinary English mantram. But he didn't call it a mantram. The magic English mantram, in a moment. First, let's see how, in this case, our Western scientific paradigm actually took us away from something that worked and substituted something much more complex.

To solve the mysteries of the brain, Western man has been pulling and pushing and analyzing and dissecting. Descartes had brain drawings, the eye sees here and the perception comes here. Camillo Golgi in the 1890's devised a stain and now you can see a neuron, a nerve cell. Golgi said these neurons were continuous through the brain, and the great Spanish microscopist, Santiago Ramón y Cajal, disagreed and said each cell was separate, and when they gave them a Nobel prize jointly in 1906 the fellas wouldn't speak to each other in Stockholm, threw pillows and sulked. Golgi stains are very pretty. A lady in physiology in Berkeley was making shirts with Golgi stains, very pretty, must be real conversation stoppers, what is that interesting pattern on your shirt, oh, those are neurons from the cerebral cortex. Oh. Must be one of the world's great in-groups when you're wearing a Golgi-stain shirt and you see another one in the airport.

So here is the neuron looking like, printed in black and white, a star or a rhombus, some say, but to me like a fried egg, a little too much pepper in one part of the yolk, and the white splatted out into fingers, as if the pan were really hot and the egg was dropped from a couple of feet. Between the end of one finger and the beginning of the next, on the next fried egg, is a gap, called a synapse by the British neurophysiologist Sir Charles Sherrington, 1897. Sherrington is a semi-poet of neurophysiology, as well as a great teacher who keeps asking his students at Cambridge to bring him something new to learn, and to whom the brain is an "enchanted loom." Nice. The synapses, the gaps, are devices for processing information, lots of neurons in the cortex, 10^{10}, and even more synaptic contacts, 10^{14}.

So an Impulse comes chugging down the axon, the long finger coming away from the cell body. Tra la la la la la la, and now it gets to the edge, and how is it going to get across the gap, the synaptic cleft, to the other side? A cliff-hanger. Just as the Impulse is about to give up, a Chemical Transmitter appears, naturally secreted by a vesicle, and gives the Impulse a ride. (That's if it's an Excitatory Transmitter; an Inhibitory Transmitter backs up and lets the Impulse just sit there.)

Otto Loewi in Germany and Sir Henry Dale in England in the 1920's tell about the chemical transmitters, and so does Sherrington's pupil Adrian in Cambridge, and neuron/neuron is too hard to do at first so they study a neuromuscular junction where the Impulse is going to tell the muscle to do something, and later Bernhard Katz in London is going to say the transmitters get released in little packets, or quanta, and the technical equipment gets more sophisticated, electron microscopes, and the synapse gets measured and the impulse clocked, and John Eccles becomes Sir John and E. D. Adrian becomes Lord Adrian, and the work goes on and Nobel prizes come fluttering out of Stockholm.

And in the biochemistry lab they have found some of the transmitters, norepinephrine and serotonin and dopamine. Reserpine, from the *Rauwolfia* root in the story of the dumb Nigerian, cuts down the norepinephrine, and the chlorpromazines that the Swiss made so much money on blocks its release. No Chemical Transmitter, no ride for the Impulse. No ride for the Impulse, fewer messages, c-a-l-m, that's the idea. But that's a little heavy-handed, so the fellas keep working on MAO inhibitors, which is not political because MAO is not Tse-tung but monoamine oxidase, monoamine being the transmitter and oxidase being the enzyme that breaks it down, and the MAO inhibitors are more specific, mood elevators as they say, because you can pick what you're transmitting and what not, and you get into alpha blockers and beta blockers, very clever indeed, if still controversial.

But somebody in the lab spots a flaw in the MAO's. Oops,

doctors are going to prescribe this and warn the people not to eat cheese, and you know some of those jerks are going to eat cheese, and then what do we do? Because there's an amino in the cheese, tyramine, and the MAO inhibitor is going to block the enzyme degradation—never mind what all this means, keep going—and the tyramine won't get deaminized and everybody's blood pressure is going to go up. Back to the test tubes, Harry. Let's see what we can do with that molecule, what did we have last time, carbon hydrogen carbon carbon nitrogen nitrogen, let's give it a pop of fluoride and see if we can change the benzine ring, nitrogen nitrogen *nitrogen,* because sure as hell those tensed-up anxious jerks are going to forget, they're going to feel very virtuous about turning down the Camembert and then they're going to have a cheeseburger with their kids, let's see, increase the budget, turn up the Bunsen burner—we're really huffing and puffing in the paradigm now—

—and along comes a character in a bed sheet stepping off the Air India flight and he says, "Why don't you say gazoom gazoom gazoom, twenty minutes twice a day but not before bedtime, shut your eyes, don't try, gazoom gazoom gazoom"—

—and *it works! Rauwolfia* time.

NOISE

WHY? Why does it work?

Start with noise. Even animals, say the ethologists, spend a couple of quiet hours a day, grooming and picking among themselves.

In our culture, the noise level is incredible. I don't mean just the jackhammer in the street outside your hotel room, or banging the garbage cans early in the morning. Look at it from the point of view of one of your neurons. There's something to do all the time.

A lot of people get up to an alarm radio, or even TV. Then maybe they read the paper with a cup of coffee. Then they get into their cars and turn on the radio, and they're so habituated to the noise they don't even listen. News: there is a tornado somewhere and traffic deaths somewhere and a house burned down somewhere. Every once in a while some paper runs the same story every day for a month to see if anybody notices, a hill in Korea or Vietnam or wherever the war is that month, or a running fight on Capitol Hill, every day for a month exactly the same story, nobody notices. All that noise goes pouring through the neurons like syrup through pancakes. And it starts very early. The average kid, say the child experts testifying about TV advertising, watches twenty-five thousand commercials a year, *twenty-five thousand* reinforcements for sugar-coated Popsy Flakes, Captain Goo, it's a tribute to the plasticity of the human brain that the kid can still talk and read—maybe he can't, but you can see why he will have his transistor radio clamped to his ear in Yellowstone Park. The pines and the sky are only partly real: real reality is a Popsy Flake commercial. Our experience shapes our perception.

So we have a lot of practice, a lot of conditioning, in what Huxley called "inquietude for the sake of inquietude." St. John of the Cross wrote about that, you get junked up just on the inquietude.

My favorite biology watcher tells how animals and insects use noise. Termites make percussive sounds by beating their heads against the floor; the sound is said to resemble sand falling on paper, but an analysis of the sound reveals a high degree of organization in the drumming; the beats occur in regular rhythmic phrases. Rabbits, mice and prairie hens drum with their feet, the deathwatch beetle makes a ticking sound with a bump on his abdomen, fish click their teeth, blow air, and drum muscles against special air sacs.

And all this registers with the respective termites, beetles and fish. Leeches tap on leaves and other leeches tap back. Animals with loose skeletons rattle them, and even earthworms emit faint, staccato notes.

Lots of music going on. Maybe some of it is just for practice, but most of it carries information; a certain click of the point-man termite turns the column, the dancer bee indicates the clover.

And what of us? Well, we are gifted with speech, and we have supercommunication, in fact we have so much of it we come close to losing the meanings in the cacophony. I suppose we need the information about which streets are torn up, and how to take tax deductions, or what foods are cheaper this season. But so much of our noise is distorted, and designed to keep us off balance, the noise about office politics and school politics, the noise, well, the television commercials are a cliché but there they are, five hours per family per night saying you are not okay, your floors do not shine, your coffee tastes lousy, you are exuding odors from fourteen parts of your body and further: health is something you as a consumer have to buy, from the dispensers of health, otherwise you're going to be up all night and your stomach's going to churn, never mind the natural self-corrections in the body, you better get in there and do the job. You do not have health, you have to buy it. That one alone costs hundreds of millions, not only over the counter, but as a matter of public policy.

And so—almost instinctively—we don't believe it, or don't believe much of it, and the tension of sorting out, amidst all the noise, what is true and what is not true takes extra energy—we are not even aware of the tension. If the dancer bee said, clover, three hundred yards, north by northwest, but none of you jerks can fly by any means known to aeronautical science and furthermore you're too fat and your mother-in-law doesn't like your face and this whole hive is being transferred to Arkansas, the rest of the bunch could try, at some expenditure of bee energy, to extract the information from the dancer bee's neurotic goings-on, or they could, one day, commit him to the attention of a large bee-eating bird and try another dancer.

And that's just the exterior noise; the confusing messages in the exterior noise are quite enough to produce a need for a quiet interior place. But we also have the *interior* noise, being language-using, conscious, conceptualizing animals, and the interior noise is even louder.

Ratcheta ratcheta ratcheta, Molly Bloom's soliloquy, me my mine, that guy in the office is and I shouldn't have said that yesterday and the prices keep going up and when the phone rang I thought and so on. Even if you turn off the TV, thereby missing the possibility of a baseball game, a football game, a hockey game, a tennis playoff—no matter *what* time of year, lots of noise there—the interior noise will get you, you've had so much practice at it. Say Mommy, baby. Say Mommy. Say Grammaw. See Grammaw? Smile. Say Grammaw to Grammaw. The neurons have been twitching so long they think not twitching is abnormal. Once in mid-Arizona a friend of mine got up in the morning bleary-eyed and said he had had no sleep. Why no sleep?

There was a beagle outside my window.

I thought it was a great phrase, something worthy of Joyce, *Finnegans Wake* maybe, God is a shout in the street. There is a beagle outside my window. What kind of beagle? Friendly, tri-colored, tail-wagging, did it sit on the roof of its doghouse flying a Sopwith Camel and dodging the Red Baron?

This damn beagle, said the friend, must have been after a jack rabbit, yawp yawp yawp yawp. All night, yawp yawp yawp yawp. Ah. Well, we all have beagles outside our windows, yawp yawp yawp, and the sound echoes in the neuronal pathways even when we're asleep, even when there is no beagle there and even when we are asleep *we will talk to ourselves constantly*. Not only does that talk limit the perceptions of reality, it gives the neurons busy-work. So: the mantram gives you a bone for the beagle, you can throw it right out there, and once you've thrown it there's nothing much else to do. You may hear some growling and clicking, but if it works you won't hear yawp yawp yawp. Of course, the beagle may not pick up the bone.

But maybe it will.

Rest deeper than sleep? Some of the neurons are quieter when you're asleep, and others work even harder, trying to get things organized for tomorrow, all lined up and consistent. If you can wind up this phrase and send it through on its own momentum, balam balam balam, waking does not matter, it becomes a lullaby for twitchy neurons, they turn up their little toes and snooze.

Why does it work? "A good vibe," said a counter-cultural voice. "A mantram is a sound whose effect is known," said the telephone company.

Wallace had a guess. Wallace and I spoke in Physiology, in which he was fluent and in which I knew just enough to say, I wish please to cash a traveler's check, where is the bathroom, I wish to speak to the manager.

"Some structure in the brain creates order," said Wallace. "We know the reticular system gates out inputs."

"So far, so good."

"As you decrease the activity in the sympathetic nervous system, the system gets more orderly."

"Is that true?"

"Sure, not only do you have synchronization between the brain hemispheres, which you don't normally see, but you get *harmonics* of alpha as well as alpha, ten twenty forty eighty."

I said I must have missed an issue of my favorite head-bump magazine.

"The inward focus and the passive direction allow the thalamus to fire at its natural rhythm."

Firing in natural rhythm! Lovely.

"And that affects the hypothalamus."

Thalamus, the seat of all that sensorimotor activity in the midbrain, the word comes from *thálamos*, nuptial couch in Greek. Imagine that. And hypothalamus then is under the nuptial couch, and the instructions to fight or flee thus come from under the nuptial couch. Very insightful, Dr. Freud.

"I think in meditation," said Wallace, "there will be an analogy like superconductivity in physics, a place where there is no resistance at all." The rishis who invented the mantrams did not have in mind that you could go to the office and see the boss differently, or move the new warehouse to South Carolina without raising your blood pressure, or watch the portfolio go down another 15 percent with equanimity. They had in mind merging consciousness with Consciousness, they said. "Well, they study infinity in physics," Wallace said. "The purpose of the machinery is higher consciousness."

The beagles of the mind are well known to all philosophies, though they are called by many names. TM gives you an immediate device for beagle-soothing, but other schools want you to be aware first of how your mind works. It is always a different matter to recognize something conceptually and to *experience* it. The year before I got to TM, I was in a course called Arica, which was a full-time esoteric school. One of the exercises—you could call it a meditation— went like this. You get a rock. (Some people got very pretty rocks, since they were going to be doing this exercise six days a week, four hours a day.) Class exercise. You put your rock on the floor in front of you; you can sit on a pillow. You put your consciousness in the rock. I was confused. How do you do that? Now you take a breath, pick up the rock, hold your breath, and move the rock in a circle in front of you.

Your eyes are shut. And while you move the rock, you think, Om namo naraya naya, which you can spot immediately as a Sanskrit mantram. Then you exhale and put the rock down, take another breath, and do the same thing left-handed, two repetitions of the mantram per circle of the rock per breath. That's the beginning; it goes on. The last motion—same mantram going—is to circle your head with the rock, and visualize a white light making the same circle inside your head.

Then you start over. Four hours. Nobody ever said that was a relaxation exercise, though you would think with all those circles and mantrams and breathing the beagles would all be occupied. And you weren't supposed to think anything else; just Om namo naraya naya.

My first reactions were: my knee hurts, this is silly, this is very boring, Om namo naraya naya, I lost the count there, what time is it, now my other knee hurts, Om namo naraya naya, this is the dumbest thing I've ever seen, Om namo naraya naya, my nose itches, Om namo naraya naya, what shall we have for dinner, look, that guy is already circling his head with his rock, Om namo naraya naya, I think I'll quit this whole business, this is the most *boring* invention since *piano* lessons, these are the piano scales of the mind, dum da da da da da dum.

I went to lunch with two classmates on a third day, a physician and a psychologist. Physician, B.S., M.D., and psychologist, B.A., M.A., Ph.D. And you know what we talked about? How big do you make *your* circle? Is it better to have a big rock or a little rock? Is it better to have a pretty rock or a plain rock? Isn't this the most boring thing, I wonder what it leads to? Can you make a white light go on at the same time the rock is going around your head? Can I see your rock when we get back to class?

Along about the second week, I got very Prussian and conscientious. I was only going to think Om namo naraya naya, and nothing else! Just like the good Germans in Autogenic Training. Enough of the chitter-chatter! No more: what time is it, my knee hurts, it's so pretty outside why am I in here. No more!

And I couldn't do it. It was like reading the sentence: don't think of an elephant, by the time you've read "elephant" it's too late. Something always popped up; it wasn't a verbal thought, it was an image, and not a white light image, either.

So I decided to do the opposite: I would *not* say Om namo naraya naya, I was just going to go over a list of stocks and review what each company had earned the previous year and what it was expected to earn this year. That was more successful, except for the occasional Om namo naraya naya that crept in uninvited.

I went home that night and I looked up all the stocks and their estimated earnings and their prices, and I was rarely more than a nickel off. Reaction: first, a little flutter of pride; second, an absolute wave of horror. All those numbers are already in the books, and that's what I'm carrying around in my head! It was like opening the attic door and this foul air comes out and there's all this *junk* lying around, bits of pictures, pieces of papers with old phone numbers, legs of old toys, bicycle tires for vanished bicycles, wishes, inhibitions, dreams, old conversations, conversations the way they should have come out, junk! Who is that who has all that junk in his head?

By chance, a friend came by and we went off to meet an ex-psychologist called Richard Alpert in his old incarnation—the ex-sidekick of Leary—and Baba Ram Dass in his present, and he said what is it you're doing, and I said, well, we have an hour of sort of hatha yoga and an hour of Tibetan chanting and then we turn this rock in a circle for four hours—"Ah," he said—and I said, I am very depressed because my mind is a pile of junk.

"That's nice, that's nice," said Baba Ram Dass. "You're doing well. The Indians say the mind is a drunken monkey, you know. When I went to India, I went to this monastery, and they showed me into this little cell, and they said, count your breath, and we'll bring the food right here. And I said, well, I don't think I want to do that right now, and they said, okay, that's what we do here, so if you're not ready, let us know whenever you're ready. So I said okay, breathe in, breathe out, one, breathe in, breathe out, two. And I thought of all the ice-cream sundaes I had ever eaten, and old movies I had seen, and old conversations, and future conversations, and in the afternoons I would think, there's an afternoon flight from Delhi to New York at three-thirty, I could walk out of here, I could be in Delhi tonight, I could be on that flight tomorrow."

"But you didn't."

"No, I didn't."

"So your mind is a drunken monkey, too."

"Everybody's mind is a drunken monkey, but they aren't aware of it. Now you're aware of it."

"I may have been just as happy not being aware of it."

But too late; don't think of an elephant. I went back to Om namo naraya naya, only now there was a little distance between me and the drunken monkey, enough so I could say, what is the drunken money going to come up with now? Let's get back to work? What's for dinner? This whole exercise is dumb? What?

If you could see into the minds of the president of U.S. Steel and the president of the AFL-CIO, if those gentlemen were sitting turning a rock and going Om namo naraya naya, their minds would be next year's budget and last year's budget and old golf scores and children's marks, images of faces, images of secretaries, obsolete airline schedules, disjointed columns of numbers already in the books—the whole array. Czech poetry. Scandinavian drinking songs.

The lesson that seeps through can be a little chilling: *your head is not your friend.* Not automatically. "The mind," said St. Theresa, the fifteenth-century Spanish mystic, "is an unbroken horse." That gives us beagles, monkeys and horses, but you get the idea.

Not all religious disciplines want to teach you to still the mind, especially not in two weekends; some want you first to see its nature, or their version of its nature.

But perhaps religion to altered states to relaxation to lowered blood pressure is a bit cumbersome. TM had taken much of the doctrine out of its technique; now Benson, the Harvard Medical School half of the old research team, was to take out the rest. But first he had to review the physiological benefits religion had had when it and not science was the paradigm:

"In the Western world today," wrote Benson and his associates, in *Psychiatry*, "there is a growing interest in nonpharmacological, self-induced, altered states of consciousness because of their alleged benefits of better mental and physical health and improved ability to deal with tension and stress. During the experience of one of these states, individuals claim to have feelings of increased creativity, of infinity, and of immortality; they have an evangelistic sense of mission, and report that mental and physical suffering vanish. Subjective and objective data exist which support the hypothesis that an integrated central nervous system reaction, the *'relaxation response,'* underlies this altered state of consciousness. Physicians should be knowledgable of the physiologic changes and possible health benefits of the relaxation response."

A Nobel-winning Swiss physiologist, Walter Hess, had delineated the location of the fight-or-flight or "ergotropic" response, and its opposite, called the "trophotropic," in the brain of the cat. A relaxation spot in the brain! " . . , the anterior hypothalamus," wrote Benson, "extending into the supra- and pre-optic areas, septum and inferior lateral thalamus."

As Hess had said, there were no specific foci for isolated responses "but a collective representation of a group of responses."

And how do you get to the anterior hyopthalamus to get the message to relax?

Benson delineated four elements:

(1) *Mental Device.* "There should be a constant stimulus, e.g. a sound, word, or phrase repeated silently or audibly, or fixed gazing at an object. The purpose of these procedures is to shift from logical, externally-oriented thought."

Benson did not mention "mantram."

(2) *Passive Attitude.* Don't worry about how you're doing, and if thoughts come, go back to the technique.

(3) *Decreased Muscle Tonus.* Sit in a comfortable posture and take it easy.

(4) *Quiet Environment.* Shut your eyes (except for meditations in gazing at an object).

Benson was eager to show that many religions contained techniques leading to "the relaxation response," but in fact the techniques might have been associated with mysticism, and mysticism has been greeted by repugnance. The Trappist author

Thomas Merton wrote, "The tendency of Christians has been to regard all non-Christian religious experience as so obviously suspect as to be either too dangerous to study or else not worth the trouble . . . Sufism is shrugged off as 'sensuality' and 'self-hypnosis,' Hinduism is pagan pantheism, Yoga is considered a technique for inducing contemplative trances . . . even professedly Christian mysticism is tainted with the pagan eros."

It should be noted, too, that the Eastern religions distinguished between the mantram and prayer. The mantram was Benson's "mental device, a constant stimulus to shift from logical, externally-oriented thought." Prayer is prayer in any religion, and some of the prayers are quite elaborate, in the East as well as the West. In his enthusiasm, Benson blurred the differences.

ECUMENICAL
RELAXATION
TECHNIQUES

"**P**ERHAPS one reason for today's decline of interest in these more organized religions is that the stress on altering awareness has been largely muted," it says in *On the Psychology of Meditation*, Naranjo and Ornstein. "And, although the techniques for altering awareness still persist, the practices have become 'automatic,' part of a set of ritual, lacking their original purpose."

You want to know what's gone from everyday life?

How to attain an altered state of consciousness, by an unknown fourteenth-century Christian author, in *The Cloud of Unknowing*: eliminate distractions, pick a single syllable word, such as "god" or "love":

> Choose whichever one you prefer, or, if you like choose another that suits your taste, provided that it is of one syllable. And clasp this word tightly in your heart so that it never leaves it no matter what may happen. . . . with this word you shall strike down thoughts of every kind and drive them beneath the cloud of forgetting. . . .

Here is the "Prayer of the Heart," or the "Prayer of Jesus," from

Gregory of Sinai at the monastery in Mount Athos in Greece, also fourteenth century:

> Sit down alone and in silence. Lower your head, shut your eyes, breathe out gently, and imagine yourself looking into your own heart. Carry your mind, i.e. your thoughts, from your head to your heart. As you breathe out, say "lord Jesus Christ, have mercy on me." Say it moving your lips gently, or simply say it in your mind. Try to put all other thoughts aside. Be calm, be patient and repeat the process very frequently.

Gershom Scholem, the Hebrew scholar, writes that practices leading to altered states extend as far back as the second century B.C., in the days of the second temple. In these practices the subject sat with his head between his knees, whispered hymns and songs, and repeated the name of a magic seal. Rabbi Abulafia, thirteenth century, developed a mystical system of contemplating the Hebrew letters of God's name, in the cabala. Scholem:

> . . . an important part in Abulafia's system is played by the technique of breathing; now this technique has found its highest development in the Indian *Yoga*, where it is commonly regarded as the most important instrument of mental discipline. Again, Abulafia lays down certain forms of recitation, and in particular some passages of his book, "The Light of the Intellect" give the impression of a Judaized treatise on *Yoga*. The similarity even extends to some aspects of the doctrine of ecstatic vision, as preceded and brought about by these practices.

Then there is Sufism, a part of Islam, which made use of rhythmic breathing, music, gestures and dances, and the constant repetition of God's name. Yoga has many variations, some of which involve staring at a geometric design called a mandala, and some of which involve breathing, positions or repeated movements.

Here is an example not cited by Benson, a Zen breathing exercise from *What the Buddha Taught*:

Bring your mind to concentrate on your breathing-in and breathing-out, let your mind watch and observe your breathing-in and breathing-out; let your mind be aware and vigilant of your breathing in and out. When you breathe, you sometimes take deep breaths, sometimes not. This does not matter at all. Breathe normally and naturally. The only thing is that when you take deep breaths you should be aware that they are deep breaths, and so on. In other words, your mind should be so fully concentrated on your breathing that you are aware of its movements and changes. Forget all other things, your surroundings, your environment; do not raise your eyes and look at anything. Try to do this for five or ten minutes.

At the beginning you will find it extremely difficult to bring your mind to concentrate on your breathing. You will be astonished how your mind runs away. It does not stay. You begin to think of various things. You hear sounds outside. You may be dismayed and disappointed. But if you continue to practice this exercise twice a day, morning and evening, you will gradually, by and by, begin to concentrate your mind on your breathing. After a certain period you will experience just that split second when your mind is fully concentrated on your breathing, when you will not hear even sounds nearby, when no external world exists for you . . . that is the moment when you lose yourself completely in the mindfulness of breathing.

The Eastern world, said Benson and his colleagues, had made these techniques a way of life; in the West, they had belonged to the mystics. The necessity of a trained teacher was always emphasized, but Benson's "relaxation response" was "a simple, non-cultic technique."

If the effects of the relaxation response held up long-term, Benson and his associates wrote, the effect on the economics of therapy would be profound, "since it is practiced at no other cost than time."

"You're talking about the $125 mantram at TM," I suggested.

"I think TM is fine if that's what you want," Benson said. "But other things work, too."

"Prayer?"

"Well, not prayer quite in the conventional sense. But if a Catholic comes in, say, and wants to use some childhood prayer, that's fine, although most of those prayers have a lot of syllables. We don't propose it voluntarily, because a lot of prayers aren't neutral, the way they were taught has left some emotional residue, guilt or tension."

"Do you have an alternate mantram, neutral and free of meaning?"

"Yes. You sit quietly, close your eyes, relax all your muscles, beginning at your feet and moving up to your face—"

"—like progressive relaxation—"

"—like progressive relaxation, and you become aware of your breathing. You breathe through your nose, and as you breathe out, you think to yourself, One—in, out—One—in, out—One."

"Your mantram is One? How did you pick that?"

"Well, we were looking around the lab, you can't use pen or pencil, some people might have hang-ups about pens or pencils, you can't have people count very high, if they're really relaxed, they'll lose the count, and if they start to worry they lose the passive attitude, and the Zen breathing exercises had people counting to some low number like three."

"So you picked One. No other numbers?"

"Well, the next one up that's euphonious, that doesn't have sharp sounds, doesn't require effort, is Nine."

"What about the religious significance of One?"

"What religious significance?"

"Well, there's the One in Oriental philosophy, as opposed to the Nothing, there's the One in Meister Eckhardt, the mystic, and there's the One in Indian religion of the Being, the All, the Unity, there's the Hebrew, 'The Lord Our God, The Lord Is One—' "

"Oh, Lord, we didn't think of that," Benson said. There was some silence on the phone for a minute. "But I don't think that's going to hang up too many people. If they're hung up on One, we'll find another sound, but One is neutral to most people."

I called up Wallace. Wallace had been away, and hadn't seen the latest *Lancet*, or *Psychosomatic Medicine*.

"One?" he said. "One?"

"One," I said. "Maybe, in extreme emergencies, Nine."

"What was the drop in blood pressure?"

"It looks like about eleven millimeters of mercury in the mean systolic, and about five diastolic."

"What was the drop in oxygen consumption?"

"From 258.9 to 225.4, and carbon dioxide down about 12 percent."

Nobody said anything.

"That's nice," Wallace said. "That's very nice."

"I have this slightly used mantram—" I said.

"It may be that a lot of things will work," Wallace said, "though we were the first to test this technique, and we'll have the first long-range studies. Other techniques may produce relaxation, but there is a difference between a mantram and other sounds, a subtle but real difference. And we have classes and free checking, and the support of other meditators, people need that, people like that."

(In fairness, the TM fee is the initiation fee, and subsequent classes and checking are indeed free. In addition, TM runs retreat weekends in the countryside at nominal cost.)

In most (but not all) of the experiments, there were also "control groups"—a similar group of people who didn't meditate, measured for comparison. Sitting still in a quiet room with eyes closed obviously cut down their exterior noise, but there was nothing to dampen the interior noise. There was, then, a big gap between the control group and the meditators, even though obviously the control group sitting still was quieter than the control group before it sat still.

I did a little informal polling. Both Benson and Wallace were right. Benson's mantram—One—was cheaper, but Wallace did indeed have teaching and checking and group support. In the poll, I told people I had a meditation technique. The technique was the same, but one version of it came from the Harvard Medical School and the other version came from India. The Harvard Medical School version was free and the Indian one cost $75, a white handkerchief, some fruit, and two weekends. Which one works?

Nobody wanted the Harvard Medical School technique. What

does the Harvard Medical School know about meditation? And free? Why free? How can it be any good if it's free? No, let's have the Indian technique. But what impressed the pollees about the Indian technique was not the fruit, the white handkerchief, the incense and so on, but the reprints from the Harvard Medical School! They wanted the mantram validated by the doctors!

Some further research showed that: Benson was right, TM had no monopoly as a relaxation technique, and Wallace was right, a *system* of meditation had many subtle gradations. It was true that meditation was a relaxation response as Benson said; many people fell asleep during their meditations. But it was more than just relaxation. Benson had stopped too soon, or had been too general. A Harvard psychologist, Daniel Goleman, got the wires out for a group of meditators and a control group, and showed them both an extremely stressful safety movie, in which fingers were lost in machinery, circular saws bit into workers' stomachs, and so on. The mediators perceived more quickly, and recovered their equilibrium more quickly. "Meditation practice is not simply a relaxed state, but the capacity for focused attention," said the report. It speculated that what this capacity for focused attention did was to unlink the cortical and limbic systems, that is, the thinking and perceiving system and the automatic and emotional system. Thus the meditators were not only quicker to return to equilibrium and more at home in that state, but more alert. "A wakeful, hypometabolic state," Benson and Wallace had written, but the emphasis seemed to be on the relaxation, on the word "hypometabolic." The meditators were also "wakeful," though there was not as much attention on that.

Of course, for busy people, there was the problem of when and where to meditate. For commuters in buses and trains, the commuting time was ideal. It looks like you're just catching a little nap. But for commuters who drive to work, there's a problem: you have to keep your eyes open while driving. (Advanced meditators in other techniques might be able to do it.)

What about non-commuters? What about busy people in midcity?

"We have the solution," said some friends. "Churches."

"Churches?"

"Sure, churches are the one place in the middle of a city that are quiet and respect silence. Some of them even say, enter, rest, and pray. So you go in, you slip into the last pew, and you do your mantram for twenty minutes. It's terrific. You can do it on the way to lunch, or after work."

I tried it myself. Churches were indeed the solution—the only place open in mid-city that respected silence other than the public library. Fabulous! Sometimes the organist would be practicing—that didn't hurt the meditation at all. Sometimes I looked at the very few other people in the church—what was in their minds? Mantrams in what language? Were they asking for something or were they meditating?

We meditators were so grateful for the churches that we began dropping dollar bills in the collection box. It seemed proper and felt good.

Benson published his article—same article—in the *Harvard Business Review*. He added one point: a coffee break, he said, was better spent as a meditation break. Corporations should encourage meditation, instead of coffee, he said. He didn't say where you should meditate in your coffee break, but when you get good enough, it doesn't matter where.

Were there, then, no problems created by these techniques? None so far, when done for limited amounts of time, said Benson. If the meditation was increased in time to several hours a day over a longer period, "some individuals have experienced feelings of withdrawal from life and symptoms which range in severity from insomnia and incontrolled movements of the limbs to hallucinatory experiences." (Interesting: the uncontrolled movements are shaktipat in the Indian religions, welcomed as an advanced state in the presence of the guru.) But these effects were difficult to evaluate "because individuals with emotional problems might be drawn to any technique . . . which evangelically promises relief from tension and stress."

I started musing about those symptoms from too much meditating.

WHY FRANNY
FAINTED

REMEMBER Franny in J. D. Salinger's *Franny and Zooey*?

The artists and writers, the real artists, generate some special harmonic that is a generation ahead of consensus logic. Franny came out in *The New Yorker* in 1955, and everybody talked about her. Franny went to see her rather stuffy boyfriend Lane on the Yale weekend at his unspecified but presumably Ivy League university, And they went off to the restaurant that served snails and frog's legs and they ordered martinis.

Franny is in a state of real upset. She hates the section men who *ruin* Turgenev and all the small-time people who are knocking everything in their casual, small-time ways, and she has dropped out of the play she was in.

"All I know is I'm losing my mind," Franny says. "I'm just sick of ego, ego, ego. My own and everybody else's. I'm sick of everybody that wants to *get* somewhere, do something distinguished and all, be somebody interesting. It's disgusting—it is, it *is*. I don't care what anybody says."

Lane says, isn't Franny just afraid of competing? And Franny says she's afraid she *will* compete, she's been "horribly conditioned to accept everybody else's values," and she's sick of it. "I'm sick of not having the courage to be an absolute nobody. I'm sick of myself and everybody that wants to make some kind of a splash . . . my teeth go funny. They're chattering. I nearly bit through a glass day before yesterday."

What's the little green book Franny is carrying? It's *The Way of a Pilgrim*. ". . . it starts out with this peasant—the pilgrim—wanting to find out what it means in the Bible when it says you should pray incessantly. You know. Without stopping . . . so he starts walking all over Russia, looking for somebody who can tell him *how* . . . he meets this person called a starets—some sort of terribly advanced religious person—and the starets tells him about a book called the 'Philokalia' . . . written by a group of terribly advanced monks who sort of advocated this really incredible method of praying."

And the starets tells the pilgrim that if you keep saying "Lord Jesus Christ, have mercy on me" over and over—"you only have to just do it with your *lips* at first—then eventually what happens, the prayer becomes self-active. Something *happens* after a while. I don't know what, but something happens, and the words get synchronized with the person's heartbeats, and then you're actually praying without ceasing. Which has a really tremendous, mystical effect on your whole outlook . . . you do it to purify your whole outlook and get an absolutely new conception of what everything's about . . . but the marvelous thing is, when you first start doing it, you don't even have to have *faith* in what you're doing. I mean even if you're terribly embarrassed about the whole thing, it's perfectly all right. I mean you're not *insulting* anybody or anything. In other words, nobody asks you to believe a single thing when you first start out. You don't even have to think about what you're saying, the starets said. All you have to have in the beginning is quantity. Then, later on, it becomes quality by itself. On its own power of something. He says that any name of God—any name at all—has this peculiar, self-active power of its own, and it starts working after you've started it up . . . in the Nembutsu sects of Buddhism, people say 'Praise to the Buddha' over and over . . . and in 'The Cloud of Unknowing' . . . you just keep saying 'God' . . . did you ever hear of anything so fascinating in your *life*, in a way? I mean it's so hard to say it's absolutely coincidence . . ."

But boyfriend Lane is a real 50's clot.

"You actually believe that stuff or what?"

Franny says she doesn't say she believes or not, but isn't it a peculiar coincidence that "all these really advanced and absolutely unbogus religious persons keep telling you . . . even in India, they tell you to meditate on the 'Om,' and the same result is supposed to happen . . ."

Lane says, what is the result? "All this synchronization business and mumbo jumbo. You get heart trouble? I don't know if you know it, but you could do yourself, somebody could do himself a great deal of real—"

"You get to see God. Something happens in the non-physical part of the heart," Franny says.

Poor Franny, a generation ahead of her time. Franny had spent five minutes in the ladies' room crying, and come back to Lane and the martinis and the frog's legs, and then she fainted.

I can remember very well the reaction to Franny and her fainting. Why did Franny faint? That was the mystery. The cadences of Franny's speech were so perfect we thought we knew her, the pretty girl going through a kooky phase, okay, but why did she faint? Franny fainted, said the consensus at the time, because she was pregnant. That shows that we didn't listen to what Franny was saying, and even if we had listened we wouldn't have known what to make of it.

And now we know. End of literary mystery. Franny put herself into a heavy meditation and very successfully, with the Jesus Prayer. (Also, she hadn't eaten and was a bit of a hysteric.) That synchronization she talked about would have made a nice EEG and EKG, head and heart, lots of alpha. The teeth chattering and crying show she couldn't quite handle the altered state; she was probably ahead of schedule, and she didn't have anybody to talk to about it, so she thought she was going crazy. Poor baby, she wasn't going crazy at all, she just didn't know about altered states of consciousness, they hadn't invented the phrase, if she had reported back to her meditation class they would have been envious at her progress, some of them would have thought, gee,

I haven't cried yet and my teeth haven't chattered. Of course, a true meditation would have left Franny serene even with a clot of a boyfriend and stupid instructors, she could have separated her emotional, limbic response from her acute, cortical perceptions. The Prayer of the Heart was working for Franny, but she was certainly in some sort of transitional state. A generation later, Franny seems to have seen things the way they were, and she was so sweet, and vulnerable.

There is an obvious difference in a way of life that supports meditation, and the workaday world that doesn't. It's one thing to do a lot of meditation in a retreat where the very rhythms of life are set up to include the meditation, and another in a busy household or a crowded schedule that doesn't. If you are going to participate in the busy household or the crowded schedule, you need a little bit of fight or flight just to get going. A lot of meditation can wipe out the fight or flight so that the effort seems silly. It may or may not be: that is another topic entirely. But too little fight or flight is not, these days, most people's problem.

The repetition of a prayer or a phrase has its effect physiologically, but not everybody, it should be pointed out, agrees that this is the way to meditate. The Indian sage Krishnamurti is scornful of the techniques of TM and the Prayer of the Heart. "By repeating Amen or Om or Coca-Cola indefinitely you obviously have a certain experience because by repetition the mind becomes quiet . . . it is one of the favorite gambits of some teachers of meditation to insist on their pupils learning concentration, that is, fixing the mind on one thought and driving out all other thoughts. This is a most stupid, ugly thing, which any schoolboy can do because he is forced to."

Krishnamurti didn't say it didn't work, he just didn't think it was a high-class meditation. His own meditation was nothing: a blank mind, "empty, not filled with things of the mind. Then there is only meditation, and not a meditator who is meditating . . . the mind must be clear, without movement, and in the light of that clarity the timeless is revealed."

I don't think anybody argues with that, but a really blank

mind is even harder than keeping only Amen or Om or Coca-Cola in the mind. Coca-Cola is Krishnamurti being snotty. It wouldn't work. Psychophysiologically, the hard c's would stub the mind as it settled down, not mellifluous enough, and psychologically in order for the process to work you have to, if not believe, at least suspend disbelief long enough for the images to clear, and while Coca-Cola has claimed many things in its history, quieting the mind has not been one of them.

It's so hard to say it's absolutely coincidence, said Franny, that here all these different people, the Indians doing Om, and the Russian pilgrims saying "Lord Jesus Christ, have mercy on me," and the Nembutsu Buddhists going Namu amida butsu over and over, and the *same thing* happens.

The same thing happens, leaving aside for a moment the question of where the vibe comes from, because a lot of different groups empirically found their way to the anterior hypothalamus extending into the supra- and pre-optic areas, septum and inferior lateral thalamus, according to Benson. And everybody has an anterior hypothalamus. Naturally the differing groups did not have the cold Western physiological language so important to our own ability to believe. Belief is important. Some people believe better if they use a word designated as holy, and some people believe better if they know this is a scientific process checked out by the Harvard Medical School with lots of fancy equipment. Remember, the placebo believers were rewarded by having their stomachs cured and their asthma clear up, and the scoffers are still taking Alka-Seltzer and wheezing. Nobody has checked out whether Ba-na-na Ba-na-na works, with catheters and EEG's and so on, and by the time you've read this it's too late to try, but if you could find somebody who didn't think bananas were funny or that the word banana meant something profound or holy, the odds would seem to favor it and the Swami Suchabanana could be right after all.

Whether we use the language of religion or the language of physiology, the end is the same: to quiet the mind.

The object of quieting the mind may be, in the West, to go back to work with your blood pressure down and your stomach calmer, but that was not the object in the religious techniques, it was simply a by-product, or a stepping stone, a preparatory phrase. The instructions were to lose yourself in the contemplation of the object, whether the object was a prayer, a symbol, or a set of movements. One branch of yoga makes use of ritualized movements; the Orthodox Jew uses a rhythmic nodding called *dovining*. The Moslem equivalent of the Jesus Prayer is *La ilaha illa'llah*, there is no God but God. The devotee, in one set of instructions, repeats the prayer frequently: "banishing every distraction . . . with *La ilaha* he denies and excludes all competing objects." The object of contemplation in a visual meditation can be a cross in Christianity, a geometric symbol in Islam, the portrait of a guru or saint; the six-pointed star is not only the Star of David but a symbol in Tantric yoga.

Such are the intolerances of humanity that through most of history people have only been able to use the socially approved method of damping down and turning off. If you went whirling like the Mevlevi Sufis in Yankee America, they would have though you were a witch or a warlock and taken appropriate action. The Shakers, who did whirl, were persecuted. If you wandered through old Russia saying the Jesus Prayer, they admired your piousness and welcomed you to table, but if you uttered a parallel Hebrew prayer you could have been in a lot of trouble. This is a more tolerant age, but if you say banana banana for twenty minutes a day, you better let your friends know it's all right.

Continued meditation leads to a state called, in Zen, one-pointedness, and in Indian terminology, the Void, or "emptiness." St. John of the Cross, a Spanish mystic, called it "the annihilation of memory." The *object* of the meditation—the syllable or the figure—has disappeared, leaving a state of blank, the blanking-out being a much desired end. This state can also be expressed in physiological psychology. Normally, we hardly ever look at anything steadily, as a meditator would gaze at a mandala or a cross or what have you. We have larger eye movements, saccades, and also very small involuntary ones, nystagmus, and both movements keep the image on the retina in constant motion.

A group of psychologists were testing the theory that the brain needs continuous change. They fixed tiny projectors on contact lenses, and tried out the apparatus on some volunteers. No matter how the eyes of the volunteers moved, the same stable image fell on the retina. The images disappeared! The volunteers did not "see." "Stabilizing" the input eliminated the continuous changes.

The same sort of thing happened in another group when the observers looked at a totally patternless visual field, a "ganzfeld" in psychologic jargon. Like a totally whitewashed surface, or the halves of a split ping-pong ball placed over the eyes. Here the experimenters reported that after about twenty minutes there was no visual experience, which they called "blank out." "Blank out" wasn't merely seeing white, or seeing nothing, it was a complete disappearance of the sense of vision; the volunteers didn't know whether their eyes were open or not.

So there is a similarity between "blank out" and the state of losing the object of meditation and arriving at one-pointedness or emptiness or Void. Franny said: all you have to have in the beginning is quantity, and it becomes quality by itself, on its own power. Blank out. If you're going to do the Jesus Prayer in the ladies' john, you can blank out on the Yale weekend.

And here we get to one of those gaps in communication. Obviously there is a big difference in set and setting for (a) a meditator involved in a belief system, and (b) a volunteer in a psych lab with a split ping-pong ball taped over his eyes. The vocabulary of the first says that if you meditate well and really cut off the outside, you can merge with Infinity. The vocabulary of the second says you are in blank out. The first seems vague and spooky, and the second seems like, if not a put-down, an outside description of an inside experience. It repeats in physiologic terms—he's showing lots of alpha, look, he's not registering any stimuli—what the meditator has been trying to do.

Meditators report that colors seem brighter and the world fresher. The world is the same as it was, whatever that is—the redness of the rose is in the eye of the meditator. We become habituated to things so well that we do not see them. Manufacturers know this, so they put New! New! on the giant-size box of detergent, and they change the clothing styles, and so on, otherwise nobody would really *see*. The first time we go into a room we can hear a clock ticking, or the traffic outside, or whatever, then after a while we don't notice. Another psychologist measured people's eyes—these guys are tireless—looking at the same picture every day. Sure enough, after a while, the people's eyes didn't really look at the picture. When they first looked at it, their eyes went tracketa tracketa tracketa all over it, and on succeeding days the eye movements became stereotyped. They hit a few spots, enough to match the model of the picture already held in the brain, and quit. That's why Jerome Bruner—still another experiment—got the answers he did with his crazy deck of cards. It had a red six of spades, among other things, and everybody called it a six of hearts. The little brain model said, spades are black, hearts are red, and the eyes didn't look closely —tracketa pop!—because what the hell, everybody's already seen a deck of cards, why look again? Why are there proofing errors in every book, when presumably a professional proofreader has gone over the copy word by word? The proofreader has to fight his optic system which "corrects" and adjusts as it goes along.

The turnoff from the meditation provides a little mini-vacation from the continuous input, and you know that when you get back from vacation, you look things over with more interest on the first day.

One of the concomitants of meditation is to open the doors of perception. "We must become like little children." Not just that the rose is redder, but that you thought the six of spades was black, and we put this red six of spades right before your very eyes and you didn't say, hey, that card is the wrong color, you said, that's a six of hearts.

Maybe your whole world is made up of these models, and every day you're betting that today is the same as the past, and that the symbol represents the same reality. But what is really real? Where are you living? The symbols are all there to help us get a grip, but maybe they're not reality.

If you can get used to this concept of symbols and reality, it can make a big difference. Of course, habituation does protect you from registering freshly the same commercial for the thousandth time.

Language and symbol divide up the world so we can grab it.

Language goes with the action mode, getting ourselves fed and clothed, the eyes scanning, focusing, and establishing boundaries. The sympathetic system is dominant. (Sympathetic is a lousy word for the system, because sympathetic in another context means warm and comforting, but the medical vocabulary has stuck us with it. It is the sympathetic system that gears up to fight or flee. Sympathetic is arise! and shine! Parasympathetic is now, now, there, there, cool it.) In the dominant sympathetic system, the future and the past are important, and the mode—language, construct—is one for control, hanging on to time, hanging on to the symbol. Rather than let go of old constructs and old images, this mode will hang them on to the current scene, the current relationships. You're just like my first wife, Zelda, you're a red six of spades.

The other mode is nonverbal and parasympathetic: letting, passive, feminine so-called, now as opposed to past or future. The other mode is what the good Germans meant by it breathes me, what Benson meant by a passive attitude, and what the Maharishi meant by we do not try, and so on.

It's not an easy concept to get across—even oversimplified like this—because it comes in words which are themselves symbols. You are reading in an active, past-and-future, sympathetic mode. What are you when you are not doing? they ask, in some meditation instruction. If you spend all your time there, anything else is as hard to imagine as antimatter.

Sympathetic/parasympathetic, active/passive, X chromosome and Y chromosome, the symmetry of twos, Yin and Yang you could say, if you were into the *I Ching*. The old gentleman with the flowered sleeves wasn't laughing at *everybody*.

THE BALLAD
OF THE ZEN COWBOY

WHILE I admired Benson's ecumenical approach in his historical roundup of altered states, I suspect it may be hard for Westerners to utilize a prayer and be in the receptive, parasympathetic mode. In many prayers you *ask for something*. "Lord, grant us victory," says the pro football coach. Victory is something. Learning the prayer was something you had to do, therefore it has associations of rewards and punishment, as in school. Meditation, then, is something you attack to achieve. In that case, "one" would certainly be better, or a Sanskrit sound with no meaning to the user. "Lord, grant us victory, let us beat those bastids" is no mantram. If there is something you lack, such as victory, that's not equilibrium.

The meditative techniques we have so far looked at are the beginning ones. In Zen, this is *bompo* Zen, ordinary Zen, you can do it just for your health and well-being and stop there if you want to. The word *zen* itself is a Japanese word meaning meditation. It began as *dhyana* in Sanskrit, went to China and became *ch'an*, went to Japan and became *zen*.

All right, meditation, blank out in ganzfeld, it sounds like a German motorcycle movie. What happens after the first step of meditation, turning off, ka-zonk, but staying awake?

That depends. Naranjo and Ornstein, psychiatrist and psychologist one each, say there are two kinds of meditation: concentrative, or damping down, and opening up. The Zen scholars have five stages, the Maharishi has seven, yogas are even more numerous. Let's try Zen for just a moment, since D. T. Suzuki, one leading authority, says Zen is not mysticism and Zen is a way, not a religion. This is from Philip Kapleau's *The Three Pillars of Zen*:

First step, for *bompo* people, count breaths. That's all. Very good for the blood pressure, ulcers, asthma, and dying twenty years too soon.

Second step, follow the breath. Don't count any more. Just follow it.

Third step, shikan-taza. Which means just sitting.

I know, it sounds crazy. Forget anything you may have remembered about Zen from the days of "Beat Zen." Just sitting is very hard, you can only do it a half-hour at a time. It's really hard because you don't have the support of counting breaths or even following breaths. Here is Zen Master Yasutani Roshi, giving instructions that sound like one of the flashbacks in *Kung Fu*:

In this type of Za-Zen [just sitting] it is all too easy for the mind ... to become distracted ... the mind must be unhurried yet firmly planted or massively composed, like Mount Fuji, let us say. But it also must be alert, stretched, like a taut bowstring. So shikan-taza is a heightened state of concentrated awareness wherein one is neither tense nor hurried, and certainly never slack. It is the mind of somebody facing death. Let us imagine that you are engaged in a duel of swordsmanship of the kind that used to take place in ancient Japan. As you face your opponent, you are unceasingly watchful, set, ready. Were you to relax your vigilance even momentarily, you would be cut down instantly. A crowd gathers to see the fight. Since you are not blind you see them from the corner of your eye, and since you are not deaf you hear them. But not for an instant is your mind captured by these sense impressions.

That's the state of mind behind the martial arts, judo and jujitsu, aikido and kung fu. Alert, relaxed, and no-mind. Stage three, just sitting, gets you to unified mind, one-pointed concentration, dynamic power, even, says the roshi, certain supranormal powers. He doesn't say what. "One who has developed *joriki* is no longer a slave to his passions, neither is he at the mercy of his environment. Always in command of both himself and the circumstances of his life, he is able to move with perfect freedom and equanimity."

Now your knees hurt from all that sitting, but you do not fight pain, you say hello, pain, how are you, and you go into the pain and it disappears. Next stage, Enlightenment. Now in the monastery there they are really chasing your shredded ego, physically and mentally, you are sitting facing the wall, no-mind, and the guy creeps up behind you and wap! wap! with the *kyosaku* stick, and now your mind has a koan, or impossible question: what was your face before your parents' birth? The koan is not a riddle that can be solved by any sort of linear thinking whatsoever. So the scene of the student and the roshi can be sheer Marx Brothers.

The Master says, "What does one's Buddha mind look like?" and the student says, "The fish play in the trees and birds fly in the sea." The Master says, move that boat on the lake with your mind, and the student turns a somersault and bumps his head. The Master is experienced enough to know how the student is coming along in this nonverbal, irrational procedure. What is the sound of one hand clapping? The student is to keep the koan in his mind, turning and turning and turning. A contemporary American master asks: how can driving on the freeways lead to enlightenment?

There is a somewhat shocking axiom for those not familiar with this: "If you meet the Buddha on the road, kill him!" If you think you and the Buddha on the road are separate objects, then you still have shadows in your mind.

Sometimes the whole process takes years. Do not let go of your koan, says the roshi, even though you feel "like a mosquito attacking an iron bowl."

All right, you keep turning and turning this koan, what was my face before my parents' birth, and you run through every possible permutation and finally, the rap goes, your ego-mind, your conceptual, language-using mind, just throws up its hands, gives up, which is very tough because the ego-mind thinks every-thing will stop if *it* stops, death. But, the rap goes, you have to die in order to be born again. When the ego-mind has busted itself on the koan, not to mention having been set up with all that breathing and counting and not counting and just sitting, then you have ken-sho, enlightenment, in psychologic terms a direct perception, or perception without the model you were carrying.

That is why, if you think you got it, you didn't get it. If you think you got it, that implies not only that there was something out there to get, but that you could know you got it, which gives you away instantly because how would you know unless you were checking the old model, six of spades, there's something there to get.

If you don't get *that*, forget it, it will flash on you some morn-ing when you're brushing your teeth and give you a little giggle.

When written up, the experiences of the Zen students sound just as far out as the koans. "I have it!" says one, overjoyed, as he bounces into the roshi. "Everything is nothing! I am every-thing! The Universe is One!"

The Zen master may not be impressed. "Everything is Buddha-nature?" he might say.

"Right, right."

"Your mind is liberated from everything that fits over it like a strait jacket?"

"Right, Master."

"Show me Buddha-nature. Divide it into two parts, sprinkle one part over your food and fly the other part like a kite."

Here's an interesting example, an American psychotherapist in Japan. First they have him counting, ugggghhh, so boring he can hardly stand it. "I had perhaps never been so frustrated in my life." It goes on, one, two, three, hi-tot-su hu-tot-su, mi-it-su. His knees hurt, he counts, he listens, he falls asleep, his knees hurt some more. A couple of days later they give him another sound, "mu," nothing. And very exact, very exact ways to do it. Pretty soon he has stopped noticing the trains that come by this place periodically, and the other outside sounds, and late one morning:

—a white, clear screen came before my eyes. In front of the screen passed, or rather floated, simple images—faces, objects. I have no clear recollection of the images. A rush of feeling came over me.

I burst into tears; the tears became quiet sobbing.

I do not remember at what point I had stopped the exercise.

I can state my feeling but I am not sure I can communicate it with any real meaning. I would like not to be mysterious; I would like to communicate it clearly, at the same time knowing that it may be possible.

My feeling was that I was seeing something of great importance, as if everything fitted together for the first time. What had all my life struggles been about? Things were very clear and very simple.

They walk our psychotherapist up to see the roshi, and the roshi gets very close to him and goes "Ah!" so sharply the psychotherapist almost jumps out of his skin.

"What did you feel?" he asked.
"Surprise."
"And after that?"
"Nothing."

The roshi has him walk around, and he looks at the place where the psychotherapist walked.

"Are you able to see the footsteps?" the Roshi asked.
"No."
"They were not there before and are not there now. There was nothing in your life before and nothing in the future, only AH!"

The next day the roshi gives him a little scroll that says, congratulations, J. T. Huber has seen unconditional nature. The roshi has two seals which he presses into red ink and then onto the card. One seal is his signature. The other says, "No moving mind."

What did all this do for J. T. Huber?

I seemed almost to have a new pair of eyes, new ears, new abilities to taste and smell and feel. I had learned to give my full attention to whatever I was doing at any one moment and I wondered if I had ever really done this before.

Gradually I began to see I was eating when I was hungry, not when it was "time to eat." I began to eat what I wanted to eat, not because it was placed before me, because others were eating, because we must have three good meals a day . . . I was seeing and choosing what I wanted to do.

Mr. Huber's peak experience seems to have been something like that of Larry in Somerset Maugham's *The Razor's Edge*. Surprising more counter-culturalists didn't read *The Razor's Edge*, but then Maugham is out of favor. Larry had his peak experience in India and went home to drive a cab happily in New York.

The experience seemed to have a permanent effect on Larry. There's no indication as to whether the effect on J. T. Huber was permanent. Sometimes such experiences produce a change, and sometimes they don't. "Though there is an afterglow from this state," writes one authority, "on emerging from meditation one is still susceptible to the patterns of old mental habits. For this reason, in Abhidhamma [a Buddhist manual], this experience is seen as relatively trivial."

Back at the beginning I promised a meditation that would shed pounds. That was gimmicky but true. Spiritual materialism, says Chogyam Trungpa, the Tibetan lama. He's right, absolutely right. But I think it provides a good ordinary example for attention, so here goes.

"I had learned to give my full attention to whatever I was doing at any one moment," said the Huber account. That attention is the key to the whole process of continuous meditative action. You can see that kind of attention in the furniture made by the Shakers of nineteenth-century America, each simple box or stool now prized because the essence of attention shows up as the quality of the object, "concentrated labor" being part of their devotion. It is the opposite of schlock and shoddy.

Be mindful of everything you do, physically or verbally, it says in *What the Buddha Taught*. People do not live in the moment, they live in the past or future, "though they seem to be doing something now here, they live somewhere else in their thoughts . . . therefore, they do not live in nor do they enjoy what they do at the moment, so they are unhappy and discontented with the present moment, with the work at hand. Naturally they cannot give themselves fully to what they appear to be doing."

In a much repeated Zen story, the fella asks the Zen master for a maxim, and the Zen master writes, "Attention." "Is that all?" says the fella, and the Zen master writes, "Attention attention." Doesn't seem to be much to it, what's it mean? says the fella, and the Zen master says, "Attention means attention."

Okay, a little spiritual materialism here, to good end. Dr. Smith's guaranteed weight loss.

(1) Pay attention. If you're alone at the lunch counter, don't read while you eat, don't review the morning, don't preview the afternoon, just eat.

(2) Slow it down this way. With each bite, you go:

Reaching; reaching. Lifting; lifting. Taking; taking. Chewing; chewing. Tasting; tasting. Savoring; savoring. Swallowing; swallowing. Digesting; digesting. Pause. Reaching; reaching. Lifting; lifting. Taking; taking. Chewing; chewing. Tasting; tasting. Swallowing; swallowing. Don't eat it all just because it's there on your plate, because somebody once planted in your brain eat everything on your plate, or because somebody once said food costs a lot, don't waste it. If you're with somebody, don't keep eating because you want to keep talking, in fact, don't eat and talk at the same time because that isn't paying attention. Eating will come in second. The food will disappear without passing through awareness. You always get a signal at each meal that says, that's almost enough, that's enough. You can move the signal forward in time by paying attention. It's that simple. I think I'll skip the medical and physiological references. The medical references say fat people eat faster, their appestats are out of whack. The physiological references say taste habituates, that is, the seventeenth bite doesn't taste as good as the first. (Smokers say the last drag doesn't taste as good as the first, but smoking is usually an unconscious activity.)

People who eat too much have fouled up the signal-to-noise

ratio, the noise being what else is going on, or lack of attention. If you've cleared some of the noise, you can start listening to the signal on *what* you eat; you don't crave a big slab of roast beef and a pile of mashed potatoes on a hot summer day.

I used to see executives in lunch clubs all the time, which is nothing striking since I was one. The reason you were having lunch with somebody was to talk to him and listen to him. A certain information exchange, and with it a certain tension. All morning had been spent sitting still, no movement except for opening a desk drawer or lifting a telephone, and now some motion and breathing are craved but nothing's available to move except mouth and stomach. The waiter plunks down a plate of bread and pats of butter. Not one man would voluntarily buy those mass-produced chemical rolls, but unless everybody says for the waiter to take the bread basket away, everybody will sit there buttering the rolls they don't want, and talking. They are eating not because they want the rolls but because they're a little excited with the vibrations of learning and self-expression. They are giving attention to the talk; somebody else is doing the eating. I ate a roll? What roll? I don't remember eating any roll. Who ate all the rolls? Waiter, I'll have a martini and the low-cal special.

If you go on a diet you have this terrific battle, you and you, and you feel good when you stick to it and bad when you don't, and at the end of the diet the weight comes back. Zen doesn't have renunciation, said the Zen master, so you don't have to give things up, *you have to accept that they go away*. Reaching, reaching; lifting, lifting; just accept that they go away, don't get into a fight. It's because we want to be on one side or the other. Psychologists would say, that's behavior modification, you see, you broke the stimulus/response pattern there, maybe you have gone and changed all the road signs so that when the impulses come roaring down the neuronal pathway all of a sudden it says detour, and then it says no left turn, no U-turn, right lane must turn right, and by the time the impulses get all this they want to stop at a gas station and get a map.

If the impulses are all back at the gas station poring over the map and squabbling with each other, the traffic patterns get changed. The eater is different. His only problem is to discard the model of what he always has for lunch, and how much is enough.

The Zen master told us a story. I had already read the story, there are only so many stories in English and this one is right at the top. Disciples of two famous masters meet. The first one says, the miracle of my master is, I stand on one side of the river, he stands on the other, and he can write on a scroll I hold up. The second disciple says, the miracle of my master is, he eats when he is hungry and drinks when he is thirsty.

I heard a tune. Words came with the tune. I was filled with ecumenical spirit: why, this very same philosophy is in an old cowboy ballad. I have even heard a real cowboy sing it in a saloon in Nogales, Arizona. So I went up to tell the Zen master of this American example.

> *I eat when I'm hungry*
> *I drink when I'm dry*
> *If the sky don't fall on me*
> *I'll live till I die.*

There are other people who have come up after the lecture and they are looking at me quite strangely. They want to know more important things, how long will it take them to get to satori, what should they be eating, why is Philip Kapleau, *Three Pillars of Zen*, so down on Alan Watts, *The Way of Zen*, and this crazy is standing here singing a cowboy ballad to the Zen master, we get all the crazies in here.

The Zen master frowned a little, as if he didn't get it. And I had to stop, because I remembered suddenly the verse that went

> *Whiskey, rye whiskey*
> *I know you of old*
> *You rob my poor pockets*
> *Of silver and gold*

and that didn't sound very Zen. I didn't sing that. So I repeated,

I eat when I'm hungry
I drink when I'm dry
If the sky don't fall on me
I'll live till I die.

I concentrated on the two yellowing beaver front teeth of the Zen master, to avoid the stares, and then up: a little stubble in the mustache from a not quite clean shave, and the brown eyes with the frown between them and the bald head, he is concentrating on the crazy American, I watch *sssss* an intake go under the beaver teeth as the song ends and he does "Ah!"—a bark, a grunt, out goes the intake, I jump, they must teach them that at Zen school.

"People believe?" he said. "Believe this song?"

I thought about it. Do people really eat when they are hungry, or believe that they will live till they die, of course they do, but do they have that *attitude*?

"Not really," I said. "They eat when it's breakfast, and again when it's lunch, and a little bell rings for the coffee wagon and—"

"Ah," he said. "So. So."

Then he didn't say anything, I didn't say anything, he nodded vigorously a couple of times, and somebody who didn't have the attitude and was in one hell of a big hurry to get to satori plucked at his elbow, and the ballad of the Zen cowboy died right there.

The sleeve-plucker should have known you don't get anything for getting to satori, or enlightenment. I know, they gave the visiting American a seal that said "no moving mind," but they were being nice. The axioms run: before satori, chop wood and draw water; after satori, chop wood and draw water. Or: before satori, a river is a river and a mountain is a mountain; during satori, a river is not a river and a mountain is not a mountain; after satori, a river is a river and a mountain is a mountain.

Or how about: "It takes seven years to get over the stink of enlightenment." You thought you had tenure, did you. There can't be any tenure if it's always now.

Well, not to dwell on Zen, for all its intellectual and physiologic attributes, this is just a handy example, not even a thumb-nail sketch. The handy example does not have "just-sitting" because they have always done it that way, no other reason, or corrupt monks selling the answers to koans, and it doesn't have even the basic elements of centering, move that center from your shoulder blades down to just below your navel.

All disciplines, they say, have a place for attention: karma yoga makes of each daily activity a sacrament; Western religions used the occasion of a meal.

But not many busy Americans are going to sit for hours facing a wall, or pursue a koan. (I wonder if "How do I pay the mort-gage when the taxes are going up so fast" would count as an insoluble question. Too linear.)

We could move logically from here to the existentialist phi-losophy of Martin Heidegger, who indicated that man's freedom is in *Gelassenheit*, or letting go, letting be, which parallels the non-Aristotelian qualities of Zen and all the other—

—or we could retire to the playing fields, to see into what spaces the powers of attention can lead us.

IV: "Sport Is a Western Yoga"

QUARTERBACKING
IN AN ALTERED
STATE

MURPHY, the great mystic, alumnus of Stanford and the Sri Aurobindo ashram, founder of Esalen, Murphy has been Rolfed and Alexandered and grouped and Zenned and yogaed and *gestalt*ed and God knows what, there is no trip he hasn't been on, every one that wants to surface has to check in with him, and serious, too, shelves of books on mystics and philosophers, lots of meditation every day, marvelous enthusiasm, and what is Murphy into? Jogging. No, not jogging, *running*, jogging is only eight minutes to the mile, Murphy wants to run a mile in five minutes, five miles in thirty-five minutes, the mystical long-distance runner. The aikido black belt has checked his centering and Murphy is out there on the running track, what's-his-name the middle-distance runner who almost made the Olympics is running alongside of him, three miles, four miles, here comes the pain, pain is a cultural attitude it says in *Principles of Psychophysiology*, it is only as real as we make it, the Italians and Jews make it more than the Yankees it says, hello pain—Murphy is in his mid-forties, bound to be pain, hello pain, go into the pain, don't fight, see if you can come out the other side and—

"Five minutes and seventeen seconds!" Down the coast in Murphy's own famous ashram, Esalen, the gurus are guruing and the *gestalt*ers are *gestalt*ing and Bob and Carol and Ted and Alice are sorting out their hang-ups, people are screaming screams, letting it all hang out, getting out of all that linear crap, sitting on cushions listening to the residents with M.A.'s in psychology —academic market a little tight these days, no jobs there—rap on what it's all about, and where is Murphy? On the golf course, and since there is no golf course at Esalen that means the president of the ashram is far away, teeing off with John Brodie, the quarterback, because golf is a kind of meditation too—

—it is? And tennis? And bowling? Hunting? Swimming? Hey, this is going to be easier than sitting and staring at the wall, hi-tot-tsu, hu-tot-tsu, mi-it-tsu—how can I attain the mortgage if the taxes go up?

I should have known Murphy would bring East to West through sports, his imperatives are all from sports. "We *have* to go to Pebble Beach tomorrow." "Why do we have to go to Pebble Beach tomorrow, Mr. Bones?" "*Nicklaus* is playing, we have to follow Nicklaus around the course."

Who am I talking to, that Good Ol' Boy my junior-year roommate, or the great ashram leader? Murphy is in awe of Nicklaus not because of the money he wins or how far he hits the ball or any of that; Nicklaus has the *greatest powers of concentration* in golf. "I've followed him around the course lots," Murphy says. "Nicklaus *plays in a trance*. He and the club and the ball are all the same thing, and there isn't anything else. He can lock right in, real one-pointedness. I think he can influence the flight of the ball after it's hit, even."

Murphy has been into this in his book, *Golf and the Kingdom,* which is a mystic book about golf, or a golf book about mysticism, same thing.

"What Nicklaus needs now is a challenger, somebody to keep his concentration on the absolute razor's edge, the way he was to Arnold Palmer."

So Murphy cancels all his appointments to walk behind Nicklaus, where he can pick up the right vibes. And vibes there are, let me tell you, "energy streamers" that the golf ball rides toward the hole. When the golfer can visualize and execute his shot in a moment of high clarity, the ball rides the energy streamer right up to the green.

John Brodie, ex-Stanford star, seventeen-year quarterback for the 49ers, most valuable player NFL 1970, second most all-time yards gained passing, and so on, is not one to dispute the energy streamers.

"I would have to say that such things seem to exist." Brodie's white teeth flash into a perfect smile. "It's happened to me dozens of times. An intention carries a force, a thought connected with an energy that can stretch itself out in a pass play or a golf shot or a base hit or a thirty-foot jump shot in basketball. I've seen it happen too many times to deny it."

Murphy: "Can we develop this? Practice it? Can you learn to develop clarity and strengthen your intentions?"

Brodie: "Yes."

Brodie is six three, two fifteen, big shoulders, moves gracefully, and as far as I know does not know a Zen master from a rubber duck, but he is about to sound like one:

"The player can't be worrying about the past or the future or the crowd or some other extraneous event. He must be able to respond in the here and now, I believe we all have this naturally, maybe we lose it as we grow up. Sometimes in the heat of the game a player's perception and coordination improve dramatically. At times, I experience a kind of clarity that I've never seen described in any football story, sometimes time seems to slow way down, as if everyone were moving in slow motion. It seems as if I have all the time in the world to watch the receivers run their patterns, and yet I know the defensive line is coming at me just as fast as ever, and yet the whole thing seems like a movie or a dance in slow motion. It's beautiful."

Stoned John Brodie. The defensive line is coming at him in slow motion, like a ballet, the crowd is screaming for twelve hundred pounds of linemen to gobble him up and spit out his white, bleached bones, and he is dancing along, the ball in one very large but somehow dainty hand, in this altered state, stoned on all the vibrations of the moment, seventeen years is a long time to have those tackles coming at you but Brodie stays with it because it's so beautiful—

—Murphy's Esalen has gathered a lot of jocks and coaches together in San Francisco for a sports seminar, Murphy suspects these moments in sport are all unarticulated but similar to the awareness of the Zen master staring at the guy in the sword fight—

—the NBC man nudges me at the seminar. "I heard Brodie was getting a little wiggy," he whispers.

Clot, I think, you do not know Zen from a rubber duck.

Brodie is telling how he has four chances on every play to communicate a pattern to Gene Washington, his wide receiver. First, the play itself, in the huddle. Brodie comes up to the line, the defense shifts, he has a second chance, an audible, a shouted signal. Somebody moves in the enemy backfield, he has a third chance, a quick hand signal. And fourth—"Sometimes I let the ball fly before Gene has made his final move, *without* a pass route exactly, it's sort of intuition and communication, Gene and I are good friends, of course, then you don't know what the cornerbacks and safety men will do, that's part of the fun, you don't know where those guys are going to be a second before something happens, you have to be ready for the sudden glimmer—"

"The pass pattern is from your collective unconscious," Murphy suggests.

Brodie doesn't know about that. "I know the *feeling*," he says. "You can get into another order of reality when you're playing that doesn't fit the grids and coordinates most people lay across life."

I am getting a little worried for Brodie. I am adding to my list of altered states: you can take a chemical, you can run balam balam balam through your head, you can just sit, and you can stand with a football in your hand and twelve hundred pounds of linemen coming at you while you look for your receivers. They all work.

But will the fans understand? The telepathic pass pattern, won't the fans say, *yuhh bum, yuh goddam yogi* if he misses? And then he will end up a well-paid TV commentator, that was a real fine play, just a super play, let's take another look at it from the end zone camera.

"If I were an effect of the fans it would affect me, but I am not an effect." Scientology talk, Big John could only lift his arm to *here* and then Scientology rearranged his perception and he could lift it to *here*.

I asked Murphy why Esalen was getting involved in sports. The Esalen track team, for God's sake, here is Esalen on the frontier supposedly and what are they doing? Sending their own track team to AAU events for seniors. That has to be where they lose all the psychiatrists who don't hate them already. Thank you, Dr. Freud, but could you give us your times in the 220 and 440?

"Isn't this exciting?" Murphy says. "Sport anticipates what the Divine Essence is. Sport is a Western yoga. The Dance of Shiva. Pure play, the delight in the moment, the Now. We need a more balanced and evolutionary culture. We already have physical mobility, why shouldn't we have psychic mobility, the ability to move psychically into different states?"

Sure enough, the athletes are beginning to talk to each other about funny spaces which they have trouble describing. "There isn't any language." It's all a bit ambiguous, but it seems they are talking about sports equivalents of the "peak experience" described by Abe Maslow, the late psychologist who hung out at Esalen. Moments of exhilaration and clarity and awareness, the click that tells you the shot is good before you know the shot is good.

We don't have long hours of meditation like they did in the exotic East, and we don't have martial arts, kung fu and judo, but when you're preparing for the Olympics and swimming six hours a day, thousands of miles a year, you get yourself to something of the same state, only you have no roshi or guru to tell you what's happening while your times are getting faster.

The California track coach tells how he does it. First he gets all these sprinters out there, every one of them can travel ten yards in less than a second, a hundred yards splitting somewhere between the ninth and tenth second, all of them straining at the leash. Now he has them run the middle part of the sprint, a running start, then forty or fifty yards that "count," then they keep on another thirty or forty. "Okay," he says, "now do it with four-fifths effort." Really? Cut the effort back? *The times get faster.*

"Okay, now run at four-fifths speed and relax your jaw." The sprinters don't believe it, they think the timer's thumb has slipped on the stop watch, four-fifths is faster than five-fifths.

Funny spaces. We're all sitting around the room, coaches, athletes, some of the athletes feel a bit strange, they wouldn't want anybody to hear them talking this way, so it helps to have a big quarterback like Brodie saying it's a ballet, the linemen coming at you in slow motion.

A gentleman gets up who is a well-known diver, deep diver, not fancy diver. He has set up a "surfing and diving ashram." No breathing in and out and looking at the wall, you put your scuba gear on, *then* you can count your breaths. "I had a diver who was skeptical, and then one day, in just thirty feet of water, something happened, and he said that suddenly he felt absolutely at one with the ocean, and *he could hear grains of sand on the bottom.* He spent almost an hour listening to the grains of sand, and his life had been changed ever since."

Nitrogen narcosis, I suggested. Not in thirty feet of water, everybody said angrily.

What is the click that tells you the shot is good before you know it's good? Maybe that isn't so mysterious. Maybe it's right-brained information that usually gets suppressed by the left brain, but sometimes it gets through before it stops to be translated into words.

And that total concentration, some psychologists say we crave it almost instinctively, damping down and focusing, and then opening up with a new state of concentration, that's why people take on activities that demand *total attention*, mountain climbing and tobogganing and skiing and car racing, where the penalties for non-concentration are so great that even the language-using mind shuts up for a minute because it understands that at least for a few minutes it better get out of the way. (The language-using mind gets to come back and write the whole thing up for the Sierra Club journal, how time slows down, and the climber is suddenly aware of all the crystals in the rocks—)

We all may crave that sort of focusing, but a lot of us pay our dues to the feeling by watching the crazies toboggan down the mountain on TV, while we have a beer can in hand.

ZEN AND THE
CROSS-COURT
BACKHAND

I signed up for "yoga tennis." Yoga tennis surfaced at Esalen, and then I pursued it other places. *Sports Illustrated* wanted to know about it, and secretly I hoped to fix my serve while exploring this new frontier. I had one yoga tennis teacher who wore a blue jogging suit and a Sikh beard and a turban; he was a former business-forms salesman who talked a lot about *ki,* energy. And another there was yoga tennis instructor who hoped to have "a tennis ashram."

But Tim Gallwey did not wear a beard or a turban. Gallwey had been the captain of the Harvard tennis team, and he had been brooding about tennis while following the Guru Maharaj Ji. He was very articulate, and eventually I took him to see my publisher, and Gallwey wrote *The Inner Game of Tennis.*

"We learn tennis element by element," Gallwey said, standing on a tennis court at the California junior college where Esalen was having a sports seminar. "If we learned it as totality, we could learn it in one-hundredth the time. Our biggest problem is Ego, is trying too hard. We know how to play perfect tennis. Perfect tennis is in us all. Everyone knows how to ride a bicycle, and just before we really ride for the first time, we know we know. The problem with Ego is that it has to achieve; we are not sure who we are until by achieving we become. So we hit the ball out and the Ego says, 'Ugh, out.' Then it starts to give commands, 'Do it right.' We shouldn't have a judgment. The ball goes *there,* not out. Ninety percent of the bad things students do are intentional corrections of something else they are doing. We have to let the body experiment and by-pass the mind. The mind acts like a sergeant with the body a private. How can anybody play as a duality?"

I recognized the sergeant's voice right away; in my mind, it says, "Move your feet, dummy," and "Watch the ball." What to do about the sergeant?

"You have to check the mind, to preoccupy it, stop it from fretting. Look at the ball. Look at the *seams* on the ball, watch the pattern, get preoccupied so the mind can't judge. In between points put your mind on your breathing. In, out. In, out. A quiet mind is the secret of yoga tennis. Most people think concentration is fierce effort. Watch your facial muscles after you hit the ball. Are they tensed or relaxed? Concentration is effortless effort, is *not trying*. The body is sophisticated; its computer commands hundreds of muscles instantly; it is wise about itself; the Ego isn't. Higher consciousness is not a mystical term. You see more when all of your energy runs in the same direction. Concentration produces joy, so we look for things that will quiet the mind."

I could see that parking the mind would be essential. I sat next to Jascha Heifetz once at a dinner party and asked him what he thought about when he was giving a concert. He said if the concert was, say, on a Saturday night he thought about the smoked salmon and the marvelous bagel he was going to have on Sunday morning. If he was thinking about the bagel, then who was thinking about the concerto? His hands.

Don't you have to know the right form before you park the mind?

The body seeks out the right form if the mind doesn't get in the way, Gallwey said. No teenager could do a monkey or a locomotive or whatever teenage dance is now rampant from a set of instructions, but he can do it in one night by observing.

Ah, observing. You didn't say observing.

"You have to talk to the body in its native language," said the tennis guru. "Its native language is not English, it is sight and feel, mostly sight. The stream of instructions most students get are verbal and have to be translated by the body before they are understood. If you are taking a tennis lesson, let the pro show you, don't let him tell you. If you want the ball to go to a cross-court corner, get an image of where you want the ball to go and let the body take it over. Say: 'Body, cross-court corner, please.'"

"Let the serve serve itself," Gallwey said. "When I first used this technique my serve got hot. Then I thought, wow, I've mastered the serve and immediately it got cold because it was me, not the serve, serving itself."

This imagining the ball into the corner, was this the power of positive thinking, Norman Vincent Peale?

"Oh, no. Positive thinking is negative thinking in disguise. If you double-fault six times in a row your positive thinking will flip to negative. So I try not to pay compliments because the compliment can always be withheld on the next shot. What we are talking about is *no thinking*."

It seemed a marvelously Rousseauistic philosophy. Man is born with a perfect tennis game and he is everywhere in chains. Rousseau was influenced by the sunny Polynesians brought to Europe by the eighteenth-century sailors; what if they had sailed a little further over, and brought back fierce and aggressive Melanesians? You don't need a tennis pro with negative instructions, you need a movie of each shot and a ball machine to drill with. It was hard for me to see the difference between the instruction "Be aware of your racket head," from the tennis guru, and "Follow through, where is your racket head?" from the ordinary pro.

"The distinction is, the pro says, good shot, bad shot," Gallwey said. "I just want to focus awareness, not make a judgment."

It occurred to me that yoga tennis was a misnomer. Hatha yoga has breathing and movement, but what the "yoga tennis" pros had come up with was a version of the Japanese and Chinese martial arts. *Zen in the Art of Archery* would be closer. The student was a middle-aged German philosophy professor in Japan, Eugen Herrigel, and he suffered through the same agonies as a yoga tennis student. He tried to tell his right hand to release the bowstring properly with his sergeant mind. The Zen master never coached him at all. The master said, "The right shot at the right moment does not come because you do not let go of yourself . . . the right art is purposeless, aimless! What stands in your way is that you have a much too willful will. You think that what you do not do yourself does not happen." The breathing exercises were to detach the student from the world, to increase a concentration that would be comparable to "the jolt that a man who has stayed up all night gives himself when he knows that his life depends on all his senses being alert." Nothing more is required of the student than that he copy the teacher: "The teacher does not harass and the pupil does not overtax himself."

One day the Zen student of archery Herr Professor Doktor Herrigel loosed a shot and the master bowed and said, "Just then It shot," and the Herr Professor Doktor gave a whoop of delight and the Zen master got so mad he wouldn't talk to him, because this wasn't the student's achievement and there he was thinking he had done it and taking the credit.

There are some pros playing, said my Zen tennis teachers, who are well into these forms of concentration without articulating them, just as Jack Nicklaus may never have gone hi-tot-tsu hu-tot-tsu mi-it-tsu. Billie Jean King, it is said, meditates upon a tennis ball. Ken Rosewall gets mentioned all the time, a perfectly balanced, classical game. And Stan Smith—if you asked Stan Smith what he was thinking about during one of those booming serves he would say the bagel he had for breakfast. (Nobody would be foolish enough to ask Jimmy Connors.) A grooved game means you can play without your head.

I told some friends about watching the patterns on the ball. One of them said later: "I tried that. It worked, it really worked. But I got so much into watching the patterns on the ball that I didn't get to play tennis, it was like a lot of work, I'd rather be lousy and not watch the patterns on the ball."

There was no immediate impact on my game, but then, the Zen archery student got restless in his fourth year of instruction,

Stones are one of the natural ma
just about anywhere you live. Form
years ago, they were made by volca
by the settling of ancient ocean bo
and pressure. Stones have many di
from shiny to gritty. If you have a
stone, it was probably worn smooth
river or stream for thousands of yea
can be found everywhere, some sto
or have such beautiful colors that t
We use them for jewelry and call th
stones. Some stones are very hard a
a diamond saw into shapes that spa
reflect light. We call these cut stone

Look carefully while searching for
may find a real fossil which is the r
of a living creature, left in stone. Th
shell dissolved over time as water a
filled the imprint and turned to sto
millions of years to form.

I'm At the store

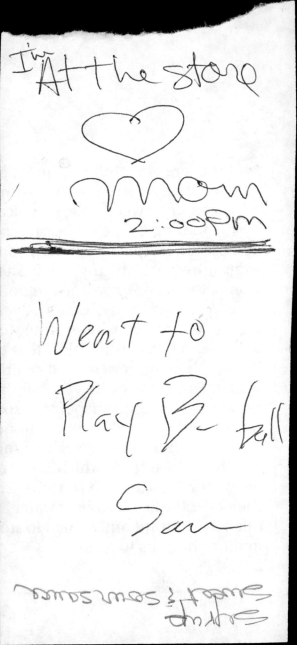

♡

mom

2:00pm

Went to

Play Be ball

Sam

when he still had met with no success. Depressed, he said to the master that he hadn't managed yet to get one single arrow off right—four years, and not one single arrow off right—or It had just appeared to loose the arrow—and his stay in Japan was limited and four years he'd been at it.

The master got cross with him. "The way to the goal is not to be measured!" he said. "Of what importance are weeks, months, years?"

Zen has gotten to be a good word now, the true thing, the thing itself. We have *Zen and the Art of Running,* and *Zen and the Art of Seeing,* and an autobiography, *Zen and the Art of Motorcycle Maintenance.* We still have to go through *Zen and Turning Your Spares into Strikes,* and *Zen Your Way to Higher Earnings;* the Zen books are getting shorter and more flowery, with any luck they will soon be mostly soupy photographs and we can be done with it

I went back to my tennis guru. My requirements were simple: I wanted a serve, that's all, with the power of a rocket, accurate to within six inches, one that would zing into the corner of the service court and spin away with such a dizzying kick that the opponent would retire nauseated.

We went out to the court with a basket of balls. I hit a couple. The Zen master didn't say anything. Some went in, some went out. The Zen master didn't say anything. I hit some more.

"Okay," he said. "Breathe in with your racket back, and out when it moves."

That was easy.

"Okay, now, where should the ball go over the net? And where should it land?"

I pointed.

"'Okay, ask your body to send it there, and get out of the way."

"Please, body, send it there."

A miss.

"It's not listening."

"Slow it down. Visualize the whole shot before you hit it. Listen to the sound the ball makes against the string."

It's amazing, but if you really visualize, and you really listen to the sound, you can't go ratcheta racheta with your mind, which is very uncomfortable, mutiny in the enlisted men's quarters.

We set up an empty tennis ball can in the corner of the service court. I know, those fierce kids in California and Florida who are out hitting three hundred sixty days a year, who hit five hundred serves a day for practice, can knock over the empty can a couple of times a day, but weekend players can't even get the ball in the court.

"Slow it down more. More. Please, body, send the ball—"

"Please, body, send the ball—"

"Slower. Slower. Make time stand still. No time."

"Please, body, send the ball—"

Zank! The empty tennis ball can went up into the air and bounced metallically.

"Who did that?" I said.

The tennis guru said nothing. He handed me another ball. It went into the corner of the service court, on roughly the same spot. So did the next one.

I began to giggle wildly. I danced around a little, the scarecrow had a brain, the cowardly lion had courage, I had a serve. "I did it! I did it!" I said.

Immediately it went away.

The next five balls went into the net.

"I shouldn't have said that," I said. "That sonofabitch is sure sensitive."

"Please, body, send the ball—"

"Please, body, send the ball—"

"Visualize. Don't use words. Don't think. Use images. In between shots, count your breath."

Now the afternoon began to take on a very eerie quality indeed, an underwater, slow-motion quality. Who-o-o-ck went the ball to its accustomed place in the service court; I had to consciously fight the exhilaration. It went away. My breathing sounded like the breathing in scuba gear. The ball was going into the service court, into the corner, but I wasn't feeling anything, no joy, no sorrow, and this was so uncomfortable I came up for air. I felt greed.

"It's going in, but it isn't going in very *hard,*" I said. "I want power, more power."

"Power comes from the snap of the wrist. Ask your wrist to snap at the top of the arc, and don't try. Use images: please, wrist, snap at the top—"

The serve began to pick up speed.

"I don't know what this is," I said, "but it isn't tennis and it isn't me."

I didn't feel at all well. The next afternoon I went out alone at a tennis club. A guy came up and asked me if I wanted to hit some. We rallied. He was very strong. He asked me if I wanted to play. I thought: he doesn't even know my name, I can lose six–love, six–love, and no one will ever know. I put on my mental scuba gear. I wasn't very nice to play with, because you can't say "Oh, nice shot" when you are breathing into your scuba mask. I watched the pattern on the ball, the serve went in, and far, far away I could hear my opponent talking to himself: "Oh, watch the ball, stupid! Don't hit it out! Don't double-fault! Move your feet, idiot!" He began to hit the ball harder and harder. Some of his hard shots were winners, but more of them began to go out. He began to get better at the end. Six–love, six–two.

"I don't know what was the matter with me today," said my opponent.

I was afraid to say anything, but I shouldn't have been afraid —the serve packed its bags and went away as soon as I got back to playing with people I knew. Sometimes it would reappear for a flash, like a tiny acid rerun. Once, on the court, I shouted, sounding like a madman: "I know you're in there, you bastid, come on out!" Please, body, send it there, please, body—and nothing. Nothing. It is on Its vacation. If I wanted It, It wouldn't come, and if I didn't want It, it might, but then who cared? And gradually it began to seem like there was tennis and Something Else, very difficult to do both at the same time even if Something Else has one hell of a serve.

And this was a bit spooky: It was living in there with me; It could bring the music back on with a thumb twitch, without telling me; It could make the biofeedback machine switch from beep beep to boop boop without letting me know; It wasn't taking any orders from me, and, in fact, It would go away if I even pretended to notice, sensitive bastid, It had a much better serve than I did but wouldn't play with any of my friends, It could take over but only if I would go do some idiot child-task like breath-counting; why does It only like me if I will play idiot? It was actually a bit frightening, was It.

THE SWEET MUSIC
OF THE STRINGS

"THE siddhi is a by-product of the process, not the process," said Torben. "That's what the yogis say."

Siddhis are powers, odd powers, spooky things yogis can do, or people can do, that are sort of impossible: materialize objects, read minds, knock over empty tennis ball cans at the corner of the court.

"But what does that mean?"

"We-l-l, it doesn't mean anything, does it? It's what the yogis say."

Somehow, I was always asking Torben what does that mean? and Torben would say, it doesn't mean anything, does it? which would make me feel as though the question had been the wrong question.

Torben Ulrich is described as a Danish touring pro, a member of a Danish family that always played the Davis Cup for Denmark—that's not who Torben is. I don't know who Torben is, I get a feeling—very hard to stuff into words—well—

Torben walked into the seminar, the one where the guy was talking about listening to the grains of sand on the bottom of the ocean, and I thought who is *that* because here is this character with the Old Testament beard and lines around the eyes and all the tennis pros stir and ruffle a bit, Torben is also described as a blithe spirit and not like anybody else, that is, I suppose, because he has this ponytail down to his waist tied with a blue ribbon and he is out playing Newcombe and Laver and Smith and—

I wish I could capture that Danish lilt, Torben can bend "no" over three syllables, nooo°°° °° ₒₒₒₒₒ—

Torben wasn't part of the weekend, but he belonged. He stopped by with Jeff Borowiak, former NCAA singles and doubles champion, ex-UCLA captain, top-twenty ranking, haircut like a tall Renaissance prince, Torben is in his mid-forties, these young players pick him up as a guru sometimes—

Torben said: "The egoless game goes further than the ego game. 'I would like to become a better tennis player' really has nothing to do with winning. The Western world is so oriented to winning that the temptation of winning is there almost always. The tennis court, seen as a mandala—"

A mandala, you already know, is an object of meditation, a geometric figure, a representation of the cosmos—*the tennis court is a mandala?*

"What does that mean?" I said for the first of a hundred times. "What does that mean, the tennis court is a mandala?"

"It doesn't mean anything," said the soft lilting voice. "It is a mandala if you choose to see it as a mandala, a confined space made an object of activity. If we are centered around the court as an object, the court is a mandala."

"You mean if you're in it or if you look at it?"

Wrong question again.

"Noo°°°°° ₒₒₒₒ," Torben said, "it doesn't mean anything because you can see the court as anything you like. No°°° ₒₒₒ, I don't think it has much meaning. But if you take it very far, sooner or later you have to see the court as a mandala, sooner or later."

"But what does that mean?" I said, for the third of a hundred times.

Borowiak had gone to Denmark to hang out with Torben. They got up at four in the afternoon—Torben likes to get up at four in the afternoon, and everybody in Denmark likes Torben —one wonders about Mrs. Torben's schedule, after all they have a kid who gets up and goes to school and plays soccer—and every other day they would jog a little, twelve miles or so, through forests that Torben named Forest #1, Forest #2, Forest #3, running through the snow, two-foot drifts sometimes, and then to the saunas and whirlpools of the public baths, and then they would come home and play tapes, Torben is an accomplished musician and a jazz critic for a Copenhagen paper, music with strange instruments like the Indian veena, hours of ragas, or Tibetan monks singing—and have dark bread and cheese, Torben eats a lot of cheese—then they'd play their flutes along with the records, Borowiak's father was a musician, Borowiak had years of music, Torben can play all the reeds—and then, from three to six in the morning they would play indoor tennis— that's three to six in the morning, must be easy to get on the courts then—and then talk

"Torben would delve into long discussions on such things as light producing waves in the air creating noises that the ear is not sensitive enough to decipher, certain lights give off sour notes. Or he might wander into his feelings about the longer muscles, he'd demonstrate with diagrams and pencils with rubber hands."

Torben tries these things out—say, twenty-five minutes to open a door—so he can make a map of his muscles, his fingers go onto the doorknob and slowly, slowly, twenty-five minutes later—

—it blew Borowiak's mind. "An explosion of horizons," he said. "There are few people in sports who have this quality, this sense of unification—"

Torben was in the Eastern U.S. to play a couple of tournaments and then Forest Hills—it wasn't easy. I would call up—

"Can we get together today?"

"Hey, hey. We might get together today. Would that be a good idea? Maybe we won't. I wonder if we will."

"Sure we will. We just make up our minds to do it, that's all. We say, we'll meet each other at such-and-such a time, at such-and-such a place—"

"Y-e-es, ye-e-es, that would be nice, if we could both be at the same place, then we could get together, we could say ten o'clock, or four o'clock, or nine o'clock, or no time at all—"

"Noon?" A little early for Torben, but he has a match that afternoon—

"Noon," said Torben, testing the word, "noon, no-o-o-o-oon, nooo°°°₀₀₀oooon. A very nice quality, noon."

Torben practically never made a date, so I would go out to where he was playing, or where he was staying, and appear—"Hey, hey," Torben would say, without surprise. One time in Torben's room, the books were *Asian Journey*, Thomas Merton, a book on acupuncture, and *Buddhist Wisdom*. Another time it was the Tibetan *Book of the Dead*.

Torben Story #21:

Torben has made it to the semifinals of the National Indoor, playing Ismail El Shafei, the Egyptian. Torben beat El Shafei's *father* in the 1948 Davis Cup.

The reporters gather in the press trailer, Torben enters, his hair down past his shoulders, really an Old Testament prophet now, in a gown, his tone lilting and saintly:

"How old are you, really, Torben? Forty-one? Forty-four?"

"How old is old?" says Torben. "What is age? Am I forty-one or twenty-one or sixty-one? Who knows?"

"Do you think you will win tomorrow?"

"No, noo°°°°ooo, I will not win. What is winning?"

Torben Story #36:

"Torben, you are playing Pancho Gonzalez tomorrow, how do you feel about his fast serve?"

"What is speed?" says Torben. "Is speed fast or slow? Speed is relative to observation. A big serve can come in slow motion."

"Pancho is very hot right now. Will you have trouble with his serve?"

"Pancho's serve is a thing of beauty. How can a thing of beauty be trouble?"

Torben Story #51:

"Torben, you are playing at an age when most players are teaching or running something else, how long will you play? What are your plans when you stop?"

"I could play or I could stop. That assumes a structure to the future. I hate getting involved in schedules and specifics. If we don't eat, we will get hungry. Then we will eat."

"How do you stay so young?"

"Young? How young you are depends on when you died last. If you die every minute, you can last a long time. If you don't establish a past . . . then when you lie down to sleep and journey into night, you can wake up as a new person or whatever you are in the morning. But you're not dragging the day before you along so that you're staggering under this bag of yesterdays: scores, bad shots, rankings. I don't always succeed."

Torben story #62: (the classic)

Torben is at Forest Hills in the fourth round, leading the great Australian, John Newcombe, two sets to none. On a vital point a butterfly flutters into his face and forces a weak volley. Newcombe goes on to win in five sets.

"Did the butterfly bother you on the crucial point?"

Torben quotes the ancient *Tao*, Chuang-tzu:

"Was I then a man dreaming I was a butterfly, or am I now a butterfly dreaming I am a man?"

"They sure ask about your age a lot," I said. I really wanted to know, myself, why Torben continued to tour the world. In the hotel lobby, the players—they seemed like such kids—would stop him—are you going to play in the Australian Open, Torben? Will you be in India this year? Why did Torben keep it up, all these hotel rooms, all these plane flights, Buenos Aires and Melbourne and London and Calcutta, when he could be running through the snow to the sauna in Denmark, or whatever?

"Well, we will have to change the idea of aging," Torben said. "A fifty-year-old musician is not out of it, why should an athlete be, if we learn not to burn up our bodies?"

We went to dinner with Tomas Koch, a left-handed Brazilian pro who also wears his long hair in a ponytail. Koch wanted to know if Torben would come and play in a tournament in Brazil. Tomas seemed a little down.

Tomas pushed the glass of water in a circle, in the restaurant, an Indian place which Vijay Amritraj, the lanky Indian, had found.

"Torben, tell me the part again about how there is no opponent."

"No opponent, only the ball."

"No opponent, only the ball."

"The ball moves to you and the ball moves away from you, no opponent. Even when you think you watch the ball, you don't watch it all the time, you see like, in a movie, only the fourth frame and the fifteenth frame and the twenty-sixth frame —when the play goes well, it is a better performance than each actor."

"Is that the click that tells you?" Tomas said.

I kept thinking I had missed a line.

"Are we talking about playing in some sort of altered state?" I asked.

"Oh, Western athletes only get into this for a few seconds, in a crude way," Torben said.

"The grass," Tomas said.

"Very bald and spotty," I volunteered. "I understand they're going to phase it out."

"The grass in Calcutta opens like a flower, you can put your face on it, so many groundskeepers for each blade, the grass in Wimbledon is very lush, such professionals, and each place has a sound," Torben said.

Now I will collapse several conversations, because I stopped asking Torben direct questions, you can't really have much of a conversation with Torben anyway, I was just there, *each place has a sound,* "All the movement can only be best if it is in harmony with the tonic, the keynote sound of the chord. So I don't think, this is music and this is tennis because everything is, traveling, tennis, music, theater, dance, if I am on a plane then this is part of the music, the sound of the engines and the pilot's voice, some tournaments it is hard to find the sound, in the Indoor the air conditioning and the crowd did not make the right sound together—"

"They talk about the home court advantage in basketball," I said, "the vibrations are part of that."

Torben stopped and was staring far away—

"They asked me, you know, to endorse a steel racket, a French company, but I tried it and I couldn't make it work because I couldn't find the sound, the sound of the ball against the racket has to be—"

Torben's voice trailed off, and it was some minutes before he spoke again.

"In music I try to let the sound take over and consume my concentration, and the same in tennis."

In the humid, ninety-degree atmosphere at Forest Hills, a Czech called Vladimir Zednik, all shoulders, looking like a draft choice for the Chicago Bears, overpowered Torben. Overpowered may not be right, because Torben was never out of it, full of deft touches and spins and surprising bursts of power. He did not seem at all upset.

"I could not find my song today," he said.

Laver was playing well.

"Rod is over his trouble," Torben said. "He is so goal-oriented, remember, after the Grand Slam, he won everything in the world that year and then he couldn't play well because he had lost the reason for playing. Poor Rod."

"Poor Rod is right up there," I said. "I don't feel a bit sorry for him."

"The goal is to be free of a goal," Torben said. "Who is that who is playing? Who is that who is making the stroke? Who is that who is making the next stroke? Until they all disappear. If you succeed at tennis then you hang up the racket because you are beyond all that, everything like that."

I had a glimmer of what Torben was talking about, but it did not make me feel at all secure. It would be playing; It would be gliding into Its perfect shots, and I would be out counting daisies somewhere. But maybe this is just the savage irony of I, fighting a potential threat, or an illusory threat.

"Once," Torben said, "Louis Armstrong was in Sweden."

Crinkly lines in the weathered, tanned Torben face, spaces between the big front teeth—

"And," Torben said, "he was going to come to Denmark. And we went to meet him in Göteborg, and we took our instruments, and we played on the ferry with Louis Armstrong all the way across, like the ferry was a Mississippi riverboat with those great jazz musicians, and the *sound* went out over the water and over the freighters and over the ferryboats, and the *sound* came back again, and that was a *wonderful* day."

Torben lost to Pancho Gonzalez in the finals of the seniors'; somebody is always winning and somebody is always losing. And my curiosity—why? why?—had long since dissolved, for obviously if you are alive you are out amidst these textures and these sounds, the sweet music of the strings, and if the music is there then you are the music while the music lasts.

V: | Vibes

AMBIGUITIES
AND VIBES

ON the Road from the City of Skepticism, I had to pass through the Valley of Ambiguity.

Here are all these devices aimed directly at shutting up the left-brained, language-using mind. I was being given a hard time by my own left-brained, language-using mind just because it liked language so much. Maybe it is easy for people who aren't word people, dancers or sculptors or mimes, but my left brain, for heaven's sake, will get so fascinated by a single word it will track its origins all the way through Middle English to Indo European. And read! It will read anything, the label on a ketchup bottle, Reg. U.S. Dept. Agriculture, Article 4 of the Warsaw Convention on the back of the airline ticket about lost luggage, anything. So that was a fight.

On the other hand, my mind was clearly a drunken monkey full of obsolete football scores and rusted bicycles, and therefore certainly not to be trusted, in spite of its verbal facility. And the verbal mind itself was getting very distrustful of everything *it* read in this field, because it was very obvious that the writers who wrote the articles were governed by drunken monkeys, and so were the editors who assigned them. The editors of the Establishment press were continuously reviewing the Alchemist; they would say to the writer, go see this latest guru and tell us why the Dupes are falling for it this time.

(Only in children's stories do the Dupes come out well. Remember that the Wizard of Oz—twenty-fourth descendant of the Alchemist—was a fraud, but he did give the scarecrow a diploma and after that the scarecrow had a brain, and the cowardly lion got a medal for courage and after that he was brave, and the tin woodman got a heart that went ticktock. But then placebos work, we know that.)

Clearly there was something going on that you missed if you simply went to see what the Dupes were falling for.

But the Dupes were really falling for a lot of nonsense, too, by even the most charitable standards. Sweet children were leaving school and home and—three drops of vinegar in the nostril and cry hum!—following the newest Oriental preacher and expecting the world to change next Tuesday. The counter-cultural press erred the other side of putting down the preacher and the Dupes. Everything not rational was true, Saturn was coming into the sixth house of Venus, and sunspots were about to cave in the economy.

So I was ready to believe, or to experience and not judge, but I wanted all my teachers to be perfect. Chogyam Trungpa the Tibetan lama is smart as a whip and he is giving a lecture—a very good lecture too, and he sips from his water glass and I know damn well that is vodka in the water glass. How come he isn't getting high on what he's teaching? I am going to these private sessions with this noted Indian religious leader and he is snuffling. Snuffling? Hay fever? Allergy? A cold? I want to give him some antihistamine. What is the problem, Sire, I ask, and he says, it must be the smog. But I'm breathing the same smog, and I'm not snuffling, hay fever and asthma have some degree of psychogenic causes, could I give him a placebo? If he does all this yoga, how come he's tense?

And I have the same problem with the psychologists. Will Schutz is a great encounter leader and a nice guy, especially once you get to know him, and he wrote a book called *Joy* and he has JOY on his California license plates and when you meet him he is dour as a Scotch accountant. Stanley Keleman writes these books and says, "The body never lies," and his own body the last time I saw it weighed two hundred and fifty pounds and was barely capable of a deep breath, much less a push-up. But I guess it didn't lie.

And then there was the incident of the Senoi. I was in a class and some of my classmates were into Senoi dream theory. The Senoi are an aboriginal people in Malaysia. They use dreams as a part of community life and they try to influence their dreams and get messages from dreams. If you dream of falling, you tell the dream at breakfast and everybody says, wonderful, where did you fall to and what did you discover? If you didn't discover, go back and dream the dream again and see what you come up with.

An anthropologist called Kilton Stewart wrote about the Senoi, and it's his Senoi chapter in Tart's *Altered States of Consciousness*. The Senoi, Stewart said, are the most adjusted people on earth, no war, no crime, their psychological achievements are better than ours in nuclear physics. Wow! Senoi seminars sprout up in colleges, and Senoi communities, too, nice young California people telling their dreams, and having their children tell their dreams, and I have a problem.

I have a problem because many years ago the U.S. Army put me on a study team in Southeast Asia, and the Senoi were one of my tribes. I dig up the notes. Sure enough, the Senoi, dream culture. But Kilton Stewart has somehow left out that thunderstorms terrify the Senoi, the women peel off their clothes, screeching like banshees, and offer themselves to the thunderstorm, and when you die, if you're a Senoi, your soul goes into the left armpit of a gigantic old woman called Sankal, who lives on an island in a lake at the bottom of a pit. And in present-day Malaysia, the Senoi children are riding the school bus to the government school where they don't get to tell their dreams, and the adults are hanging out trying to cadge tips from the tourists by getting their pictures taken. And the anthropologist who found the Senoi, these peaceable people, who in fact introduced Kilton Stewart to them, Dr. Noone from Cambridge, well, poor Dr. Noone got blowpiped by a poisoned dart from his best

Senoi buddy. Southeast Asian version of the Saturday Night Special, a little fracas over a lady.

I really want the Senoi to be this marvelous dream culture, and I don't want my California classmates to be mad at me, but it influences my enthusiasm for Senoi dream culture to recall how you had to hire a shaman to get your soul back out of Sankal's armpit. Now my classmates are mad, they think I am a narc or something. What do I do with my Army notes?

And then there is the Guru Maharaj Ji, the teenage guru. Some of my nice friends are following the Guru Maharaj Ji. Off we go to a *satsang*, a spiritual discourse, delivered by a mahatma, one empowered to spread the Knowledge, a shaved-head, berobed Indian with a singsong delivery. It is a pep talk for the big rally in Houston, the Millennium.

"A man comes back next life as what he meditates upon this time," says the Mahatma. "A man who meditates upon God becomes God. A man who meditates upon wealth is clutching the earth like a snake, a snake loves the earth, and wealth is like the earth, so a man who spends his time thinking upon wealth comes back as a snake. So do not be attached to wealth. Use wealth for the benefit of humanity, bring money for the Millennium even if it is only ten dollars or twenty dollars—" It sounded like Marjoe, the kid preacher—"You've got five dollars, ten dollars under the coffee can in the kitchen, oh, bring it here, bring it here for *Je*sus."

Rennie Davis, the Sixties activist, tells us how the Millennium is going to awaken consciousness that will allow us to plug into the Ground of Being and usher in a thousand years of peace, but it's going to take some money, "so each one of us has to go out and hit our parents—a hundred dollars, fifty dollars."

Hit our parents? Hit our parents? Rennie lost me.

The Guru Maharaj Ji was a setup for the Alchemist-baiting press. He had a Rolls-Royce and all those Hondas and Shri Hans Productions for films and records, and Divine Travel Services, and *Divine Times* (THE LORD IN LONDON! HOLY FAMILY NOW IN ENGLAND!) and vegetarian restaurants—De Tocqueville wrote: "Strange sects endeavor [in America] to strike out extraordinary paths of eternal happiness . . . religious insanity is very common."

"It's natural for the kids to turn to the Second Coming of Santa Claus," said Paul Krassner, the editor of *The Realist,* in Houston.

"He's no Santa Claus, he's the Lord," said Rennie Davis.

"This is the Knowledge you can't get in College," sang Bhole Ji, the Guru Maharaj Ji's brother, who leads the Divine rock band.

"When I got the Knowledge," said Rennie, "I saw this incredible light in the middle of my forehead, a diamond was spinning and getting larger, then the divine music, a heavy roar for a while, then dinnnnnnng, every fiber of my being began to vibrate . . . an incredible wave of bliss shot through me, my mind began to play this incredible rock and roll . . ."

"This is like being with the Nixon CREEP people," said the editor of *The Realist.*

Rennie Davis said Guru Maharaj Ji is "the Lord, the universe, the power of creation itself," and the Guru's followers speak of him with Buddha and Jesus. Not everybody agrees. Agehananda Bharati, the Indian-born chairman of Syracuse University's anthropology department, who has written on Indian religions, says he is "a typical Asian phony."

Along the lines of shaking the techniques out of the disciplines, I wanted to know about the Knowledge. Usually I go on the trips myself, but I had been on enough of them by the time I ran into the Guru Maharaj Ji's crowd. The rite of the Knowledge is secret and those who describe it risk demotion in future incarnations to all sorts of base things, but there have been enough defectors now to give something of a description:

The mahatma is sitting against the middle of a wall, with a very bright light shinning on him. First he satsangs you for about two hours about the retribution you're going to suffer if you ever reveal the secret of the Knowledge-giving. Fire and brimstone, suffering and gnashing of teeth, eternal damnation. Then he starts giving Knowledge. First he does your eyes. He presses his knuckles very hard upon your eyeballs and keeps them there until you see the *light.* Then he plugs up your ears with his fingers in a certain way until you hear the *music.* Then he tips your head back in a certain way for the meditative position, and that nectar you taste, that's your snot. Then he tells you the secret word to meditate on, and that's kind of a breath sound that's supposed to represent the divine energy of the world, ah-ha, ah-ha.

The guru's followers weren't happy with that particular account, needless to say. But they knew I was trying to find a Western vocabulary for various phenomena, so we talked about the white light.

"The pressure on the eyeball could certainly get the retinal cells to fire," I said. "That would give you a white light. Lots of things can give you a white light, neurochemical transmitters, hallucinogens—"

"It's not knuckles on the eyeballs, it's *thumbs* on the eyeballs, gently," said a devotee.

"That would stop the saccades, or small involuntary movements of the eye," I said. "Very good for quieting."

"But what about the pineal gland? asked a pleasant, wide-eyed girl. Every Eastern trip gets to the pineal gland at some point. The pineal body is in the middle of the brain, above the pons, developing from the diencephalon. Its functions, says the textbook, are obscure, as if it were the vestige of something we have evolved away from.

"Descartes said it was the seat of the soul, and it appears in a lot of esoteric disciplines as the Third Eye," I said. "And this was considered so much esoteric baloney, but in 1965 some neurophysiologists found that the nerve to the pineal is a branch of the sympathetic nerves receiving impulses from a branch of nerves that transmit impulses from the eye to the brain."

I was reading from my pineal paragraphs.

"Thus the pineal gland responds by a very indirect route to light in the environment. Though not organized as an eye, it can function as a light receptor."

"Oh my God, there *is* a Third Eye," said the pleasant girl.

The Third Eye stuff got me when I first found the pineal papers. A secret eye in the middle of the brain! What would you see with it?

"Remember, we don't see with our eyes," I said, the anatomy professor, "we see *with the help of our eyes*. What we think of as seeing is a brain function."

I went back to the text.

"The light receptive qualities cause changes in the secretion of the hormone melatonin, which causes the concentration of melanin in pigment cells. In small vertebrates and mammals, seasonal light changes can influence sexual behavior."

"Far out!" said another devotee.

My neurophysiology text didn't have the celestial music or the nectar, but I had scored a lot of points with the Third Eye. We were all agreed on the effects of mantrams.

"Even though you know this," said the devotees, "you don't have the Knowledge. Why don't you get the Knowledge?"

"How long would it take?"

"Oh, if you're really ready, as little as half an hour. Maybe ten minutes. Some people have done it that fast."

The guru's followers were well-scrubbed and smiling and sincere. I did not get the Knowledge.

Almost a year later, some of the devotees told me the Millennium had been a bit disappointing. "We were all so worked up, we really thought flying saucers might land. Rennie Davis said there might be beings on other planets who wanted the Knowledge."

Flying saucers or not, the devotees I met were still there a year later, still in service. They stayed in service even after the guru's mother fired him, saying he had become too Western. Like Eleanor of Aquitaine, she attempted to favor another of her sons, but many of the American followers stuck to the teenage guru. The Guru Maharaj Ji adopted a lower profile.

There remains the unfortunate incident of the blackjacking, not necessarily only as a comment on the people of Divine Light. I wouldn't even bring it up but it shows the *certainty* that seems to come from the evangelical nature of religious enthusiasms.

A reporter for an underground newspaper in Detroit threw a pie in Guru Maharaj Ji's face. "I always wanted to throw a pie in God's face," he said. A week later he was visited by two men, an older Indian and a young American. The Indian zapped the young reporter with a blackjack, causing six skull lacerations, and necessitating a plastic plate in the cerebrum. There is a felony warrant out in Detroit for the two men; the blackjack-wielding Indian turns out to be Mahatma Fakiranand. Was Mahatma Fakiranand stripped of his mahatmadom? No, he was sent to give Knowledge in Europe. "There are no hard and fast rules for being holy," said a Divine Light official. "In India there have been gurus who have led their followers into full-scale wars."

Not just in India. I think of the archbishop leading his troops in the Albigensian Crusade, crying, "Kill them! Kill every man, woman and child! God will reveal who are the true Catholics!" Closer to home, I met a young man who had just defected from the service of the Reverend Sun Myung Moon, a Korean who received a visitation from Jesus Christ on a hillside in 1936, and began preaching his own brand of gospel. The Reverend Sun Myung Moon began collecting not only his own followers from city to city, but hecklers, Jesus freaks who had some dispute in theology with the Korean. At one dinner, the Reverend passed out billy clubs to some of his followers, to aid in the theological dispute with his fellow Christians. Not that this is new. There is a famous letter from Cotton Mather to the commander of the brig *Porpoise,* suggesting that he "waylay the ship *Welcome* near the Cape of Cod, carrying that scamp William Penn and his heretic Quakers and sell the whole lot as slaves to Barbados, thus performing a service to the Lord." And keep the money.

It is said, in the intellectual sections of the counter-culture, that our society has been too linear and rational and unfeeling, and in the less intellectual sections *stoned* is good, the uptight Establishment does not know stoned. In 1934 the Nazis in Germany held a tremendous night rally at Nuremberg. The stadium was ringed with antiaircraft searchlights, giving the effect, said the British ambassador, of "a cathedral of ice." Drums beat a hypnotic rhythm; drums and music have been used in many cultures to alter consciousness. Observers said the master orator, Chancellor Hitler, played the crowd like an orchestra, a frenzy of energy. In short, *everybody at Nuremberg was stoned.* A couple of years later they went out to impose the benefits of their certainty on as much of the world as they could reach.

It may be true, we have been goal-oriented, linear, mechanical, unfeeling; but stoned also does not work out well sometimes for the unstoned.

So I had ambiguities. Occasionally my schedule would compound the ambiguities. Nine A.M., Tibetan chanting. Eleven A.M., classwork on smiling to a count of six, or flaring one nostril to a count of six. Stuff to drive the left brain crazy, show the drunken monkey it doesn't run you. One P.M., catch the shuttle plane to attend three P.M. portfolio meeting, bring left brain back in a hurry, read *Wall St. Journal* and briefs on the plane. Make notes for meeting. Seven P.M. catch shuttle plane back, turn left brain off with breathing meditation; breathe in to a count of six, hold one, breathe out to a count of six, visualize breath.

It helps to reassure the language-using mind that it can come back even after it's turned off. Maybe get some help from the rest of the body, skin talk, say. Jung anticipated biofeedback monitoring the skin, wired up his patients while he tried word associations. Subsequent experiments showed that skins could remember, and mirror, and know things before the language-mind translated them.

And this brings us to Vibes. The TM people and the Harvard Medical School people said, meditation can relax you by dropping the level of activity. The incremental idea says, if you turn down the noise in your mind, you can hear what else is going on. Skin talk, stomach talk, heart talk. It's almost the opposite of some kinds of psychiatry, where the waking self is the sober rational one writing out checks to the psychiatrist, and the hidden self is considered an unruly child. "Emotional parasites thriving in the human body," wrote Barbara Brown, a biofeedback researcher, "can be traced . . . to a socially created barrier between the conscious and subconscious worlds. The entire body is reacting one way, crying out signals to a consciousness that is listening only to the consciousness of another society-evolved human product."

Vibes doesn't necessarily mean vibes the way the kids mean it, because that covers their own perceptions, which can be just as red-six-of-spades as those of people who don't use the word vibes. This idea is that your skin or gut is perceiving—perception isn't only through the eyes—things important to your survival. Not that this is so radical, it's in the language, I have a gut feeling, he get under my skin, she is certainly a pain in the ass.

I have two personal Vibe stories from the money world. After my first six months of chanting and sheer movement and so on in esoteric psychology, I went to the giant glass slab in downtown New York to see my partners. I was limited, meaning I had left my money with them, and they were general, meaning they were doing something with it, and with their own. We sat in the small paneled private dining room. In the other dining room, the bigger one, same floor, the dancer bees were humming with indications of pension-fund clover and the air was heavy with electrical money excitement. I could feel the rhythms of the place like a narcotic in the blood, the same giddiness and rush.

In our dining room, that narcotic excitement was being translated into vigorous buttering of the rolls. The gross national product was going to be this, the interest rates were going to be that, there was thirty billion of cash in the mutual and pension funds, the market was going to turn around—and I noticed something.

There were four of us there and I was not smoking and *there were four lit cigarettes.*

"—the market is as low as it was in fifty-five, it is at the bottom end of its swing," said Leon—

"—as low as it was in fifty-one, I am adjusting for the Korean upsurge in commodity prices—" said Chuck, and I am sitting there starting to see how people can smoke four cigarettes at the same time.

"Leon is smoking two cigarettes," I announced after a while. "One rests on the ashtray while he puffs on the other one, and then he switches them, and sometimes one of you also switches the cigarette you're puffing on with Leon's reserve cigarette in the ashtray, and nobody notices."

Even after I said it, nobody noticed. Leon stubbed out one of the cigarettes and called the waiter, he thought I was complaining about being left out of the smoking.

"Give our guest a cigar," he said to the waiter.

Then we went to the offices and looked at the green-and-white computer sheets that had the portfolios, and something was wrong, the brasses and the flutes and the tympani weren't all together, even though there was high excitement and an estimate for each stock and a Beta rating from the computer, the portfolio had scabs and everybody was picking at them.

"I don't like it," I said.

"What? What? What should we do?"

I said—it was hard to say, because I was trying to translate these vibes—that there was too much activity, everybody was working too hard, pushing and pulling and tugging at the portfolio, and thinking up sixty-seven different reasons for everything, as well as what somebody heard somebody say in the Fed, and what the guy said who came in from the Coast.

"So what should we do?"

I said everybody who ran a portfolio should stand on his head ten minutes a day—I was improvising—and one day a week, Thursday, say, they should not come to work and not work at home and walk barefoot in the grass and think about something else, biology or physics or music, what does the music say, how corn grows—or geraniums, anything—and then on Friday morning first thing before they talk to anybody they should see whether the portfolio looked the same as Wednesday night.

They listened respectfully but I wasn't translating the vibes well enough, so they slapped me on the back and I left, and here is what I thought when I left.

I have been in this group that sits chanting Ra-a-a-m a couple of hours a day, and practices smiling to a count of six, and has a vocabulary so arcane none of them understands it, and they think a Great Cosmic Wave is coming. Plainly, *they are crazy.* And I have just spent the day with people that smoke two cigarettes at a time and make three phone calls at a time, and the portfolios reflect this entropy, and *they are crazy, too.*

Aha, everybody is crazy, there is only thee and me, and thee has been acting a bit queer recently.

The vibes, as it turned out, should have been paid attention. One of the gentlemen smoking two cigarettes had a heart attack within a year. And the portfolios had heart attacks, too, from going down so fast.

But I learn slowly. I opened the mailbox a year later, and here was another portfolio from another group, and when I opened the envelope I got an incredible rash on the skin. Just from reading a list of names and numbers. By now I was more respectful of Vibes, so I tried translating verbally. The message said: *Risk. Flee.*

I called up, and I translated *risk, flee* into boring everyday terms: say, you fellas seem to have a big percentage bunched up in just two situations and not much liquidity or flexibility.

And the managers said, you don't understand, you're out of touch, we have all the facts, here are the facts, blah blah blah.

I had a conflict between my skin, which was continuing to flash *risk, flee,* and the ol' left brain, which said: "These guys are probably right, they're there every day, they get all the information, you're out of touch, they wouldn't be there if they didn't know what they were doing."

So I had to take the responsibility for the Vibes, and I didn't. The conceptual mind has years of practice against some momentary skin flush, and the skin flush is dumb and emotional, so it loses.

That portfolio went into a spin, too. The skin flush was smarter.

It might not have been. Skin flushes and heart bumps are only signals on our own survival, they do not necessarily keep an accurate score on some game taking place in society, what they have is a personal component that says, *hey, listen.*

"Listen" is not even the right word, it simply transfers to the ear what we mean when we say, perceive more than you see. Or hear. If you perceive, you're smarter than you think you are. But perceive isn't a very dramatic word.

EXERCISES OLD
AND NEW

WE have been looking at techniques from a variety of uncommon disciplines. Most of the techniques are a bit left-handed. Right-brained, nonlinear, nonverbal. That makes them easy to read about—they seem almost idiotically simple—and not hard to do, but hard to keep doing. They're hard to keep doing because we are pitched at a more restless level; they require internal quiet and balance, and there's always something more interesting to do, certainly something more exciting, than exercises like these. Some authorities say that our culture became so lacking in imagination, intuition, mystery, and altered states that it left the opening for Eastern religions and "fundamental" Christian sects to expand.

But these techniques do not always come dressed exotically. Doctors and management consultants commend the therapeutic effects of moving attention from work to something that isn't treated like work and which mobilizes the body differently. The cardiac specialists who wrote *Type A Behavior and Your Heart* wanted their patients to read Proust. No hard-working, compulsively competitive businessman could possibly read the entire *Remembrance of Things Past,* the pace of Proust and all that detail would drive him nuts—or slow him down, and that's the idea. Peter Drucker, the authority on management policies and techniques, warns the rising executive in *Management* against preoccupation with the job and its goals and office politics. What else should the rising executive do? Well, maybe play in a string quartet, said Peter Drucker. Music is indeed right-brained, and would have a mobilization different from sales projections. Furthermore, the playing in the string quartet should be *important,* important enough to demand concentration and attention. But the ranks of American business are noticeably bereft of fingers used to the viola da gamba. Not many cellists, either.

Here are two contemporary exercises gestalt psychologists will recognize immediately, which are so easy to read about it's hard to believe they could work. Their etiology is uncertain, but they are obvious cousins to the meditation techniques. The first is called Create a Space. It runs something like this:

Create a Space

Think of a time when you were absolutely, totally relaxed. Maybe you were in bed on a Sunday morning with nothing to do and rain on the roof. Maybe you were at a beach, or in a meadow on a summer day. Review all your most relaxed scenes, and pick the one that seems to make you go ah-h-h-h when you remember it. Now try to get back to that feeling, imagine all the details of how that total relaxation felt. The details are important: how did your eyes feel, how did your hands feel, how did your head feel.

When you can put yourself into that space, bring the space with you. Have the space three feet on each side of you wherever you go. And then, when you're sure of the space, imagine a stressful situation. Now take yourself, and your space, three feet on each side of you, into the imagined stressful situation and let all the details play out.

Create a Space is used in some courses we will come to a bit later. I had a classmate who was a prison psychologist, and he had been teaching Create a Space to his clients, the prisoners. I don't know how he did that, but I went to visit him one after-noon when I was in his home state, and we took a tour. I couldn't tell how well it worked—the vibrations of con and counter-con go on at so many levels between prisoners and pri-son psychologists—but my classmate, who had been working in prison programs for twelve years, said the prisoners had taken to Create a Space more than anything in his tenure, and they wanted to know more. We talked to some of the prisoners. They all seemed to be named Billy Jack and Jim Bob and Bobby Joe. They were not self-conscious about the exercise.

"It takes a while," said Jim Bob, "but I wear my space past this one guard and he don't bother me no more."

The Wise Thing in the Cave

Like Create a Space, this comes from contemporary rather than esoteric disciplines, gestalt psychology and psychosynthesis, but the roots are the same. The point is to use those intuitive and subsurface powers that get drowned by the noise in the mind, or by the automatic actions of the mind. It helps to have a part-ner take you through the first couple of times, so that you can lie down with your eyes shut and pay attention to all the details.

The Wise Thing in the Cave also creates a space in imagina-tion. The first time I did the exercise we imagined a field, and walked across the field, and noticed the grass, and the flowers, and then there was a cave, and we went into the cave, and there were stalactites and stalagmites and the sound of water running —and on and on for about fifteen minutes.

Great details once inside the cave, the feel underfoot, the sound of the cave, the echoes. If it's done right, it can be as ab-sorbing as, say, a good movie.

And at the end of the cave is a person or an animal or any-thing you want, who is very wise. Anybody or anything you want. You get to ask the Wise Thing one question, any question. And you see what It says.

When I told this exercise to some friends, they couldn't understand it. Aren't you just making up the answer? What's such a big deal?

But the voice in the owl or the wise old man or whatever archetype appears is not the voice you're used to, if the exercise works. The voice belongs to It from outer space, the one whose thumb twitch turns off the grating sound, who has a big serve if nobody is looking. It's still you—so is the thumb twitch, or the serve—but another part.

"You do not actively imagine anything in the cave," said our instructor. "You let appear whatever wants to appear, and you let it say whatever it wants to say. You have access to all sorts of material within yourself which you usually ignore."

MEDIUM SHOT

Along the cave, the cave walls tannish and moist, SOUND of gurgling water.

VOICE-OVER

The Instructor's Voice: Now, at the end of the cave is a shape, it is the wise symbol you have picked, go a little closer.

MEDIUM SHOT

There's a shape there all right, but it's hard to see what it is—it's—it's a man, it looks like—

VOICE-OVER

The Instructor's Voice: All right, move a little closer, and now I am going to leave you, proceed at your own pace to the end of the cave and ask your question whenever you are ready—

MEDIUM SHOT

—yes, it's a man, sitting there, that face is familiar, but not too familiar, who the hell?

ZOOM, CLOSING IN

—the face is very distinct, who the hell is that, it's an oldish man, a distinguished face—Claude Rains, in *Caesar and Cleopatra*? Almost, no, it's—Walter Lippmann, the old columnist, he used to get annual visits from *CBS Reports* and deliver wisdom on the state of the world—

That's who appeared for me, Walter Lippmann.

I couldn't think of anything to ask Walter Lippmann.

A voice came out of the character playing me and said, "How do I get out of this cave?"

Walter Lippman was old, wise, and kindly.

"You will have no trouble," Walter Lippman said. "You know the way. Go back the same way you came."

But I didn't. As soon as Walter Lippman said that, I did the equivalent of waking up and looking around the room, people still had their eyes shut talking to their Wise Things, I thought: I blew it, that's really dumb dialogue for Walter Lippmann, I could have asked him anything and all I wanted to know was how the hell to get out of there.

I thought the whole thing was such a flop I hoped the instructor wouldn't call on me, but he did. Other people had owls and grandmothers and religious figures. The class didn't think Walter Lippman was a flop at all. From my question and Walter Lippmann's answer they knew all about me; it was a little frightening how much they knew. The only thing they thought was dumb was how quickly I dismissed Walter Lippmann's pearl of wisdom.

"Our society worships a seventeen-year-old swigging a Pepsi at the beach and does not listen to its grandfathers," said the instructor.

Carl Jung, the great, pioneering Swiss psychiatrist, had just such a wise old man, whom he called Philemon. The Wise Old Man is an archetype anyway, a symbol from the collective unconscious that Jung said was common to everyone in all cultures. Jung has a dialogue with Philemon, the other-Jung, for much of his life, and recorded it, kept a memoir of the talks.

I could hardly wait to get back and see Walter, but the next time into the cave he wasn't there. It was another Walter, Cronkite. My channel seemed to be permanently tuned to CBS. Hardly fair. The image disintegrated before Walter Cronkite could even say good evening

The Great Central Philippine Headache Cure

I made that name up. First I was in a course which used this attention technique, and then I was reading Kilton Stewart, the anthropologist, who had by then moved from the Senoi in Malaysia to the Central Philippines, and lo and behold, there are the shamans in the Central Philippines curing headaches with this, an obvious cousin to autogenic training, it breathes me, to the meditations that use color, and to Create a Space. You need two people, one to ask the questions.

Close your eyes and look at your headache. Tell me about it. What color is your headache? Where do you see the color? Where is the headache in your head? Do you still feel it's there, or is it moving? How big is your headache? If it were liquid, would it fill a quart jar? A gallon jar? A bathtub? Can you pour the headache into one of those containers? When I say pour, start pouring, and see if it overflows. Pour.

What does your headache make you think of? Look at that. Now look at the color of your headache. Is it the same? Tell me about the color. A dark shade or a light shade? Is the headache still the same size as when we started? Would you say it's as bad as when we started? No? Keep your eyes closed, breathe evenly, and tell me how big your headache is now. Describe the experience of your headache exactly. All of life is experience and this is experience, what is the experience? What color is the headache now? What does it feel like? How big is it?

And so on. I have seen, in one startling demonstration after another, the Great Central Philippine Headache Cure work. Why on earth does it work? Is it a relaxation technique, or some form of hypnosis? Is it because pain is a signal, and this technique says to the signal, thank you, message received, over and out, go home now, in a physiological rather than a verbal way?

The narrator, or question asker, has to be relaxed, attentive and cool, so that the headache victim's mind doesn't tense itself against the visualizations. Some people say the technique works but the headache comes back later. Why it should work at all is fascinating. If you try it for ten minutes without the headache getting smaller, take two aspirin, breathe evenly, watch the black velvet on the inside of your eyelids for three minutes, and go on about your business.

Mantram as a Block

Now we go back to esoteric psychology for the example, but the process is still the focusing of attention, just as in the headache cure. Earlier we had the mantram as a bone for a yapping beagle, a device for a turnoff which, it seems, drops metabolism and lactate. Mantram as a Block comes out of the Oriental martial arts, as far as I know. The Zen master said, if you're in this sword fight you have to be there, unhindered, every molecule vibrating, as if it's your last moment alive, otherwise you might get cut up and it will be your last moment alive. Mantram as a Block lets you get out of your own way, like breath-counting on the tennis court.

We don't have sword fights any more, we have departmental meetings, or dinner parties for the boss, or confrontations between parents and children. I actually found Mantram as a Block in two courses, neither of which called it that. In one, the master said he had learned it from a martial arts master, and the mantram was meaningless syllables with a very intricate hypnotic rhythm, but repeated in different orders and cadences. It took almost a week to learn with class drills, so there's not much point in putting the exact syllables here, you would have to score it like music.

The mantric syllables have no power of magic; you could do the same thing with "The Night Before Christmas" if those words didn't carry a meaning. You need something with a beat and a pattern and a degree of intricacy; if you blow it, start over. You have to focus your mind's eye on the intricacy while you continue with the department chairman or your spouse or your children or your parents. Contrapuntal music is good—try to hear several lines, not just melody. I don't really believe "The Night Before Christmas" would work, but if it did, it might be like this:

CHAIRMAN: Mr. Jones will now tell us why his report is late when everybody else was on time—

JONES: (Twas the night before Christmas, and all through the house)

I don't want to say that it was computer error, but the fact is
(Not a creature was stirring, not even a mouse)
that we were ready two weeks ago, and then—

Jones keeps cool, at the risk of saying something about eight tiny
reindeer. Better just abstract "The Night Before Christmas" to
its rhythms. Or "Hiawatha." If the Chairman calls on you, get
the rhythm revved up and running before you talk.

One of the editors of *Psychology Today* told me Mantram as
a Block had ruined the fights he had with his wife. She had
taken the course; he hadn't, so he only knew abstractly what was
going on. "All I know is," he said, "she gets that damn thing
running, and I say the same old things, and she says the same
old things, but that damn thing is running in her head, I can
feel it, it drives me right up the wall."

The block only has to work once or twice to have some permanent value. If you can get it to work twice, you will have
your mind cued: just as the relax-mantram cues *relax*, this cues
centered and ready and calm, centered and ready and calm. I
have used Mantram as a Block in traffic jams outside the airport, with flat tires that weren't supposed to happen, and in
verbal scraps. It doesn't disperse the traffic jam or repair the
tire or end the fight, but it helps your nerve center of gravity
down from your shoulders to your navel, and if your center of
gravity is lower you don't tip over so easily.

Fair Witness

This is a yoga exercise which sounds the easiest of all and is the
hardest. You create a witness who walks around behind you and
notices every single thing—it is, in fact, you—*and does not judge.*
It just reflects. I Am a Camera.

There she is reaching for a cigarette, not there is that nicotine
addict reaching for a cigarette, or whoopee, I need a cigarette.
There he is, going to the refrigerator, he is opening the door,
his hand is around the beer can, he is taking it out—not, I need

one, no, I already had a couple, the hell with it, I pay for them, I drink them, and so on.

This is an exercise in mindfulness or awareness, and most people can't do it for three minutes. I can't. People start to play scenes for their Fair Witness, as if it were a judge, or they treat the Fair Witness as a biographer, which is another form of judge, or they get tired of the point of view of the Fair Witness, and go back to their own, or shuttle back and forth.

By plucking these exercise out of their courses, I am guilty of all sort of things, not the least of which is spiritual materialism and reductionism. They are meant as illustration, not as how-to, but if they work, they work.

We have seen now the confusion caused by noise in the mind, the healing effect of quieting the mind, the way the body can send messages that might be true but to which nobody is usually listening, the protecting or integrating of the whole organism by preoccupying the mind, the power of reacreating a calm feeling in a stressful time, and the power of imaging.

Eastern psychologies treat all of this, though not in a coherent way to the Western mind, and some Western syntheses also use them.

But you don't have to go to a mountaintop in the Himalayas.

The wisdom that follows is from Satchel Paige, a great black pitcher, denied the opportunity to compete in major leagues for much of his life but certainly one of the great athletes in American history. It is doubtful whether Satch knew the Upanishads, the Bhagavad-Gita, the Vedas, Roberto Assagioli's psychosynthesis, or gestalt psychology. He didn't have to.

Satchel Paige's Rules for Right Living

Avoid fried foods which angry up the blood.

If your stomach disputes you, lie down and pacify it with cooling thoughts.

Keep the juice flowing by jangling around gently as you move.
Go very lightly on the vices such as carrying on in society—the social ramble ain't restful.
Avoid running at all times.
Don't look back. Somethin' might be gaining on you.

See what ol' Satch knew. *Avoid foods that angry up the blood*; diets are common to many disciplines, and when you become sensitive your instincts lead you right, and the food is part of you. *If your stomach disputes you, lie down and pacify it with cooling thoughts.* Psychosynthesis, gestalt therapy, progressive relaxation, autogenic training, meditations, power of mind and the autonomic nervous system. *Keep the juice flowing by jangling around gently as you move. T'ai chi,* the concepts of subtle energy, *chi* or *ki,* centeredness. *Go lightly on the vices . . . the social ramble ain't restful.* Do not become attached, do not identify with what you do, turn down the noise in your mind. *Avoid running at all times.* Where are you going so fast, and what do you get when you get there? *Don't look back, somethin' might be gaining on you.* Stay present; clear the karma, something *is* gaining on you, and on everybody, from day one.

I wish ol' Satch were still around, he could be a guru with a big following. And as refreshing as another gentleman of my acquaintance, Swami Hal.

SWAMI HAL AND
THE YOGI MAFIA

"**I**F you're going to talk about yogis, you better learn about the yogi Mafia," a friend said.

"The yogi *Mafia*? There is one?"

"We have a swami friend, Hal, who will tell you about it."

But it was no easy task to get to see Hal. For one thing, his ashram was deep in the woods of the Northwest, and not well serviced by public transportation. For another, introductions or no, he did not seem eager to see me. As I bumped along in my rented car in the pine woods, peering amidst the cabins that looked like something left from the CCC, a giant, bearded, berobed figure appeared with the following salutation:

"What the hell do you want?"

I told him I wanted to know about the yogi Mafia.

"Get the hell out of here."

Hal had a gravelly whiskey voice, and a Falstaffian figure. He was an American who had gone to India to become a swami and now ran this little ashram. Hal had a very abrasive manner, but I began to feel, after the first half-hour, that he also had a peculiar honesty. His is one of the few names I've changed. Hal said if I didn't, he would stuff my tape recorder down my throat, and I believed him. He lived in the woods with a few followers and some juvenile delinquents who had been farmed out to him by despairing civil authorities. I asked him what the young incipient hoods did.

"They meditate," Hal said. "Nobody makes them meditate. They do it. And they work on the farm."

"Because it's a religious principle?"

"BECAUSE I'LL KICK THEIR ASSES IF THEY DON'T AND THEY KNOW I CAN DO IT," Hal boomed. "Nobody makes them come here, they pick it, the word goes out, this is a straight place, no liquor, no dope, nobody hassling them, and the word is also out, NOBODY MESSES WITH THE SWAMI. We got alumni who come back and visit. ALUMNI!" Hal boomed. I could see that nobody who didn't weigh two hundred and sixty pounds should mess with the swami. I asked Hal how he got to be a swami but he wouldn't tell me any details.

"What the hell do you care? I went to India, I took my vows, I'm a renunciate, that's what a swami is, and that's what I am. I don't ask anybody for anything, and I'm not proselytizing! Proselytizing! Eastern religions don't seek converts! You want knowledge, you have to stand outside the monastery for a month in the rain! Then they say, okay, you're sincere, you can work in the kitchen for a year! Now look what we got! Instant samadhi! We got Eastern religions in this country out looking for converts, just like the Fundamentalists! Christians proselytize, okay. Moslems, they just tell you, there is no God but Allah, believe it or we'll kill you. That's how Islam spread. The sword! They rode out and held a sword to everybody's throat, and said, this country's gonna be Moslem, right? And everybody who didn't say, yassuh boss, was dead, so they had unanimous acceptance! But what is this, hustling the Eastern religions? What's going on the past ten years in this country?"

"What is going on?" I asked.

"I go to hear Baba Ram Dass," said the swami. "I like Richard. He's a screwed-up guy, but he doesn't rip off the kids. He's working on his sex problems, he's so enthusiastic about his guru, but all right, he's sincere. And outside the hall where Baba Ram Dass, Richard, is speaking, every freak in the world is standing, passing out pamphlets! The Jesus freaks hit me with the Gospels of John. All right, I know the Gospels of John, but I'll take one, thank you. Six freaks are dancing in orange robes singing Hare Krishna, banging their tambourines. Two more cults hand me pamphlets. Now mind you, I'm in my swami robes, sandals, no leather, MY SWAMI ROBES and this freak comes up and starts hassling me about Krishna consciousness. That's too much. I say, GET OUT OF MY WAY YOU ASSHOLE I'M BEYOND KRISHNA CONSCIOUSNESS CAN'T YOU SEE I'M A SWAMI? I'M AN INCARNATION OF GOD YOU STUPID YOUNG PUP! These kids are all so ignorant of everybody else's trips they're trying to sell me—ME, A SWAMI—on their trip."

"Why are so many kids into all this stuff?"

"I know one answer," Hal said. "Their parents are killing themselves with materialism. Okay, you didn't have to drive through the Oregon woods to hear that. Another reason is, they take materialism for granted, times have been so good they can afford to try these trips. In a Depression everybody is hustling jobs and nobody is trying out Hare Krishna. And there's another reason. They like to hassle their parents. Look, Ma, I'm a Jesus freak, nya nya nya! And the old lady sticks her head in the gas oven."

"Kids really do it to annoy their parents?"

"They don't think of it that way, they do it because it shows independence, but they like to see their parents in a flap. You don't see many thirty-five-year-old freaks because by that time the parents are either dead or have stopped giving a damn. That's only one reason. A lot of kids want to break away, to try another way of life, so they pick something that separates them from their parents but not by so much that their parents want to blow their brains out."

"Like?"

"Like, in India there's a high proportion of Jewish kids. The kid comes back, he's in sandals, he meditates, all right, he's strange, but he's quiet and he's not a Jesus freak screaming into a microphone in some Texas stadium, he's almost acceptable. Like Richard, he lands at the airport, his father sees him in his robes, he says, quick get in the car before anybody sees you, but now his father, the railroad president, is quite proud of him because Richard is very *successful* at his Indian gig. The Protestant kids go to the Jesus freaks, stomping and hollering, a lot of them go to things that are like that, Guru Maharaj Ji or Scientology, secret orders, that bit, and the Catholic kids cause their parents the pain when they first leave the church, they can go in any direction at all that doesn't seem Catholic, with a hierarchy and bossy nuns, but they like things that have mystery and ritual. Now you can see with all these kids roaming around THIS HAS BECOME QUITE A BUSINESS."

"And that's why the yogi Mafia?"

"It's not a real Mafia, more like a gentlemen's agreement."

"But you have meetings?"

"Not formally, but sure, there are conventions and gatherings and whatnot. When I was inducted into the holy order of the Mafia one of them walked over to me and said, we have to stop hassling each other, it's our bread and butter, he slapped my hand. Our bread and butter! That's a good old American term! For an Indian religious leader!"

"How does it work?"

"Well, if I want to get going and, say, Satchadinada is strong in New York, I don't butt into his territory. I go somewhere where the territory is more open. Except Los Angeles, all rules are off for Los Angeles, the place is so freaky that the agreements are suspended for Los Angeles. Those must be some meetings, when the brethren gather, smoking their hash pipes and talking good hard numbers, I wish I was the travel agent for Air India. You gotta realize, some of these movements have sixty, eighty ashrams, and each ashram has fifty or sixty kids, *it's a business.*"

"You sound mad about it."

"Why should I be mad about it? That's not my bag. I don't like these swine who rip off the kids, but otherwise, what the hell do I care? Let everybody take his own trip. A lot of these places, though, are full of sick kids. My God, it's like a chain of clinics."

"Are the kids helped?"

"Some are, some aren't. It depends on the trip, too. A lot of kids are very ignorant."

"Are you saying some of the spiritual leaders are okay and some aren't?"

"Sure."

"Can you tell me which ones?"

"You want to get me assassinated?"

"You're joking."

"I am joking, and you should remember there's just as much ripping off going on under good old Christianity as in more exotic places."

So Hal wouldn't tell me who he thought was okay, and who wasn't, except that I noticed he would refer to some yogi as "that punk" or "that fraud," and when I brought up another name Hal said, "HEY! You leave him alone! He's a real scholar! He's a goddam saint! Gimme that tape recorder!"

He turned it off. I asked Hal if the spiritual quests were part of something permanent.

"It started with the drugs," Hal said, "Leary and the LSD Leary is one of the smartest people I've ever met. They're still using his interpersonal tests in prisons and hospitals. It's a crime they framed him into a fifty-year jail sentence, for what? enough marijuana to make one cigarette? Leary thought psychedelics would change the world. Leary was the Magus, the manipulator. If Leary was the Magus with the white clothes and the rose in his teeth, then Richard had to be the guru. Some pair they were. But he got a power thing, and if you think you're the messiah, somebody is sure as hell going to try nailing you to a cross just to make the myth come out right.

"The drugs did lead the kids to the spiritual quests—not the narcotics, not heroin, but the psychedelics. I think the drugs are fading out. Kids are always going to blast themselves with something to freak out their parents, as long as everybody isn't pulled into one great society, like China, all moving one way, but look how much attitudes have changed in twenty years, attitudes toward sex, and the military, and the government. Some good things are happening. I don't know where it goes, and I doubt if the ruling families will change, but other things do."

I had my usual engineering questions for Hal. Did mantrams really vibrate parts of the body?

"Sure. They clear the mind of thought. Even the Egyptians used Om."

Could you vibrate parts of the body with English?

"Sure, but you'd have to construct it. Sanskrit is a conscious language, built around the vibrations. Look, in English—O-o-o-mmmmmooonnnney, M-O-N-E-Y, see what vibrations? Try money! Money! Hawr hawr hawr!"

Hal's booming laugh went echoing through the woods.

"Other cultures have explored the nervous system, and the levels you can get to with it," Hal said. "And you know that, so why are you asking me? Now beat it, and let us get back to work."

I walked back out to the car. I had inched forward about fifty or sixty yards over the ruts when HEY! H-E-Y! went rolling over the car and into the woods. I looked in the rear-view mirror. The sandal-clad, heavily bellied Falstaffian figure was puffing toward the car. I stopped. He caught up, and leaned down to the window. There was sweat in his beard.

"You gonna come back here?"

"I don't know," I said.

"Well, you can if you want to," Hal said.

I didn't know why I would come back, but I was curiously touched.

"Come back sometime and see what my kids have done," he said.

"Okay," I said.

Hal stood up, and slapped the door of the car as if it were the flanks of a horse he wanted to get moving. I put the car back in gear.

"DON'T TAKE ANY WOODEN NICKELS!" he shouted, and I drove away. In the rear-view mirror I could seem him standing, legs apart, hands on hip, in the middle of the road, watching.

VI: | Packagers

Practices we call out of the ordinary have given some psychologists new fields to study. By bringing the practices into a contemporary vocabulary like that of psychology, we make them lose some of their strangeness, which reduces both attraction and repulsion. Once we have a vocabulary for the exotic, we have made it seem more "real," or at least "real" in the terms that we can handle.

Given the appetites and needs for some of the techniques, it is not surprising, in a business society, that, as Swami Hal says, this has become a business. The gurus et al. don't put it that way, and most of them are teaching something quite traditional and specific.

But in addition to the people passing out something very traditional, there are also people who cut across the fields, synthesizing and packaging, interpreting, considering not only the source but the audience.

Some kids are out following gurus, but there are also people signing up for self-help courses that take a weekend or two, or a couple of nights.

> The mind-cure principles are beginning so to pervade the air that one catches their spirit second hand. One hears of "The Gospel of Relaxation," of the "Don't Worry Movement," of people who repeat to themselves "Youth, health, vigor!" when dressing in the morning. . . .

That is not from yesterday, it is from 1900, William James, *The Varieties of Religious Experience.* So packaging in this country is hardly new. Then, as now, the "mind-cure principles" were activities chiefly of the middle and upper classes, discretionary income diversions. What is interesting is that—though the packagers do not always know it—the ideas and processes they dispense are three to five thousand years old.

MEETINGS WITH
REMARKABLE MEN

GURDJIEFF is dead, and I have no idea whether he thought of himself as a packager. Certainly not the kind of packager who can take ideas, or exotic processes, and sell them in a course. Yet Gurdjieff's ideas filter down into contemporary courses, as we will see; and they are not even Gurdjieff's ideas, they are much older than that. Gurdjieff's processes and exercises are designed to bring people out of their ordinary consciousness, to "wake them up."

Some years ago I had a brief correspondence with a former research biochemist, Robert de Ropp. De Ropp had written a very interesting book called *The Master Game*. Seven years after the brief correspondence, I went to see him in Santa Rosa, California, where he was leading a small Gurdjieff group and getting ready to survive the end of the world.

What people demand from life, De Ropp wrote, is not comfort, wealth or esteem, but games worth playing. People who can't find a game worth playing fall prey to accidie, defined by the Fathers of the Church a long time ago as one of the Deadly Sins, paralysis of the will, generalized boredom, total sloth, now a prelude to what is called "mental illness." Among the broad games that De Ropp listed were the wealth game, the fame game, the glory or victory game, the householder game, the games of art, science and religion. All games played according to rules, trials of wit or strength with definite aims. At the time I had just finished observing that many people in the world of money did not pursue money as the object but rather as a process in a game to be played. This was only one of De Ropp's games, which left me with my ace trumped and the nice correspondence with De Ropp.

The aim of the Master Game is "the attainment of full consciousness or real awakening," wrote De Ropp. Man's ordinary state of consciousness, his so-called waking state, is not the highest level of consciousness of which he is capable. "In fact, this state is so far from real awakening that it could appropriately be called a form of somnambulism, a condition of 'waking sleep.'" Today, De Ropp warned, in this culture, players of the Master Game are regarded as "queer or slightly mad." Further, he warned, teachers and groups involved in the Master Game are difficult to find: "They do not advertise, they operate under disguises. Moreover, there exists an abundance of frauds and fools who pass themselves off as teachers without having any right to do so." So it isn't easy. But "there is in some, not all, men a distinctive hunger for experience in another dimension, for an elevated or expanded state of consciousness." Huxley had said, "The urge to transcend self-conscious selfhood is a principal appetite of the soul." Hence the false track, De Ropp said, of the drug trips.

The idea of a group with a non-advertising Master quietly waking themselves up was very intriguing, I told De Ropp, in the mid-Sixties. I could spare, say, Thursday afternoons from 5:00 to 7:30 for such a venture. De Ropp said it wasn't that easy, you had to devote all your efforts and possibly leave the country to play such a game, and he sent me a little booklet with a picture of this exotic Levantine with black handlebar mustaches called Gurdjieff. I couldn't make head or tail of the little booklet and sent it back, and it was years before I even got to review the Gurdjieff literature.

"Wherever did you get this stuff?" I had asked De Ropp, and that was apparently a question that people also wanted to know of Gurdjieff, for some who have written about it went tracking over Asia Minor and Central Asia to find sources. Gurdjieff himself never gave anybody a straight answer. He was born George Georgiades in Kars, in eastern Turkey; the name Gurdjieff is the Caucasian form of the Greek name, and Gurdjieff grew up in the swirl of Greeks, Armenians, Yezidis and Assyrians that moved in one direction or another, depending on whether the Russian Army or the Turkish Army was in the valley of Kars.

Gurdjieff's father, said Gurdjieff, could sing the ballads of Gilgamesh that had been sung in the valley of Kars three thousand years before. His aphorisms have the wisdom of peasant aphorisms everywhere in the world:

> If you wish to be rich, make friends with the police.
> If you wish to be famous, make friends with the reporters.
> If you wish to lose your faith, make friends with the priest.
> If you wish to be full, make friends with your mother-in-law.
> If you wish to sleep, make friends with your wife.

Gurdjieff could speak Armenian, his mother's tongue, and Turkish, which everyone spoke, and in that era a knowledge of Turkish could take you from Albania to Tibet, a range of 6,000 miles. One who follows the Work, said Gurdjieff once, "must be able to make his living with his left foot." That presumes a certain living by the wits. In one account, Gurdjieff worked in the building of a railroad in Greece, and though the plans for the railroad were already drawn, he sold to several towns the right to get the railroad. He seems to have been a healer, and in fact earned half a ship by curing a Greek youth, and he seems to have been enough of a hypnotist that he described one of his tasks as that of freeing people from suggestibility, the mass hypnosis to which they were so prone. He certainly knew carpets and antiques, and when he and a small group of followers were caught, in the Russian Revolution, between the White and Red armies, Gurdjieff was able to raise money by doing some carpet trading. In another account, while traveling he comes across some Russians who are about to throw away barrels of herring because they have been pickled, and he buys the herring and sells it a couple of days later to people who love pickled herring. That aspect of Gurdjieff does not seem uncommon to the area. An old Lebanese joke has a grandfather asking a four-year-old how much is two and two, and the four-year-old says, are you buying or selling?

Buying and selling was not Gurdjieff's preoccupation. He also studied the origins of Christian liturgy in Cappadocia. As a Czarist Russian agent, he traveled as far as Tibet, and one of his biographers, J. G. Bennett, was the British intelligence officer, fluent in central Asian languages, who kept a dossier on him. And on the travels, Gurdjieff is supposed to have spent time in the centers of the Masters of Wisdom.

The Masters of Wisdom are an old tradition of central Asia. There are, it is said, some people with extra powers, who affect the destiny of mankind from time to time, changing the course of events, averting calamity, injecting new modes of thought into the needs of the changing age. In Tibet, the Masters of Wisdom would be reincarnating Rimpoche Lamas. Gurdjieff's route took him to Samarkand, Bokhara, Tashkent, Afghanistan and Tibet —marvelous names, suitable for the British Victorian adventure stories. Gurdjieff's route is speculation, because he never gave people a straight answer and operated by allusion. And in Samarkand and Tashkent and Balkh, Gurdjieff hung out with some of the teaching schools of Sufism. Sufis are Moslem mystics, and we will come back to them in more detail in a moment. Some schools seem more mystic than Moslem; the Yesevis developed music and exercises for the emotional and physical centers in man that had shamanistic origins. The Mevlevis—there are various spellings—were the whirling dervishes. There is a hierarchy, according to some of this doctrine, which receives revelations of Divine Purpose and transmits them through Transformed Ones to mankind. The Transformed Ones have the gift of transmitting *baraka*, or grace, a word similar to *baruch*, or blessing, in Hebrew.

Gurdjieff and some of his followers eventually went to Berlin, then to Paris, to New York, and back to Paris. What Gurdjieff taught certainly had the Sufi techniques—in New York they put on a demonstration of dervish dancing that left the audience somewhat confused—but almost nothing of Islam.

What did Gurdjieff say? "Man is a machine. He is asleep. He can control nothing; everything controls him." Mechanical man, mechanical desires.

Gurdjieff is not easy to read; he wasn't attuned to writing, and what he does write comes in "legominism," or the transmission of wisdom in a baser form. He had some talented writers around him: Katherine Mansfield died at his Paris mansion, and Kathryn Hulme, who wrote *The Nun's Story*, gave an account of her years with Gurdjieff in *The Undiscovered Country*. So the stories about him have a good deal more charm than those by him. Miss Hulme, for example, decided to give up smoking. Mechanical man; mechanical desires. After a year and a lot of conscious struggle she told Gurdjieff she had licked this particular form of slavery, whereupon he handed her one of his Russian cigarettes. "Anybody can *not* smoke," he said.

In other words, if you're not a slave to smoking, and you're not a slave to not-smoking, *then* you're not a slave any more and you can do whatever you want with your freedom. But being free is harder than being a slave to either smoking or not-smoking, the perils of attachment. Sufi story:

> Two men are sitting in a café, and a camel walks past.
> "What does that make you think of?" says the first.
> "Food," says the other.
> "Since when are camels used for food?"
> "I haven't eaten today, everything makes me think of food."

Translating from the psychology of perception, we perceive literally what we need to perceive, and tune out what we don't want.

One account of life with Gurdjieff was written by Fritz Peters, who was eleven years old when his aunt took him to live at Gurdjieff's "Institute" outside of Paris. Peters and the other children were bored, so they played pranks, tormenting one old Russian by stealing his false teeth and his reading glasses. The governess in charge of the children brought them up on appropriate charges before Gurdjieff. He rewarded them, peeling off ten francs for each offense. " 'What you not understand is, not everyone can be troublemaker, like you,' said Gurdjieff. 'This important in life, like yeast for bread . . . people live in status-quo, live only by habit, automatically . . . people not understand about learning, think necessary talk all the time, learn through mind, words. Not so. Many things only learn from feeling, even sensation.' " The children shocked the Institute, and the Gurdjieff shocked the children—and the governess. Shocks were to be welcomed; they kept one present-tense and unattached.

"Accustom yourself to nothing," Gurdjieff said, but he did his best to accustom himself to roast baby lamb, extraordinary vegetables, exotic candies, and marvelous liqueurs. His activities were financed by donations: "shearing sheep," he called it.

Sometimes it seems as though there was a mountain in central Asia somewhere with the river of these concepts coming down, splitting, and flowing in different directions, east to China and the Tao, south to India, west and southwest to Asia Minor and the Middle East. The Zen archer has his student start with breathing, to eliminate the "I" and become the same as the arrow and the target. Chuang-tzu tells of Prince Hui's wonderful cook, who is so in harmony with the Tao, the cosmos, that when he wields his meat cleaver the stroke he makes is the very essence of the motion to be made with the meat cleaver. An ordinary cook changes his chopper once a month because he hacks, a good cook once a year because he cuts, but Prince Hui's cook's chopper is as fresh as if from the whetstone after nineteen years, and from the precision and single-mindedness of the chopping Prince Hui learned how to live.

"Do one thing at a time," said Gurdjieff, and he had his followers work at handicrafts, cobbling and tailoring, but it is doubtful from the accounts whether any of them ever learned to repair a shoe. Gurdjieff taught that men were three-centered, the three centers being roughly the head, the heart and the "moving center" below the navel, the *hara* or center of gravity in Zen. To educate the "moving center" and draw energy away from the "noise machine" in the head, there were rhythmic activities—sawing wood, spading the garden—and "sacred gymnastics."

Nobody has tested, psychophysiologically, the effect of prosaic rhythmic activities, but we could almost predict the results. In times of great stress, instinctively, Rose Kennedy would go outside and bounce a tennis ball over and over. Digging in the garden has been known to relieve the pressures of commerce, and the circadian rhythms of nature are sought by people on vacations. Jack Nicklaus has probably never heard of Gurdjieff, or Prince Hui and the wonderful cook, but he plays in a trance and has a golf stroke that is the equivalent of the perfectly balanced motion of the wonderful cook's cleaver whistling through the air. Prince Hui's golf pro. It gets less mysterious when you think of mundane examples, and if you think of it as educating the right-brained activities and the muscle hungers and muscle memories that don't get much of a chance in our sedentary world, it gets almost scientific.

Not that Gurdjieff ever gets scientific; science demands communication, and Gurdjieff didn't think people valued what came too easily. If that were all there is to Gurdjieff, then we could enjoy the fables.

But Gurdjieff is also full of astral spirits, and the earth being food for the moon, and the law of octaves, and incredible chemistry involving carbon and hydrogen and oxygen—not the way they are in the chemistry textbook, but as alchemical symbols, I suppose, back to "legominism."

The Alchemist, 1610, faces a complaint from Master Surly that his terms are "a pretty kind of game, somewhat like tricks o' the cards, to cheat a man, with charming." Sir? says the Alchemist.

> *Was not all the knowledge*
> *Of the Egyptians writ in mystic symbols?*
> *Speak not the Scriptures, oft, in parables?*
> *Are not the choicest fables of the poets . . .*
> *Wrapped in perplexing allegories?*

"Two hundred fully conscious people," said Gurdjieff, "could change the whole world." From time to time groups gather to do the Gurdjieff exercises, to educate other parts of the body, to study all the vibrations, to remember themselves. Remembering oneself is one of the prime Gurdjieff exercises, not so far from the instructions of the Khwajagan Sufi masters: be present at every breath, do not let your attention wander, learn not to identify yourself with anything, remember your Friend, i.e., God. (The Khwajagan instructions, possibly from the twelfth century, were written up in Persian in the fifteenth century, and in English in 1958. From some cultures there is a time lag into ours.)

But as the distance from Gurdjieff increases, the spell diminishes. The Gurdjieffians I met turned up in other disciplines, after years of waiting for something to happen, having woven their baskets and done the "stop" exercise so long.

De Ropp's small group lived in a dramatic contemporary house in Santa Rosa, given by an oil-service heir. Posters: mechanical men, mechanical desires. "I spent twelve years with Ouspensky in England," De Ropp said, in clipped British tones. Ouspensky was Gurdjieff's chief pupil, and the author of a number of books about Gurdjieff. Don't go to Gurdjieff, Ouspensky told De Ropp. "Gurdjieff's quite mad."

We took a small tour. "We're practically self-sufficient here," said De Ropp. "We grow all our own vegetables, we have our cows, we churn our own butter, we press our own cheese. When it all blows, we'll still be here." When it all blows? When there is no more Pacific Gas & Electric? I was admiring the electric mixer, which served when the butter churn broke, and the splendid ivy-green double-sized refrigerator. "Some of these things will run on methane gas," said De Ropp, "and we're going to get a windmill. Why don't Americans make good windmills? Why should we have to go to Australia or Switzerland?"

De Ropp called his group the Church of the Earth. His chief delight was taking his kayak out into the Pacific and fishing. He wanted to take me kayak-fishing. The fish were going to provide good protein after the collapse, after the energy crisis and the resource crisis and the other crises had finished their work.

"You poor fellow," he said. "The water is already around your ankles, there, in the cities. Like the *Titanic*, just a little brush, hardly felt by anybody, the orchestra keeps playing. Oh, can't you see what will happen to New York? The elevators will stop. The subways will stop. It will be a dead city in twenty or thirty years. And the owl and the bittern will be heard in the streets. The owl and the bittern will be heard in the streets."

De Ropp had been a scientist at Rockefeller University in New York, as well as a research chemist at Lederle.

"I gather you don't like New York," I said, "but must you wish it complete destruction?"

"The owl and the bittern will be heard in the streets," he said firmly. "You better come kayak-fishing with us."

He seemed very cheerful about it and very healthy. "We need more people here with technical skills, carpentry and plumbing," he said.

"So do all the communes," I said. "They're long on English majors and short on carpenters."

"This is just the right place," De Ropp said. "Right climate, not too far from the ocean. Gurdjieff would have found some rich widows, and told them, 'I shall fleece you.' They loved that, rich widows. We should do that, I suppose."

"Carpenters and rich widows," I said. "If I meet any, I'll send them along."

"You don't have too much time," De Ropp said.

A year later, I sent him the windmill catalog from another commune.

But that day, when I got to San Francisco, I told some friends I had been visiting De Ropp.

"Oh, yeah, *The Master Game*, that's a good book," they said. "Is he still doing the Sufi number up there?"

WHO'S A SUFI?

I am not sure how "Sufi" got to be such a good word on the consciousness circuit. "I have just come back from India," said Baba Ram Dass in one of his lectures, later published, "and next I am going to Chile to study with a Sufi master." Maybe it is the idea of these fully awakened, conscious people, operating from power centers in the high plains of central Asia. Any certainty is better than the uncertainties of life; it is really nice to have a They who are secretly running things. Every once in a while I have a qualm myself. Here is the International Monetary Fund which meets in Basel and tells the Bank of England to shape up, and warns the Bank of Italy that Italy is falling apart, and raps the U.S. Treasury over the knuckles for the Eurodollar overhang, some international leverage there, and who's the new chairman? A Dutch Sufi. Dutch? Sufi? What the hell are they planning in Samarkand?

A Sufi—he said he was a Sufi—came to one of my classes with a set of drums, which he played with his hands. We all formed a circle and danced around, while he chanted: *La illaha il'l Allah.* For two hours. He was one hell of a drummer. Also, when he really got going, his eyeballs rolled up into his head so that only the whites were showing. Very restful, he told me later. As for the rest of us, our palms got very sticky, the movements got more ragged, and finally some people fell down. I suspect that's something of what you get if you go to one of the Sufi weekends advertised amidst the yoga retreats. (Amidst the same ads now are those for Pentecostal churches and Hasidic Jewish retreats. We have chanting and dancing, say the latter, almost wistfully, more to recapture their own than to proselytize, and of course they have chanting and dancing, and have had for hundreds of years.)

Or you can go to weekends where Sufi stories are read aloud from the collections of Idries Shah. You hear them aloud, over and over, so they can sink into level of consciousness other than the normal linear one. Most of the stories are teaching stories, but unlike parables they are funny, at least the first time. The hero is a wise fool called Mulla Nasrudin, pronounced Nas-ru-DEEN. Nasrudin is down on his hands and knees in the street, and his friend comes along and says what are you doing, and Nasrudin says looking for my house key, and the friend starts to help him, saying where did you drop it, and Nasrudin says by the door, and the friend says, but why don't we look there, then? And Nasrudin says, but there is more light here.

Then you are to think: in your own life, do you look where the light is, or where the key is?

Nasrudin is sprinkling bread crumbs in the street. Why are you doing that? says the straight man. To keep the tigers away, says Nasrudin. But there are no tigers around here, says the straight man. Exactly, says Nasrudin. Effective, isn't it? Do we do that daily, in some way?

In the Hasidic stories of Judaism, there are *rebbes* and beggars. The beggar comes to the door, and the Hasidic Nasrudin looks around, sees a ring lying on a table, and gives it to the beggar. The *rebbe's* wife screams at him, you dolt (wives are always screaming you dolt, in both Nasrudin and the Hasidic stories)—you dolt, that was a very valuable ring. The householder runs after the beggar and says, hey, friend, that ring is really valuable, don't let the jeweler cheat you when you sell it.

Once I mused, in an article, on the phrase "Sufi master." One was supposed to know a Sufi master by coming into his presence, the baraka would zap you. But how would you know otherwise? "Sufi master," I wrote, "is not like Berkeley Ph.D. You cannot call up and check, because there is no Sufi U." I got a letter signed in flowing Arabic script, but when I went to see the gentleman he turned out to be an American executive, tall, blue-eyed, blond, Scottish-surnamed, not a flowing Arab at all, with an office on Fifth Avenue. He had gotten the Call and gone to Teheran and been initiated, a serious Moslem, fasting, Ramadan, bowing five times a day to Mecca (back to Fifth Avenue, face toward the East River); I asked his secretary if he still bowed to Mecca five times a day when his schedule was crowded and she said yes, he just closes the door. The executive wrote to me because he wanted me to be aware that there was a lot of baloney around, that Idries Shah wasn't a descendant of the Prophet Mohammed, like he said, he was the son of the chauffeur at the British consul someplace in Pakistan, and true, he had written down some of the Nasrudin stories, those he hadn't made up and so on.

So I began to work on the Sufis. I had lunch with two Middle Eastern diplomats. They wanted to talk about the price of oil. They were both scholarly fellows, so midway through lunch I brought up the Sufis. You have a lot of Sufis in your country, don't you?

Well, er, yes, mystics, aren't they, Hassan? Yes, mystics, rather quaint old fellows, chant a lot.

It was as if they had asked me with great intensity what I knew about the ghost dancers of the Sioux.

And then, gradually, I met serious scholars who gave me serious books; there are Sufis all over the world, and, though it gets to this country only in the Department of Asian and Middle Eastern Studies at the University, quite a bit about Sufism. So you go through *The Sufi Orders in Islam*, and Jalal ud-din-Rumi's Math-nawi-yi Ma nawi, and various books all titled *The Mystics of Islam*, and *The Life and Times of Shaikh Farid-ud-din Ganj-i-Shakar*, and pretty soon you can tell the widespread and moderate Qadiriyah from the Sanusiyah and the Mevlevis and Bektashiyah from the Haddawah, who "do not spoil God's day by work." And something's missing. It's become Islamic History, or Comparative Religion. Out on the consciousness circuit nobody wants to know how Al-Ghazzali pulled a whole synthesis together in the eleventh century, they want to know the Secrets of the Sufi Masters. How to get high. Does that pattern in the carpet really change your consciousness, thus the "flying carpet"? See, if you stare at that special geometry, it will pop the bounds of that left-brained pattern you impose upon the world, and if you don't, it's just a carpet. The sober, left-brained books Rumpelstiltskin away the mystery, and the techniques become "autohypnotic states, hal, plural ahwal, through certain practices of concentration or frenzied dancing and chanting of certain formulas." That fixes it, just a little autohypnosis, from concentration and frenzied dancing. Black Elk doesn't make it rain, Black Elk does his thing and it rains anyway; we have a lousy weatherman and that's why he was predicting continued fair and hot.

A couple of scholars had furtive looks about them, as if dabbling in this stuff was messing with djinn. You remember the djinn, when Aladdin rubbed his lamp, another symbol you see of sleeping powers, and you have to consider quite seriously before you dive into these depths of mind, because when the djinn gets out of the lamp—I liked that uneasiness. I missed the mystery coming out of the power centers over the mountains on the high plains of central Asia. Somebody somewhere ought to know how to get to super-consciousness.

Thanks for the books, gentlemen, I read the ones in English, I have to give the ones in Turkish and Persian back to you as regretfully I am not equipped, and by the way, have you ever tried some of this stuff? Well, er, furtive look, one shouldn't speak too lightly of these things.

There is, of course, a Sufi story to cover this feeling. (It also appears in Russian as the bishop and the pious staretzki.) A scholarly Sufi is walking along the edge of the lake, pondering moral and scholastic problems, and he hears a dervish call coming from an island in the middle of the lake. The scholarly Sufi listens for a while and keeps walking, and it bugs him because the recitation is all wrong, the pronunciation is wrong, and finally he hires a boat and rows out to the island; and there is a dervish sitting in a hut, chanting this chant all wrong. And the scholarly Sufi says, friend, I know you'll appreciate this. And the scholar recites the correct way. I have rowed out here because you're doing it all wrong, this is the way it goes. The island dervish thanks him, and the scholarly one starts rowing to shore, and he hears splish splish splish and turns around, and the second dervish is running across the *surface* of the water to catch up, and says, "Say, friend, could you give me the right way again, I didn't quite get it."

NEXT WEEK,
SATORI 24

OF all the gurus that there are, surely we must have had the only Oscar.

Oscar Ichazo was the "sufi master" that Baba Ram Dass said he was going to Chile to study with. Baba Ram Dass didn't go, but several dozen Americans did. They knew of Oscar from Claudio Naranjo, a Chilean psychiatrist, co-author of *The Psychology of Meditation*, who led groups at Esalen. Oscar had developed a training that could take people to new levels of consciousness, a super package. The Americans spent ten months in Chile, and then forty-two of them decided that the experience was so important they would form a teaching house in New York, to start the spreading of the word. Why New York? The energy of New York excited Oscar: "New York," he said, "has more people prepared for reality than the world has previously seen in one culture." The teaching group took a full-page ad in *The New York Times* headlined THE MOSQUITO THAT BITES THE IRON BULL, and mentioning such exercises as "proto-analysis," and "psychocatalyzers" leading to "the awareness of the tiger," "Permanent 24." A very mysterious ad indeed. Oscar's program was called Arica, after the town in Chile where he had been teaching.

Arica had a drumbeater other than Claudio Naranjo, and that was John Lilly. Lilly had perhaps more academic credentials than anyone on the consciousness circuit. He was an M.D., a psychiatrist, a research neurophysiologist, and after a lot of work on the brain and sensory deprivation he worked with government and foundation aid on communicating with dolphins in a special lab in the Virgin Islands. The dolphin work had brought him a certain degree of fame. Lilly was very enthusiastic about Arica at that point, both in interviews and in a book he wrote called *The Center of the Cyclone.* "Successful heads of corporations," Lilly said in his interview in *Psychology Today,* "already operate at Satori 24. They are joyfully locked into their work. But they have never had maps which suggested to them the possibility of achieving more blissful levels of consciousness."

If I had to translate that Satori 24, I would say it was Jack Nicklaus' golf stroke, or Prince Hui's cook's meat-cleaver stroke, in everything, all the time. The number came from Gurdjieff's levels of vibrations, and as translated by Oscar and John Lilly, the normal state is 96, or ego with a vengeance, getting along, but with pain, guilt, fear, and sometimes alcohol. Forty-eight is neutral, getting and receiving information, 24 is professionalism that can be done without the verbalizing mind. From there down it gets more mystic: 12 is "blissful state, making the Christ, the green qutub, realization of baraka, cosmic energy, heightened bodily awareness"; 6 is "point source of consciousness, energy, light, and love"; 3 is "classical satori, fusion with universal mind." Lilly had, Lilly said, been through all those levels.

(To Gurdjieff's levels of vibrations, Oscar added six more, ranging from 192 to 6,000, all quite disagreeable. Society is in 6,000 most of the time.)

The course was for three months, six days a week, fourteen hours a day, and it cost $3,000. That program certainly did assume an affluent society. It seemed about as far out as you could go, and the very intensity attracted me. Why not start far out, and work one's way back, in the explorations of mind?

"You seem to have created," wrote one of Oscar's interviewers, "the nearest thing we now have to a university for altered states of consciousness." But unlike university, we did not know, at any time, the name of the course we were taking. We would simply show up and do what the trainers told us, rather like falling out into the company street in the Army, awright you guys, first platoon, get in the truck. The Army simile would occur to me again and again—first the lack of a verbal framework, then the physical qualities of the experience, and finally some of the qualities of shared experience.

Among the trainees were a handful of psychologists and psychiatrists, another handful of writers and critics, and a number of Esalenites. But the bulk of the class of sixty were either students and/or women who, through divorce or otherwise, had reached a point of some confusion in their lives. We didn't live together, though many of the trainees shared apartments.

The lack of verbal framework was quite deliberate. If we had started with that, it was said, then we would have experienced the experience through the construct we had already set up verbally.

So: we went on a high-protein diet. No white sugar, no alcohol, low carbohydrates and no animals that are scavengers, e.g., no pork or ham, no crab. We did weeks of largely physical activity: an hour-and-a-half gym, most of whose movements were adapted from hatha yoga. "You do not do the exercises, they will do you." Not surprisingly, the trainees began to lose weight and look better. We did hours of chanting. We did breathing exercises to the *Bolero*. Sit on the floor, open your arms gradually, breathe in all through the ascending phrase, out in the descending phrase. That's hard to do at first. "The *Bolero* is Sufi music," said the trainers. "Different phrases vibrate parts of the body."

We did a lot of dance and movement exercises. That is when I thought, American men get short-changed, because most of their physical activity is competitive and in sudden, tensed bursts of movement. The men are supposed to play football and basketball and golf and tennis and bowling, but it is okay for the women to take a dance class. If you look at the men's sports, you see that it is the warm-ups that have the rhythms and the centering, not the games themselves (the lazy pitches in the bull pen, the ball being tossed around the infield.)

We had some talented musicians drumming for these classes in movement, and videotapes to watch ourselves. We had imagination exercises to sensitize parts of the body—feel your feet gold, your calves gold, your knees gold—that I later found in the Christian mystics. Each of these body parts was supposed to have a mind function, the nose senses possibilities, the hands and feet, goals, and so on. Thought, the trainers reported, does not only belong to the brain. The head must cease its tyrannical control. Consciousness is to be homogenized into the whole organism. If your wires are crossed, say, between your needs (mouth and stomach) and your goals, you make goals of your needs, like sex and hunger.

And we began to do group work that had overtones of encounter. We were given nine types of ego, a kind of personality that we had adapted vis-à-vis the world. The Indolents are lazy and manipulate people, the Plans always live in the future and never quite get around to what they're going to do, and the Go's believe that work is everything and they are their work and they work three times as hard as they have to, very thorough and Germanic. The staff had already assigned each of us into a group, with the help of a questionnaire, but in the guessing game many people guessed correctly.

My group turned out to be Go. "I'm so glad we're Go's," said a matron in my group. "I certainly wouldn't have wanted to be anything else. Now, let's get organized."

"But we have to *give up* this fixation," said another woman. "We work so hard because of our *lacks*."

The antidote to the fixation was a posture, or asana, for meditation. In our case, it was holy law, or: the universe will run without you.

(Later, when it came to administration, the Go's quickly took over much of the work, and the Indolents somehow manipulated them. The Plans lay on the floor planning, and the Stinges hid in the corner. Everybody seemed very relieved to be playing his role in the open, and nobody was in a hurry to give up the role he was used to, even though that prevented him from being "free.")

There is nothing particularly radical about a personality grid, and the "Pygmalion effect" says that if you try an experiment in a classroom and tell the class that brown-eyed children are smart and blue-eyed children are dumb, by the end of the semester they start testing that way.)

All of this, so far, without Oscar. He appeared one evening— in his socks, like everybody else, all shoes left always at the door —looking not at all like a guru but like, well, a Latin-American, smallish, balding, mustached, sport-shirted. He spoke with a heavy Spanish accent.

Oscar's talks—we saw a lot of him from that point—always had something of the air of a Presidential press conference because there were always twenty microphones in front of him. Everybody with a tape recorder wanted his own cassette. Oscar surprised us. This training, he said, was not for self-improvement, it was for humanity, because the planet faced a great crisis, a great cosmic wave, in the next ten years. The crisis was related to the wounding of the earth with pollution, depleting resources, and wars. Humanity had to come to consciousness, or face extinction.

Further: the training we were being given would never be given again. Its purpose was to train *teachers*; it would go on another two months beyond the original three, but that wouldn't cost anything, and in fact those who needed money would be paid. (I spent thirty minutes on the Finance Committee, possibly the shortest time I have ever been in any job. I was used to post-Renaissance bookkeeping: if you don't have the money in the bank, you don't pay everybody a lot, you set up reserves. One stalwart said, "I can't be in *satori* on less than $1,000 a month," and so everybody was paid $1,000 a month until the money ran out.)

The physical and experiential sectors of the training declined in favor of hours of theory, the traps for each ego type, the asanas for each ego type, and finally a theory of what Oscar called "trialectics," everything is process. Oscar liked making up compound words: kinerhythm was moving the rock with the mantram, psychocalisthenics was the adopted hatha yoga gym, psychocatalyzers were the virtues we were to seek, "cutting the diamond" and the Ark were group exercises. Group work, Oscar said, enabled us to progress much faster than individuals in Oriental disciplines.

Arica, said Oscar, would have to become a tribe. Eventually all humanity would have to become a tribe. With the tribe taking care of needs, the individual ego trip could be given up.

The tribal community took care of some needs so well that most of the couples split up. We went through exercises to rid ourselves of the karma, or consequences of past actions, of money, sex, and power. Some of those who had money and had freed themselves of its karmic powers made contributions that supported the group, like the good tribal members they were. "Karma cleaning" was basically confession and desensitization. A sure cure for prurience is to listen to people telling the sexual story of their lives incident by incident. We would gather in small groups, sit in a circle on the floor, and recite. After three or four days the groups would change, and the stories began to sound more and more ordinary. Some people could tell such a story in two hours, and some took all day.

"Let's see, that was the year I was fourteen," said the pleasant blonde, "and then when I was fifteen I left this convent school and went to the high school. I guess I smoked a little dope and when my parents were away I moved in with my old man—"

—it took a minute to grasp that her old man was not her father, but what Grandmother would call her beau—

"—and we didn't get along so I got another old man, and toward the end of that summer I got into a very bad space with my mother because I told her I might be knocked up, and I wasn't sure which of my old men, oh, and there was Charlie, he was black, that got my mother very uptight because my mother is, you know, country club, and my father was working all the time, and then one night—"

I remember rousing myself from my torpor on the floor to think of these California rich conservative parents, poor bastards pacing the living room, where did we fail? She had riding lessons and ballet lessons and tennis lessons and the best parochial schools and we loved her, where did we go wrong?

"—and then in my junior year in high school, I balled this guy, George, he was—"

—let's see, we ought to be in college by lunchtime, we could be through by three-thirty with any luck because she's only twenty-two, by ten o'clock tonight we could get Harry from thirteen to college, that would bring us to Louise tomorrow morning—next week, money—

—yet there is an effect. Why, said the women to the men, look at all the energy you have put into this feeling that you had to perform, like a contest. And the effect of stony silence on recitations that people thought were quite dramatic reduced the drama. We had spent all that energy for sex, money and power, and here it sounded like an oral reading of the *Congressional Record*.

But even in the fusing tribal activities, all was not love. For one thing, there was an A group and a B group, A being higher level, faster progress, B holding up the caravan, yet, Alice in Wonderland, there were no rational criteria for who was in A and who was in B ever articulated, a vibrational level, more, and people moved from B to A and A to B, or were told they had moved, and when they got to A they were a little cool to the B's who were holding up progress.

I have the feeling there was a lesson in all this, that A's and B's are quite arbitrary, and that Oscar was yanking everybody around to show there is no day-to-day tenure in life. But some people got to stay in A all the time. And then there was always the threat that people could be fired from the school. No reason, no appeal, they would simply be gone in the night, one less body in the company street the next morning. As the training went on, and the trainees had to decide not to go back to school, or to their jobs, this threat became more serious.

As long as the course was simply a course, this wasn't too much of a problem, but many were swept up in the Mission to save Humanity. "This school," said Oscar, "is the most important thing going on in the planet at this time. Arica is going to reconcile mysticism and the modern world. We are talking about a different psychological order of man, with a different psychological structure. Totally balanced, instincts in harmony."

Underlying the mission were quasi-religious overtones, though not distinctly from any one creed. "Essence" in Arica, as in Gurdjieff, as in who knows what before, is the natural state of man, divine unity, but—like the Fall—he loses it, falling prey to the Ego and its fears for survival, its traps and its passions. "There is no peace short of being within the divine consciousness," said Oscar. "The Western secular attempt to live without knowledge of the sacred unity of all things is a failure." Is this a new religion? Oscar was asked. A new church? Oh no, Oscar said. The disciplines are old: Buddhist, Tao, Islamic, Christian, but we don't ask for belief or faith, we just say, try these things and see what happens.

So being fired from the school was not only being dropped along the wayside on the road to Satori 24, it was being dropped from the mission that would save the world. ("Two hundred fully conscious people," Gurdjieff had said, "can change the world.") But alas, where there is a Utopian vision there is frequently a Grand Inquisitor. We have to live in an imperfect society. The Perfect Society has Secret Police, to make sure everything stays perfect.

There was a word in Arica, *chich*, from Oscar's Spanish, *chicherero*, chatter, the trivial talk of the mind. That's what we had to lose. And certain authors and composers and people were more *chich*-y than others—Beethoven had a lot of *chich,* said Oscar. And one night, after a drop to B by an unusual number of people, a committee announced there was too much *chich* in people's minds, and that the committee was proposing that it come to people's apartments and weed out their books and records, taking away the *chich*-y ones, just out of tribal spirit and group love, and then the group's consciousness could be pure again and we could make rapid progress.

And that was too much. Here was Arica barely two years old, and about to have an Index, just like the Roman Church! "Well, Oscar *was* trained as a Jesuit," whispered one mutineer. "I don't want to live in Dublin," I said. "Church censorship. Half the good movies never get there." Somebody else sarcastically suggested a great book-burning on the steps of the Public Library, and the committee beat a humiliated retreat.

That was an important moment. As much as everybody wanted

to live in Satori 24, they wanted to live even more in the U.S. Constitution. I went home and read the Constitution, which nobody does after they leave school, except lawyers. The Constitution seemed bigger than the *B-Minor Mass*. It is a fantastic document. All the transactions going on between the gentlemen who wrote it produced a state of extremely high energy, they were stoned just doing the job. In fact, they wrote it in Satori 24.

"Where did you get all this stuff?" I asked Oscar. Some things I had heard were murky with legend. Oscar was from a wealthy family in Bolivia and during World War II they put up some Japanese on the estancia who had to leave the coastline in Peru and Chile, and among the Japanese was a Samurai master who, for room and board, taught Oscar and his brother martial arts—

Oscar was ripe for all this because, if he was not an epileptic, he had attacks which certainly seem like epilepsy, starting at six and a half. "I would experience a lot of pain, my heart would pound, fear I was going to die, then . . . I would die, after a while I would return to my body and discover I was alive. I was terrified, I became very lonely . . ."

Oscar was going to a Jesuit school, and he hoped Communion and prayer would help; it led instead to his disillusion with the Church. And he did learn the martial arts from the wandering Japanese, and his family owned some land so he sought out the Indian shamans, and they introduced him to psychedelic drugs, and then there was hypnotism and yoga and William James and reading in anatomy and physiology, still trying to find out about his condition, and when he was nineteen he left the University at La Paz and became the coffee boy in a Gurdjieff group in Buenos Aires. "About two-thirds of the group were Orientals, strong on Zen and Sufism," said Oscar, "and the cabala."

Eventually Oscar became a full-fledged group member, and then he went to the Orient, "to Hong Kong and India and Tibet, and studied Buddhism and Confucianism and alchemy and the *I Ching*." Some of Oscar's stories sound like early *Terry and the Pirates*.

FADE IN: *Terry and the Pirates* music, beaded curtains parting, a gong. Oscar is studying the *I Ching* in Kowloon. Through one *I Ching* master, Oscar meets another, this one also in the martial arts, the second one throws the *I Ching* to see what future portends and then stares at Oscar, the hexagrams haven't come up before like this, Oscar is the one who is to be taught, he is to go to his hotel and get his things and move in with the very old master, who is maybe ninety-six. "I couldn't believe it," Oscar said. "His skin was like a baby's. I could never catch him, in any exercise. He told me, you have to live like you are living your last second. This idea of awareness is very old. He taught me to go inside sleep without sleeping, not so far out, animals do it, we did it ourselves in the jungle, you are sleeping but you are awake. I learned psychoalchemy from the martial arts."

I was trying to have a hard-nosed interview with Oscar. (*Psychology Today* thought they had a scout in the interior and they hadn't seen a smoke signal in six months.) Where did you get the money for these travels? From my uncle. When you would stop in all these exotic places, how did you know where to go? I had people to look up, from the group in Buenos Aires, and from other people along the way. Now, you stopped with Sufis, who spoke Arabic and Farsi, or Persian, and then other groups spoke Hindi, and Chinese—how did you talk to them? In English. In *English*, Oscar? (Oscar's sentences in English were frequently preceded by the phrase, "Now here come another thing.") Well, language wasn't important. Oscar had an impatience with word culture. Words words words words words. Words were used too much as a screen. "We are in transition to the planetary culture, psychology is the most important thing in the next culture."

Plainly, Oscar's psychology had little to do with rats. "Psychology is the knowledge of the interior of the human psyche. Western psychology is discovering what we already did. A culture starts when man rediscovers Void, what the game is. In the Occident, that isn't part of the culture."

In one respect, Oscar was right. Things had certainly gotten planetary. Here is a counter-tradition, swirling from the Hermetic in Egypt, the Gnostic in Greece, a dash of Zoroastrianism from Persia, the Masters of Wisdom in Central Asia teaching Gurdjieff, a Gurdjieff group appearing in Buenos Aires, where a mustached Bolivian takes it to Arica in Chile, to which come Americans from California, and it ends up on West 57th Street in Manhattan, an escalator goes up from the street through a purple paper tunnel and there in this ex-computer facility are representations of tarot cards on the wall, and the Sanskrit tonic sound, Om, in Sanskrit ॐ . Far out, as my old classmates said so frequently.

But no one ever put it that way. Oscar got his indications by Direct Revelation. That's traditional, too. "I spent forty days in the desert in Cordova . . . I was in a space without connection, my consciousness went inside the enneagram, I returned from the experience and each enneagram was complete, but it was very hard to put into words. Of course, this was my psychic projection." A student from the West pointed out it was within a century and a half since Joseph Smith had gotten a Direct Revelation, and look at the Mormons today, he said.

At that time, all the students who had ever studied with Oscar were gathered for this crash course, pilgrims who had gone to Chile, the ten-month course, the five-month course —was there anybody, I asked, who had reached the state of total clarity and awareness, the one called "Permanent 24" in that ad in *The New York Times*?

"No, nobody," said Oscar. "Not really. Not yet. Permanent 24 takes much more work."

As for me, I went from A to B to C, the last being a group of secondary citizens who were doing some work on the outside, and hence not committed to the Work totally. The C team was kept insulated so as not to drag down the group level. More people were fired from the school. I had to go to Chicago, and the phone in my hotel room rang and said the Work will begin again tomorrow morning, fly back, and I suddenly had to pick between Studs Terkel's radio show and flying back. I didn't fly back. (In Chester Barnard's *Functions of the Executive*, an absolute classic from many years ago, it says that the decision not to decide is a decision.) Also, on my own I had found an appropriate Sufi saying. "Trust in Allah," it said, "but tie your camel first." But I didn't want to miss anything. I really didn't. I took a make-up when I got back, and limped through graduation.

Oscar was true to what he said in one respect: the big course was never given again. Everybody who took it was now expected to go out and teach. And most of them did. They spread around the country, Los Angeles, Atlanta, Boston, Denver, groups of five and ten. They rented houses, put ads in the paper, and started teaching. What they taught was little mini-courses, some for an evening, some for a lunch hour, the longest for forty days. Arica bought rock commercials on the radio and it received a burst of publicity, but it never took off like Transcendental Meditation, or even like the Guru Maharaj Ji. The package was class, not mass.

I knew about the new courses only by hearsay, as I had been dropped unceremoniously even from the mailing list and the newsletter, for what sin I cannot imagine, except perhaps lack of evangelism. (Even the most interesting of esoteric courses have distressing overtones of evangelism.) But then Arica calmed down, the newsletter began to arrive again, and after an absence of about two and a half years I went back to sit in a beginner's course. The spooky talk had all been cleaned up. The chanting was just like breathing, "Ah-h-h" (inhale), "Tu-u-u-" (exhale). The meditation was a *kasina,* not called so, staring at a symbol on the wall until its colors began to swirl psychedelically. The "karma cleaning" or confession was done with a deck of cards, each of which had a statement for which we were supposed to supply an example, e.g., "A time I felt ashamed, socially," "A time I felt spiritually confused." Everybody warmed to that. Each participant faced the room and said, "I want to change!" and the whole group would cheer and holler and stomp. It was the most applause some of them had ever had and it was hard to get them to sit down. Oscar had not lost his talent for inventing polychromatic and multitonal experiences. And still to come was the Hypergnostic Awareness—still in the future—Oscar had not lost his talent for naming processes, either. Our old moving meditation, "From Thee we come, to Thee we go," had developed a thumping country-and-western beat that had everybody clapping and stamping and hollering—

—clapping and stamping and hollering? Good heavens! Mid-Manhattan Pentecostalism! The Pentecostalists lost members when they went, upwardly mobile, into the white-collar middle class and got embarrassed by the glossolalia, speaking in tongues, and coming forward for Jesus, and repenting, and now the upper middle class found its bluejean-clad youth clapping and stomping in a package from Samarkand, via Buenos Aires, with music scored for the new age. One Arica song with a contemporary beat was "My Dear Mind, You Don't Exist." What fun!

I sat in on a seminar in Behavior and Change at a major university, taught by a friend. A graduate student was reporting on his experience at Arica. He counted himself an Arican, but he confused the seminar with those vibrational levels—"See, 6,000 is where society is, 784 is a very depressed state, and 192 is practically suicidal"—and then he began to tell of Oscar's background, how Oscar had learned these mysteries in Hong Kong and Afghanistan and Tibet—the legend was well on its way—and had studied with this very old master—Good heavens, it was my very own hickory-flavored Terry and the Pirates stories from *Psychology Today!*

And I visited headquarters. The furniture looked like Proctor & Gamble's ad agency. Films, I was told, were replacing lectures, there were audio-visual teaching aids, management consultants, cash flow charts on the walls. The staff was going to publish the "psychocalisthenics" just like the Royal Canadian Air Force exercises, and Oscar was writing his autobiography. You could take an Arica course on a sunny beach in Florida during the winter, or on a wilderness trip in the summer, or on a raft floating down the Colorado river, and you could charge it all on Master Charge. (The days of the A group and the B group and looking for the *chich* in people's books were so long ago, I was told, they were regarded with some nostalgia, like hip flasks).

Long before the Road to Satori 24 became eligible for Master Charge, I met a Chilean economist who had been in a simultaneous training group in Chile. It was like a reunion meeting of the Thunderbolt Pilots Association.

"They told me you were in it," I said.

"They told me *you* were in it," he said. "Are you a Go?"

I felt I could admit such a failing to an old Thunderbolt pilot, even though Go's are deceitful.

"So am I. I was Director of the Budget in Chile at twenty-six, and Minister of the Interior in my thirties," he said, "so of course I am hung up on work. Terrible."

"But don't you feel the rest of them didn't quite value work enough?"

"Yes, no question. See, we are both still hung up. But they don't get enough work done, in fact they never start till ten-thirty in the morning. The bunch that runs it must be rather crazy, but I thought it remarkable how these differing people—truckdrivers, academics, lawyers—would all come up with the same thing about my persona, how I came across."

"I like the physical stuff best," I said, "and it bothered me that the people who got fired were more interesting than those who stayed."

"Ah," said my friend. "Those who left were still in Ego, there was no room. One mountain, one tiger. One mountain, one tiger."

"Did you ever know anybody who made it out of Ego, into Satori 24?"

"No, never. But we always had such expectation. After all, the diet, the physical stuff—you began to feel differently, lighter—"

"—maybe you would know something with your liver, or your feet, any day—"

"—exactly, you *are* feeling different, and they say, next week, a new exercise! Very powerful! This tremendous sense of *expectation,* next week, the group energy rises and consciousness is transformed, next week, next week—"

"Satori 24!"

"Next week, Satori 24! It sounds good, even as we sit here!" We sat for a moment.

"It's too bad there isn't one more week," I said, "even though I know what I know, and I don't think anything would be different."

"One more week? Next week?" My Chilean friend burst into laughter. "All right! Maybe it's next week! I'll go if you'll go!"

THE HIGH VALUE
OF NOTHING

ARICA had its people doing moving exercises and breathing exercises; EST had them sitting still on folding auditorium chairs for fifteen hours at a stretch. EST stands for Erhard Seminars Training, Erhard being Werner Erhard, the founder. Oscar Ichazo had come from the mystery schools: Werner Erhard came from Sales Motivation and Dale Carnegie. Oscar used Sanskrit mantrams and Sufi geometric symbols, and Werner used plain English, more or less. Werner's package had no chanting, no movement—in fact, not much theory—just two hundred fifty people sitting on chairs, an instructor with a microphone, and portable floor mikes in case anybody wanted to talk back. Oscar's course is never over, Werner's is two weekends, $250 now, though I suppose Werner's isn't over after the two weekends, either. (After the two weekends you can take one-night-a-week seminars in Sex, Money, Power, What's So, and Be Here Now.)

Yet, oddly, many of the antecedents of these packages are complementary, and not indigenous to the elementary schools in this country. Midway through Arica, playing the game of where-does-this-come-from, I was reading Ouspensky and the Tibetan *Book of the Dead* and the *Sufi Orders of Islam*, and after EST I had to go back to semantics, the semanticists and philosophers, Korzybski and Ludwig Wittgenstein, because EST is at least partially a linguistic pop.

Werner did not care much about the antecedents. He went straight to Motivation and Development from high school in a Philadelphia suburb, where he was called Jack Rosenberg. He took the courses, and in a short time was teaching them. His rather unusual *nom de commerce* was put together from Ludwig Erhard and Werner von Braun. Werner, as he is now called, is good-looking, aggressive and forceful—the salesmen taking his courses must have charged out of the room, confident they were the best salesmen and they were going to sell enough to win the prize trip to Hawaii.

"I could show people how to get what they wanted," Werner said, "and I could act like I was okay, I could produce symbols, but when the people get what they wanted it wasn't what they wanted because they weren't *experiencing* it."

"Experience" is the keynote word in Werner's vocabulary. "Language is terrible, psychology is terrible, how come there's no statement on what experience is, how come I, with no background, have to make one up," Werner said. In a dim way I knew what he meant—Werner has to strain sometimes for what he means, but his forcefulness and enthusiasm do not diminish.

"No," I said, "if there were a statement on what experience is, then people would know the statement and not the experience, they would have one more statement but they wouldn't have experienced the experience."

"Gee, that's right," Werner said. I was talking like a good EST graduate. "Let's see," Werner said, "maybe we can do it with money. Money is the symbol of security, right? It's not the *experience* of security. Some people want the experience of security so they pile up money, but they still don't have the experience of security, they can act *as if* they are experiencing security, they can buy things that *go with* security, but they haven't experienced *out* the barrier between them and feeling secure. Now, if they experience out the barrier between them and feeling secure, they may or may not have more money or less money, but they will have the feeling of security."

"Experiencing out the barrier would be something like a Freudian analyst getting his patient to be aware of unconscious factors he wasn't aware of?"

"Sure. I don't know. Partly. I never know exactly where I get these things."

Werner must have been one of the unlikeliest pilgrims on the consciousness circuit. He did Scientology—itself a mishmash of Freud and Eastern ideas—and yoga and Zen—"I was lucky enough to be stunned by Zen"—and Subud—"that latihan in Subud is like Bedlam"—and encounter and attack therapy and sensitivity, and Dale Carnegie—

"I guess I was looking for Truth, but I was also using each technique in my business. I was lucky, because Business only cares about results. In a university, I would have been crossing departmental lines and getting everybody mad, in a seminary I would have been burned as a witch, but business only cares about results. So if it worked I used it, and if it didn't work I dropped it, and if it worked I used it some more. See, Business could care less. I would say, 'I've added something, I'm going to try some Zen with this group,' and they would say, 'Sure, Werner, just don't get any on the floor, and have our men back to their Division Chief by four-thirty.' Of course, I had to translate from religion or therapy into business, but I had the advantage of not knowing anything, you see, I just said, how can I use it? I'm a mechanic, I know how things work. I could out-Carnegie Carnegie and out-Peale Peale. But those guys just buried the problem."

And then? Werner had mentioned a particular incident that changed everything, ken-sho, sudden flash.

"I was sitting in my wife's Mustang on a hill in San Francisco and I realized, what is, is, and what was, was. Now that sounds absolutely stupid. And what isn't, isn't. It was stunning. See, an archbishop is an archbishop and very important, but an archbishop in Zen, the name, translated, means 'trash can,' that's Zen telling you the way it is. How can you tell people what is, is? It doesn't mean anything. It's nothing. You can't define nothing because that's a definition, but what's valuable in my training is nothing. Nothing is the element of transubstantiation."

"And that was the beginning of EST? So EST means 'it is,' as well."

"Right. EST is—well, a not completely thought-out unified theory—"

"But you started teaching it—"

"Yes. No—you can't teach it, that's what's wrong with teaching, nobody knows what learning is—you can't teach, all you can do is to create a condition that allows experience, but to the degree that it's *believed,* it fails."

I didn't know whether Werner had read Carl Rogers or picked that up out of the air.

"Because then it's belief and not experience?"

"Sure, experience is what's there before the form and structure are applied. See, all we want to do—the transformation is to change the notion of who you are. So that you can see, who is it that thinks, who is it that feels, and if you de-identify not only from things but experiences, from your own experiences, when you reach a critical mass of de-identification, things make sense. The Bible makes sense. Other things make sense."

It's a bit dizzying, all this rap about nothing and experience. It's dizzying like turning over the sentence "This very sentence is false," which is one of the early paradoxes in semantics, because if the very sentence *is* false then it's true, but how can it be true if it's false? "There are only two things in the world," Werner said once, "nothing and semantics."

The metalinguist Benjamin Whorf wrote on how our conceptions molded our perceptions, how difficult it was to perceive what we had no word for. The semanticist Alfred Korzybski, in *Science and Sanity*, wrote, "Every language, having a structure, by the very nature of the language, reflects in its own structure that of the world as assumed by those who evolved language. In other words, we read unconsciously into the world the structure of the language we use." The heaviness we give to nouns in English helps to make our world a world of *things*, more object than process. The structure of the language, in fact, helps us to think that semantics is only words, and therefore not very important, certainly not as important as machine tools or jumbo jets.

The Zen master said, rivers are rivers and mountains are

mountains, and we say, of course, how quaint. Then a psychiatrist comes along with some Zen training and a difficult patient, neurotic we would say because of her illegitimate birth. The psychiatrist says, "Who were you before you were an illegitimate child?" The patient bursts into tears and says, "I am I! Oh, I am I!" That enables us to shrug and say, well, it does some good, in the odd case.

The Vienna-born philosopher Ludwig Wittgenstein has some statements that get to sound very Zen-like, though Wittgenstein never sat counting to three in his life, and in fact went through the heaviest of exercises. *Tractatus Logico-Philosopicus* is one tome, and *Philosophical Investigations* is another; either would do as something to chew on if you are sitting on the runway at O'Hare with the air conditioning off for five hours sometime. Wittgenstein was one of the most influential contemporary philosophers, a Cambridge professor, and in the *Tractatus* he says: "The sense of the world must be outside the world. In the world everything is as it is and happens as it does happen." Wittgenstein, in philosophy, arrived at a position in which the subject-predicate analysis of propositions is abandoned, and to get students to follow he would devise linguistic pops. "The method," wrote one commentator, "consisted in constructing or calling attention to examples of linguistic behavior in such a way as to shock the mind into noticing something which had not been noticed and thereby to free it from what might be called the bind of conception."

"Werner," I said, "you don't by any chance know Ludwig Wittgenstein's *Philosophical Investigations?*"

"No," Werner said firmly. "Look, the general semantics people come to my seminar and say, it's general semantics. The Zen people come and say, it's Zen. But see, all the techniques are bullshit. Understanding it is something you do if you don't get it, you know that. See, enlightenment has no value. You can't be right with it, you can't sit on it, you can't sell it, you can't use it to survive with, and to the degree you value it, it isn't enlightenment."

Werner went to India. Not seeking enlightenment?

"No. I went for a couple of reasons. First of all, in my business, people should go to India."

"You mean credentials, like the Harvard Business School or the Stanford Graduate—"

"Sure." Werner's candor was always disarming. "And second, I wanted to hang out with some of the Indian saints. Because just hanging out opens a space for you."

"Opens a space" is another keystone in Werner's vocabulary. I had asked Werner, in some correspondence, why he had gone to India, correspondence between our several conversations. MY PURPOSE IN GOING (Werner's letters come in capital letters, but that may be the machines he likes) WAS TO MEET AND SHARE WITH SOME OF THAT COUNTRY'S SPIRITUAL LEADERS. MOST OF THE TIME WAS SPENT WITH SWAMI MUKTANANDA AND SATYA SAI BABA, BOTH OF WHOM I THOROUGHLY ENJOYED AND REALIZED BENEFIT FROM.

What benefit?

"Just being around opens a space. See, masters don't give you rules. A master just tells you what is."

That's one of Werner's aphorisms: This is it. There are no hidden meanings. All that mystical stuff is just what's so. A master is someone who found out. Werner's aphorisms are printed in a handy little booklet no bigger than the sayings of Chairman Mao: Life is a rip-off when you expect to get what you want. Life works when you choose what you got. Actually what you got is what you chose. To move on, choose it.

"Take responsibility for" is another keystone phrase. There's no gray area. Once you say you'll take responsibility for, you *will*, in EST. If you say you're coming to the midweek lecture and you don't turn up, someone will call your house and ask for you to look at the barrier between you and taking responsibility for, because if you experience out the barrier, you'll take responsibility for.

Werner has no good words for the Ego, either. Another stream of aphorisms: The purpose of the mind is survival. Ego starts when a being stops considering itself a being and starts being its own point of view. It thinks survival is maintaining that point of view. An ego, therefore, is a point of view attempting to cause its own survival. So its purpose is domination of everything and everybody. An Ego will sacrifice its own body just to be right.

It makes more sense if you let the totality sink in, and don't analyze each component.

The EST course has a little swatch of guided meditation, and variations of Create a Space and The Great Central Philippine Headache cure, and dollops of Scientology theory, and some acting exercises, and some fantasy, pieces borrowed from other courses, especially Dale Carnegie, but what is most characteristic is the rap, so I have tried to give a sampling of the rap:

"See, the whole idea of making it is bullshit. Life is a game, to have a game something has to be more important than something else; if what already is, is more important than what isn't, the game is over, so life is a game in which what isn't is more important than what is, let the good times roll. Life is a game, but living isn't a game, living is what is, experiencing right where you are. Nothing mystical about it."

I said: why couldn't some dropout simply stay in bed all the time, if what is, is?

If he does, then he didn't get it, Werner said, because that's not why people stay in bed all the time, it's unexperienced experience that keeps them there, anxiety or fear, and if they experience out the anxiety, then they either get out of bed or don't get out of bed, but they don't stay in bed because they heard somewhere that what is, is.

"Who's on first, What's on second, and I Don't Know is on third," I said. "I wish Ludwig Wittgenstein could have taken this course. Do you know what the two things were I heard about the course before I took it? That you don't let them eat and you don't let them go to the bathroom."

"People are so strung up in their games that they're crazy," Werner said.

Anybody, said the instructor, one of Werner's verbal Marines, could have their money back in the next ten minutes and leave, but after that everybody who stayed had to agree that they would do what they were told for the rest of the weekend: we had to check our watches at the door, we could only eat if there was a food break, and sure enough, only go to the bathroom if there was a break for that, and we would sit on these chairs as long as necessary, maybe till one or two in the morning, it then being nine A.M. A couple of people left. The portable floor microphones were passed around anytime anyone wanted to talk, to share what they were feeling—but the first hours were slow, and mostly attack: "You people are *turkeys*! A turkey is an animal so dumb it lifts up its head to drink the rain and drowns! Because you don't *experience,* you haven't ever experienced, and you take all your non-experiences and classify them and keep them in a silver box, if you got laid the first time you put that in a box and the next time you opened the box to see if that experience was like the experience in the box—"

A hand goes up, a dignified, pleasant lady with gray hair— "I think you could make your point without all this vile language, it doesn't add to the communication—"

"Fern, honey," says the instructor, "these are only *words,* you don't want to let words run you, Fern, why do you grant the words the power to make you an effect, Fern, there is no difference between fuck and spaghetti!"

Fern gasped with the brutality of "fuck," belted out by Werner's Marine.

"And by the time this course is through, you will be able to go to Mamma Leone's and order a plate of fuck! Or sing this whole bunch a dirty song!"

Fern said if the doors weren't locked and if she hadn't made an agreement, she would leave.

The next morning Fern signaled for a microphone, got up, said she had been thinking about things overnight, and she was going to sing a song—the only dirty one she knew, she said: "Two Irishmen, two Irishmen, were sittin in a ditch," sang Fern to a standing ovation. "I've never done a thing like that in my life," Fern giggled, when the applause died.

"You people," said Werner's verbal Marine, the first day, "don't even know who you are, you have yamayamayama going in your head, all your actions are strung together on your racket, your game, whatever manner it is you found you can survive with, you're interested, you're indifferent, you're ingratiating, some of you are so hip your act is I Don't Have an Act—"

Sure enough, from time to time a hand would go wandering up—when were we going to get a break, I didn't have any breakfast, when are we—

"What is all this?" roared the instructor. "You people are *tubes!* In one end and out the other, you let that run your lives! Who runs your life? You or your body?"

Mechanical man, mechanical desires—

"I wish the people in the courses wouldn't get so hung up on that," Werner said later to me, "but people really *are* tubes. At least we make them look at their tube-ness. At least if you don't let them pee, *you begin to get their attention.* If I could talk to teachers, I would tell them that. See, the truth puts people to sleep. It goes right to the unconscious in them, and most people are unconscious, for the truth to get to the truth that is in people, it has to get through the unconsciousness. So if you can make them uncomfortable in their unconsciousness, enough just to make people aware they *are* unconscious, then you have a better chance of letting some truth strike the truth in them."

"All right, tubes, we will have a thirty-minute break," said the sergeant, along about five o'clock. "Thirty minutes doesn't mean thirty-one minutes. The doors will be locked in thirty minutes."

Nobody had peed on the floor. The hunger pangs had come and gone. But at midnight a lady in front of me kept taking a pack of Viceroys out of her purse, and extracting a cigarette—there is no smoking in EST at any time—and tapping it on the back of her hand, and then putting it back into the pack, and putting the pack back in her purse. Then she wept quietly. I had never seen anybody weep for a cigarette, but I guess you can weep for whatever you're really attached to. However, it is okay to weep. "The doors are locked, we have tigers outside them to scare people away, so in here you can let go."

"Enlightenment," belted the instructor, chalk in hand, before the blackboard, "is the knowledge that you are a machine. YOU ARE A MACHINE!"

A hand went up, a microphone got passed—another resistant,

another declaration of independence: "I am Milton Drexler"—Milton had a mustache, Milton is perhaps an accountant, a C.P.A., and this disturbs him, dehumanizes him—"and I AM NOT A MACHINE."

"Don't get me wrong," said the instructor. "Your voice says you have been attacked, your face says you are defending: *I didn't say a Milton Drexler Machine was bad.*"

"We attack their beliefs," Werner said. "Because as long as they look out through beliefs, that's all they see, so maybe you get a belief crumbled for a few minutes."

Sometimes the class would turn on the instructor—this is stupid, this is a rip-off, you don't make any sense, whaddya mean, reasonableness is of a very low order, and I Don't Know is a form of certainty?

"Thank you," says the instructor, "I acknowledge I hear you." But he doesn't react. Can't we make the bastard react?

"You are the worst, coldest bastard I have ever met, you have a lot of problems you ought to look at yourself, and this is all a rip-off."

"Thank you, I acknowledge that I understood you."

"Oh, you could say, what's that thing from aikido—give the other guy the space," said Werner. "You know."

"The guy comes at you," I said, reciting from my aikido class, "but, see, he doesn't want you, he wants the space you're in, so you move out of that space and let him have it, and then he's off balance, and should he happen to want to fall down you push him down."

"Something like that," Werner said. "But that isn't it, either, you can't make a rule like give the other guy the space."

"Because then you have the rule and not the experience, and rules are bullshit."

"You're getting it."

"Don't say that. I don't want to get it, because it might create a problem."

I could say we played Create a Space, and did our acting exercises, and went through more semantics, but that wouldn't communicate the boredom or the Enlightenment. I don't feel so bad about my inability to communicate because sometimes Werner can't do it, either. John Denver, the country-and-western star, went through EST, and one night he was a TV talk show host, and had Werner on, and they asked him what was EST and what did it do, and he said it was a series of techniques to Open Spaces for people, which sometimes increased their aliveness. Werner said this with his usual Dale Carnegie crisp firmness, and John Denver beamed, and everybody went: wha?

EST does not advertise, but it does tell its graduates that they can get their friends to share their own aliveness and well-being by bringing them to a Guest Seminar, from which they can sign up for the Full Seminar, $200. However, graduates are abjured from explaining the course, as "UNDERSTANDING IS THE BOOBY PRIZE AND THINKING THAT YOU KNOW IS AN ACTUAL BARRIER TO EXPERIENCING," as Werner wrote, in a general communication to all graduates. If you do *not* bring a guest, you are asked to look at the barrier between you and bringing a guest. Graduates are also asked to "assist," which means working for free at EST offices from time to time. "Assisting" helps to promote the experience.

EST may have borrowed from Zen, but it was not to be corrupted by selling the answers to the koans. Werner, in fact, wrote a letter warning graduates that they deprived future trainees of the experience if they told them the answers to the koans, the koans having been translated from the traditional to the American, from the puzzles of the Sixth Patriarch to vanilla and chocolate.

What was curious to me was that a high proportion of the EST seminars I attended were filled with verbal people enthusiastic about this course that told them that understanding was the booby prize and thinking was a barrier and everything was so much bullshit. They loved that. You knew they were verbal people because they would signal for the portable microphone and express themselves very well. They would come to the EST seminar, having "looked at" some part of their life—we quickly got used to the Games People Play—and they would tell this role they had discovered like it had never been seen before, and everybody else in the audience who had played that particular game would strike a note of resonance. The games were a real tribute to Eric Berne—See What You Made Me Do, and You're Doing It Wrong, and It's Not My Fault, played between bosses and employees, and parents and children, and husbands and wives. The recognition of the games changed people's points of view. Some swore it changed their lives. At any seminar, the attendees were encouraged to tell how EST helped them that week. Every self-help course from Dale Carnegie on does that, and the Dale Carnegie course is sixty-five years old, and that one works, too.

EST is spreading all over the place, Los Angeles, New York, Hawaii, Aspen, and "graduates" can attend seminars anywhere for a nominal fee. EST's ability to spread is only limited by the availability of trainers. The "training," the two weekends sitting in a chair, demands of the "trainer" that he be up on a podium before the audience from nine A.M. to midnight, armed with only a pitcher of water, a glass and a microphone, two days in a row, in control and responding. That takes talent, as well as training. Good instructors aren't so easy to come by, because they have to play off the audiences, handle attacks and deliver them, read voices and faces. In my postgraduate seminar, the seminarians would call up and try to find out who the preacher of the evening was, because there was a dramatic fall-off in quality between Broadway and the road show, between the stars and the understudies. The further from the initial training, the thinner the talent. Some of the seminar leaders were young trainees who could not manage their audience, even though they were repeating the rote formulas. The first string had considerable poise, stage presence—the stuff needs a good actor—theater, at its most perfect, also provides catharsis, exhilaration, moments of illumination—theater—actors—

—actor! Jock MacGowan, famous in his Beckett roles, on the stage in the old tramp's raincoat, transferring marbles, counting them, from one pocket to another, and then counting them, and then transferring them back again, sixteen in this pocket and

seven in this, it's excruciating, this scene from *Molloy,* because
he keeps talking and he isn't saying anything; dialogue, like action, is a game to pass the time, as Hamm says in *Endgame.* Or:
the two old tramps wait by a tree on a hopelessly acrophobic set,
on a road, for Godot, who doesn't come, "nothing happens, nobody comes, nobody goes, it's awful." And each statement by
one of the characters is hedged, and qualified, in rustling, mur-
muring voices until it falls away and falls away and doesn't
mean anything. Doesn't mean anything, but—the language-
using, stimulus-hungry, left-balanced brain fidgets, *this is boring,
this doesn't make any sense,* who the hell is Godot and what happens if he gets here, Theater of the Absurd! Yet something does
creep through, around the language or despite it, or because of
it, because Beckett is a Joycean master, the first critics de-
nounced *Waiting for Godot,* "a farrago of pointless chit-chat,"
but the convicts at San Quentin sat transfixed, "Godot is the
outside," and now it's almost too late, Godot has been marked
literary classic, so when the viewer's interior voice starts up, *this
is boring, this doesn't make sense,* it gets a slap on the wrist
from the second interior voice, *shut up, they say it's a classic.*
And what creeps through is that self-canceling definition, the
unarticulated experience.

> For to know nothing is nothing, not to want to know anything
> likewise, but to be beyond knowing anything, that is when peace
> enters in, to the soul of the incurious seeker,

it says in Beckett's *Molloy,* and in his own voice, in his essay on
Proust, says Beckett:

> Life is habit. Or rather life is a succession of habits, since the indi-
> vidual is a succession of individuals . . . habit is the generic term
> for the countless treaties concluded between the countless subjects
> that constitute the individual and their countless correlative ob-
> jects. The periods of transition . . . represent [the moment when]
> boredom of living is replaced by the suffering of being.

And this "recognition of illusoriness," says the theater critic Martin Esslin, "and prefabricated meaning . . . far from ending in

despair . . . is the starting point of a new point in consciousness. . . ."

At the end of each of the first two acts of *Godot,* the same lines
occur:

> Well, shall we go?
> Yes, let's go.
> *(They do not move.)*

They do not move. In the end, these fellows all disappear up
their own tails. Beckett's play *Breath* is eight seconds long, and
consists of a breath. Like the artists who hang up a blank can-
vas, or a sign on the museum door that says THIS MUSEUM IS
CLOSED FOR TWO WEEKS, and that's the art. It must be pretty close
to the end of the line, crossover time into something else, but it
doesn't get us to the something else.

Nothing! In 1924, the General Electric Company conducted
an experiment at its Hawthorne plant to improve production.
The women in the experiment did the same work they did before, but experimenters fooled with the lights and the pace. One
work break, three work breaks. Hot snacks, no snacks. No matter
what they did, production improved. Yet nothing had been
added. The "Hawthorne effect," it was called, because, though
nothing had been added, the point of view of the women working had changed, they were not just women working in a plant,
they were part of an experiment, *they were aware of what they
were doing,* and so nothing became something.

Goodness, from work theory in sociology to Dale Carnegie to
the existentialism loosely—very loosely—underlying the Theater
of the Absurd—

"Beckett," I said.

"Who?" Werner said.

"Beckett, Samuel Beckett."

"Nope, don't know him. A lot of people say the same thing. I
just stand there where they want to hear it."

Well, if Werner doesn't know Beckett and Wittgenstein and Whorf, then what the hell *was* all that stuff? It sure takes up a lot of linear space here on the page.

"Nothing" did work for EST. Some of its graduates left exhilarated; it was hard to tell which of the derived and distilled exercises produced the exhilaration. Maybe it was the whole package. Or maybe it was the reverse spin: for years, much of our liberal society has told people that whatever is, isn't their fault. Their parents were mean, or indifferent, or overloving. Their teachers were hopelessly stereotyped, their jobs just weren't designed for humanity, the President—any President—is a bum. And here was a message that people created their own experiences and were responsible for themselves! Wow!

Forty thousand people graduated from EST. The waiting list for trainings grew to several months. Werner piloted the company plane, a Cessna 414, around the country, He was so busy he barely had time to train the trainers, much less give the trainings. EST had Facilitators and Communicators, and free programs for schools and prisons, and a summer camp EST training for teenagers. Werner moved up to Chairman; the new Chief Executive Officer was Don Cox, a former Harvard Business School professor, a more recently Vice-president for Planning of Coca-Cola. The San Francisco *Chronicle* ran a front-page series on this hometown product. Its tone was irreverent. EST replied in the hurt tones the oil companies used when they defended themselves against making too much money. Making money? Certainly not: EST designed itself to break even. It really did. The *Chronicle* did not understand that money can only produce money, but enthusiasm can produce enthusiasm. It sounded for the moment as if the old Zen equation, archbishop = trash can, had slipped away. Werner sent all his graduates a valentine: I Love You. We knew he did; we knew those phone calls pursuing us when we did not come to Meeting was because: They Care!

EST got itself an absolutely blue-ribbon Advisory Board, educators and psychiatrists who had taken the training. When it encountered the media, it assembled its media graduates and its Advisory Board for a symposium, and abstracted the lessons with astonishing rapidity. EST alumni were a literate bunch; 40 percent of them had some graduate school.

In San Francisco, the EST organization headquarters had all the élan of a growth company on the steep part of the curve. Sometimes it did seem as though we belonged to a United Air Lines that didn't have any planes, only stewardesses and reservations clerks. Every EST graduate became a first name to the staff phoning. EST must have a big phone bill, for its big extended family. When you phoned back, you got a cheerful first-name greeting. "Hi, this is Nancy," said the voice on the phone. "How may I assist you?" Sloppy old conversations were broken into Communications and Acknowledgments. The charts at headquarters showed that at the present growth rate, the one million mark would be crossed in—

Plainly, something would happen to EST. It would get too big too fast and have computer trouble. Parkinson's Law would replace the koans of the Sixth Patriarch of Zen. What would happen to EST? It would disappear, I mused. Not because angry parents descended upon it, not because people tire of arcana, as happens in other movements. It would disappear right into United Air Lines, or the Telephone Company. No telling which will be the survivor. A very American ending.

"I guess EST will keep growing because the demand is more than the supply," Werner said. "But don't get me wrong, I don't think the world needs EST, I don't think the world needs anything, the world already is, and that's perfect."

"If nobody needs it, why do you do it?"

"I do it because I do it, because that's what I do."

I bet Satchel Paige said something about fish swimming and birds flying, but nobody wrote it down.

From the EST leaflet:

There is no note-taking; there is no written material to study. There is no discipline to follow and no system to use. When the training is over just the result is left.

REGISTERING
THE PACKAGES

ARE the packages effective? There are many testimonials from happy alumni and some from disgruntled alumni, but there are more alumni all the time. (A multiple alumnus like myself is absolutely inundated by computer-directed mail, because you go onto the mailing list once you "graduate.")

There are no long-range studies to determine effectiveness, any more than there are really long-range studies that determine whether the ladies and gentlemen who switch their deodorants and their toothpastes immediately register success with the opposite sex.

To be properly registered in the paradigm, the effectiveness would need other quantitative measures: aliveness and Satori 24 and so on, which is difficult with either quantitative or verbal language. The meditation people did *quantify* relaxation, and as time goes by they will have longitudinal studies, and all the courses have elements of meditation. So we're on our way.

The demand is more than the supply, Werner said. That means that they don't have to be sold, they are bought. People tell other people. They don't have to tell other people unless something works. Of course, people operate from what one leading psychologist called "cognitive dissonance"; they justify what they have already chosen a little bit, and they weed out conflicts so that they have a totally consistent picture, and they really believe it themselves. Even so, it is a demand-pull field. Sex, Money, Power, What's So—what's so, alone, is what everybody wants to know. If the demand is more than the supply and the old paradigm's rules still go, the supply will rise until an equilibrium is reached.

The packages here may be superseded or they may grow. They are schools unlike our others.

We have been paying some fleeting attention to language and semantics, because we are coming to the end of the paradigm in these accounts, and at the edge, language becomes even more important than from safely in the middle.

I wished, in fantasy, not only for Ludwig Wittgenstein as a traveling companion to the edge of the paradigm, but for Benjamin Whorf. Wittgenstein was the heir to an Austrian steel fortune. He trained as an engineer, got intrigued by philosophy at Cambridge in 1912 and then by Bertrand Russell and mathematics. His *Tractatus,* through the Vienna Circle, helped to create a movement in philosophy called logical positivism. But Wittgenstein dropped it, gave his fortune away, and went to teach in an elementary school in a mountain village in Austria. Later he came back to a professorship in Cambridge, but he didn't like being a professor . . .

. . . and Benjamin Whorf turned down opportunities to become one. He was, of all things, a fire inspection engineer; a Massachusetts Yankee, a chemical engineer from MIT, B.S., '18, who spent his working life rising in the Hartford Fire Insurance Company through fire prevention technology, at which he was expert. His avocation was languages—Indian languages, Hopi, Shawnee, Choctaw, even Aztec—and he wrote his papers and continued in the insurance business, a couple of blocks away from where the poet, Wallace Stevens, was also becoming a vice-president in the insurance business, some Hartford they had in those days if they could have put it all together, Whorf giving his chalk talks at the Children's Museum . . .

And why is Whorf so intriguing here at the margins of psychology? It may be because of his suggestion that you have been tricked by your language into a certain way of perceiving reality, and that possibly an awareness of the trickery gives you an insight. (The Whorfian thesis is sometimes called Sapir-Whorf, for the contributions of Edward Sapir, an authority not only on Indian languages but the science of language.) The Hopis could create a consistent universe without our meanings for time, energy, space and matter, Whorf wrote. Each language performs an artificial chopping up of the continuous flow of existence in a different way. Children repattern every day, Mississippi is not Mrs. Sippy, the equator is not a menagerie lion but an imaginary line. "A change in language can transform our appreciation of the Cosmos"—"The lower personal mind, caught in a vaster world inscrutable to its methods, uses its strange gift of language to weave the web of Maya or illusion, to make a provisional analysis of reality and then regard it as final . . . Western culture has gone farthest here, farthest in determined thoroughness of provisional analysis, and farthest in determination to regard it as final. The commitment to illusion has been sealed in western Indo-European language, and the road out of illusion for the West lies through a wider understanding of language than western Indo-European can give."

Did the TM people read Benjamin Whorf? Maybe they did, but bogged down in Choctaw tenses, or in the learned comparisons of Bergsonian time and Hopi time, or Newtonian space and matter coming from language, not intuition. If they'd kept going, they would have found something familiar—the mantram, "repatterning states in the nervous system and glands, [assisting] the consciousness into the noumenal pattern world." The noumenon is the thing itself, rather than the phenomenon as which it appears.

Wittgenstein the influential philosopher, Korzybski the Polish-American count, Whorf the Yankee engineer—we could use them in the material ahead, for much of it relates to experience and language. How do we communicate experience if the language is inadequate? Which is really real, the language or the experience?

Let's first, using blunt old English, see where we have come from. We perceive the world from a certain point. The sociologist

Talcott Parsons called the total system of language and perception a "gloss." We lump together isolated perceptions into a totality—we have to be taught this—and what we are taught is what everybody agrees on. The world is an agreement. We have seen from little flicks of semanticists and metalinguists and philosophers what language can do: English, for example, has two genders, masculine and feminine, which these word-people would say leads us to either-or, binary views. You're not losing a daughter, you're gaining a son. Instead of "gloss" I've used "paradigm," which has an element of time, all the glosses day after day, and assumptions of causality and predictability. Our paradigm is largely thing-oriented, materialistic and rational—verbal and intellectual.

Along come some experimental psychologists who tell us that we perceive our own paradigm and that's it. We discard what we perceive outside of it, so we don't even know it's there. (We *still* don't know what's there, because just saying well, we're in a paradigm all right, doesn't show us what's beyond.) Because of the nature of our paradigm, what can be described, it is agreed, is more real than what can't be described. And what can be *measured*, with numbers, is even more real than what can be described verbally, in our paradigm.

Physiologically, say some other experimental psychologists, this leads our culture to be more left-brained than right-brained, and the left hemisphere of the brain controlling analysis and speech, and the right, music and movement.

Even though all these assumptions may be true, there is great plasticity, or capacity for change, in the human organism. The optimistic view is that people can certainly grow and use parts of themselves they haven't used.

Meditation, which used to belong exclusively to religion, was a loose end in our paradigm. Now the loose end is being folded in, because meditation has been *measured* and its effects have been given a hypothesis and some level of predictability. Medical researchers have found that, possibly, meditation is an aid to the parasympathetic system, which helps to cool the agitation of the sympathetic system, in which many of us live much of the time. What the measurers did was to bring the language describing meditation from just beyond the paradigm to just within it, and now it wouldn't be surprising to see the borders of the paradigm extended.

Biofeedback has brought a high degree of measurement to the conscious control of the automatic nervous system—even to the firing of a single neuron. This work was also done by experimental psychologists. The autonomic nervous system was supposed to be beyond conscious control, and now it has crossed that filmy line, a change in a sub-paradigm, with effects in medicine and psychology.

Both meditation and biofeedback have helped to change the view of our ordinary, waking consciousness. The view is not new—it had been espoused by nineteenth-century psychologists such as William James, and in other cultures and other languages, but it is not the track we have been on recently, and certainly not scientifically, insofar as "scientifically" means accurately measured, and with a covering hypothesis and elements of predictability. We can now consider elements beyond this ordinary consciousness, and its limitations as an instrument.

Other cultures have given us traditions we can explore now as psychologies. They are not necessarily coherent alternatives, and frequently they come in bizarre—to us—language, and they do not have our symmetry. But they have elements that can move the edges of our paradigm. By the process of articulation, translation, description and measurement, we may be able to relate to them, though we do run the risk of missing their true natures in the process of applying our traditional analytic mode.

Now we are going to consider some explorers who are right out of the paradigm—they have gone through the holes in it, like Alice down the rabbit hole, and come back to tell us, but so far there is no way to work in what they have said, so it stays just beyond the edge of the paradigm, orbiting discreetly.

From within the paradigm, what some of the explorers have to say sounds, well, wiggy. Bizarre. It would help to have, as first-round choices, Whorf, Wittgenstein and Korzybski—they even sound like first-round draft choices—but they are all of them gone. Maybe we could get Noam Chomsky.

VII: The Far Side of Paradigm

THE SENIOR
ASTRONAUT:
YOU GOTTA KNOW
THE TERRITORY

EVEN though years had gone by, as an astronaut of inner space I was still a weekend warrior, and John Cunningham Lilly was a real no-foolin' space traveler. First of all, there were all those qualifications—Cal Tech, a medical degree from the University of Pennsylvania, training as a psychoanalyst, research in biophysics, neurophysiology, neuroanatomy—you couldn't design a better program for an Astronaut of Inner Space.

"I have spent much time in rather unusual, unordinary states, spaces, universes, dimensions, realities," Lilly wrote in an autobiography that was to become a cult book. "I speak as one who has been to the highest states of consciousness or of Satori-Samadhi, and as one who has returned to report to those interested. Some who went to these highest levels stayed there. Some came back and taught. Some came back to stay, too awed or frightened or guilty to teach, report, or ever return there ... it is my firm belief that the experience of highest states of consciousness is necessary for the survival of the human species."

"The old theories," wrote the doctor and neurophysiologist who certainly knew them, "about the action of the brain, of the mind, and of the spirit do not seem to be adequate." And he laid down his axiom: "In the province of the mind, what is believed to be true is true or becomes true, within limits to be found experientially and experimentally. These limits are further beliefs to be transcended. In the province of the mind, there are no limits."

In the Fifties, Lilly worked in Washington at the National Institute of Neurological Diseases and Blindness, mapping electrical activity in the cerebral cortex, and working with the brains of laboratory animals. Then, at the National Institutes of Health, he began to study sensory deprivation. Some neurophysiologists had postulated that if you cut off all stimulation from the brain, it would go to sleep. Lilly built a sensory-deprivation tank. The temperature of the water was 93°, experimentally determined as the temperature at which there is no sensation of hot or cold, in which tactile sensations disappear if you don't move. The water solution was buoyant, to remove the pull of gravity. No sound. No light. Lilly climbed in, and began his trip from the natural to the esoteric sciences.

Cut off from stimulation, the brain, Lilly found, did not go to sleep. Observing his own brain, Lilly found "dreamlike states, trancelike states, mystical states." He was joined, for example, by another person in the tank. And "at other times I apparently tuned in on networks of communication that are normally below our levels of awareness, networks of civilization way beyond ours."

Wiggy. Schizy. Lilly knew exactly what people would say, and he had nothing but contempt for the comments.

"I think the attempt to define all mystical, transcendental and ecstatic experiences which do not fit in with the categories of consensus reality as psychotic is conceptually limiting and comes from a timidity which is not seemly for the honest, open-minded explorer." We have, Lilly said, a built-in survival program, full of fears, and we have to fight through the survival program to find what's beyond. In other words, you're so scared and so determined to perceive the world in a comfortable way that you never get beyond the fear. Lilly had, he said, worked with schizophrenic and psychotic patients. In the tank he was examining *belief structures,* our belief structures imposed limits on what we perceived and experienced; what were the principles governing the human mind?

In the tank, "I began to experience a super-self level, a network of inter-related essences, yours, mine, everybody's, all hooked together. The Universal Mind . . . though it was only later in reading that I found the states I was getting into resembled those attained by other techniques."

A decade later, when LSD was still legal, he dosed himself with it and climbed into an even better tank. There were the Two Guides, now quite famous in the literature, who had appeared each time he had a brush with death, previously when he had been in a coma through a faulty injection, and when he was five and had TB—"Every time I have a job to do, these characters show up and tell me what the job is."

The Two Guides were from universes Lilly didn't necessarily believe existed when he started, but "I defined them as existing" in order to remove the barriers. And out went Lilly, three hundred micrograms of LSD and floating in a sensory deprivation tank, to outer space: high-intensity light . . . "as they approached their presences became more and more powerful, and I noticed more and more of them coming into me. Their thinking, their feeling, their knowledge was pouring into me. They stopped just as it was becoming almost intolerable to have them any closer."

The first time Lilly wrote of the Two Guides, he protested, "It is very hard to put this experience into words, because there were no words exchanged. Pure thought and feeling was being transmitted and received by me and by these two entities—I am a single point of consciousness, of feeling, I have no body, I feel their presence, I see their presence, without eyes, without a body. They tell me I can stay in this place, that I have left my body, but that I can return to it if I wish . . ."

The body, Lilly decided, can take care of itself when one leaves it, and "one can return if things get too tough out there." He continued to experiment with LSD doses and the tank, talking of "earthside time" as different from tank time. It took tremendous energy to control all the fears. With subsequent trips he was able to let go of some of the fears, and use the energy that had been holding the fears to explore further—you must go *beyond* the limiting belief, Lilly said, there are no final, true beliefs, compulsion is being trapped in a known psychic reality, a dead-end space.

On subsequent trips the Two Guides began to sound like the tape in *Mission Impossible*. Lilly had managed to get to these spaces without fear, said the Guides, now "your next assignment, if you wish it, is to achieve this through your own efforts plus the help of others . . . there are several others on your planet capable of teaching you and also learning from you. There are levels beyond where you are now and where we exist to which you can go with the proper work."

Lilly had, at the end of the Sixties, become so fascinated by the personal exploration of inner space that he did not view his dolphin experiments as proper. He had a laboratory in the Virgin Islands, and a staff, and grants, and scientific papers to do, but he began to see the dolphins not as scientific objects but as real entities, and being real, in some sort of prison. He turned the dolphins loose, and went to study with Oscar in Chile. And to write the account of these explorations of all his trips. "You become a point of consciousness, love, energy, warmth, cognition." That was the good trip. There were also the bad trips—demons, absolute blind frantic terror and panic.

The acid crowd had a new guru, and an M.D. neurophysiologist psychiatrist dolphin expert at that. They recognized both the ecstasies and the terrors. When Lilly left Arica, he began to give his own seminars. They were not the usual raps; scientific vocabulary cantered through the sentences, micrograms and dendrites and millivolts. The wandering Lamb Chops did not dig him too long, they said he was "cold." He put people down who asked dumb questions, and verbally rapped people over the knuckles like an old nun when they hadn't done their homework. One of our keys to opening consciousness in our seminar was a book called *The Laws of Form,* which properly you would have to classify as mathematics, Boolean algebra. All things are: true, false, as if true, as if false, and meaningless. Lilly was eventually to add five more categories to this description of existence, of which #8 was love. I sent *The Laws of Form* to some friends, renowned mathematicians at the Institute for Advanced Study. They said it was a nice exercise in Boolean algebra, but what was all this about changing consciousness?

That's the problem with vocabulary. Does the phrase "change consciousness" imply a great expectation or a small one? Perhaps learning mathematics changes your consciousness. Wouldn't learning Chinese, too? Maybe the renowned mathematicians had already had their consciousness subtly changed—they could, after all, speak to each other in Boolean algebra and numerous other disciplines, chalk in hand at the blackboard. Lilly also used chalk in hand at the blackboard.

And what of the Two Guides, and the outer space, and the points of light? Sometimes Lilly later denied the experiences except as in his imagination, and at other times "I felt they had a very secure reality. The two guides warned me that I would go through such phases of skepticism, of doubt . . . during the experiences, I knew this was the truth. At other times I was not sure." And later he said, "The two guides may be aspects of my own functioning at the superself level, they may be helpful constructs or concepts, they may be representatives of a hidden esoteric school, I don't know."

No one who had ever been on a similar trip, altered state however arrived at, doubted the Two Guides as feelings and experience. But were they really "real"? A large number of people—upwards of a million—had experimented with hallucinogens, a much smaller number, alone. Very few people had been in a sensory deprivation tank, and no one had ever plopped into the tank with pure, legal Sandoz LSD. "If you want to be an expert," Lilly said to me once, "invent the territory."

I had my own problems with Lilly's accounts. They read, first of all, as though dictated while jogging. And the Two Guides seemed very much like the angels a small Catholic boy in St. Paul, Minnesota, would have seen—and as a matter of fact did see, but a horrified nun put him down and said only saints saw visions. Norman Mailer once said we should send a poet among the astronauts to the moon; I began to feel we should have a poet on the labyrinthine, murky explorations of inner space. I had such problems with the language. On one Lilly trip, "I was listening to Beethoven's Ninth Symphony. I literally left my body and went to Heaven" ... wait, wait, literally? Sure, what one believes to be true either is true or becomes true within limits to be found experientially—true, false, as if true, as if false, meaningless ... love. Well, the *experience* was there, everybody has the same experience of the certainty within the experience, and of course the metaphor is only a metaphor, but ... first team! Korzybski! Wittgenstein! Whorf! Off the bench and in there and dig in! We may have to punt!

Lilly bought a place in the Santa Monica mountains and turned it into a tank farm. That was his seminar now. The Samadhi Tank Company began to make them to Lilly's specs. A professor friend of mine, a classmate in a course, acquired a Samadhi Tank and used it in a psych course, the students in pairs, safety man outside the tank in case somebody should freak out and beat on the sides, subject inside, then switch and everybody write a term paper.

I was not put off by the maintenance man who said, "Wouldn't catch me in one of those things," or by signing releases, I undertake all exercises, experiments, and use of the tank at my own sole risk, and neither ... nor shall be liable for claims, demands, injuries, damages, action or causes of actions whatsoever to my person arising out of or connected with use by me of the tank ...

I took off all my clothes. Usually we have a safety man, said my professor friend, I have work to do and you don't need one. I'll be back in an hour and a half. It won't seem like an hour and a half, it may seem longer, but I won't forget. Oh yes, some people think there isn't enough air and they're choking and so on, that's just a panic excuse, the air system is fine, so I won't accept that from you.

The lid came down. It seemed quite heavy. Thump thump thump THUMP. What the hell is that? Oh, it's my pulse. Why is it going so fast? Just because that lid seemed so heavy. Is the water really buoyant? Yep, you really have to work to sink, and then you can't stay down. Certainly is black in here. Yessir, eyes wide open and can't see a single thing, weird. Thump . . . thump . . . thump, that's better. *Quiet* in here. *Very* quiet. Certainly is dark. Yep. Wonder how much time has gone by. Thirty seconds? That leaves eighty-nine minutes and thirty seconds, if the sonofabitch doesn't forget I'm in here. No, he wouldn't forget. What if he gets hit by a truck? He wouldn't get hit by a truck either. Now what's *that* little sound?

There was nobody in the tank but me, and the little sounds were all me. Thump thump thump, and little gurgles in the stomach and intestines, and something in the ear, amazing how many little sounds there are that normally you don't hear because the outside world is making so much noise . . . so what. The sergeant-voice arrived, slightly breathless from the tennis court. You dummy, you're not supposed just to lie there, you're supposed to Have an Experience. Lilly got all the way to Arcturus III, for Chrissakes.

Well, here I am in the tank, where the hell are the Two Guides?

I let everything go. I had been holding my head up, unconsciously. It didn't drop as far into the salt water as I thought. Nothing to do. Probably eighty-six minutes to go . . . I couldn't stop thinking about Lilly. Dammit, that was *his* trip, I don't know any angels, that's not my metaphor anyway.

Thump, thump, gurgle, gurgle. Let's do a meditation. What color is your left foot? Where *is* your left foot? Left . . . there it is.

Hey, let's go, said the sergeant-voice. You dummy, you're using up your tank time with the same old ratcheta ratcheta. Go somewhere! Inner space! Outer space! But stop that!

Certainly is *black* in here. Wherever you go normally, you're never in complete blackness, there's always *some* light . . .

I had a momentary vision of some bicycle riders at twilight, a country road. Ah, Altered State of Consciousness. Let go, let go, let go, let's go . . .

. . . and so on.

The building with the tank room was new. The main hallway connecting the several college buildings was several stories high, quite striking architecturally, with kiosks for various college notices. Big posters with bold colors broke up the spaces. Outside, a sunny day, the leaves of the shade trees making nice patterns on the grass. A bit of a breeze. Some people on the college tennis courts, in the distance. I couldn't remember whether my car was in parking lot 3 or parking lot 4, they looked almost exactly alike. I had to walk down one line of cars before I saw it. I got into my car. The speedometer said 15279. I had a fleeting worry—what if I have a flat tire? Then I thought: that's a bit silly, why should I worry about a flat tire, I don't normally. Now, where are the keys, the car keys, I had them—in my right-hand pocket, of my pants, my pants, my pants are on the chair, the chair in the tank room, the tank room? THE TANK ROOM? EEEEEEEEEEEEEEEeeeeeeekkkkkkkkkk I'm still back in the tank! Zoooooooooooooooooop!

THUMP THUMP THUMP THUMP thump thump thump . . . thump. . . thump. Whew! Eyes, that's right, my eyes are open but I'm not seeing anything because tank, this is a tank, this is, let's see, Friday afternoon, see, water, salty, thump . . . thump . . . thump car, what was that, 15279 . . . body, am I here? I'm here.

Where the hell are the Two Guides?

Ah-h-h-h, shut up about the Two Guides. Where are the bicycle riders on the country road?

Where's the bottom of this tank?

Let's go back, let's go . . .

I heard footsteps. The lid opened, a silhouetted figure in dim light up there.

"Hi, how you doin?"

"Not ready yet."

"That's an hour and a half. Blink your eyes. In a minute, I'm going to turn the light on in this room."

I said the last hour had certainly gone by quickly. I climbed out. My professor friend was grinning.

"Why are you grinning?" I said.

"Why are *you* grinning? You're giggling. You look ver rested."

I said I felt somewhat rested. My fingers and toes were quit wrinkled. I got dressed.

"This course has turned out well," my friend said. He de

scribed the reading list for the course. Some of the papers written by the students had been quite interesting. "Some of the kids logged a lot of time, three, four hours at a stretch."

"No bad experiences?"

"Not one. The administration was worried, but the course turned out extremely well."

I told him how Lilly's trip got in my way. "The damn Two Guides," I said. "Of course, he had been on lots more trips. And with pure Sandoz LSD. I'm not sure I'd go back in there with three hundred micrograms of LSD. That's guts ball."

I took a couple of psychological tests. We chatted.

"You look much more serene than when you got here," said my friend. Well, they always say that, the people that run the resort, when you're leaving.

Bold posters in the corridor. The sun was still out, the shade trees making nice patterns on the sunny grass. Some people on the college tennis courts, in the distance. The car was in lot 4. I got in. My keys were in my right-hand pocket, and my pants were on. The speedometer said 15279.

Lilly, the senior astronaut, seemed to be able to move effortlessly, almost dizzily, among vibrational levels: here he is doing an exercise in Chile with another man, involving a lot of spooky staring:

"I went automatically into Satori #6 yet holding in #12 and #24. The part of me in #6 took a look around and saw that part of him was peaking into #6 but that he didn't know it. I came back down and reported this to him . . . 'he' was in 48, he became extremely angry, going into 96 immediately . . ."

It always seemed to me that there were verbal definitions of subtle feelings, but no parameters, one man's #6 is another man's #12, I was wishing for road signs: WELCOME TO VIBRATIONAL LEVEL #12. PLEASE DIM LIGHTS. DO NOT LITTER.

In Chile, Lilly went into the desert as part of the program. Alone in the desert in a little hut, five days and nights, "I started to cry, lonely at first, for me. I went with the grief. It changed to grief-joy combined and it was for all humans—later [Oscar]

called this a special region, making the Christ, the green qutub."
(The last word is Arabic, meaning special powers, or one with
special powers.)

That's the senior astronaut. When the National Guard goes
camping—first of all, we didn't do it in the desert, because there
wasn't a desert handy. The instructions were to find a small
room with plain walls, remove the pictures, hang a blanket over
the window, remove all furniture except a sleeping bag or cot,
no reading material, not a word, nothing to listen to, one can-
dle, bring the food for three days, cold food, obviously, nothing
to prepare, put the food and water on the floor in the corner,
the room should be one where you can be alone undisturbed for
three days, the room should be next to a bathroom or handy to
one but use the bathroom only in extreme necessity—

—camping in the city. I took: one barbecued chicken, toma-
toes, carrots, grapefruit, hard-boiled eggs, cans of tuna, and at
the last minute, half a bag of Granola, the cereal, utensils, and a
can opener.

Three days, three nights. Very instructive sidelight, not intended as the main part of the exercise: if the exterior stimulation is reduced like that, and you ask yourself whether it's your
stomach or your head that's hungry, you really only eat when
you're hungry. I emerged with the chicken and the tuna intact.
All I had eaten for three days was the grapefruit, the vegetables,
and part of the cereal thrown in impromptu at the last moment.

But there was to be no free time. All to be taken up with exercises. Even the more experienced National Guardsmen giggled nervously when handed the programs they were to do alone:
first day, jnana yoga. (All yoga is not breathing and twisting.
That's hatha. Jnana is with the head, the imagination.) Two
hours: inhale cold, exhale warm. That's it. That's the warm-up.
Inhale warm, exhale cold. Then, four hours: imagine a flower,
inhale the flower, exhale the flower. Okay, but *four hours*? Four
hours: blow a note on your $1.98 G. Schirmer recorder, chant
the note, draw the petals of a lotus in the air, blow the note,
chant the note, draw the petals in the air—

—not much there for the left side of the old brain to do. In my case, it arrived with the following message: you know what you're doing? You're sitting in the middle of a blank room, a ganzfeld in perception, and you look like a nut there with your goddam recorder and your imaginary flower; in fact, you *are* a nut and this a crazy, help, help! Inhale the *universe*? Wha?

Midway through the second day, the over-voice had begun to dim. Fading away: you know what this is like? This is like being stuck in the airport hotel in Toledo in a blizzard with no lights and no food and no planes taking off and the radiators are stuck and the phones are out, so big deal, next time you're stuck for three days in the airport hotel in Toledo you'll know some exercises to do—

Flower exercise. The old enneagram, or symbol, from the Masters of Wisdom:

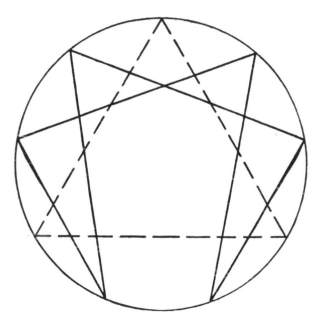

At each point where the interior lines touch the circle, there is a flower of a specific color. So you go from red flower at point one to green flower at point two, and so on, nine points, and back to red flower. Four hours.

Then a rather curious phenomenon began. The mechanism began to run by itself. That is, I did not direct it to go red flower, green flower, but it did anyway. Furthermore, I could just sit there and watch, because I wouldn't know what *shade* of red or green was going to turn up. Oh, that's a pretty green. Say, that's a very deep purple, deeper than the last time around.

The mechanism got to the left lower point, the yellow flower, and nothing appeared. Then the yellow flower appeared, just a syncopated beat late. Red flower, green flower, I just sat there staring, childlike and dazzled, Oooh, that's a pretty one, and the flowers appeared *before* the words I could use to describe them. Faster than words! Wow! And when we got to the yellow point, a large *carrot* appeared.

You're no flower, get out of there, I said.

The carrot changed, cartoon-like, back to a flower. I thought that was very funny. Red flower, green flower, purple flower, and this time the yellow flower appeared upside down. The sonofabitch was a real prankster. I laughed right out loud. In fact, I began to feel very good. So I sat there, laughing, not controlling, this flower charade running through its routine, and left-sided, I thought, now isn't this interesting, you're stoned but you're not stoned, you're not stoned because you can still think all these things clearly, this is Tuesday afternoon and you haven't had anything to make you stoned, Granola doesn't do that, and yet there's no question that a very funny flower routine is being run in here.

It got darker after a while, and I found I could make a white spot appear on the black, shadowy wall and move it around by moving my head, that was pretty funny, and the old verbal brain, pretty well beaten back, would appear occasionally with some dry psychological professorial comment: it is well known that language does not appear until the age of umpteen months and that it is cumbersome, images do, physiologically, travel faster than words, but we do admit that the preverbal or non-verbal state is very interesting, More Research Is Needed.

That's not all I saw, but it will do for a start.

Then there were the sounds. Birds. A cardinal, then a robin, then a jay, then something I couldn't identify but something like a song sparrow, then a meadowlark, but more like a Western meadowlark, wasn't he pretty far from home? It wasn't too strange to hear birds, your hearing becomes more focused without distracting sounds, we were only a block from the park, but then I noticed: always in the same order, these birds, first the cardinal, then the robin and the others. It must be a mockingbird, the order is all rigidly the same. In fact, that's quite a compulsive mockingbird out there, he never even mixes them up. The bird sounds ceased when it got dark, and they came back the next day: cardinal, robin, jay—

At the end of the third evening, an instructor came to get me, and perform some closing ceremonies. I wanted to know about my carrot in the lower left-hand corner. I had decided it was an Achievement. I simply wanted to know what satori it came from: #24 didn't seem quite good enough, more like #12, but no no sign of a green qutub. No answers on that. "You look peaceful," said the instructor. I decided the whole exercise was so nice I would do it again sometime, but I never did.

Retreats, of course, are very old. The people who thought of them were quite smart.

The bird sounds, as it turns out, were irrelevant but a funny footnote. It took two days after the end of the exercise to care about the headlines, or get riled or stirred up, which shows you can have a vacation with nothing but Granola, carrots, water, a blank room, some exercises, and your own head. Then I was walking down the street near the apartment and wait—what's that--a cardinal, a robin, a jay—the same damn birds, in the same order, what the hell? And now I'm walking down the street, the buses are roaring up Madison Avenue, taxis are honking, and I am, believe me, alert: I am looking for a compulsive mockingbird in mid-Manhattan. I walk a little further, and the sound is—coming from—a flower shop, a flower shop, and I go into the flower shop—the bird sounds are louder, very loud—in fact, they're somewhere amidst all these plants and ferns and greenery, up there, behind the ferns, a loudspeaker, bird sounds from the speaker—

"Uh, excuse me, I hear birds in here, that loudspeaker, you have a bird record on?"

The proprietor, a small man with a mustache in a gray vest, smiles. "You like birds?"

"Sure, sure, I used to know all about them as a kid—"

"It's a tape. From the Audubon. The bird society. It makes it more—peaceful, in here, you know, like a woods."

"It's very nice. I just thought I would stop in and tell you how much I liked it."

The proprietor beamed. "That tape plays over and over. It's not like music, you get tired of certain music, but bird sounds blend right into the plants. It's funny, I had that tape three— no, four years now, all the time, and in all that time you're the first person who ever noticed."

There is a traditional way to view these phenomena from well within the paradigm. A generation ago, the distinguished McGill University psychologist Donald Hebb, together with his associates, did a number of experiments on the effects of sensory deprivation. The volunteers were paid to stay in an environment where there wasn't any stimulation at all. Their vision was restricted by translucent plastic visors, their hearing was impeded by an earphone-like pillow, and so on. They were to stay in their cubicles as long as they could.

Hebb's experiment was sponsored by Canada's Defence Research Board. That board was seeking information on two problems among others: the first reports of "brainwashing" were beginning to come back from the Korean war, and radar operators spent long hours watching for Russians coming over the North Pole. Hebb, as a leading psychologist, was interested in motivation, but basically the interest of the experimenters was directed to the effects of monotony and the lack of stimulation. As an example, why did radar operators sometimes fail to see the blips after long hours at the screen? Long-distance truck-drivers had accidents sometimes, according to studies in France and at Harvard, because the drivers began to see "red spiders on the windshield, and non-existent animals running across the road."

Hebb's volunteers were not explorers or meditators, and they did not enjoy the experience. They were planning to do some work in their cubicles, think over problems, write speeches, etc. But they couldn't concentrate. Their minds began to drift. With that set and setting, and with the attitudes they brought in, they began to think the experimenters were against them. Their left hemispheres fought the experience. Also, it could be noted that the deprivation apparatus was physically uncomfortable: cotton gloves, cardboard cuffs, translucent visors.

"The subjects reported something else to which we at first paid no particular attention, but which was to emerge as the most striking result of the experiments," said the report. "Many of them, after long isolation, began to see 'images.' Several subjects seemed to be 'having dreams' *while they were awake*. Not until one of the experimenters himself went through the isolation experience for a long period did we realize the power and the strangeness of the phenomenon."

The subjects got light-headed, and then irritable. What did they see? "Rows of little yellow men with black caps on and their mouths open. Eyeglasses marching down a street. These scenes were frequently distorted, and were described as being like animated movie cartoons. The hallucinations were not confined to vision. Occasionally a subject heard people in the scene 'talking.' One . . . heard a choir singing 'in full stereophonic sound.' One . . . had a feeling of being hit in the arm by pellets fired from a miniature rocket ship he saw. Some subjects reported that they felt as if another body were lying beside them in the cubicle; in one case the two bodies overlapped, partly occupying the same space."

Now this is very useful for the long-distance truckdrivers. Any truckdriver who sees a twenty-foot rabbit hopping across the road should pull up, he has been staring at the image of his headlights on the road, and the white line on the road, and he has put himself right into blank out in ganzfeld, he has stopped registering what is out there and is creating other images.

And the experiments also give us a Rumpelstiltskin for the results. Hallucinations. That takes care of that. (Maybe not true hallucinations. I didn't think the carrot was *really* there in midair, and the gentleman fired upon by the miniature rocket ship didn't think it was a real rocket ship, but hallucinations enough to classify, Rumpelstiltskin.)

From the popularized results of the first sensory deprivation experiments grew some lurid spy stuff. One night my wife was watching *Hawaii Five-O*. The Sinister Foreign Power was picking up our agents and dropping them into a sensory deprivation tank, whereupon they would crack immediately. Only the super-hero was able to withstand a couple of hours. I looked up from my reading.

"They have the wrong bunch of agents," I said. "All the kids in Shelby's course have logged more time than that. They fight to get into the tank. You have to sign up three weeks ahead of time."

"Shhh," my wife said.

The hero's own iron brain was about to crack when the good guys from Hawaii Five-O burst into the room and fished him out. He recovered enough, I think, to slug a couple of the bad-dies in the donnybrook before the commercial, but don't hold me to the details.

Now here was something strange. In Shelby's course, the kids were elbowing each other to get into a tank. But Hebb's associate Woodbury Heron had called his report "The Pathology of Boredom," in *Scientific American,* and that article had been reprinted many times. Pathology is the study of disease. "A changing sensory environment seems essential for human beings," Heron had written. "Without it, the brain ceases to function in an adequate way." Sensory deprivation was equated with boredom, and boredom with disease, as in the pathology of boredom. And that's how it got to *Hawaii Five-O,* though there may have been some intermediate stages.

Clearly, expectation and attitude were important factors in determining the experience. "In modern society," John Lilly had written, "most people have been programmed to avoid soli-tude, isolation, and confinement. Television sets in homes are anti-isolation and anti-solitude devices . . . thus, there is a nega-tive attitude toward solitude, isolation, and confinement in most persons. This attitude has been reinforced by those doing research on so-called sensory deprivation . . . the psychiatrists who came into the field . . . made judgments about the phenomena . . . without careful experiment analysis. . . . Negative expectations generated negative results."

(He could have said, yogis go up to the Himalayas and spend two years in a cave, and when they come down sometimes they start a whole new movement and head straight for the Johnny Carson show, where they talk volubly, but that wouldn't have been his style.) Lilly, of course, knew all the sensory deprivation literature. He never used it in his seminars; I suppose he was too irritated by it.

But not all the sensory deprivation research suggested plots for *Hawaii Five-O*. There were literally hundreds of experiments, some with positive results. But they did not surface above the general din produced by 224 technical psychology journals.

In 1975, however, one of the sensory deprivation researchers, Peter Suedfeld of the University of British Columbia, rounded up the research, rather pointedly, as "The Benefits of Boredom." For some subjects had stayed in a dark, soundproof room for as long as three weeks! The visions, the hallucinations, were due "largely to spontaneous neural firing in the retina," and the "auditory and olfactory perceptions are affected by residual stimuli from the subject's body."

Simple tasks such as memorization were actually performed better by the volunteers emerging from the dark room, though complex tasks were not. Sensitivity to sounds and colors increased. But perhaps most interesting, time spent in a quiet, dark room, even just twenty-four hours, made it easier to change bad habits. Some smokers quit smoking. "In sensory deprivation," said the report, "heavy smokers are not stressed by the absence of cigarettes." Further: sensory deprivation had been used in treating drug addiction, hypertension, snake phobia, and stuttering.

(The sensory deprivation literature, so-called, refers mostly to a quiet, dark room. Lilly's tank, called HHDE, or hydro-hypodynamic environment in the jargon, is too stressful for most subjects because of its strangeness.)

Time goes by! The world turns! Sensory deprivation is good

for you! (Somebody is probably getting ready to merchandise a Magic Closet right now.) But whether you find the experience useful, or even tolerable, depends on whether you think you can come out whenever you want. Much as I liked the quieting feelings produced by both the ganzfeld room and the tank, I have not been back to either, and if someone had said, "Marine, you die," before dropping me into a tank, I would have found it very stressful.

Buddhist psychology had already recorded the little yellow men with black caps and the stereophonic choirs that arrive with time spent quietly and alone. If you are into meditation, the *makyo* arrive, phenomena. That shows your journey has begun. Everybody gets *makyo*. Don't get interested in them, they will hold up your progress. Don't fight them, just notice them without judging, they will go away. You want to get your mind to one-pointedness, and the *makyo* are just a little test on the road of the pilgrim.

A woman of my acquaintance, getting a doctorate in Oriental religions, spent several weeks meditating in a cell at a Buddhist retreat in India. After a number of days, she began to hear voices.

"First of all," she said, "I could really hear the voices, they weren't voices like when you *imagine* voices. I could hear them. And the voices weren't noble and profound, I am no Joan of Arc, nobody told me to go out and lead France. The horror, the absolute horror, was that the voices were all everyday *trivia*: move to the back of the bus, please. Put on your rubbers, it's going to rain. Why haven't you written lately? Please fill out both sides of the form, please fill out both sides of the form, please fill out both sides of the form. Did you want the ground chuck or the ground round? How much is this? That price is too high, they called again, you didn't return the call.

"I sat there with my knees under my chin, my hands over my ears, but *I couldn't turn them off*. It was awful, horror, sheer horror, yet it was what goes on all the time, this trivia is existence. Finally I fell asleep, exhausted, the voices were gone.

"At the end of the next day I had an interview with the priest who was supervising. I told him about the voices. He said, 'Oh, good, good, this garbage has to come to the surface every once in a while to be cleaned out.'

"When I left there I felt so light I could walk on treetops. It was exhilarating."

"And now?" I asked her.

"Now there are ups and downs. The voices came back. But I like to get my garbage cleaned out once or twice a year."

Lilly, the senior astronaut, was not particularly interested in the way of the pilgrim. "I prefer understanding rather than devotion," he said. "I prefer fellow seekers rather than charismatic disciples. I am a scientific observer."

The scientific crowd, I ventured, didn't think all of this was so scientific.

"They're hung up in the pre-quantum mechanics world. Where is the observer? They think the observer is here, the reality is there. Ask them: is mathematics science? Where did the math come from? Where does each advance in math come from? It comes from the inner mind, it can't be explained as a natural science."

So Lilly went on exploring. Into the tank, at least every other day.

"Sometimes I go into these spaces and get instructions and They say, you'll forget these instructions until it's important to use them, but that's the kind of thing you don't like to talk about because somebody might pop you into a strange corner."

"Just tell me one more time," I said, "what's the difference between you and a schizophrenic who also goes to strange spaces?"

Lilly fixed with with a cold blue eye.

"I can come back. Schizophrenics wander into spaces by accident, some of them like it, some of them hate it, but it makes their relationship with other people precarious, and they can't control it. When I climb out of the tank, I'm back. You know the emphasis we put on consensus is the main enemy of investigation in these regions. Safety first, status quo. I have it myself. The fear that the universe is not what you assume it to be is very basic, especially when you know damn well it isn't what you assume it to be. So you struggle with teaching enough people to appreciate that what you think the universe is, isn't true, enough unsure so they don't panic, but so they're not content— then you'll have a first-class investigation."

I pressed on about the spaces. Had I read, Lilly said, *Stranger in a Strange Land*? Or *The Starmaker*? Science fiction. The first has become a cult book, but I am not a science fiction fan. Lilly sometimes seemed an example of Kuhn's criticism of scientific education, very specific in its area but with little experience of the rest of the tradition, maybe that was the problem with the language: did he notice the gap between experience and expression?

"Oh, all the time. I call it coming back through the screen of words."

And the spaces—the tank was a comfortable enough experience, no?

"It can be terrifying, not the tank, but the spaces. I'm uneasy when I get there. It turns your realities around, and when I'm allowed in, most of the time I want to get out. I don't emphasize the terrifying spaces because there are too many people afraid of simple spaces."

From time to time I would check in with the senior astronaut. Sometimes he was grumpy about all this tank time.

"They can get somebody else to go on these trips," he said. "I got out of the tank the other day and I looked in the mirror and I said, you're a retired hero, you've had enough."

Then he found a new drug, entirely legal, that permitted a cold-eyed exploration of inner spaces without panic, a dissociative drug. I won't even tell the name, lest it start a run on both the drug and the FDA.

"You told me six months ago," I said, after he described the new drug, "that you were a retired hero, and now here you go again."

"Almost retired," Lilly said. "This is very interesting."

I had gotten a bit fond of this remote and complex man. Sometimes—rarely—he had touches of humor.

"One of these days," I said, "the battery in your survival program is going to run down. There will be just one last faint message—*don't go on this trip.* When you get that one, cancel the trip, otherwise you'll be off with the Two Guides and that will be the last voyage."

"Survival programs always say don't go," Lilly said. "The territory's still there."

BABA RAM DASS: PILGRIM, PREACHER

"I prefer understanding rather than devotion," Lilly had said. The way of the pilgrim was, anyway, already brilliantly represented in the person of Richard Alpert, Baba Ram Dass. I first heard the story on a tape cassette, that was how it spread, people would go hear him and tape it and copy the tape and mail one to their friends, and they would copy the tape and mail it again, an old story with a new technology. Then I heard it in person, several times, and even now, I can turn on the warm cadences in my ear—

"I had an apartment in Cambridge that was filled with antiques and I gave very charming dinner parties. I had a Mercedes-Benz sedan and a Triumph 500 cc motorcycle and a Cessna 172 airplane and an MG sports car and a sailboat and a bicycle. I vacationed in the Caribbean where I did scuba-diving. I was living the way a successful bachelor professor is supposed to live in the American world of 'he who makes it.'"

Thus it begins. It has within it the same sense of expectation that "once upon a time" carries. We know there is going to be a story, and in fact the story is worth attention here not only for its charm but because it became a metaphor, an archetype, bigger than itself.

"I was blessed by everything that Western society could offer: affluence, and love, education, the fruits of advanced technology, including drugs, the best drugs. All that was part of my preparation to now know something else."

The Harvard psychology professor, the ex-sidekick of Tim Leary, the son of the president of the New Haven Railroad, kicked out for the drug experiments, years more of drug experiments, LSD, hashish, cocaine, who knows what—this gentleman is now sitting amidst banks of flowers facing an audience, most of them in jeans and boots, or the girls in the long granny dresses and sandals, and this gentleman is now balding, with a graying beard and long hair in the back, and the one-stringed instruments have ceased their sound and he just sits there and smiles. And after the longest time, he says, "Well, here we are." And his voice is so warm and he is so relaxed and he smiles and gradually everybody starts to smile, "Here we are," he says again, and here we are, not just in this room but all together on the surface of the planet—"Here we are, and we'll just talk a little, I'll talk some, and then we can get up and walk around and maybe have some cider, and you can talk, or ask questions, and we'll all just hang out for a while."

Ah-h-h-h. And we settle back, because we are going to have Buddha's Four Noble Truths, in this relaxed, funny way. Maybe with some of St. John or St. Theresa, some nice passages read to us. Or some of the cabala. And the Four Noble Truths come out so relaxed, life is suffering because you don't get what you want, or if you get what you want you might lose it, so the cause of the suffering is attachment, or desire. The fourth truth is Buddha's eightfold path for giving up attachment, which comes out to "work on yourself," not in the old Ben Franklin–Horatio Alger way, because that's in the service of the ego, but to where there's still some little bit of divine spark even though there's no body, no feeling, no thoughts, no behavior: "a complete perceptual reorganization of who I am, formless, unlimited, beyond space and time, I am light, love, consciousness, energy. It's a hard one. I'm still working on it."

The audience is rapt because it is not some odd Indian preaching at them, but this colloquial charmer who still has the language of psychology and the metaphors of his generation. So he can say "perceptual reorganization" and we're comfortable. And to explain the name Ram Dass, Servant of God, we have to have the story of Ram, but that's comfortable too, not quite the way it comes out in Hindi, probably:

"So Ram is going through the jungle and he meets these naked ascetics. And they say, 'Hey, Ram, you're God and we're really being bugged by these demons; we can't meditate. Would you mind giving us a mantra because they really make a lot of noise, you know, it's like cats making love on the back fence.' So Ram goes to see his guru, to get the mantra to help the ascetics, and the guru says, 'Come on, baby, what do you mean? I mean, you're God, if you're God, you're the mantra and the demons and the whole business'—oh, I forgot, we're in an incarnation and we have to play this out so here goes—"

Or there are the chakras, physical localizations of psychic energy in the Hindu system, expressed in terms of places, people get hung up in them, the first is survival, that's Africa, the jungle, and the second is the Riviera, sensual gratification, sex, that's the one Freud got hung up in, and the third is power, Washington, Moscow, Peking, London, that's where Adler hung out, and the fourth is the heart chakra, that's Jung's territory, still three more chakras to go—

If you go to the right places, they have Ram Dass's picture on the wall, even outdoors among some of the street vendors of Telegraph Avenue in Berkeley.

And there is always this ability to speak the language: Ram Dass comes back from India and now he is in these funny Indian clothes and so he goes to speak to the psychiatric Grand Rounds, he knows what they are thinking, here is poor Dr. Alpert, used to be at Harvard, took all those drugs, a very interesting case, schizophrenic, because Alpert is sitting *on* the end of the conference table cross-legged working his beads, but when he speaks, he speaks of himself as the case, hallucinations, dissociative experiences, he tells the whole journey in psychodynamic terms, the mandala is "a heuristic device for cognitive centering," and now what the hell are the Grand Rounds to do, but be charmed, and get the message?

In 1967, after all the drugs and all the psychoanalysis, Richard Alpert went to India—I have to summarize the story, he tells it much better himself if you want to hear it—and came into the presence of the Maharishi, a funny old man sitting on a blanket, who knew everything in Alpert's head. (Do not confuse this maharishi, Neem Karoli Baba, with the TM Maharishi or the Guru Maharaj Ji.) He knew what he was thinking, all the time. Alpert's mind raced—CIA? Underground?—and then "like a computer with an insoluble problem, my mind gave up. It burned out its circuitry." A wrenching in the chest, an outpouring of tears, "all I could say was I felt like I was home. The journey was over."

Six months of cold baths of four A.M. and exercise and breathing and communicating only by writing on a slate, and then he came back to the U.S. as Baba Ram Dass. His father the railroad president was much relieved, he called him Rum Dum but it was better than the drug trip, his elder brother the stockbroker called him Rammed Ass, but he began to move around, college campuses mostly, staying only a few days at each place, no set schedule, a sort of Johnny Appleseed of the consciousness story. If there was anything you were hiding, or harboring, that was holding you back, any pain that was difficult to share, you could tell him—he would sit, facing you, running his own mantram through his mind —free, no catches. The crowds began to grow.

Another trip to India: his guru detached him from the Johnny Appleseed role by sending all the wandering American college kids after him, as if to overwhelm him. "I'm good at describing things, but I have no conceptual understanding of what happened, Marishi kept changing roles, a nice old man, an old fool, a wizard, divine. Each label crashed immediately. He took me through fierce trips about anger, jealousy, sex, greed, attachment to the body. I said, 'I don't want to be enlightened, I just want to be pure enough to do whatever work I'm supposed to do.' He gave me a mango, hit me on the head, and said, 'You will be.' "

Another college auditorium, another group, flowers, stringed instruments:

"I didn't want to end up on this path. I wanted something more esoteric, more exquisite, secrets, special powers, to be able to do things to people, I'll go into Mao's mind and Brezhnev's mind, we'll have peace—just have a little shtick to go with it, but all I know is what my guru told me, love everyone, serve everyone, remember God. I have no sense of social responsibility. I do this just to work on myself, no scrapbook, I don't have any model of why I am doing this, I'm not collecting anything, I don't have a goal, the game is just to stay in totally free fall. Ultimately the laws of the universe are not rationally knowable because they are not within the logical rational system, since that is a subsystem, and there's a metasystem of which that's all part, which includes paradox and opposites.

"It sounds very Mickey Mouse to the Western, sophisticated mind to say love everyone, serve everyone, remember God, I know that. I see part of my role as that of a gnostic intermediary, to bring metaphors from one system into another, without attachment, that is, I'm doing it because I'm doing it because I'm doing it. I can't write the script. This is very difficult for our Western culture, where you usually have a model of what you're going to do and you're collecting this for that and you're living in time. See, when Christ said, 'Had ye but faith, ye could move mountains,' he was speaking literal truth, but were you able to move mountains, you wouldn't be you any more, you would be the Being who created the mountain in the first place. At some level as real as this physical plane, there is only one of us, and at another plane there aren't any of us."

There were parts that were difficult for the audiences: reincarnation, the three-year-old child who dies but then maybe its work was done, maybe next time—and it's scarcely arguable, Ram Dass would simply say, "A lot of things are not in the Western model." Like the miracle stories: Maharishi reading Ram Dass's mind. Or: a barber is shaving Maharishi in midmorning, and Maharishi says how are things going, and the barber says, I have a son in Madras and I haven't heard from him in a year. Two days later the barber's son arrives to see his father and says, the craziest thing happened to me, in the middle of the morning two days ago a nutty old man with shaving lather over half his face walked in, said, "Here, go see your father, he wants to see you," gave me the bus fare, and disappeared. Or: Ram Dass goes to see Swami Muktananda, who gives him a mantram and shows him into a meditation room and—sort of like a dream—Ram Dass is on the astral plane and flying in the room and then tilts a bit and gets frightened and says what am I doing down there lying on my back and zooop back into his body, and when he emerges from the meditation room, Swami Muktananda says, "Enjoy flying?"

How did he know that?

I asked Swami Muktananda. It was a couple of years later, and Swami Muktananda was in the United States, and his followers set up an ashram in an old school, and he sat, cross-legged, in his socks. With his beard and his beret and his sunglasses, he looked like a stoned jazz musician. But he didn't wear the sunglasses and the beret to receive people. We had been through an "intensive," one day, chanting and discourses, and now we could all approach and ask questions. People would come up, bump their heads on the floor, and ask their question. I was too uptight to bump my head on the floor. People's questions were: should they quit their job, should they leave their spouse, how should they meditate, could they have a mantram, please?

I asked: "You remember when Baba Ram Dass was in your meditation room in India and you were outside of it and he went flying around outside his body and when he came out you said, 'enjoy flying'?"

Muktananda frowned while the translator translated, and midway through he smiled.

"I don't know how I knew, but I remember when he did it," Muktananda said. "Come to my ashram, we'll have you flying in no time."

"I don't want to fly, I just want to know how you knew he was flying," I said.

Muktananda spoke rapidly in Hindi. Then he got up, and

grinned. He looked suddenly very, very familiar. Like a long-lost uncle or something. It was bizarre. Then he came up to me, put his arm around my head, and trotted around the room with me in this semi-wrestling hold. Then he scratched my back. It felt good. It would be nice to have a guru around the house, I remember thinking.

I was still trying to collect my perceptions—how did he get to look so familiar so fast—when the translator spoke again.

"Baba really wants to see you again," he said. (Baba was what they call the Swami.) "Really. And he says, do not get hung up in flying, that is not what it's about, it just happens sometimes."

"I don't want to fly," I said. "But if I do, and he knows about it, will he tell me how he knows?"

Ram Dass tells this story: his VW Microbus breaks down one day in India, full of Western kids following him, and everybody gets out to push but a couple of girls. Ram Dass is mad, why shouldn't they push, too, they're young and healthy, Ram Dass gets back and walks into the ashram, and Maharishi says, "Oho, Ram Dass is mad because the girls wouldn't help push the VW "

The rational mind immediately scrambles for plausible explanations: in other cultures there are all sorts of ways information gets transmitted, tom-toms, the way twigs are bent, who knows what, we accept that, even though we can't read broken twigs and tom-toms ourselves, so Maharishi got the word somehow about the VW, or about what Ram Dass was thinking, maybe he's very good at perception, in the tom-tom, broken-twig sense, a flicker from a face tells him something. Does that do it? Not quite.

A psychology professor I know had a visit with Maharishi. "People would come in, and he would make a lot of probes: you have a brother in Bombay, and the guy would say, no, Maharishi, my brother is in Delhi. Sometimes he'd guess right, and sometimes he'd guess wrong. He did have some uncanny perceptions. But all the time, I felt it was a game with him, of no importance, something he used to put people on because the word was around that he had all these strange powers."

"I know I'm pushing you hard," Ram Dass, Dr. Alpert, told

a group of psychologists and psychiatrists, "but I'm just trying to give you a feeling. The game is much more interesting than we thought it was. You begin to see this entire physical plane as a training school. The minute you stop treating all of the experiences that every single being has had which don't fit in with your conceptual model of who you are and how it works as hallucinations or irrationality or psychosis or deviance, you understand it as, really, information—all of us are judging all the time, we run these things through rationally, but there are other ways of knowing."

"Who *is* this guy?" I said, to Ram Dass, of Maharishi, sounding like Butch Cassidy squinting at his pursuers.

"I don't know." Ram Dass smiled. He tapped his head. "There's nobody home."

Ram Dass had become an archetype, a metaphor himself. Kids followed him to India, around India. The Indians were a bit bewildered. "The young Americans," they said, "dance and sing kirtan all day." Kirtan are religious chants and songs. "But they're so young. Don't they know the stages? First you're a student, then you go into a profession or a business, then you become a householder, then your household grows up and doesn't need you any more, and *then* you go do kirtan all day."

At home, Ram Dass always had an audience, even with little advance notice. But the audience, like all of us, was fixed in time: now it was no longer kids, it was the kids turning thirty or even thirty-five, in other words the same group, and one day my friend the psychology professor asked his class—and this in psychology, not engineering—how many people had heard of Baba Ram Dass and only one hand went up. "It was stunning," he said, "five years ago it would have been every hand."

But that isn't the end of the story.

Some of the young journeyers to the East, rooted in the Sixties —Ram Dass's audience, Ram Dass's followers—came home and got Ph.D.'s in the psychology of meditation or in Oriental languages or something else related. And they went back to the East on postdoctoral fellowships and began to study the Eastern teachings with the tools of the paradigm, and to chart the more exotic areas of consciousness. It is interesting to read their papers, and see them translate the Eastern metaphors into the language of psychology: "hell" in the Therevadan scriptures meaning anxiety, "the hungry ghosts" meaning cravings or deficiencies, and "the frightened ghosts" meaning irrational fears. Then they found the Eastern stuff went on and there wasn't anything to translate it with, or into. In other words, the Eastern psychologies extended on into areas not covered by ours. "The gross stuff, the heavy stuff where you can use the EEG and the EKG and so on, is all in the early stages," said one.

By pruning away at the distractions, says one paper, one could arrive at a stage with: a brilliant white light, rapturous feelings, goose flesh, the feeling of levitating, tranquillity of mind and body, devotional feelings, energy, happiness, quick and clear perception, equanimity. That stage is called Pseudo-Nirvana.

"*Pseudo*-Nirvana?" I said. "It sure sounds like the real thing."

"That's only halfway there," said my friends. They were not only into the *Visuddhimagga*, the summary of Buddha's discourses leading to purification, but, being scholars, they were into all the commentaries on the *Visuddhimagga*.

"What comes after Pseudo-Nirvana?" I asked.

"Then there are some of the darker sides of the mind, pain, dread, and so on."

"I might stop at Pseudo-Nirvana. What's beyond pain, dread, and so on?"

"Cessation of pain, dread, and finally, the cessation of everything, total consciousness, consciousness with no object. Beyond time and space."

I am so little advanced that Pseudo-Nirvana still sounded better.

And even drawing on the feelings of my most altered states, I couldn't grasp consciousness without an object. And beyond time and space, I find myself imagining, like science fiction, but there's always an observer, and a "real" time and a "real" space to come back to, and if there really isn't any observer and any time and any space, I start to get a headache and have to stop and think my hands warm.

. . .

"The supernormal powers that Western parapsychology is looking for are in the *Visuddhimagga*," said another young friend. "Telekinesis—moving objects with the mind, super-hearing, knowing the minds of others, knowing the past and future, materializing things. It describes these technically, in detail, but only as a caution that they crop up in advanced mastery, are hard to maintain, easy to break, and they're a hindrance on the path. They're a great danger to people who are still in ego and not ready for them, and masters are forbidden to display them to the laity."

"We're going to have a problem," said one scholar, "because there just aren't very many people in what we call this fifth state." The first four being waking, dreaming, sleeping, meditation. "They are hard to find and harder to deal with, and then when you do start to deal with them, the Western techniques of objectifying and cross-validating don't seem to work unless you're in some state yourself that approaches that of the one you're trying to study."

Watching my own mind, I found it saying, well, isn't that interesting, this quaint old document the *Visuddhimagga* is full of parapsychology, but then probably so are the stories of the Andean Indians and the Tibetan stories, Milarepa and Marpa, and the Bible has walking on water and isn't this all interesting Cultural Anthropology and Comparative Religion, and then a second voice would say, you're Rumpelstiltskin-ing it, if you name it and classify it, it will go away.

"There's even another problem," said the first scholar. "If you really get into this, you can lose your point of view, and then writing a paper for some academic journal seems very unimportant."

Poor Reggie has gone native, the regimental commander says of his wandering surgeon—

"Do me a favor," I said. "Just before you decide never to write about it, drop me a post card."

But I know the post card, if there ever is one, will not be like Stanley finding Livingstone.

CARLOS: I MET A MAN
UPON A STAIR

CARLOS Castaneda was an anthropology student the day he met Don Juan, the Yaqui sorcerer, and Carlos became the sorcerer's apprentice. Carlos became to non-ordinary reality what Dickens was to the Industrial Revolution. Carlos' first book was full of acknowledgments to professors, and it was copyrighted by the Regents of the University of California: "Space does not conform to Euclidean geometry, time does not form a continuous unidirectional flow, causation does not conform to Aristotelian logic, man is not differentiated from non-man or life from death," non-ordinary all right, from the moment Carlos first met Don Juan outside the bus station in—was it Yuma? The book didn't say. The first book was really only noticed by the counter-culture Californians, my goodness, there was Mescalito, the spirit of the mushrooms, and the hundred-foot gnat; everybody who had ever been stoned had found another commentator.

But Carlos went on, four Don Juan books, best sellers worldwide, and Don Juan became as well known as Charlie Brown and the other Don Juan and Oliver Twist, and the more famous Don Juan got, the more obscure Carlos got. You couldn't find him: no photographs, no address—"erasing personal history."

"The art of a hunter is to become inaccessible," Don Juan told Carlos. "To be inaccessible means that you touch the world around you sparingly. To be unavailable means that you deliberately avoid exhausting yourself and others. To worry is to become accessible."

Sometimes I crossed Carlos' trail, but he was inaccessible—a hunter, a warrior. When I read the books, and reread them, Don Juan sounded wise—wise as, say, a yogi or a Zen master. "What makes us unhappy is to want," said Don Juan, just like the Zen master. "To be poor or wanting is only a thought." Sometimes Don Juan also sounded like an existentialist, Albert Camus in *L'Étranger,* perhaps: "If nothing really matters, how can I go on living?" Don Juan is setting this up: "For me, there is no victory and no defeat or emptiness. Everything is filled to the brim and everything is equal . . ."

Carlos learned his "power spot," and the art of "not sitting," sound shamanistic practices. The parodists leapt into action: one found a mystical ski instructor whose "power spot" was in the bar on a stool; what he was doing was "not skiing."

Yet what Carlos was learning and what Don Juan said were by no means inconsistent with all the other visions of non-ordinary reality, funny as they sounded to the parodists. Carlos knew the UCLA anthropology library very well, and his ambition was to have a Ph.D. in anthropology, which, indeed, he did finally get for one of his books, *Journey to Ixtlan.* And now he would really like to lecture in anthropology, he set the whole field on its ear, except these freaky kids descend upon him, not listening to the anthropology jargon, but trying to see if he has mystical feet, or can disappear—

Some people bothered themselves. Was Don Juan made up? Was it a put-on? Carlos said: I could scarcely make up somebody like Don Juan. No one has ever met Don Juan, though Mexican students have scoured the State of Sonora. Carlos certainly met *somebody*, said Carlos' friends, because he is very changed, he was very shook up by Don Juan even if Don Juan doesn't turn out to talk exactly like Carlos says he does.

Unlike the students scouring the Mexican hills, I didn't want to meet Don Juan because I don't speak Yaqui or Spanish. Anyway Carlos' books stood by themselves, a dazzling performance. It was Carlos' rare interviews that interested me.

Carlos had learned the sorcerer's tricks, the terror and wonder of being alive. He had talked to a coyote and the coyote talked back. ("Coyotes are tricksters," Don Juan warned. "Snakes make better friends.") That sounds strange in cold print, though not so much to the people who had met Mescalito.

But Carlos did not live in Mexico with Don Juan, he lived in Westwood, in Los Angeles. What lessons had he brought back?

He could stop his internal dialogue, even in Los Angeles—in fact, using Los Angeles. "You can use the buzzing of the freeway to teach yourself to listen to the outside world. When we stop the world, the world we stop is the one we usually maintain by our continual inner dialogue. Once you can stop the internal babble you stop maintaining your old world. The descriptions collapse. That is when personality change begins. When you concentrate on sounds, you realize it is difficult for the brain to categorize all the sounds, and in a short while you stop trying. This is unlike visual perception which keeps us forming categories and thinking. It is so restful when you can turn off the talking, categorizing and judging."

Carlos disrupted his routines. "It is a challenge to live with no routines in a routinary world." (Gurdjieff and the Zen master would nod.) Carlos certainly did live without routines. When he turned in a book, he would not make an appointment with his editor in New York. He would simply appear. "I think he must come in from the stairs, the fire exit, because he never passes a secretary," said Michael, his editor. If you made a date with him, he would smile, say "Wonderful," and then not show up. If you did not have a date with him, he might show up and be very funny, absolutely delightful. I missed two encounters with Carlos, one on each coast. I said to Michael, the next time Carlos comes in from the stairs, will you let me know? Certainly, said Michael. But he didn't.

"Once," Carlos said, "I read a bit of the linguistic philosophy of Ludwig Wittgenstein to Don Juan and he laughed and said: 'Your friend Wittgenstein tied the noose too tight around his neck so he can't go anywhere.' "

Very good description of Wittgenstein. Wittgenstein? It would be fun to talk to Carlos. That must have been a good evening. Carlos and this wrinkled old Mexican wizard are out on the ramada of Don Juan's house, maybe smoking Mescalito's mix, or ingesting something else, or maybe Carlos is in the stage beyond that, and they are discussing reality and nonreality. Carlos is reading him Wittgenstein as evening falls. Certainly beats the port and the sherry in the crusty common rooms of Oxford.

I called Michael once, but he was out. The secretary I had been nice to said, "*He's* here." I didn't have to ask who *he* was. I was close by. I walked to the building, pressed the elevator button, and got in. I was wondering, when he calls United or American does he give his own name? What does he read on the plane? Anthropology, maybe, he does like to lecture about phenomenology and membership and socialization.

I had an odd impulse. I got out of the elevator immediately, found the EXIT sign, and started up the stairs. A secretary passed with an armload of paper work, saving elevator time by walking one flight. Another flight—and then, down the stairs came a small, dark man, maybe five five, one forty, with a rather humorous face. Carlos? Hard to know, there are so few pictures of him. I decided it was.

I turned around and began trotting down the stairs side by side with the gentleman.

"I was just on my way to Michael's office," I said.

The gentleman nodded and did not break his pace.

"I just wanted to say," I said. I stopped. That certainly sounded feeble. "A terrific contribution. Communicates experience, not just reading about it."

The gentleman nodded and continued down the stairs.

We were going downstairs at a rapid rate, and it was obvious that this interview would not last too long.

"Wittgenstein," I said.

Now I had his interest.

"When you and Don Juan were sitting at his house reading Wittgenstein, was it the *Tractatus* or *Philosophical Investigations*?"

The gentleman grinned. "Did I say we read it? I just told him the ideas one evening. I didn't have the book along."

"Which book?"

"Either book."

We were almost to the lobby. In Carlos' last book, Don Juan teaches him the most difficult feat of all, to make a double of yourself. Another person, your duplicate. That was how Don Gennaro could be two hundred miles away and also right there, at the same time. It occurred to me that perhaps this was not Carlos. Half humorously, I said: "This may seem a silly question, but are you Carlos or Carlos' double?"

"I'm Carlos' double," said the gentleman. He laughed.

I did not want to intrude. I could have kept up with him in the lobby crowd if I had really tried, but I didn't.

PARAPSYCH

The Phoneless Message from
Cousin Josie

WELL, what about this: can people really wake up at night and know that something has happened to some member of their family somewhere else? Or get some glimpse into the future? Or cause objects to fall off the shelf?

The status of parapsychology—the word loosely used to cover such events—can only be described as peculiar.

On the one hand: public interest is avid. Not only has there been a revival of interest in witches and demons, but anyone who claims some sort of extraordinary powers can usually get a public hearing on all the TV talk shows. Might even be able to get a TV show of his own going.

Such interest is probably the descendant of similar fascination with magic and with seances and wobbly ouija boards and talking to the dead.

But also: there is some growing respectability to the study of parapsychology, insofar as a hundred or so educational institutions now have a course in it, or have it as part of another course, and the study itself was finally voted into the American Association for the Advancement of Science in 1969, and a former astronaut, Edgar Mitchell, decided to devote himself to it.

I talked to Mitchell in his office in Palo Alto: Apollo 14 pictures in the background, phones ringing, crisp manner, the moon trip was a "peak experience"—Mitchell had learned the vocabulary of humanistic psychology—maybe even a mystical experience, seeing the earth sit out there like a big blue ball made Mitchell think of all the insanity on the planet, and a need for a radical change in the culture: "I knew we have untapped intuitive and psychic forces which we must utilize if we are to disregard these forces." So Mitchell formed a foundation, the Institute of Noetic Sciences, to "fuse the two modalities of organizing the universe, the objective, pragmatic modality of Western science and the subjective, intuitive approach of the great spiritual doctrines."

And, on that one hand, while parapsychology made it into the science societies and young assistant professors of psychology began to teach it to earnest and curious students and Edgar Mitchell sponsored Uri Geller—

On the other hand, the scientific establishment is still scornful enough that to work in the area labels you as slightly tetched in the head, a poor Reggie due to be sent home, and almost nobody is doing any real work at all in the area. I mean nobody. It was stunning to find out that, while *The Exorcist* could gross $70 million, and while mind readers and nail benders could reach 60 million people a night on television, there weren't twenty-five people in the country, there weren't forty in the Western world, working on parapsychology full-time.

Obviously, parapsychology is beyond the current paradigm. To extend the borders of the paradigm, or at least to look at it the same way we ordinarily look at the universe, we would have to do the following: be able to control some parapsychological events, be able to repeat them, have a hypothesis that would encompass these odd events, a theory with some predictive power, and then further experiments and events would come along and confirm the previous events and, the structure of scientific revolutions, pretty soon the borders of the paradigm would be modified and extended or, if the revolution were big enough, the old paradigm would go right into the museum and the new paradigm would tell us how to explain the world to ourselves.

The handful of serious researchers are working that way, setting up experiments that would hopefully be repeatable, but they have almost no funds. The total funding of parapsychology is less than the cost of a commercial break on a talk show where people are discussing the marvels of telepathy and psychokinesis.

So: if you woke with a start dreaming that cousin Josie was in an auto accident, and she was, just at that time, or if some flash hit you, unreasonably, about some future event which then turned out to happen, or if things fall off the shelf around you, that might be statistical chance or the powers might be real but you are way out there in the blue with a paradigm to sit in.

We've already seen that some things are possible—even repeatable—that previously weren't. Biofeedback showed that the autonomic nervous system could be consciously controlled, and very precisely, without the use of the left-brained, language-using part of the mind. Further: language shapes the way we see the world, and not all cultures have our view of time and space. (The Greeks call anyone who is exactly on time "the Englishman," you don't come for dinner at eight, you come over, and eventually dinner happens.) Maybe our language, our set, and our expectations are excluding us from what's there.

We also know that our perceptions are not only culturally conditioned, but not totally trustworthy. A single word repeated will begin to dissolve into other words. A flashing strobe light on a blank wall will make patterns begin to seem to appear on the wall. A red six of spades will be called a six of hearts.

Out of all there is to be perceived, we know we perceive very little. Here's a chart from physiological psychology, showing how much of the spectrum we can perceive:

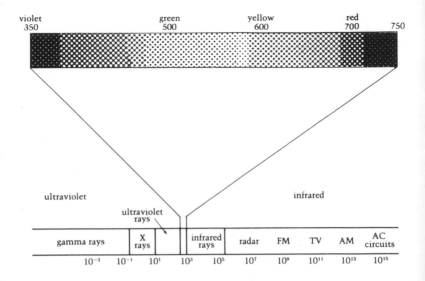

Our brains and nervous systems, it seems, act as a filter. In perception studies there is a famous paper, retitled "What the Frog's Eye Tells the Frog's Brain." Some scientists at MIT wired up frogs—brains, eyeballs and all—to see what the frog actually saw. Frogs do not see what we see; no leaves rustling in the wind, no beautiful sunsets. The frog's eye tells the frog's brain of overhead light interference—could be the shadow of a predator and that something small nearby is flying by, which could possibly be eaten. In other words, the frog's universe is screened down to the minimum needed for survival.

(Add somewhat irrelevant information from perception which might come in handy someday: elephants turn right more easily than left, if you are ever chased by an elephant, and the cobra sways back and forth to get a fix on you, and if you sway in exactly the same arc presumably he can't quite see you.)

The frog's eye/frog's brain experiment supported a more elegantly stated philosophy, coming from the French philosopher Henri Bergson and the English philosopher C. D. Broad, which says that, like the frog, we screen down. "Each person," said Broad, "is at each moment capable of remembering all that has even happened to him and of perceiving everything that is happening in the universe. The function of the brain and nervous system is to protect us from being overwhelmed and confused by this mass of largely useless and irrelevant knowledge, by shutting out most of what we should otherwise perceive or remember at any moment, and leaving only that very small and special selection which is likely to be practically useful." Aldous Huxley wrote that screening down—his metaphor was a reducing valve—left only "a measly trickle." To express the measly trickle, we had symbols and languages, which did give us the benefits of accumulated experience. "Most people," wrote Huxley, "know only what comes through the reducing valve and is consecrated as genuinely real by the local language." The reducing valve, said Huxley, could be by-passed to some extent by "spiritual exercises," drugs, and "innate gift." "Our narrowed, individual minds regard [the measly trickle] as a complete, or at least sufficient, picture of reality," but even by by-passing the reducing valve, we only get a glimpse of the Mind at Large.

Huxley and Broad, in fact, anticipated the world-renowned neurophysiologists Moruzzi in Italy and Eccles in Australia and the U.S. "There is now evidence," wrote Eccles, "that at any one time we are only conscious of an extremely small fraction of the immense sensory input that is pouring into our brains. In fact, by far the greater part of the activity in the brain, and even in the cerebral cortex, does not reach consciousness at all. However, we have the ability to direct our attention apparently at will to one or another element in the input from our sense organs."

Parapsychology attempts to measure the stuff outside the filter.

Some years ago, a botanist-turned-psychologist, J. B. Rhine, got a grant from the Rockefeller Foundation to work, in his lab in Durham, North Carolina, on people's ability to sense what card is about to be turned up. (Durham has been the center of research in parapsychology ever since.) Rhine's experiments said that some of his subjects guessed the right cards far beyond the range of probability.

There was some controversy about both the method and the statistics, but the experiments were repeated with better controls. At one point, there was even an argument by mathematicians:

perhaps the laws of probability were wrong, and needed some tuning up.

The handful of serious parapsychologists, knowing the suspicion that greets any experiments which have no paradigm to support them, set up quite careful controls. Helmut Schmidt, a former physicist working in Durham, tested the ability of subjects to guess which of four lamps would light up, the lighting up of the lamps being random, and the source of that randomness being the emission of elementary particles from radioactive materials. No hands, no chance for cuing or human error. Some of the subjects, said Schmidt, made predictive guesses with the probability against chance being 10 million to 1.

At Maimonides Medical Center in New York, Dr. Montague Ullman designed an exponent to cut down on the distraction by all the other noise; such as we don't perceive the signals of telepathy. Ullman tried two undistracted states for his experiments, sleep and blank out in ganzfeld.

In the sleep experiments, a "sender," or a volunteer, a student, a research assistant, a doctoral candidate, would concentrate on a particular picture or print. When the sleeper's psychophysiology showed that he was dreaming—the right EEG reading, and rapid eye movements—he would be woken and would dictate his dreams into a tape recorder. In the morning he would be asked to rate various prints and pictures according to the way they most matched the dream material; various double-blind procedures would be set up to protect the experiment.

I offered myself as a subject for the blank out in ganzfeld. Over the eyes went the split ping-pong balls. Over the ears went the earphones to produce the "white noise." I sat in an easy chair. The "sender" went into an electromagnetically shielded soundproof room. You can't see anything but a diffused white light with those ping-pong balls over your eyes. You get some instructions on the earphones and then off you go, dictating into a small microphone around your neck, free association, anything you see or think.

If your eyes are open but can see only a diffused light, you still get images. I got some geometric shapes, some V's, some interlocked circles flowing by. I dictated continuously, there go some more forms . . . look like birds flying . . . geese, maybe . . . shrinking circles, imploding.

But by this time, after two years of full-time research and a dozen years of guinea-pigging, my language-using, classifying mind arrived quickly, sounding, as usual, professorial and knowing—

—yep, here we are with geometric shapes again, now that might be from some ocular pressure, as in Barber's paper on the hallucinogens, or that might be from the phosphenes on the eyelids, isn't that interesting.

There goes a shape, I dictated, looks like . . . Mickey Mouse . . . Mickey Mouse's ears, floating by. There are . . . Mickey Mouse's ears again . . . south-southeast, five knots . . .

After a little less than an hour, the ping-pong balls were untaped and the earphones taken off, and I went to look at the pictures the "sender" had been sending. One looked terribly familiar. It was a Disney character, Pinocchio. I reached out for it. Wait, said the interior voice in my ear. Is that close to Mickey Mouse? Mickey Mouse's ears? It really looks the most familiar, but cartoon images are common in sensory deprivation experiences, Mickey Mouse isn't Pinocchio, Pinocchio looks familiar because almost all Disney characters look familiar, especially if you once saw the movie, that black crow in the second picture, we had a black crow shape, didn't we? Looks certainly like one of those black shapes, pick the black crow.

The "sender" had been sending Pinocchio. First hunch right.

Another writer, Francine Gray, saw, once they taped on the split ping-pong balls, images of Arabs in robes, long-gowned ministers, Orthodox priests, and immediately picked, once her experiment was over, a slide of Arabs in long white robes. That was a "direct hit"; my scores were only five out of ten. Her reaction to her "direct hit" was one of anxiety: "a serious headache, blurred vision, perspiration, dizziness, trouble sleeping." "When my view of reality is undermined by something as anomalous as a psychic event, I am in a world of chaos in which no place seems safe," she said. "I realized that this was one of the reasons why parapsychology has tended to remain such an ill-funded, fragile, suspect field of science. We are increasingly titillated by

Edgar Cayce, pop ESP courses at the local Y, showman spoon-benders on TV and the whole surge of paperback occultism; but the experience of having our latent psychic capacities confirmed in a laboratory leads to a deep and primitive anxiety from which we tend to withdraw very quickly."

The Maimonides experiments were one of only two ever to be funded by the National Institutes of Mental Health, but they, too, ran out of money. There was money available from rich widows who wanted to talk to their dead husbands, but little for experiments. Somehow the experiments were boring, except to people interested in parapsychology. The "direct hits" seemed open to other interpretations, and the statistics were, well, statistics.

I have an innate bias about statistics anyway, which comes from watching very learned economists miss the gross national product by $150 billion. There's always one more equation. But that's my problem; if the chances of a hit are one in 10 million, the only defects can be in the definition of a hit, and in the probability statistics, but even if the chances aren't one in 10 million, they're certainly better than fifty-fifty.

Parapsychology wasn't helped, in its fragile state, when one of its most promising experimenters was found to have tampered with the machine that produced random impulses for shocking rats on a grid. And, ultimately, the whole Uri Geller adventure may have been a setback.

Uri: Instructions from the Saucer

Uri Geller, a handsome, six-foot three-inch former Israeli para-trooper, left a trail of broken forks and bent nails across the television talk shows, all done with some mysterious powers. His credibility came, at least in part, from the fact that he had been tested at the Stanford Research Institute, a think tank in Menlo Park, California, that was once associated with Stanford University, and now works on the things that think tanks largely supported by the government work on—Russian missile capabilities, and so on. His credibility was further enhanced because it was Captain Mitchell who brought him to both Stanford Research and the TV shows.

I asked Mitchell what the reaction was of NASA to his current project.

"NASA has an engineering mentality," he said, "so they're slightly embarrassed by it. It doesn't fit the paradigm of engineering. They come in from time to time, because all the astronauts had some sort of experience like mine, seeing the earth as a tiny insignificant globe in a vast cosmos, knowing there is some sort of direction where science says there isn't, and that knowing isn't intellectual. Not all the astronauts had reactions like mine—as soon as the heavy tasks were over, on the way home, I had this alternating pathos and ecstasy, hard to describe—but all of them had something, only it surfaced through whatever belief structure they had."

Captain Mitchell had a Ph.D. in engineering; if the so-called "Geller effects" turned out to be true, what was that going to do to engineering and physics?

"Oh, it will expand it like Einstein did to Newtonian physics I see it as bimodal, rather than as opposing points of view."

And why was he leading Uri to TV?

"The networks say it sells, and it helps to get the point of view across. I don't think Geller has any idea of why his things work, there just seems to be some sort of channel open that normally gets blocked."

That was the way Geller was regarded at Stanford Research, too, as a kind of *naif*, a prima donna, very difficult to deal with, but who had a channel open that normally gets blocked. The rest of us all have corks in our channels. The scientists who were testing Geller were no rat-runners, they were laser physicists. In the unwritten hierarchy of science, laser physics gets more points than rat-running. Physicists Hal Puthoff and Russell Targ had some funny stories about other people with ESP.

"When people heard we were working on ESP," said Hal, "we got all kinds of visitors. A wife brought in her husband, this truckdriver. He was in despair, they were about to lock him up. He claimed he could hear voices, the neighbors, talking about him. Turned out he *did* hear the neighbors talking about him.

He could also see things in other rooms. We tested him on some standard stuff, symbols in envelopes in another room. He tested brilliantly. The doctors put him on Thorazine and he stopped hearing and seeing things and went back to work, the abilities only came back if he stopped the Thorazine."

"We had a four-year-old kid," said Russell, "who would get dressed up because, he said, Aunt Pearl was coming, and the mother would say Aunt Pearl is in Cincinnati, and then Aunt Pearl would walk in unexpectedly. The mother wanted the kid turned off, it was a bother."

"ESP hasn't been trained out of kids," Hal said. "We agree on the physical universe and we don't agree on the power of thought, so we're trapped in the physical universe. But this stuff is growing. By the end of the century, everybody will be in some subculture that brings in the subjective."

Geller's public appearances were generally concerned with making metal objects bend: forks, spoons, big nails. I was surprised to find that he had never done this at Stanford Research—the impression from television, from the coupling of his metal-bending performance with the words "Stanford Research" and "scientists," was that he had been locked up in a Faraday cage, shielded from all contact and interference. There, by some mysterious power, he melted forks.

"We were all set up with rings to bend," Hal said, "but it's never happened."

"Why not?"

"Well, a lab situation is different from a public performance, where he can get people's energies working, he's used to having people watch, controlling them, being relaxed."

What had he done in the lab, if he hadn't bent any metal? Well, he'd generated a magnetic field, and affected the roll of dice, carefully controlled, and made numerous telepathic hits.

How did he do that?

"He says he visualizes a TV screen, and then he reports what comes in on the screen. He thinks the flying saucer people give him the right answers. The other day, a flying saucer was one of the images we had in another room. He kept saying, I'm not getting it, I'm not getting it, and he kept seeing the image of a flying saucer, he was supposed to draw whatever image came through, and finally the flying saucer people whirled by again and said, 'It's *us* this time, dummy, draw *us!*' He drew a flying saucer."

"He was exhibiting ESP, though, before he began to talk about the flying saucer people. Then somebody suggested that to him, and he used it as an explanation. Psychics don't know where their powers come from, or why, and they're afraid they'll go away, so they make up these things, and sometimes they cheat."

A magazine article had suggested that Geller cheated.

"He cheats, he cheats a lot, and also he's real," said one of the physicists.

We were at SRI—security guards, escorts, badges, not because of this research but because of the stuff in other parts of the buildings. Geller was happy with his day at the lab. He had scored a lot of telepathic hits.

"I am feeling good today. The vibrations are very good."

Did he, I wanted to know, use any alcohol or drugs? No, never. Was there anything he could affect besides metal? No, just metal. When he wanted to get a metal ring to break, how did he break it?

"I just concentrate and say, 'Break!' and it breaks."

Geller's demeanor was boyish and enthusiastic.

"I don't know how I do it, I don't know why it happens, I am some sort of a channel."

Right then, he was more interested in cars and girls than in academic discussion of the paranormal. I found I was more interested in the physicists than in Geller. I noted the contents of a bookcase in one of the offices: three full shelves of books on quantum mechanics, light, lasers, masers, all standard physics stuff, and then the anomalies—Jung, *Witchcraft and Magic*.

I spent some time with the physicists.

"When Uri comes to dinner," said one of the wives, "I have to be sure to put the good silver away. He melts forks unconsciously, he can't help it." She showed me a fork Uri had been eating with. It certainly looked melted and twisted.

"Things happen around Uri," said one of the physicists who

was not on the project. "We were walking to the parking lot one day, and a large rock fell at our feet out of a clear blue sky."*

"We have all kinds of crazy things on videotape, watches falling out of the ceiling, poltergeists."

"You know," said Hal, "Mitchell left his camera on the moon. It was really a bit embarrassing, they mentioned it on all the subsequent moonshots. So Uri was going to try to bring it back. All kinds of Mitchell stuff began to materialize around him. He dug his spoon into his ice cream one day and found a tiepin Mitchell had been missing for two years. Gradually, Mitchell's jewelry box in Texas began to fill up with everything he'd lost, cuff links, tieclasps, stuff gone for years."

"But no camera."

"No, the camera's still up there."

"Do you have any way of explaining this?"

"Modern physics isn't capable of explaining it. On the other hand, equations in physics permit many things that are just ignored, for the time being. Advanced potential models correspond to precognition, some of the waves would start in the future to arrive now. The equations permit it, but the physics textbooks discard the part that runs from the future to the present. Superconductivity has lots of unused equations. In wave functions, there are particles slower than light, and protons and neutrinos as fast as light, and the equations permit tachyons, which would be faster than light."

"But nobody's found a tachyon."

"Not yet."

"So the right equations might be lying dormant somewhere."

"Sure. We don't know how things happen; every year the laws get violated, and then we say, well, that was good until now."

"But aren't equations just another language, with their own constraints? There's always an equal sign in the middle."

"I think," Hal said, "what we're going to end up with is that thought is senior to physics."

---

* In the eighteenth century, the French Academy passed a special resolution saying it would reject all further reports of rocks falling out of the sky.

"Sir James Jeans did say," I said, "that the universe was looking more like a big thought than a big machine."

"It may be that what we think is real, the physical universe, is an interference pattern in the thought world, the basic ether or tachyon seed or what have you."

The boys were losing me.

"I'm convinced," Hal said, "there are Superintelligences."

"Well, who is it when they appear?"

"Oh, spirits, gods, archangels, large thoughts—"

"There was an ex-Jesuit priest in one of my courses," I said, "who meditated about five hours a day, and could leave his body, and always contacted the same archangel."

"Did he get any good data?" Russell said.

"I asked him," I said, "and he said, no, they mostly went to the beach."

"MacGowan's paper said there were ten *billion* inhabitable planets in this galaxy alone. Some of them are bound to be more advanced than us. Now what would you do if you found Earth? Anthropologists know you don't just lay one culture on another, you'd shock the more primitive one and destroy it. So, maybe they see us as a Skinner box, or like a wild game preserve—"

"Wait, wait—who's They?"

"They—they're probably part robot and part organic, we already know how to make artificial hearts and kidneys, and computers that simulate brains, it wouldn't be hard to see a more advanced being partly mechanical, partly organic, and of course with mechanical evolution time would be much less of a problem."

"So what would the Superintelligences be doing?"

"Oh, monitoring, not hitting us right off, maybe giving us little hints that they're there—some astronomers have noticed signals coming back thirty seconds later, as if they were bounced right back—"

I wanted to know more about the earth as a wild game preserve. I was charmed by the idea that maybe we were considered a national park by the gentlemen from Krypton.

"It's also possible," said one of the SRI physicists not on the ESP project, "that the earth is a prison planet."

ADAM SMITH

"The earth is a prison planet?"

"That this backwash is where entities are sent who are out of harmony."

I looked around. I was having a violent attack of ambiguity. On the one hand, the gentlemen sitting with me at a Chinese restaurant on the peninsula south of San Francisco had Ph.D.'s in physics and established reputations in physics. On the other hand, I wished that some of them hadn't been into Scientology and their subjects into it too, and some of them into Eastern stuff. Why couldn't they be 4-H Club straight, ordinary physicists? Were they kidding? No, they weren't kidding, they knew how it sounded—it was just a hypothesis, mind you—but it was obviously something they'd talked about among themselves before.

"This all sounds like *2001*, science fiction," I said.

"Whatever is real may come up more strange than *2001*," they said.

Part of me was saying, let's get out of here, they are all crazy, Ph.D.'s or no, wiggy people have Ph.D.'s, and another part was totally fascinated. I began to feel a little dizzy. It must have been the monosodium glutamate in the Chinese food.

Randi: A Prestidigitation of Magicians

I went to see Uri whenever he performed publicly and I was around; by this time I knew a lot of people in the audience. Uri was to try to guess a color we were all thinking. He turned away, and a woman wrote "blue" on the blackboard, and then erased it. "Okay, I'm going to take a chance. The color I get is blue." The audience applauded wildly. Uri cut off the applause. He pointed to one corner of the audience. "Who over here," he said, "was sending yellow?" A young man, somewhat sheepishly, raised his hand. "Please don't do that," Uri said, "it confuses me." The man apologized.

Volunteers came forward with rings and pins and keys. Uri would try to bend them, or break them. He said objects of emotional attachment would be of the most value. He couldn't guarantee success, he was tired, from trying to focus his mental powers before senior physicists. We should all be "with" him, send him our own psychic energies. He tried bending rings by putting them in the hands of volunteers and then passing his hands over theirs. It didn't work. We were watching on a television monitor. The audience got a bit restive.

"It's not working," Uri said. "It's not going to work." Plainly, it was not going to come. I knew how he felt; It had that tennis serve that wouldn't come if you wanted it. "Wait—" Uri said. "There? Isn't one broken? No?" No. "Wait—there! There! Didn't it break?" One of the rings, indeed, had broken, though it was hard to tell, on the television monitor.

For hubris, there is nemesis, for matter, there is antimatter, and for Uri Geller, there was James Randi, a bearded, roguish, saucy magician I ran into on the streets of New York. Randi's fame had taken an upward turn from being an anti Geller

"He's a magician," Randi said. "It was careless of them not to know. Physicists are easier to fool than anybody."

"All that metal bending—"

Randi reached for my keys, and began to stroke one of them.

"He couldn't perform on the Carson show because I got to Carson, and we didn't let him bump the table with all the little canisters on them," Randi said. "Then he went on the Griffin show, and Griffin said, ladies and gentlemen, here's a man who failed before thirty-five million people, and that's good enough for me, and the audience cheered."

My office key was beginning to bend.

"Cut that out," I said. The office key continued to bend.

"Bend it back, I don't have another one," I said. Randi reversed it and the office key began to bend the other way.

"We had a bunch of magicians at his last performance. We were laughing. I've videotaped all his shows so I can analyze his tricks."

The office key was bending too much the other way.

"Can't you get the damn thing like it was at first?" I said. "It won't open the door that way."

Randi handed the key back. We were sitting in a restaurant. Absent-mindedly, Randi held a spoon, which began to bend.

"He's very good, though, very, very good," Randi said. "He's one of the best I've ever seen."

"Could I learn to bend a spoon like that?"

"Sure," said Randi, and he showed me.

All of Randi's processes involve what psychologists call cognitive dissonance. You're used to seeing things a certain way, so you continue to see them, and if you have a spoon in the hands, you can make your hands appear to hold the spoon in a way other than they really are, while you give it some pressure.

"Now, watches, Geller starts stopped watches. That's easy. Would you like to move your own watch ahead an hour by mental powers? Let's see—what time have you got? Hold your watch face down in the palm of your hand—that's right—now keeping a circle going on the watch-back with your finger—that's good, that's good—"

Randi began to imitate Geller. He frowned, as if in fierce concentration. "It's not going to work, no, please, you must be with me, somebody is sending me bad vibrations, please everybody send me good vibrations, I don't think I can do it today, I was up all night with the Nobel prize winners, wait, wait, maybe it's going to work—"

The imitation was almost cruel; Randi really had the cadences down.

"Now, look at your watch. I think we have moved it an hour ahead by sheer mental powers."

The watch was an hour ahead. I was mystified. How the hell did that happen? Randi wouldn't show me. He must have gotten a thumbnail on the watch stem at some point, probably when he said, let's see, what time is it, but I sure didn't see it.

"And the telepathy?"

"Some telepathy involves a little pencil point in the thumbnail, and some a quick look at the blackboard when everybody's distracted, and some involves handling the envelopes."

"Is there anything Geller can do that you can't?"

"Yes. I told you, he's very very good—but I'm working on it."

Again I felt a curious ambiguity. If Geller was just a magician,

I was disappointed not to have a box seat when the paradigm changed. But there was also a little feeling of relief, that maybe the world was still the way we thought—

—yet the scientist who got a Nobel prize for his work in measuring and clocking impulses in the nervous system, Sir John Eccles, wrote, "I think telepathy is still a tenable belief, but if it exists at all, it provides an extremely imperfect and inefficient way of transferring information from the neural activity of one brain...."

A book came out about Geller. It said that Geller got his instructions from an orbiting computer called Spectra, from the planet Hoova. People began to lose interest.

I had a long talk with a friend of Randi's, Ray Hyman, who teaches a course called Pseudo Psychologies at the University of Oregon.

"They have me billed as a skeptic," Hyman said. "All I want is to get the kids to ask the right questions. Most people are so ignorant of the roles of perception and memory that they don't know what's rare and what's ordinary. The kids have been so oriented to think that the Establishment is lying about everything that they think anything the Establishment excludes must be considered, in this case the scientific establishment. It takes patience to know the phenomena. Young generations are very experience-oriented, and they would rather have the clarity of some experience than something empirically tested, they're almost antiscientific. Sometimes there is a causal explanation. Forty years ago the parapsychologists said bats had ESP, and the antiparapsychologists said they were crazy. Now we know the bats have a sophisticated sonar system, but before radar there was no way to explain it. Two hundred years ago, when the scientific establishment rejected Mesmer's animal magnetism, it also rejected the powers of suggestion which animal magnetism explained. There may be something important going on, and maybe the statistical model doesn't apply. But I don't see very much clearheaded work."

Some psychologists—as opposed to physicists—at Stanford Research Institute tested Geller, and reported to a psychology newsletter, without much fanfare, that they had come up with nothing. The vibes must have been bad. Wherever Geller went, a gaggle of magicians followed, eager to claim him as one of their own.

"Unlike magicians, it doesn't always work for me," said Uri. "That proves I'm real."

"Parapsychology experiments in general, and the Geller experiments in particular, have been set up without adequate controls and with many unconscious biases," said Martin Gardner, a *Scientific American* columnist and amateur magician, "and with no knowledge of magic."

Wherever Geller went, people either wanted to believe very badly or wanted to disbelieve very badly. I found myself sliding into indifference. For I know that I am very easily fooled. Show me a red six of spades and I will call it the six of hearts. Play a tape of a single word over and over and I will hear other words. Sometimes I even see carrots in midair in a ganzfeld room.

And I wasn't really interested in learning magic. I would like to be able to move the hands of your watch ahead an hour, but not enough to spend more than ten minutes learning it, and I know it's in the big magic book you can send away for, or learn from somebody else once you're in the magician's union.

These phenomena, say the ESP fans, are fragile, the people who are "sensitives" don't know where the stuff comes from, and they are frequently erratic and emotional people who sometimes even cheat because they don't know what turns it off and on.

And the hard-nosed stick-to-the-paradigm people say: no experiment yet has turned up any real psychic phenomena that can't be otherwise explained. To convince the hard-nosed, you would have to have a "sensitive" on one coast, another on the other coast, both monitored for any gismos and tiny walkie-talkies, and then one of them would send Watson-come-here-I-want-you and the other would not only get it, but would send back What-hath-God-wrought. Then the physicists would dump over a bin of unused equations and pick some pretty ones that matched up what had just happened.

Ingo, it seemed, could go anyplace, right while sitting there drinking coffee and smoking a cigar.

Ingo was described as a "sensitive" and a "talented psychic." It made a certain amount of sense that some people should be more sensitive than others. Some people have absolute pitch, they can sing you a middle G with exactly the right amplitude, and some people are tone-deaf. What Ingo could do is called "remote viewing." You give the psychic or sensitive a place, described by the coordinates, latitude thus and longitude thus, and zooop off he goes, and then describes it—it's an island shaped like this in the Indian Ocean, nobody's ever heard of it, he draws a map that's almost it, not quite, but you can see the resemblance. I didn't see Ingo do this, but I was at a seminar where it was reported having been done in the lab, and later I asked Ingo how he did it. Ingo was amused by the whole procedure. Ingo is a former clerk who is now an artist. He began by studying astrology so he could get along with people. I thought, when I first talked to him, that he was from the South, he sounds like the bachelor gentlemen you meet from the South, but he is from Utah.

"I just get the description, and then I let it happen," Ingo said.

"Does it take any time?"

"No, no time at all. It's not the same dimension."

"Did anything in particular equip you to do this sort of travel?"

"Well, your mind says it's not possible, and if you think it isn't possible, then it isn't possible. So you have to clear out your mind of its disbeliefs and open it to any sort of experience, and that takes hours and hours of work, clearing out the unconscious."

Scientology again, all those hours of "auditing," recitation, what's the last time you remember this, what's the time before that, on back into previous lives. Ingo had been heavily into Scientology, like one of the physicists testing him.

I asked Ingo when he first noticed he had some talent in this area. Ingo said his chinchilla could read his mind; when the time came to put him in his cage, his chinchilla disappeared. And then he could read his chinchilla's mind. Something like that.

Ingo was getting impatient with the lab work. "I *may* just dematerialize *every*thing," Ingo said.

Ingo, said the SRI physicists, had been to the back side of the moon before the astronauts, and described it just like they found it. Ingo had been to Jupiter, they were going to check that one out with the Pioneer fly-by.

"What did Ingo see when he went to Jupiter?"

"Oh, gases and clouds and things."

Ingo had been to Mercury, too. He noticed a magnetic field that surprised the scientists.

"NASA is very excited about Ingo's trips," said one of his fans, not a scientist.

I decided to check this with NASA, about six different officials and a lot of phone calls. NASA disclaimed any excitement over Ingo's trips. In fact, they disclaimed the knowledge of Ingo's trips.

"You wouldn't expect them to admit it, would you?" said Ingo's fans. "Not only is it secret, it might affect their funding." The files did show that a NASA official, a couple of years ago, said both NASA and the Soviet Academy of Sciences were studying "energy transfer" and "psycho-physiological information transfer," which sounds like telepathy and astral travel to those that translate that way.

NASA called back.

"We did sponsor an experiment in this area," said the NASA man, "to see whether unusual man-machine learning existed, whether a subject could determine how a randomly lit machine was going to light, determined by a computer."

The idea that it was a machine determined by a computer was important to the NASA man.

"I just wanted to see if Ingo's trip to Jupiter matched yours." I said.

"Oh, Lord," said the NASA man. "We only sponsored this thing with the random computer machine, I don't know anything about these ESP space trips, all our space trips use standard rocketry and telemetry. Those guys at SRI tried to tell us about this 'remote viewing,' but that's not part of the contract. There seems to be some controversy about the results."

The NASA official was getting more and more uncomfortable.

"I suppose we have to be open," he said, "but I have a hard time with this stuff."

"Did you know Ingo went to Mercury?"

"No, I didn't know, I don't want to know, and please don't tell me. We didn't sponsor that. All our probes use regular old rockets."

There was a certain air of put-on about Ingo, which his friends said he adopted for protection.

"Ninety-five percent of all so-called psychics are frauds," Ingo said. "You can't believe what some people will believe."

I wanted to know about the other 5 percent. Ingo shrugged. He said he didn't want to be a laboratory subject any more, he wanted to make some money. He had some premonitions about the economy, and he wanted to know how to capitalize on it. His premonitions were that a terrible depression was just around the corner, which was not an unusual opinion at that time, and that gold would go to $2,000 an ounce. That one was easy; if gold is $150 or $170 and chaos will take it to $2,000, it's a buy.

Then an opportunity did come up for Ingo to make some money. He went dowsing for oil. In dowsing for water, you carry around a forked stick, and when it turns down, you start digging. Ingo didn't carry a forked stick in dowsing for oil. He just walked around over the territory that had been mapped.

"There are so many substrata already mapped, but nobody's sure," he said, "so if I just increase the percentages a bit, that's well worth it. But the places you have to go are just awful, very muddy, Louisiana and Texas and Tennessee, and there are a lot of bugs."

To go oil dowsing, Ingo went physically, getting his shoes muddy. The man who hired him was William Keeler, the former chairman of Phillips Petroleum.

Ingo was always pleasant, but also reluctant to talk about his abilities. People would misunderstand too readily. (He is, however, writing several books.)

Perhaps he is right to be reluctant. I started to think: if Ingo can go anyplace on earth with just a latitude and a longitude, if he can go to Jupiter and Mercury and other galaxies just by having his mind clear, think what he could do with an address and a zip code. Why, he could right to my house, uninvited—not that he isn't pleasant, mind you—and not even have to ring the doorbell. The only people who have come to my house without walking in a door or a window are Santa Claus and the Tooth Fairy, who leave a quarter under your pillow if you leave him-or-her a tooth, and in a sense both of them were invited, and neither has been around for a while.

So Ingo is well advised to be cautious. A Swedish lady sued Uri Geller; his vibrations, she said, bent the metal coil she used as a birth-control device, and she got pregnant.

I know the appeal of telepathy and clairvoyance and psychokinesis; it is a harmonic of one of our myths, the toddler from the planet Krypton who grows up to be Superman, and the success of that story itself shows how well it resonates with some unconscious theme. People who are titillated by the popular occult assume that somehow the telepathy works *for* you, like a super-shortwave radio, telling you something you need to know. But what if the bad guys had the radio station, and you couldn't turn it off?

Our models for what is possible come largely from nineteenth-century physics. Parapsychology isn't possible in that physics, and if it is, it comes off as some sort of Jules Verne fiction, telepathy like mental radio and psychokinesis like a mental laser, and Jules Verne is fiction.

Two years after my first trip to Stanford Research, I was back there again. Uri and Ingo had come and gone. The magazines and newspapers that dote on psychic phenomena continued to report bent spoons and flying saucers. The editors of the Establishment press had sent the reporters to find What the Dupes Are Falling for Now, printed that story, and gone on to other things. Hal Puthoff and Russell Targ had published a paper in *Nature,* a British science journal so august its editor is addressed in the third person. The journal noted editorially that no spoons bent under laboratory conditions, repeated a criticism of the way the experiment had been set up, and then praised the effort. Science, it said, has to be open, at least this is a start. *The New York Times* wrote an editorial saying the same thing. Stanford Research, with millions in government contracts, continued to back its two oddball physicists at some risk.

I still wasn't that interested in psychic phenomena. As a real skeptic, I did a ten-minute "remote viewing" exercise. Puthoff went off into some far corner of one of the buildings and I was to describe where he was. I was sitting with my eyes shut. I had difficulty separating imagination and remote viewing. The first item that floated into vision was a metallic object, chrome-plated, hinged, attached to a vertical surface, like a door. I described it —you can hear this on the tape—as looking like a stapler, except that one part was curved. Then I went on: tan metal cabinet, large room, safety poster. After ten minutes we shut off the tape recorder and went to where Puthoff sat. I had never been in that part of the building. Tan metal cabinet, table, safety poster. So what, I said, all the offices of Stanford Research have that equipment. I had, after all, been to Stanford half a dozen times.

It was the chrome-plated stapler that jarred me. It turned out to be the handle on the door of a small refrigerator in the middle of the lab. No other lab rooms I had seen had a refrigerator, or a handle like that.

"Not bad," Hal said.

I felt like I had just seen the clock on the wall of the fourth-grade classroom. But I was still rationalizing it, and I was more interested in the possible rationale than some blip like that on a personal screen. So I was interested in the papers of Dr. Evan Harris Walker, a physicist at the U.S. Army Ballistic Research Laboratories, Aberdeen Proving Ground, Maryland 21005. It's a measurement problem in quantum mechanics, said Dr. Walker. Quantum mechanics "is entirely at odds with our common sense conception of the physical world, but this is the correct picture of reality."

It certainly is at odds. Common sense would tell you you can't have two things in the same place at the same time, but quantum mechanics permits it. And: a textbook example, you are in a car on a roller coaster, but the roller coaster has been built wrong and there isn't enough energy to get you over the next hill. Can you get there? Sure, if the next dip is lower, it's called "tunneling." It must work, the products are right at our fingertips. The telephone company's computer that direct-dials and bills the calls contains descendants of the tunnel diode.

Just in case you are into physics, Dr. Walker's rationale uses the state vector, ψ, of the Schrödinger equation. The observer can bias the probabilities, so the observer has to be quantified. It gets harder from there: "Hidden variables interconnect events in different locations in space and time but those variables do not have any functional dependence on the space-time separation of the events." This extension of the Copenhagen interpretation of quantum theory is based on "consciousness as a quantum mechanical event."

I read parts of Dr. Walker's papers to some particle physicists. "Hidden variables can explain lots of things," they said. They weren't turned on.

Dr. Walker gave a talk on physics to a TM group, and met the Maharishi. "As one might expect," he reported, "the Maharishi is an esthetic mystic who burns quantities of musk-flavored incense and speaks about the beauty of how the sap rises in the flower." Two weeks later, a TM functionary called up to get a copy of the talk. "When I hung up the phone," reported Dr. Walker, "the office suddenly was filled with the strong odor of musk incense. Of course, I was not perturbed too much by this since I am aware of the psychological factors that can cause one to reexperience characteristics of past events. As I was rationalizing on this point, my office mate, Dr. Serge Zaroodny, entered and instantly asked, 'What is that odor? Who has been burning incense?' The whole affair struck me as amusing and certainly odd."

The paper in *Nature* helped the atmosphere in the scientific community—for one thing, it cleaned up the magic tricks—but it did not raise any money. The number of serious researchers was headed in the direction of zero, and the old paradigm stood like a fortress with only tiny cracks.

The Last Paradigm?

There are some who believe we are evolving, as Teilhard de Chardin said, in some mysterious way, toward total consciousness, the noösphere, or toward a Hegelian synthesis. There are some who believe we are evolving toward hell in a hand basket, using up all the world's resources at an accelerating rate, running out of energy and the ability to control our destiny. The two views aren't necessarily at odds, though those on the hilltop waiting for the world to end tomorrow morning run the risk of looking sheepish if they have to come back down to town and buy bread at the bakery. We do know the world is changing at an accelerating rate.

It is very hard to extrapolate another paradigm because we use the one we have. Is the current paradigm the last paradigm? Maybe it is, but that was what the cardinals thought who tried Galileo and found him guilty and silenced him.

"BOSH, DR. JUNG."
"YOU ARE MISTAKEN,
DR. FREUD."

ERE on the far side of the paradigm, the air is a bit thin and inclines us to dizziness. We keep looking in the guidebook to see where we are: if we have come this far, and this is Tuesday, then this must be Belgium. We see things through the belief structures we already have.

If we are rational and skeptical, then we will be wary of the Alchemist and all his cohorts. No shortage of Alchemists these days. No experiments have been carefully enough controlled and proved. There are still some unknowns, but they will become known by the same methods that has made so many unknowns known.

If we are not so rational and skeptical, or had an aunt who could do weird things, then we forgive the eccentric psychics the way we forgive a prima donna for her antics, she still has that voice. That the Establishment frowns is all the more reason to believe; the Establishment filters out what it wants to believe anyway, just like the rest of us.

This division is not new. Carl Jung, the pioneer of psychiatry, said he refused "to commit the fashionable stupidity of regarding everything I cannot explain as a fraud." He experimented with all sorts of things, and in one famous incident, a heavy walnut table, an old heirloom, split during a seance, and soon afterwards a bread knife in a drawer snapped into four pieces "like a pistol shot."

In 1909 Jung went to see Freud, his senior and the acknowledged parent of psychiatry. They were talking about something you can't see, can't hear, and that has, in the terms of physics, no weight, no mass, no velocity—the unconscious. The skeptics considered it bordering on alchemy. And during one conversation, Jung felt a curious sensation in his diaphragm. "At that moment there was such a loud report in the bookcase, which stood right next to us, that we both started up in alarm, fearing the thing was going to topple over us. I said to Freud: 'There, that is an example of a so-called catalytic exteriorization phenomenon.'"

Freud wasn't having any. "That is sheer bosh," he said to Jung.

"It is not," said Jung.

(Nice dialogue between the giants.)

" 'You are mistaken, Herr Professor,' " says Jung, in his own account. " 'And to prove my point I now predict that in a moment there will be another loud report!' Sure enough, no sooner had I said the word than the same detonation went off in the bookcase. To this day I do not know what gave me this certainty. But I knew beyond all doubt the report would come again. Freud only stared aghast at me. I do not know what was in his mind, or what his look meant. In any case, this incident aroused his mistrust of me, and I had the feeling that I had done something against him."

Freud was, indeed, much more cautious. He wrote on parapsychology, but never published the papers; they appeared after his death.

The sober old American Society for Psychical Research, distressed by the boom in psychic interest that somehow did not extend to any serious research, did a survey of bookstores. In some anguish, it reported that 97 percent of what was on the shelves in this area was "occult" and more properly placed in fiction; only 3 percent was genuine psychical research. The rest is This Way to the Egress. Use Healing Rays to Repair the Body! Attract All the Money You Need! Influence the Thoughts of Others! Transform Your Surroundings! Predict Future Events!

I have little trouble with any of these exhortations. Influence the thoughts of others: you dolt, you really don't have it together, do you, and watch where you're stepping. Transform your surroundings: paint, soap, brush, mop. Attract all the money you need: but do you need what you think you need? what is need? what is you? Use healing rays to repair the body: they aren't rays, but the body always heals itself, the physician only sets it up, the medicine only helps. Predict future events: that's easy, the hard part is making the event match the prediction. Shakespeare, *Henry IV*:

> GLENDOWER: I can call spirits from the
>   vasty deep.
> HOTSPUR: Why, so can I, or so can
>   any man;
>   But will they come when you do call
>   for them?

WHAT CELL
GOES THERE?

THE spirits of the vasty deep are still at large, and there are mysteries that seem like ESP which fall into other sciences. Consider:

We had at our house some Baltimore orioles, the gentleman a handsome orange-and-black fellow with an abnormal space in the leading edge of one wing, where he had run into a twig while dodging a hawk or coming home late after finding some fermenting juniper berries, nothing more serious than a dented fender. Orioles have a distinctive nest which hangs like a purse on the very end of a branch, quite a piece of engineering. One day, the summer's work done, the orioles were packing up to depart. The questioners in the following sequence are children who might now be embarrassed by the purity of their questions, but happily it was recorded on a tape cassette.

"Where are the orioles going?"

We looked it up in the bird book. The orioles were going to Central America, or perhaps Venezuela, for the winter. We looked up Venezuela in the Atlas. Venezuela! All the way down there? Across the sea? How do they know how to get there?

"They go with the other orioles."

"How do the other orioles know how to get there?"

"There's always some oriole who's been there before."

"How did the first oriole know how to get there?"

"He didn't really know it was Venezuela, he was just following the bug supply south."

"How do the orioles know when to go?"

"They notice the bugs are scarcer."

"But there are still plenty of bugs around."

We looked that up. True, the bugs were still around. The birds had light-sensitive cells that told them the days are getting shorter, and they know they better get going.

In the spring, the moppet brigade announced that the orioles were back. (One was heard to ask, while standing under the hanging nest, "Did you have a good time in Venezuela?") Sure enough, same gentleman with the dented fender.

"How did the orioles come back from Venezuela?"

"They came with the other orioles."

"But how did they find this *house*? They never went before, and they never came back before, and there aren't any other orioles around, and it's very far, and even if they followed the bugs north, how did they know which state to go to, and how did they find this house?"

Now the reference material was getting more complex. *Scientific American,* we reported, had discussed planetarium experiments where it appeared that perhaps birds navigated by the position of the stars. The senior moppet was extremely dissatisfied.

"A Pan American *pi*lot," he said, "would have to have special training to go to Venezuela, and he would have known about stars from school, and he would have a radio and special signals, and the stars wouldn't help find something as small as a house in the middle of a *state*."

"That would be very precise navigation," I said, "but they have good eyesight."

"Besides, the stars are in different places in the spring than when the orioles left, so if they were following stars they would get mixed up but here they are."

Two more candidates for the occult, disillusioned with rational science.

How does a large, droopy-eyed dog, called a bloodhound not from an affinity to the red stuff but because of a long and blooded lineage, take a sniff of a thumb print on a glass slide, walk twenty miles into the middle of a woods two weeks later, ignoring all other smells, and go whoof?

How does the salmon know where to go back to? Well, he tracks the water. Wire him up, as some scientists did, and expose him to different batches of water, and he will ignore them all, but try some hometown water and he will light up the machine. Those are some receptors in the olfactory cells. The vibration of some molecule, or the geometry of the molecule, communicates. But how do the receptor cells know, and how do they communicate?

Or termites. A couple of termites, wandering around, are ineffectual. But as the termites gather, as they reach a critical mass, they form columns, work crews, disposal units, engineering cadres, committees, and throw up crystalline and vaulted chambers, termite cathedrals. How do they know that the nth termite has created the critical mass? How does the column know when to turn, and how does it have the engineering knowledge to build a vault? Pheromones, maybe, hormonal secretions that carry some molecular message to somebody else who can read the pheromones in that molecular language. But how does that communication work?

In the past few years, there has been an exciting explosion in molecular biology. The molecular biologists didn't even have an old crowd defending the paradigm to throw over, because there wasn't anything there before. So: how does one cell know how to make a whole whale? Or, in people: how does the gene instruct the cells that are going to make, say, a liver? What creates that particular shape and biochemical function? There's no command from within the cell, the patterning signal has to be an interaction between cells. The cells produce signals and the other cells pick up the chemical messages. What are these messages that go from cell to cell?

You are sitting there reading, and all the while, just under earshot, there is this absolute racket going on, cell to cell, right there in yourself, except that the boop boop and beep beep do not sound that way, they are rather pieces of chemistry traded.

And if, subliminally, we could pick that up, what else could we pick up? Doctor, lawyer, merchant, chief? Do you love me? Really?

The physiologists and neurophysiologists tell us there is a vast world out there, beeping and honking and scratching and belching, and we perceive only a small part of it, like the frog whose eyes only see dinner going by or the predator's shadow. And part of that cacophony we do perceive, but we don't know we perceive it—it's probably too far down on the survival scale. Are the vibes real or do we project them? Sometimes, we know, we project them, but sometimes, well, did you ever leave a room and say something funny about that man, or that woman? Schizophrenics, postulates one scientist, may have problems because their signals are flawed, the receptors gummed up; schizophrenics have an unfamiliar odor in their sweat, it is said, attributed to an acid called trans-3-methyl-2-hexanoic. Could we pereceive it? We perceive smaller concentrations of other combinations.

Maybe Sherlock Holmes was able to translate strange esters for himself, like the catfish that can tell the boss catfish was in these waters only a few minutes ago.

I called up a psychiatrist friend who works at a classy mental institution. Could you really smell degrees of craziness in people? Sure.

"What does trans-3-methyl-2-hexanoic acid smell like?"

"Oh, it's a rather ripe, rich smell, almost fruity."

Hot on the trail of vibes: could I learn it? Sure, why not, I had learned, ancient Chevalier de Tastevin, to sniff the differences in Burgundies, the strength of the Cortons and the mellowness of the Musignys.

So there I am, under my friend's sponsorship, making the rounds, Doctor Smith, here just for the day, in a borrowed white coat.

"And how are you today?" says my friend, to two patients. One of the patients smiles and the other one doesn't respond.

Doctor Smith is going sniff sniff sniff. Hurried smile: sniff sniff sniff. Too damn much antiseptic in here, or something with an alcohol base.

Mrs. Green is showing Doctor Smith around.

"And this is our day room, where we have supervised activities, arts and crafts."

Sure enough, one guy is making a pair of moccasins, two ladies are weaving something or other, strands are being pulled into baskets.

Sniff sniff sniff, goes Doctor Smith.

Three rather aged ladies and a young man are playing cards. Doctor Smith kibitzes: sniff sniff sniff.

Doctor Smith is getting distressed: "You let them *smoke*?" he asks Mrs. Green.

"Yes," says Mrs. Green. "Are you one of those doctors who really objects to smoking?"

"Yes," says Doctor Smith firmly, for all he is smelling is Marlboros and Viceroys and antiseptic.

"F Wing is a bit tense today," Mrs. Green says.

"Let's go to E Wing," says Doctor Smith. Sniff sniff sniff

E Wing is indeed tense. Some people scream. Sniff sniff sniff.

Doctor Smith thanks his hosts, come nightfall, for an interesting day. He doesn't think he's found trans-3-methyl-2-hexanoic acid, sniff sniff sniff.

"You really should take care of that cold, Doctor," says Mrs. Green.

Later, Doctor Smith did get a sniff of trans-3-methyl-hexanoic-acid. Another psychiatrist collected the sweat from rubber bed sheets. Ripe, all right.

Two Georgia researchers came up with a discovery: women in fertile periods produced a pheromone in a vaginal secretion. Vibes, maybe that's why all the fellas are clustered around. Good heavens, Madison Avenue just finished selling strawberry-flavored douches. Now what? Now, I suppose, we will need a douche to follow the strawberry douche, called *Naturel*. Watch

your TV commercials for further developments. "*Naturel*, forti-
fied with extra pheromones."

With all that cacophony going on, couldn't there be just one
little message from Cousin Josie about Herbie? A focusing of
enough energy to bend a nail or float a ping-pong ball into midair? A few molecular strands from tomorrow?

Maybe. But not from our paradigm. We could certainly train
ourselves within our sensibilities—people who speak inflected
languages have more accurate pitch than we do, and wine tasters
can sniff more clues than they have language for.

If you tell me that people perceive all sorts of things they're
not aware of, the geometry of passing molecules, an odd cosmic
ray here and there, I experience no discomfort. I might even get
a little ambitious: How to Tune In on Passing Molecules You've
Already Registered. There's more out there than we perceive,
and we perceive more than we know.

I know that bodies heal themselves, and sometimes they can
get a psychic push or trigger, whether from a sugar pill, a physician, or a healer. But tell me that some people can heal others
long-distance, thousands of miles, when the healee doesn't even
know he's being healed, and I start to scramble for more ordinary explanations. I know there is lots of territory unexplored
and unexplained, but trips to the moon should be on gossamer
wings or big rockets, and that goes double for Mercury, Jupiter,
and the rest of the universe.

The rules of our paradigm are: what you observe must relate
to what we know, and be simply stated, and have a theory and
a little bit of elegance, and you have to be able to do it again,
or tell why it would work again.

That doesn't mean it will turn out to be true. The astronomy
of Ptolemy could predict eclipses, and it had theory, and predictability, but it turned out to be not true. "Phlogiston" helped
to explain eighteenth-century chemistry, and "ether," nineteenth-century physics.

Jung had a theory about the bookcases that kept going off like
firecrackers—synchronicity, not causality—but since he didn't

get to explode a bookcase on cue—causality—it doesn't count as true. What is true is left-brained: you can take it apart and put it together and it will do what you predict.

"It is highly probable," writes a young and respected neurobiologist, "that in due course it will be possible to explain the 'mystic experience' in terms of neurobiology; it is highly improbable that neurobiology will ever be explained in terms of the 'mystic experience.'" The second half of that sentence is bound to be true. Historically, mystics have been very uninterested in explaining the experience in terms of neurobiology. Mostly, they tell stories, or don't say anything at all. What about the first half of the sentence? Is the mystic experience going to turn out to be the right series of nucleotides? But then what? At the edges of paradigms, the temptation to Rumpelstiltskin is very great: name it and it will go away.

The orioles settle down for the winter in Venezuela; the bobolinks go all the way to Argentina. And the position of the stars, as a young friend of mine pointed out, changes from hemisphere to hemisphere and season to season.

THE MIND,
THE QUANTUM AND
THE UNIVERSE

THE reason physics got to be king of the hill, said the French geneticist François Jacob, was that physics was the first to have its own language, and that language was mathematics. The molecular biologists are making great strides, unlocking enigmas, solving puzzles, getting neurobiology ready to take over mysticism. The neurobiologists do not think about it much, but their language, with all the inherent assumptions we have learned about language, is based on physics. And the language of physics is less certain than the conclusions of neurobiology.

For example: you remember the Impulse, going tra la la la la la down the axon and stumbling into a Cleft. All physics; the Impulse is a quantifiable charge of electricity, and what happens to the Impulse depends on the constituents of the cells and the positive charges on the sodium and potassium, and the minuses on the chloride and protein, and you measure in millivolts. That sort of physics—and its related chemistry—is elementary, and will probably serve for a long time.

But down the road it turns out that solid old physics is only valid for the medium-sized world we live in, pounds and inches, volts and seconds. Very small or very tall, it begins to make no

sense at all. Not common sense, anyway, but we are all respectful, because the next equation may disperse us all.

What follows is not really going to be about physics—it is old
stuff anyway to physicists. What follows is about language and
meaning and how we see the world, so don't try to sort it out
and certainly don't remember it.

First there were crystals, and then smaller than crystals were
molecules, and then smaller than molecules were atoms. The
atom was like a little solar system, a sun in the middle, the
nucleus, and the electrons whirling around it, like planets.

There is a lot of space in a solar system. So there came the
parable of Eddington's desk, Eddington being a great English
physicist. Looked at normally, Eddington's desk was a nice an-
tique, and looked at atomically, there was almost nothing there,
only empty space with a few incredibly tiny specks, the electrons
whirling around their nuclei, vast, vast spaces separating them.
(Thus one lecturer on the Void was able to say that we are
99½ percent Void already, so there is only a little way to go, but
the last part is the hardest.) From a survival point of view, of
course, if Eddington's desk falls on you it hurts like hell, and
dropped from high enough it will dispatch you better than
$E = mc^2$.

And these subatomic bits were already being troublesome, because they acted sometimes as if they were waves, and sometimes
as if they were particles.

And then it turned out that we weren't done by having a
nucleus, like a little sun, because there were smaller pieces than
the nucleus, first one, then two, then four—omega minuses and
neutrinos—and now we are up to several hundred of the little
pests, still hunting for the quark, the most elementary particle,
and no guarantee that a quark won't turn out to have cousins
and ghostly relatives and Son of Quark.

Quarks! The name was borrowed by Dr. Murray Gell-Mann
from Joyce, *Finnegans Wake,* "Three quarks for Muster Mark?"
Quark is Dr. Gell-Mann's second gift of poetry to physics, for it
was he, in the 1950's, who described a quantum number as
"strange," so that we could have "strangeness" as a quality of
particles. Science must simplify, and the three basic quarks,

"things postulated which clarify the world unseen," mathematically underlie all particles, the three quarks being up, down and sideways—but wait, what goes there? Very exciting, a fourth elementary particle, a "charmed quark," whose "charm" is a mathematical concept. With ultra-powerful nuclear accelerators, we may be getting there, the trial of discovery, the basic units of all matter—

"—but we hope we don't see a quark because that might stir up more problems," said my particle adviser. "In fact, we hope we don't even see a quark *track*. Quarks should stay where they are, mathematical." And indeed, no one ever sees any of the mites, nor even the particles in which the quarks may be eternally confined, all they see are tiny tracks in the snow, or, more accurately, bubbles in a bubble chamber, and then from the angles and curves they can figure out who just went by or didn't go by at some unimaginable speed.

Of the particles known today, half are particles and half are antiparticles, the antiparticle having the same mass but with an opposite charge and opposite spin. Antiparticles are rare and not very long-lived. When antiparticles meets their mirror-image they annihilate each other immediately. It is possible that other galaxies are made up of antiparticles, which has led to the speculation that their time would flow backwards to ours. (It also led one physicist to write a poem about such a place, where Dr. Edward Anti-Teller lived, and kept macassars on his chairs.)

Nor is the behavior of the mites anything for Aristotelian logic. For example, if you shoot a particle at another particle at high speed, they break apart into pieces, but *each* of the pieces is as big as the original.

On Wednesday afternoons sometimes, Dr. Richard Feynman of Cal Tech drives up to Malibu and plops into one of John Lilly's tanks. Feynman got the Nobel prize for the backwards-in-time work; a positron traveling forward in time behaves just like an electron moving momentarily backwards in time. The Two Guides from Malibu Meet the Time Machine, the Connecticut Yankee Stops Off on the Way to King Arthur's Court.

Cutest of all the particles, everybody agrees, is the neutrino. Neutrinos are very hard to detect because they have no mass, no electric charge, no magnetic field. They come charging out of the sun and go right through everything as if everything weren't there. Nothing can stop a neutrino except another neutrino, which does happen sometimes, enabling people to record the splat. Neutrinos coming from the sun could tell us things, so the physicists constructed a big vat of cleaning fluid deep in an old Homestake lead mine in South Dakota, deep enough so that other particles from space couldn't find it, and waited for some neutrino on his way through the earth to get asphyxiated. Wrote John Updike:

> *Neutrinos, they are very small.*
> > *They have no charge and have no mass*
> *And do not interact at all.*
> *The earth is just a silly ball*
> > *To them, through which they simply pass*
> *Like dustmaids down a drafty hall*
> > *Or photons through a sheet of glass—*
>
> > *And, scorning barriers of class*
> *Infiltrate you and me! Like tall*
> *And painless guillotines, they fall*
> > *Down through our heads into the grass . . .*

One can see why the proponents of ESP—the 3 percent on the bookstore shelves—like to make analogies with subatomic physics. A gang of positrons, or anti-electrons coming back from the future, might bear a message. Or, if neutrinos are accepted ghosts, what about ghosts that do not yet have an equation?

It can be dizzying to think of negative mass and antimatter and particles that aren't there except they are, and mites that go backwards in time for less than an eye blink. On the scale of the very grand, it gets worse. If you took all the space out of Eddington's desk and collapsed it down to its protons, its gravity would increase tremendously and would pull everything into it. A collapsing star becomes a mass so dense that if it became a neutron star ten miles in diameter, a tablespoon of sand would weigh 40,000 billion tons. A bigger star would squeeze itself into matter so dense that it would simply *disappear,* a "black hole," and in the act of its collapse, time isn't time and space isn't space. To a very theoretical astronaut who happened to be in a black hole, it would seem like one second, but in outside time billions of years would have gone by. Where do the items go that disappear into a black hole? Some astrophysicists postulate that the black hole is a tunnel into another universe.

Our own universe expands, reaches a maximum dimension, and contracts. "When the universe finally collapses," writes Professor John Wheeler of Princeton, "the classical general relativity of Einstein offers no way to go beyond the point. If you try to solve the problem on a computer, the computer stops. Smoke comes out. But according to the quantum principle, the dynamics should continue. We can well expect that when the universe collapses, there's a certain probability that it will start a new cycle. Another universe will leave its own track in superspace."

Superspace?

"The stage on which the space of the universe moves is certainly not space itself. Nobody can be a stage for himself; he has to have a larger arena in which to move. The arena in which space does its changing is not even the spacetime of Einstein, for spacetime is the history of space changing with time. The area must be a larger object: superspace. Superspace is not endowed with three or four dimensions—it's endowed with an *infinite* number of dimensions. Any single point in superspace represents an entire, three-dimensional world; nearby points represent slightly different three-dimensional worlds."

I get it. No, I don't get it. Yes, I get it, sort of, if I don't try. Wheeler and his colleagues were looking for the equation behind the universe: what started it? What is beyond the end of time? Would the law of physics still hold without the universe?

Superspace. Black holes where one second is ten billion years. Tunnels to another universe. Infinite dimensions. It would seem, at first glance, that solving Jung's exploding bookcases, or getting messages from Aunt Josie, ought to be a cinch.

Wheeler, a gentle, scholarly man who worked with Einstein and Niels Bohr and other atomic giants, gave a speech on the five hundredth birthday of Copernicus. Look how far we have come, it said, from Copernicus. Darwin and Freud and the double helix of life, everybody had his own list of the remaining mysteries, but his list had three.

Wheeler's three mysteries were: "the mind, the quantum, and the universe." I wrote a note. Plainly, he had been working on the universe. I had been scratching at the mind. "I will meet you," I said, "at the quantum."

"That's some list: the mind, the quantum, and the universe," I said.

"All three," Wheeler said, "threaten the clean separation between observer and observed that used to be the essence of science."

"What's a quantum?" I said. "I thought it was a kind of jump."

"I meant the quantum principle," he said. "It might be better called the Merlin principle. Merlin the magician, pursued, changed first to a fox, then a rabbit, then to a bird on one's shoulder. The Merlin principle keeps changing before us, putting on a new form every decade."

In the 1920's, a young German theoretical physicist, Werner Heisenberg, was working on some of the contradictions in physics. It was an exciting time in physics, and the pioneer group of physicists, if you read their essays and autobiographies, had an enormous amount of fun. Heisenberg visited periodically with Niels Bohr in Denmark. They had long philosophical conversations, and Heisenberg's hay fever was better in Denmark. And without going into the details of the problems, Heisenberg wrote out some pages of noncommutative algebra that were to have a great impact. In physics, the Principle of Uncertainty carries his name; his work got him a Nobel prize at thirty-one. Heisenberg's Uncertainty Principle says that you can't know both the position and the velocity of an electron, all you can have is a statistical probability. The implications went beyond physics: they affected the basic point of view from which we look at things. And that shift is this: the observer is part of the process.

That did not begin with Heisenberg, but his name is on the principle.

"In the world of the quantum," Wheeler said, "the observer and the observed turn out to have a tight and totally unexpected linkage. The quantum principle demolishes the view we once had that the universe sits safely 'out there,' that we can observe that goes on in it from behind a foot-thick slab of plate glass without ourselves being involved in what goes on. We have learned that to observe even so minuscule an object as an electron we have to shatter that slab of glass. We have to insert a measuring device. We can put in a device to measure position or a device to measure momentum, but the installation of one prevents the insertion of the other. We ourselves have to decide which it is that we will do. Whichever it is, it has an unpredictable effect on the future of that electron. To that degree the future of the universe is changed. We changed it. We have to cross out the old word 'observer' and replace it by the new word 'participator.' In some strange sense, the quantum principle tells us that we are dealing with a participatory universe."

Here are some possibly clumsy analogies:

An anthropologist goes to visit a primitive tribe. He brings pills for the drinking water, a Polaroid camera, a movie camera, insect repellent, and a rifle. Is the tribe he observes the same tribe that would have been there with no anthropologist to watch? Will the tribe really spend the same time learning to run down an animal, or will it start saving up for a rifle? And if we accept that the tribe won't be the same, how do we know what it was like before, without an anthropologist to tell us?

Or: we have a national election. The polls close in the East, and the computer projections announce the winners on TV. The people in the West still have two hours of voting time. Do they still vote? Would the score have been exactly the same?

The observation of the process has become part of the process.

"We go down and down," Wheeler said, "from crystal to molecule, from molecule to atom, from atom to nucleus, from nucleus to particle, and there is still something beyond both geometry and particle. In the end we have to come back to mind. How can consciousness understand consciousness? There's a paradox. Niels Bohr said we only made progress from paradoxes."

What is really real? That was a starting point for this trip, and the circle—consistent with the laws of conservation—begins to close on itself. It is even a bit chilling to remember that "really" and "real" come from the Latin *res*, thing, and so we are asking how much thingness is a thing, *which has already limited the answer.*

Wheeler's shelves have Pierce and Parmenides and Paracelsus and William James; the European physicists had not only James but Kant and Plato. They begin to sound more like mystics than physicists. Eugene Wigner, another Nobel prizewinner (sorry to keep listing Nobel prizes, it is to show these are serious people), wrote an essay called "Two Kinds of Reality," the first being "my own consciousness" and the second, everything else; "the universal or impersonal reality as a concept is a reality of the second type," useful for communicating, but only possibly valid. Everything but the first type is a construct.

The critics of the quantum physicists, fifty years ago, used to call it "atomysticism." The atom had been the building block of our universe, and Heisenberg wrote: "An atom is not a *thing*. When we get down to the atomic level, the objective world in space and time no longer exists, and the mathematical symbols of theoretical physics refer merely to possibilities, not facts." Now there is a good exercise for wooziness: an atom is not a thing, it is only a possibility, and we are all made up of atoms.

Any good theoretical physicist learns to let go of that wooziness, and in the process, he also learns to sound like a mystic. "When a student of physics makes his first acquaintance with the theory of atomic structure and of quanta," wrote J. Robert Oppenheimer, "he must come to the rather deep and subtle notion which has turned out to be the clue to unraveling that whole domain of physical experience. This is the notion of complementarity, which recognizes that various ways of talking about experience may each have validity, and may each be necessary for the adequate description of the physical world, and yet may stand in mutually exclusive relationship to each other, so that in a situation to which one applies, there may be no consistent possibility of applying the other."

So physicists talk about two realities. Oppenheimer called them "the way of time and history, and the way of eternity and timelessness." Heisenberg called them "the objective world, pursuing its regular course in space and time, [and] a subject, mystically experiencing the unity of the world and no longer confronted by an object or by any objective world." Wigner called the two ways scientific knowledge and natural knowledge:

> Scientific knowledge leans on, and is impossible without, the type of knowledge we acquired in babyhood. Furthermore, this original knowledge was probably not at all acquired by us in the active sense; most of it must have been given to us in the same mysterious way, and probably as part of, our consciousness. As to content and usefulness, scientific knowledge is an infinitesimal fraction of the natural knowledge.

"One may say," wrote Heisenberg, "that the human ability to understand may be in a certain sense unlimited. But the existing scientific concepts cover always only a very limited part of reality, and the other part that has not yet been understood is infinite. Whenever we proceed from the known into the unknown we may hope to understand, but we may have to learn at the same time a new meaning of the word 'understanding.' " The understanding, Heisenberg wrote in another essay, "is recognized even before it is rationally understood in detail." It is, at one place, "the unfolding of abstract structures," the "shuddering before the beautiful of which Plato speaks."

Thin air out here. The mystics have to go through all that meditation, and the physicists have to go through all that math and quantum theory, and in one sense the processes are similar because they require a letting go of daily common sense, and the ability to let the universe be some other way. They arrive at, if not the same place, one that sounds at least recognizable: Einstein's Unified Field Theory was supposed to supplant the surface complexity of nature with a profound simplicity: "Thus all man's perceptions of the world and all his abstract intuitions of reality would merge finally into one, and the deep underlying unity of the universe would be laid bare." Heisenberg saw the "faith in the central order" not only in the unfolding Platonic abstractions but in Bach.

"When is a man in mere understanding?" Meister Eckhart the mystic asked, rhetorically. "When he sees one thing separate from another. And when is a man above mere understanding? That I can tell you: when a man sees All in all."

If we seem to be spending a lot of time on time, it is because time is such a clear element in the paradigm, to show us the limitations of our paradigm. We think of time as being linear, it starts and it moves forward, whether we're there to perceive it or not. But if black holes turn out to be real, and time speeds up incredibly in a black hole, then our regular notion of time moving forward, ticktock, is just something we made up. And time moving backward would not just be the Time Machine, and the Connecticut Yankee, but an example of how we made up the original notion.

I traded some papers with the physicists. I gave them *Four Quartets*. They liked that. Next year if you take Physics 111, you may get this:

> Time present and time past
> Are both perhaps present in time future,
> And time future contained in time past.
> If all time is eternally present
> All time is unredeemable.
> What might have been is an abstraction
> Remaining a perpetual possibility
> Only in a world of speculation
> What might have been and what has been
> Point to one end, which is always present.
> The end of all our exploring
> Will be to arrive where we started
> And know the place for the first time.

"All these mystics," I said, "keep talking about the unity of everything, and the physicists, when they stop writing equations and start writing words, say they are looking for the equation behind One."

I was talking to still another physicist, another Nobel prize-winner, pictures on his walls of Einstein and Heisenberg and Dirac and de Broglie, hotshot pioneers of this century. Niels Bohr on a motorcycle. Somebody else in ski clothes. A lot of conversation seems to have gone on in boats and on mountaintops.

"Yes, if they stop to think about it," said my physicist. "And sometimes, after a burst of physics, they stop to think about it. Otherwise, not more than anybody else, you worry about grants and meetings and research assistants, but if you get away and sit in a boat on a lake and think where we have come from in fifty years, and where we might be going, maybe the tools of physics give you an extra moment."

"I don't think the public has quite caught up to the quantum," I said, "they're either in materialism or superstition or both. I get uncomfortable myself if I think we're only here as a probability."

"Yes," said my friend, and shot a wrist watch out from one gray, European-suited sleeve. I said I was relieved to see he wore a watch, since my head was full of either physics or Eliot's *Four Quartets,* four poems about time and reality, the intersection of time and timeless. And then there were the little pests that went backwards in time—

"A bookkeeping device," said my friend. "A way of looking at things."

"Like, on the books, the building has been depreciated but it's still standing and still being used."

"I don't know those things," he said. After a generation here, he still has a faint Middle European accent.

"I get very confused about time," I said.

"There is nothing to be confused about," he said. *"Physicists define time to make motion look simple."*

I felt myself slipping a bit. "Is there a real time?"

"Time is real and also time is not real."

I had fallen right into my own quantum example, I was out there with the rest of the public. Some koan, Zen is easier.

"We have satellites in space that are picking up signals from pulsars, spinning stars a universe away, a galaxy away, the signals are regular but the stars may no longer be there. The Clifford-Einstein equations led us to think the building material of the universe is curved space—"

The building material is curved space?

He had glanced at his watch again. "Einstein said, time is what you read from a clock, and my watch says lunchtime. Should we go? *Primum vivere, deinde philosophari*."

They must learn that in the gymnasia. Somebody threw my high school Latin book out, years ago. I translate that as live first, philosophize later, or maybe, no philosophy on an empty stomach. It seems as profound as anything else.

PRIMUM VIVERE

ONE day Henry David Thoreau had had enough of Walden Pond, and the little cabin he had built there. "I left the woods," he wrote, "for as good a reason as I went there. Perhaps it seemed to me that I had several more lives to live, and could not spare any more time for that one. It is remarkable how easily and insensibly we fall into a particular route, and make a beaten track for ourselves." Emerson was going to Europe, and needed a house-sitter, and Thoreau packed up and went to Emerson's house.

And one day the road into the woods from the Middle of the Journey led out again for me. Perhaps my tape recorder is still on a tree in there. When I went in, I was following a thirst, a kind of curiosity, a sense of excitement, and the experiences were fresh. I had no particular goal or intention. But in time there was an invisible line, after which the experiences were modified by language. Perhaps I would need this language to tell about the woods—and that little impulse made the experience less pure, for the left-brained language would arrive too soon with its own peculiar modes. Then the language would blanket the experience. By calling in the Observer, I was not sure the Participant was the same; the Uncertainty Principle hovered like a large black bird.

I knew that the world is not the way they tell you it is, but what else it is would have to wait. I hoped to get box seats to the Trial of Galileo, to be present when someone sent What Hath God Wrought by telepathy, or to see the first Photograph of a Quark, caught surprised and blinking in its nest. Apocalyptic cries everywhere, population and energy seemed less urgent, for all was process. Paradigms exist in time; what now would time bring?

There were some after-effects. I had followed my courses religiously, and now I had to get all new clothes. For a year I had had no alcohol, and little refined sugar, and all that awareness —reaching, reaching, tasting, tasting—produced a fuller stomach with less food. I didn't think I was fat or even bulky when I began; we never know how we look—"a stocky, blue-jawed figure," a Newsweek article had said of me. Stocky? Blue-jawed? Really? Burly, as a Canadian paper said? No more. A regular gazelle. I became a scale addict, for effortlessly, without tension, my weight was dropping, one pound, two pounds a week, past my Army weight, past my college weight, and it finally leveled off at the weight last registered when I was a skinny seventeen. So I had to get new clothes. (I kept some of the old ones, superstitiously.)

It had not been so hard to give up alcohol in the cause of pursuing awareness. It was more difficult giving up ice cream. An ice-cream chain called Baskin-Robbins moved relentlessly closer to where some of my courses met—curse them, temptation in the way, I lingered outside the window like an executive outside a porn movie at lunch hour. Creme Caramel! Burgundy Cherry! Pralines and Cream!

And Key Lime Pie! That was too much. One day I looked guiltily over my shoulder and ducked in, a single-scoop Key Lime Pie cone, and I was a sinner fallen from pure awareness. I got a rush from an ice-cream cone, a buzz in the head, a high, and a terrible down a couple of hours later as the body system used the sugar from the ice-cream cone and kept right on going into the reserves.

.   .   .

I was not going to make it to Satori #3 this trip. One day in late spring, more than a year after I began the experiential exercises, I went down into my own cellar with a corkscrew. There slept, row on row, all the noble wines I had collected for years, each in its own bassinet of orange tile drainpipe. The tile helped to keep the temperature constant. If I were to give up some of the clarity of experiences in order to record the experiences, I might as well do it here, and record my own fall from grace. On top of all the slumbering vintages was my wine book, in which I had, years ago, recorded the inventory and the taste of each wine, and how well the wines went with various foods. But what to choose? Should we make it a really big ceremony, and drink the last of the Montrachet? Or a mellow, deep Musigny, Comte Georges de Vogue? There was one Musigny 1919, a gift, probably long gone by now inside its bottle, and then 1959, 1961, 1964, 1966—or wait, here are three Lafites out of a case, 1961, 1966—no, too ceremonial. Something more everyday, let's see, Beychevelle, Montrose, Calon-Segur. I pulled a 1962 Calon-Segur and opened it.

Now began a stereo track in which the channels did not match. Channel A clicked on with the first sniff, the first taste, and said:

"This is a pleasant wine, nice bouquet, ready to drink, much less tannin than the 1961—"

Channel B as usual had no words and I had to translate, which took a moment, because involuntarily I sat down heavily. I had taken three swallows and it felt like I had fallen thirty feet. With some difficulty I wrote on page 76 of the wine book:

"Dim memory says this wine matches pleasant. But I can't focus my eyes and I can't stand up. My stomach feels bile green. Muscles heavy. Breathing uneven. Uncertain spasms in throat and stomach. Awful. I feel drugged. *Drugged.*"

And, of course, I was; alcohol is a drug even when it comes from a slumbering Calon-Segur 1962. Can we remember the body's reaction to its first cigarette? I had to sit for a while. Then I left the bottle and went upstairs and ran through the Great Central Philippine Headache Cure.

Within months, the spaces of Channel A and Channel B began to shift. When I was in the midst of all the breathing and chanting and meditating and group work, the headlines in newspapers all seemed much the same, but feelings and emotions and something beyond, which we have no language for, seemed clear. Now, in a more traditional mode of visiting laboratories and talking to brain people, the headlines resumed their sharp distinctions, and the feelings became more blurred and vague. It became easy to skip meditations. I could drink a glass of wine without getting dizzy and nauseated. Sometimes, for some minor distress, it was easier to take an aspirin than lie down and pacify it with cooling thoughts.

Pretty soon, I could read the *Wall Street Journal* without hearing messages from my skin, and I was listening to the words people uttered, and not the timbre of their voices as they talked. I knew I was losing something, but I was on the way back.

There remains the story of the Crazy Indian. That was how I thought of him. I went to a broadcast studio one day, and they said, your Indian friend is in the control room. And I said, I don't have an Indian friend. (I didn't even know whether by Indian they meant Black Elk or Krishna Dass.) I was just starting to read in this area and there is this Indian waving happily in the control room, nobody I knew. When the broadcast was over, I said, I don't believe we've met, and the Indian grinned happily and said, but we know you at the ashram, your money book. "The stock doesn't know you own it!" sang the Indian. "It is going up as long as it is going up! That is what Sri Aurobindo would have written if he wrote in American, and that is what you wrote. So I have brought you a present."

And he gave me a very handsome edition of the works of Sri Aurobindo. I did not want to say, who the hell is Sri Aurobindo, so I said, thank you very much.

But that was not the end of it. I could not lose the Crazy Indian. If I turned right, he turned right. If I jumped into a cab, so did he.

I figured this was a caper of old Suchabanana, so I called Murphy—on my credit card—the Crazy Indian standing outside the phone booth grinning—but Murphy denied any knowledge.

"That was Murphy," I said when I came out of the phone booth. The Crazy Indian did not know Murphy. "Murphy wants to know if he can be the golf coach at the ashram."

The Crazy Indian said certainly, they had a wonderful sports program at the ashram.

If it wasn't Suchabanana, and I wasn't getting paranoid, then maybe old Carl Jung was right that there are no coincidences.

The Crazy Indian did a little bob and said, "Namaste." So we walked down the street and I said, how long are you here for, and the Crazy Indian said he had to leave Saturday morning when his visa expired, and he showed me the visa in his passport. He had only been in the country a week.

"You didn't come here just to hand me that book," I said.

"No," he said, "I came to see two people. You were one. Namaste."

"What is namaste?" I said.

"Oh, that means, I salute the light within you."

"I have a light?"

"Everybody has a light," he said, with an expansive gesture to the hurrying mob outside Pennsylvania Station. The individuals in the mob hurried on, faces down, grim. I began to feel a little rerun of Altered State #6; if time is not time, if owning the earth is a game we play, if there are vibrations we are too dense to feel, well, maybe everybody has a light.

The Crazy Indian ducked away for a moment and came back with some flowers and handed them to me. I was embarrassed. What the hell was I supposed to do with flowers?

"Namaste," I said. "Namaste," I said to the passing crowd.

"Namaste," said the Crazy Indian.

I shook hands firmly and told him I had to leave now—he was about to get on the train with me—and I got on the train and walked through it and every few feet I would stop and give somebody a flower and smile and say, "Namaste." Some of them pulled their newspapers closer around them, but by the end of the train I had given all the flowers away.

Namaste.

NOTES

source of some of what follows. Shapiro has a later paper in A. E. Bergin and S. L. Garfield, eds., *Handbook of Psychotherapy and Behavior Change: Empirical Analysis.* A group at Johns Hopkins Medical School has a relevant batch of papers: see J. D. Frank; D. Rosenthal and J. D. Frank. Frank has an interesting book, *Persuasion and Healing.*

17 Colored pills: A. A. Baker in Shapiro.

17 Percentages of effectiveness: F. J. Evans in *Psychology Today.*

17 Placebo injections: F. J. Evans in *Psychology Today.*

17 "the vibes give it away": P. E. Feldman in Shapiro; also, N. Miller.

17 As for the actor in the white coat on TV telling you you'll be better by morning, or a scene on TV of people recovering quickly after some TV-advertised medication, please note the manuscript of Dr. Ranieri Gerbi of Pisa in 1794. For toothache, Dr. Gerbi prescribed that a certain species of worm be crushed between thumb and forefinger, and then the fingers held to the pained spot. An independent commission reported that 431 of 629 toothaches stopped immediately! That percentage is right up there with The Leading Pain Reliever, and independent commissions are still reporting similar statistics.

18 Blood pressure, medication and placebos: R. F. Grenfell et al., *Southern Medical Journal*, in Shapiro.

18 Asthma sufferers: Luparello et al. in *Psychosomatic Medicine* (reprinted in N. E. Miller, *Biofeedback and Self-Control*).

18 Stomach pill: R. A. Sternbach in *Psychophysiology.*

18 Witch doctors and psychiatrists: P. Torrey, *The Mind Game.*

PARADIGMS

21 *The Structure of Scientific Revolutions:* Kuhn's paradigm is itself a paradigm, and not without its critics. The more it gets to be an academic buzz-word, the less comfortable I feel with it. But it's probably better than "disciplinary matrix," which is proposed as its successor. No thumbnail reference to the history of science should leave out Karl Popper and Michael Polanyi, especially the latter.

23 "a science about the level . . .": E. Berne, unpublished speech, "Away from a Theory of the Impact of Interpersonal Interaction on Nonverbal Participation," Golden Gate Group Psychotherapy Association, June 20, 1970. A very funny and very acute speech.

Notes

Page

24 "an unconscious tendency...": See also T. Roszak, *The Making of a Counter Culture* and *Where the Wasteland Ends* for a general discussion.

24 The parallel between the selectivity of the paradigm and that of perception is made loosely in R. Ornstein, *The Psychology of Consciousness*.

24 "A team of Stanford psychologists..." Not only Stanford psychologists, of course. I started with a file called "Stanford Cats," and then "Harvard Med. Cats," and finally ended with "Experience Shapes Perception." The Stanford cats are in H. Hirsch in *Science*; also in Hirsch and D. N. Spinelli in *Experimental Brain Research* and Spinelli et al. in *Experimental Brain Research*. The Harvard cats are in T. N. Wiesel and D. H. Hubel in *Journal of Neurophysiology*. Other Wiesel-Hubel papers are fascinating on how the cells of the visual cortex encode the visual world, but they don't belong here under paradigms. Spinelli has a relevant article with Karl Pribram in *Journal of Electroencephalography and Clinical Neurophysiology*, 44:144-49 (1967). An additional article is by C. Blakemore and J. F. Cooper in *Nature*

My language about "stripes" is a bit loose. The patterns were computer-directed dots, and the change in the patterns changed the distribution of the cells in the cats' cortexes. But not only does the point remain, it's quite significant. This work on perception and experience, and the interaction of the organism and the environment, didn't begin here and certainly isn't limited to the cats here. It's fascinating, and though I sometimes get overenthusiastic about items from physiological psychology where the techniques are beyond me, I wish I had the space to do more without getting away from the story. I appreciate the direction in reading from Richard F. Thompson.

THE ASTRONAUTS OF INNER SPACE

26 Wilder Penfield: "Speech, Perception and the Uncommitted Cortex" in J. Eccles, *Brain and Conscious Experience*. See also Penfield, *Speech and Brain Mechanisms*.

32 "A Harvard Divinity School student . . .": Also a psychologist, Walter Pahnke, now deceased. Pahnke's thesis is unpublished, but see his "Contribution of the Psychology of Religion to the Therapeutic Use of the Psychedelic Substances" in H. Abramson, ed., *The Use of LSD in Psychotherapy and Alcoholism*, and "Drugs and Mysticism" in B. Aaronson and H. Osmond, eds., *Psychedics: Uses and Implications of Hallucinogenic Drugs*. W. Pahnke and W. Richards, "Implications of

Page

Experimental Mysticism," in C. Tart, ed., *Altered States of Consciousness*. The account is from Richard Alpert.

A VERY SHORT HISTORY OF SOME AMERICAN DRUGS FAMILIAR TO EVERYBODY

34   Aspirin usage may actually be much higher. See New York *Times,*
        26 (March 27, 1975).

35   Xanthines: L. S. Goodman and A. Gilman, *The Pharmacological Basis
        of Therapeutics*.

35   "xanthine addict": E. M. Brecher et al., eds., *Licit & Illicit Drugs*.
        While this is dated, the effects of caffeine continue to be debated in
        the journals. See *British Medical Journal* (February 8, 1975) and J. F.
        Graden in *American Journal of Psychiatry*.

36   " 'hard drugs' ": Summarized from E. M. Brecher et al., eds., *Licit &
        Illicit Drugs*.

THE WORLD'S FIRST ACID TRIP

Humphrey Osmond spent a number of evenings at my house. His help
is gratefully acknowledged. So is that of Jean Houston, R. E. L. Master
and Frank Berger, the latter for some tutoring in pharmacology.

38   " 'I lay down...' ": Hofmann's account, in a foreign journal, is par-
        tially excerpted in L. S. Goodman and A. Gilman, eds., *The Pharma-
        ceutical Basis of Therapeutics,* and in R. E. Masters and L. Houston,
        The Varieties of Psychedelic Experience.

39   "LSD subject": L. S. Goodman and A. Gilman, eds., *The Pharmacologi-
        cal Basis of Therapeutics*.

40   "An American authority...": E. M. Brecher et al., eds., *Licit & Illicit
        Drugs*.

40   "a review of the literature": E. M. Brecher et al., eds., *Licit & Illicit
        Drugs*, p. 357. Also see N. Dishotsky et al. in *Science*.

40   "One hospital team...": Marlboro Day Hospital, in E. M. Brecher
        et al., eds., *Licit & Illicit Drugs*, p. 361.

AND A SHORT CHRONICLE OF THE MADNESS

42   "A team of researchers...": F. N. Cheek et al. in *Science*.

Notes

Page

42   "many people who believe...": C. Tart, ed., *Altered States of Consciousness*, pp. 386–87.

42   Mushrooms: Andrew Weil, private communication.

44   Liddy, Owsley, et al.: M. J. Warth in *Village Voice*.

44   Huxley's letter to Osmond: G. Smith, ed., *The Letters of Aldous Huxley*, p. 945.

There is a fairly extensive bibliography on psychedelics in C. Tart, ed., *Altered State of Consciousness*. The dangers are broken out into a section called "Dangers," and there are sections under "General," "Therapeutics," "Legal Aspects," "Pharmacology and Botany," "Sociology and Anthropology," and so on. A good source on dangers is S. Cohen in *JAMA* and other journals. See also the bibliography in T. X. Barber, *LSD, Marihuana, Yoga, and Hypnosis.*

WHAT DID WE LEARN?

51   "neuronal pathways": J. Eccles, *The Neurophysiological Basis of Mind: The Principles of Neurophysiology*. Much easier is Eccles, "The Physiology of Imagination, in T. J. Teyler, ed., *Altered States of Awareness*. Also see K. Pribram, "The Neurophysiology of Remembering," in R. Thompson, ed., *Physiological Psychology*.
    Physiological Psychology, Altered States of Awareness, Perception: Mechanisms and Models, Frontiers of Psychological Research and *The Nature and Nurture of Behavior* are all collections in the series *Readings from Scientific American*. They are abstract, college text-level writing but the illustrations and presentation make them reasonably clear.

51   The computer metaphor rages through the sleep literature, too; e.g., E. L. Hartmann, *The Functions of Sleep*, p. 15: "Greenberg and Leidman (1966) believe that D-sleep may involve rewinding recent memories onto long-term storage tapes." To be accurate, the metaphor would have to be dynamic, and the computer as equipment is static, but it does get an idea across. Loosely.

52   "dark woods": I know at least three journals which will still publish papers on The Meaning of the Forest. It's interesting to go on and read J. Campbell, *The Mythic Image* and *The Hero with a Thousand*

Faces. *The Mythic Image* is beautiful and costs $45.00; *Hero with a Thousand Faces* is a paperback, $4.

53 Houston's "phylogenetic" speculations: R. E. Masters and J. Houston, *The Varieties of Psychedelic Experience.*

54 "V-shaped shadow": L. Thomas, *The Lives of a Cell*, p. 90, after N. Tinberger, *The Study of Instinct*. Further reading on genes: T. Dobzhansky, *Mankind Evolving*; R. Dubos, *So Human an Animal*; S. Luria, *Life . . . the Unfinished Experiment*. All paperbacks. A. Lehninger, *Biochemistry*, is clear but much harder, and $20.

54 Grof's research and theories are discussed in *Journal of Transpersonal Psychology*, 1 (1973), and in a three-part paper presented to the 2nd Interdisciplinary Conference on the Voluntary Control of Internal States, Council Grove, Kansas (1970).

55n "Two sociologists . . .": New York *Times Magazine*, 24 (January 26, 1975).

56 "A Hasidic rabbi . . .": R. Metzner, ed., *The Ecstatic Adventure*, pp. 96–124.

57 "'our normal waking consciousness'": W. James, *The Varieties of Religious Experience*. There are several different editions available; this is New American Library, p. 298.

II. Hemispheres

LEFT SIDE, RIGHT SIDE, WHY RALPH NADER CAN'T DANCE

63 It is a bit flip to call Sperry "the captain of left-right research," since every source leads back to him. Sperry's "Brain Bisection and Mechanisms of Consciousness" is in J. C. Eccles, ed., *Brain and Conscious Experience*. Sperry's classic article on hemispheres, "The Great Cerebral Commissure" in *Scientific American*, is reprinted in S. Coopersmith, ed., *Frontiers of Psychological Research*. "The Eye and the Brain" is repeated in two of the *Scientific American* readers (they do overlap sometimes). Sperry's one-time student, now professor, Michael Gazzaniga has "The Split Brain in Man" in *Physiological Psychology*, again the *Scientific American* reader, and a more technical book, *The Bisected Brain*. Sperry's "A Modified View of Consciousness" is in *Psychological Re-*

Notes

view. The patients whom Sperry and Gazzaniga wrote about were sometimes those of Joseph Bogen, the Los Angeles neurosurgeon who wrote a very interesting series, "The Other Side of the Brain," in *Bulletin of the Los Angeles Neurological Society*. One of the Bogen articles and Gazzaniga's "Split Brain" are in R. Ornstein, ed., *The Nature of Human Consciousness*. The patient whose hands battled is in Gazzaniga. "It couldn't even double the number four" is in the discussion following Sperry's "Brain Bisection" paper in Eccles, as above.

I also used sections 1, 4, 5, 6, 10 and 15 of S. J. Dimond and J. G. Beaumont, *Hemisphere Function in the Human Brain*, and Dimond's *The Double Brain*. Without specific citations as background, I have used some of *The Neurosciences: Third Study Program*, edited by Schmitt and Worden. These books are expensive and technical; *Third Neurosciences* is also heavy (nonportable).

Robert Ornstein of the Langley Porter Neuropsychiatric Institute suggested readings, sent copies of journal articles in his files and read sections of the book in manuscript, for which I am thankful.

ON THE LEFT HAND (RIGHT BRAIN), AMERICA'S LEADING ASHRAM

76   M. Murphy, *Golf in the Kingdom*.

78   "'Somatosensory deprivation'...". J. Prescott in *Intellectual Digest*, 6–10 (March 1974). Certainly a far-out thesis, but then...

THE GRANDMA AND GRANDPA OF GRAVITY

Besides Sam Keen's account of Rolfing in *Psychology Today*, see *Bulletin of Structural Integration*.

BIOFEEDBACK: WHO'S AT HOME HERE?

Virtually the only wheel in town is Aldine Publishing, which collects the annual *Biofeedback and Self-Control*. While these collections are editorially the best of what went on, as a publishing job it is terrible: photographed journal articles, horrendously priced. Pp. 59–80 of my 1971 *Biofeedback* are missing. Just plain missing. Where is my copy of *Cardiovascular Psychophysiology*, ordered eighteen months ago? I marked up somebody else's. The new annual costs $18.50.

100 "a hundred minus seven...": Old stuff from way before biofeedback. E. D. Adrian and B. H. C. Matthews said that arithmetic would reduce alpha, and that was in 1934! In *Brain*, 57:355 (1934). And H. H. Jasper said opening your eyes would reduce alpha, but closing them would

bring it back again, and that was published in 1941! In *Epilepsy and Cerebral Localization*, edited by W. Penfield and T. C. Erickson.

100 "A psychologist...": Ralph Hefferline of Columbia.

I used as a checklist *Relaxation and Related States: A Bibliography of Psychological and Physiological Research* by Richard J. Davidson and Gary E. Schwartz of the Harvard Psychology Department. Other than Aldine and above, I should cite G. E. Schwartz in *American Scientist* and D. Mostofsky, ed., *Behavior Control and Modification of Physiological Activity*.

Gary Schwartz suggested reading, supplied journal articles from his files and read the manuscript, for which I am thankful.

RESPECTABILITY, CONFIRMATION AND THE MYSTERY OF THE REBELLING RATS

Miller has a summary in A. M. Freedman et al., eds., *Comprehensive Textbook of Psychiatry*. His earlier writings are in N. E. Miller, *Selected Papers*; two more generalized articles are in *Science*. Dworkin has a summary in the first chapter of his *An Effort to Replicate Visceral Learning in the Curarized Rat*. Some of this history is counted in a small, carefully written book, *Visceral Learning*, by G. Jonas, basically a profile of Miller.

106 The difficulties with the curarized rats are described by Miller and Dworkin in P. A. Obrist et al., eds., *Cardiovascular Psychophysiology*.

107 T. Weiss and B. Engel in *Psychosomatic Medicine*; Engel and Bleecker in *Cardiovascular Psychophysiology*.

108 "two of the biofeedback pioneers": J. Stoyva and T. Budzynski, in the 1972 Aldine *Biofeedback* annual. Also, Budzynski et al. in *Behavior Therapy and Experimental Psychiatry*. Stoyva and Budzynski have other entries on biofeedback and tension headaches.

108 "Still another psychologist...": M. S. Sterman in L. Birk, *Seminars in Psychiatry*.

109 The material on the Greens is directly from them and from interviews with Elmer Green. Green et al., Menninger Foundation papers. Also J. D. Sargent et al. in *Psychosomatic Medicine* and Green et al. in J. Rose, ed., *Progress of Cybernetics*. The Greens wrote a summary in *Science Year, 1974*. Articles by the Greens and Walters are in several collections, and the Greens have been written up in the popular press, references not included here.

The enthusiasm for biofeedback was far from universal. See D. A.

Paskewitz and M. T. Orne in *Science*. And one of the biofeedback researchers who read this chapter said the comparison to James Lind's two sailors sucking on limes was "unnecessarily generous; James Lind's experiments were better controlled than most biofeedback experiments."

WIRING UP THE YOGIS

The most widely collected report on the yogis is B. K. Anand et al. in *Journal of Electroencephalography and Clinical Neurophysiology*. The electroencephalographic study of the Zen masters is in *Folio Psychiatria and Neurologia Japonica*, 20 (1966). Other yoga and Zen entries are under H. V. A. Rao et al. in *Journal of the All-India Institute of Mental Health* and M. A. Wenger and B. K. Bagchi in *Behavioral Science*.

116   "big hitters": The Greens' account of Swami Rama is also in *Science Year, 1974*. The account by the Greens of Jack Schwarz is "A Demonstration of Voluntary Control of Bleeding and Pain" in Menninger Foundation papers.

118   "And the perception of pain varies ...": See R. A. Sternbach, *Principles of Psychophysiology*. "cheerful Gurkha recruits" in the autobiography of John Masters, *Bugles and a Tiger*, and *The Road Past Mandalay*.

118   Melzack has a college-level exposition in R. F. Thompson, ed., *Physiological Psychology*, reprinted from *Scientific American*.

119   "demystify the yogic tricks": T. X. Barber, *LSD, Marihuana, Yoga, and Hypnosis*. The insensitivity to pain relates to a similar discussion of hypnosis and pain in Barber's *Hypnotism, Imagination and Human Potentialities*. See "Hypnotism and Surgical Pain," pp. 79–98. Barber is a prolific writer, and it isn't possible to list all the references; most of them concern hypnosis, but they have some relevance here. Look in the abstracts under Barber, T. X., and Calverly, D. S., and under Barber's associates, Spanos, N. P., and Chaves, J. F.

T. X. Barber suggested readings, sent articles from his files and discussed a number of points not directly cited but having a bearing on the whole manuscript, for which I am thankful.

III. Meditations

From William James to the mid-1960's, the literature on meditation is spotty at best. A physician and psychiatrist, Arthur Deikman, wrote two bridging essays: "Deautomatization and the Mysic Experience" in *Psychiatry*, which contains much of the historical material used by Benson et al. in *Psychiatry* (though for some reason it isn't cited), and "Bimodal Consciousness" in *Archives of General Psychiatry*. "Deautomatization" is reprinted in both R. Ornstein, ed., *The Nature of Human Consciousness*, and C. Tart, ed., *Altered States of Consciousness*. "Bimodal" is reprinted in Ornstein. I took a seminar of Deikman's, which provided the background in particular for pp. 168–70.

TM material from TM. TM has considerably more material than has been referenced here.

125 "not as part of religion": And this section doesn't deal with meditation as part of religion. Further, the psychologies of the religious practices in this section are known generally to the professionals but not to the adherents. Nor does this section deal with meditation as therapy, though there is a growing literature on that subject. See the excellent overview by D. Goleman in *American Journal of Psychotherapy*. Also: E. Gellhorn in *Perspectives in Biology and Medicine* and Gellhorn and W. F. Kiely in *Journal of Nervous and Mental Disease*, 154:399 (1972).

Relaxation techniques using forms of meditation, but not called meditation in W. Luthe, *Autogenic Training*, and Luthe, ed., *Autogenic Therapy. IV. Research and Theory*. Also, Jacobson, *Progressive Relaxation*. And see J. Fagan and I. L. Shepherd, eds., *Gestalt Therapy Now*, especially Naranjo, and R. Assagioli, *Psychosynthesis*.

YOU DESERVE A BREAK TODAY

130 Use of this mantram by unauthorized personnel is strictly forbidden.

134 "lactate concentrations": Not to get sidetracked on lactates, but this doesn't seem quite as significant as it first did. Lactate as a concomitant of anxiety was dramatized by Ferris Pitts, Jr., in an article with the striking title "The Biochemistry of Anxiety," in *Scientific American*. But recently it has been widely criticized. See N. Levitt in C. D. Spielberger, ed., *Anxiety: Current Trends in Theory and Research*. The other results from meditation have been duplicated extensively.

134 "hypnosis has no particular physiology": See T. X. Barber, and others.

136 Benson's *Lancet* article: I suppose the importance, to Benson, was that this was the first use of in, out, "one," with quantified results, instead of a mantram with quantified results. Jacobson had similar relaxation techniques forty years ago. A parallel to Benson's article is by J. F. Beary and Benson in *Psychosomatic Medicine*.

Notes

Page

137   "beta spikes were appearing": See J. P. Banquet in *Journal of Electro-encephalography and Clinical Neurophysiology.*

137   "TM reduced the symptoms of asthma": A. F. Wilson and R. Honsberger in *Clinical Research*, 2, 2 (1937).

138   " 'creativity and intelligence' ": G. Schwartz in *Psychology Today.*

140   Tart's reaction to TM: See C. Tart in *Journal of Transpersonal Psychology.*

144   "nitrogen nitrogen": Needless to say, these elements have been arranged for their poetry, not their biochemistry.

NOISE

146   "my favorite biology watcher": Lewis Thomas.

147   "health is something you ... have to buy": L. Thomas, "Your Very Good Health, *The Lives of a Cell*, pp. 81–86. I wish everybody would read this, Congress, the drug companies, consumers, Blue Cross ...

149   "*harmonics* of alpha as well as alpha": My counselors say TM is ahead of itself here. Wallace is referring to J. P. Banquet in *Journal of Electroencephalography and Clinical Neurophysiology.*

153   W. Hess, *Functional Organization of the Diencephalon.*

154   "The tendency of Christians ...": T. Merton, *Mystics and Zen Masters*, pp. 205–09.

154   Difference between mantram and prayer: Swami Satchidananda, *Integral Yoga—Hatha.*

ECUMENICAL RELAXATION TECHNIQUES

155   "Choose whichever one ...": I. Progoff, *The Cloud of Unknowing.*

156   "Sit down alone ...". R. French, *The Way of the Pilgrim.*

160   D. Goleman, unpublished doctoral dissertation, Harvard University, 1973, summarized in Goleman in *American Journal of Psychotherapy.*

WHY FRANNY FAINTED

165   J. Krishnamurti, *Commentaries on Living: Third Series*, quoted in J. E. Coleman, *The Quiet Mind.*

NOTES

167 "A group of psychologists...": Hebb, Heron and Pritchard at McGill. "tiny projectors on contact lenses" described by Pritchard in R. L. Held and W. Richards, eds., *Perception: Mechanisms and Models.*

168 " 'ganzfeld' "; " 'blank out' ": W. Cohen in *American Journal of Psychology* and T. C. Cadwallander in *American Psychologist.* Ornstein, in *The Psychology of Consciousness,* makes the point about one-pointedness or Void and "blank out."

169 "eye movements became stereotyped": C. Furst in *Perception and Psychophysics.*

169 "red six of spades": And other cards, other colors. See J. Bruner in *Psychological Review.* And many other Bruner references in perception and categorization.

174 "When written up...": P. Kapleau, *The Three Pillars of Zen.*

174 "American psychotherapist in Japan": J. Huber, *Through an Eastern Window.* This account is reprinted in *Asian Psychology,* edited by Gardner and Lois Murphy.

176 " 'afterglow from this state' ": D. Goleman in *American Journal of Psychotherapy.*

176 Shaker furniture: It's interesting to consider this Shaker hymn in the light of this discussion of Zen psychology:
> *Tis a gift to be simple*
> *Tis a gift to be free*
> *Tis a gift to come down*
> *Where you ought to be ...*
> *And when we find ourselves in the place just right*
> *We'll be in the valley of love and delight.*

IV. "Sport Is a Western Yoga"

QUARTERBACKING IN AN ALTERED STATE

187 Murphy and Brodie were, at one time, going to write a book together, and they had several public dialogues which I taped. *Intellectual Digest* published a Murphy-Brodie interview in January 1973 which had Brodie's statement about time slowing down, and a very odd pass to Gene Washington not discussed in the text here.

189 " 'there isn't any language' ": But the scholars will be eager to supply

their own. M. Csikzentmihalyi in *Journal of Humanistic Psychology* calls a "Flow" state one where "action and awareness are sustained... in concentration," "limited stimulus field...awareness devoid of concern with outcome," "self-forgetfulness," "skills adequate to meet... the demand," "clarity." "Flow" is "an optimal fit between one's capability and the demands of the moment."

The only danger in this is that it leads to the quantification of "Flow." Think what football announcers could do with the statistics.

ZEN AND THE CROSS-COURT BACKHAND

In very different form, I wrote an account of Esalen sports and "yoga tennis" in *Sports Illustrated*.

THE SWEET MUSIC OF THE STRINGS

The Torben stories go round and round in sports magazines: I think Torben enjoys staging them just to see what sort of event the moment will produce. In any case, they inspire lyrical sportswriting, as done by Mark Kram in *Sports Illustrated* and Robert Bradford in *Tennis*. Bradford wrote up Borowiak several years after Torben, and Borowiak's Copenhagen trip is in his Borowiak story.

206 "you are the music": T. S. Eliot was into the Dharma.

V. Vibes

AMBIGUITIES AND VIDEO

209 "The editors of the Establishment press...": The press reviews the Alchemist continuously, that is, the "story" is what is up on the story-board as a "story," and not the "story" itself. For example, on July 4, 1973 there was a large gathering of counter cultural folk in Central Park in Manhattan. They sat and chanted and formed circles and drew curious passers-by, no story there. But then came a skywriting plane that wrote "OM" in the sky over New York. A clear blue sky and "OM." I was curious. Who hired the plane? Was this the first time anybody skywrote "OM" over a Western city? What was the reaction of sky-gawkers on seeing "OM" instead of "Pepsi-Cola"? What did the skywriter intend? Did "OM" cost less than "Pepsi-Cola"? Then the sky-writing plane flew off, and this time when it came back it wrote "OM" in *Sanskrit*,   . Now my curiosity was really up. Certainly this was

the first case of Sanskrit skywriting—and right over hundreds of thousands of sky-gawkers! Who on earth was doing this? What was the pilot's reaction upon being given a Sanskrit mantram to skywrite? Right under the "OM," in both English and Sanskrit, was, of course, the headquarters of the New York *Times.* I opened the *Times*—all the news that's fit to print—on July 5. No skywriter. No "OM." Instead, several columns on the break-up of a hippie festival in Grand Junction, Colorado. As for the TV news, it went to the beach, and never turned its camera upward.

211 "poor Dr. Noone got blowpiped": The story of the search for Dr. Noone is told by his brother, Richard Noone, in *The Rape of the Dream People.*

213 " 'the Second Coming of Santa Claus' ": F. Gray in *New York Review.*

213 "The mahatma is sitting...": F. Gray in *New York Review.* Another account is in *Newsweek*, 157–58 (November 19, 1973).

214 Pineal gland: G. E. W. Wolstenholme and J. Knight, eds., *The Pineal Gland.*

216 "The Indian zapped ...": F. Gray in *New York Review.*

217 B. Brown, *New Mind, New Body.*

Packagers

MEETINGS WITH REMARKABLE MEN

243 The aphorisms are in G. I. Gurdjieff, *Meetings with Remarkable Men.*

WHO'S A SUFI?

251 The Nasrudin stories are now in a series of paperbacks, done by Idries Shah. *The Dermis Probe, Tales of the Dervishes, Wisdom of the Idiots* and *The Pleasantries of the Incredible Mulla Nasrudin* are Dutton paperbacks, and Shah's *The Sufis* is an Anchor paperback.

251 Some of the Hasidic stories are in M. Buber's *Tales of the Hasidim.*

252 "Idries Shah wasn't a descendant ...": I have absolutely no information on who is and is not a descendant of the Prophet. There is a similar attack on Shah in *Encounter* by a professor of Persian at the University of Edinburgh, L. P. Elwell-Sutton, who says that Shah has transcribed some Nasrudin stories, that his scholarship is sloppy, that

his father was "an unsuccessful medical student turned traveler and publicist" and that the descendants of the Prophet number in the millions.

NEXT WEEK, SATORI 24

Some of this material appeared, in quite different form, as "Alumni Notes, Altered States U.," in *Psychology Today* (July 1973).

256   Lilly's interview: S. Keen, *Psychology Today*.

THE HIGH VALUE OF NOTHING

273   "The psychiatrist says...": A. Kondo in *Chicago Review*.

273   " 'The method...' ": P. Wiepahl in *Chicago Review*.

281   " 'recognition of illusoriness' ": M. Esslin, *The Theatre of the Absurd*, p. 64.

289   "Maybe we could get Noam Chomsky": See *Syntactic Structures* after the first round draft-choice reading, and *Language and Mind*. Also, *Chomsky: Selected Readings*, edited by J. P. B. Allen and P. van Buren. *Aspects of the Theory of Syntax* is much harder. Interesting, but in the text it begins to stray from the story, so we have to pass Chomsky as a first-round draft choice. Maybe we can get him later on a trade.

VI. The Far Side of Paradigm

THE SENIOR ASTRONAUT: YOU GOTTA KNOW THE TERRITORY

Lilly's books are *The Center of the Cyclone* and *Programming and Metaprogramming in the Human Biocomputer* His original paper is in *Psychiatric Research Reports*. See also S. Keen's interview with Lilly in *Psychology Today*. Lilly's remarks on the false objectivity of psychologists—"the behavioral view has something to offer...but it is incomplete"—are in "Solitude, Isolation and Confinement," Lilly's contribution to a small book with a big title, *The Psychodynamic Implications of Physiological Studies on Sensory Deprivation*, edited by L. Madow and L. Snow.

W. Heron's 1957 article in *Scientific American* is reprinted in S. Coopersmith, ed., *Frontiers of Psychological Research*. An unsigned review of the research to that date is in *Lancet*, 2:1072 (1959).

P. Solomon et al., eds., *Sensory Deprivation*, summarizes a conference which Lilly felt was the Establishment view.

Two chapters of *Isolation: Clinical and Experimental Approaches* by C. A. Brownfield are relevant.

A number of articles are in the collection edited by J. P. Zubek, *Sensory Deprivation: Fifteen Years of Research*.

Peter Suedfeld's article "The Benefits of Boredom" is in *American Scientist*. The first Suedfeld article on cutting down smoking is in *Journal of Applied Social Psychology*, 3:30–38 (1973). The others are referenced in "The Benefits of Boredom."

BABA RAM DASS: PILGRIM, PREACHER

While Ram Dass hasn't written as Ram Dass, his fans have taped his talks and made the edited versions into two books that are quite unique: *Be Here Now* and *The Only Dance There Is*. Not only are they unique, they are fun.

315 "'I was blessed...'": *Be Here Now*. The other quotations are from *The Only Dance There Is*, tapes of talks made at the Menninger Foundation and the Spring Grove Hospital. And my own tapes.

CARLOS: I MET A MAN UPON A STAIR

324 "'Space does not conform...'" is in the preface by Walter Goldschmidt to *The Teachings of Don Juan: A Yaqui Way of Knowledge*, the first of the Don Juan books. The three that followed are *A Separate Reality*, *Journey to Ixtlan* and *Tales of Power*.

325 The Castaneda statements are from his interview in *Psychology Today* (December 1971).

328 "to make a double of yourself": Note this from G. Reed, *The Psychology of Anomalous Experience*, p. 53: "Shamans and witches cultivate and control their spirit doubles. The shaman double may be dispatched to round up the erring spirit of a patient, or *to bring back news of events in New York...*" (my italics)

PARAPSYCH

332 "perception studies": H. K. Hartline at the University of Pennsylvania won a Nobel prize for mapping the receptive fields of cells. David Hubel and Torsten Wiesel at the Harvard Medical School have already been cited under "Harvard cats." The earlier frog's eye/frog's brain

Notes

Page

work was done by Jerome Lettvin and his associates at MIT. See also R. L. Held and W. Richards, eds., *Perception: Mechanisms and Models,* R. F. Thompson's *Physiological Psychology* and *Introduction to Physiological Psychology.* Also P. M. Milner, *Physiological Psychology.*

332   "frog's eye/frog's brain experiment": That wasn't its purpose, of course, but it does seem to be consistent. See H. R. Maturana et al. in *Journal of General Physiology.* The popular version is under J. Y. Lettvin et al. in *Proceedings of the Institute of Radio Engineers.*

333   Eccles' statement is on p. 56 of the paperback edition of *Facing Reality.* See also the summary discussion in his *Brain and Conscious Experience.*

335   "Another writer ...": New York *Times Magazine* (August 11, 1974).

346   "Some psychologists ... tested Geller": According to Martin Gardner, *Scientific American* columnist.

350   Targ and Puthoff's *Nature* article: *Nature* also published a critique. Puthoff and Targ continued their physics-parapsychology speculations in "Physics, Entropy and Psychokinesis," SRI paper.

351   F. H. Walker, Rhine Swanton Symposium, AAAS. Not many quantum physicists are into ESP.

"BOSH, DR. JUNG"

355   "one famous incident": C. G. Jung, *Memories, Dreams, Reflections,* A. Jaffe, ed., pp. 155–56.

355   Ninety-seven percent "occult"; 3 percent research: R. A. White and L. A. Dale, *Parapsychology.*

359   Wired-up salmon: T. J. Hara in *Science.* The fish language is in J. H. Todd in *Scientific American.* Some of this derives from pp. 104ff. in *Life ... the Unfinished Experiment* by S. Luria. But you can read L. Thomas, *The Lives of a Cell,* and get it all with such pleasure.

THE MIND, THE QUANTUM AND THE UNIVERSE

364   Not only François Jacob, of course, but most recently. See "Language and Reality in Modern Physics" in *Physics and Philosophy,* W. Heisenberg, and "Discussions About Language" in *Physics and Beyond,* Heisenberg.

364   "the language of physics is less certain": S. Rose says, "The biologist, although confident of the extensions to the edifice he is creating, all

the time has to build in doubt as to whether his physical foundations may not be in quagmire." *The Conscious Brain*, pp. 292–93.

366   "half are particles and half are anti-particles": This didn't quite pass my particle advisers, who wrote, "Certain particles are their own anti-particles. Better to say: many particles come in two forms, particles and anti-particles, the anti-particle having the same mass as the particle. As to their life, particles and anti-particles of a given species are equally stable . . . our world is made up largely of the particles proton, neutron, electron. When one of the corresponding anti-particles is created, it will sooner or later run into one of its counterparts and both will disappear in the annihilation."

That's in case you want your particles straight. My point was just to create some perspective in time and space. Thanks to: John Wheeler, Tom Stix, Sam Treiman, the Joseph Henry Laboratories, Princeton University.

366   Neutrinos: A very good summary of subatomic physics is in A. Koestler, *The Roots of Coincidence*. Updike's "Cosmic Gall," from *Telephone Poles and Other Poems*, is also there, though I liked some different lines.

368   Wheeler's "superspace" is in *University: A Princeton Quarterly* (Summer 1972). "the mind, the quantum, and the universe" is in J. Wheeler, *Smithsonian and National Academy of Science*. Also Wheeler, "From Relativity to Mutability," in *The Physicist's Conception of Nature*, J. Mehra, ed.

369   " 'What's a quantum?' " Said Ernest Schrödinger, Nobel prizewinning quantum pioneer, "If all this damn'd quantum jumping were really here to stay, I should be sorry I ever got involved." W. Heisenberg, *Physics and Beyond*, p. 75.

371   "real" and *res*: W. Heisenberg, *Physics and Philosophy*.

371   " 'complementarity' ": J. R. Oppenheimer, "Physics in the Contemporary World, in M. Gardner, ed., *Great Essays in Science*, p. 189.

372   " 'eternity and timelessness' ": Oppenheimer, *Science and the Common Understanding*, p. 69. " 'the objective world' ": W. Heisenberg, *Across the Frontiers*, p. 227. " 'Scientific knowledge . . .' ": E. Wigner, "Two Kinds of Reality," *Symmetries and Reflections: Scientific Essays*, pp. 197–98.

372   " 'the human ability to understand' ": W. Heisenberg, "Role of Modern Physics in Human Thinking," *Physics and Philosophy*, pp. 201–02. "The understanding . . .": Heisenberg, "The Meaning of Beauty in the

Exact Sciences," *Across the Frontiers*, pp. 177–78. Also see "Natural Law and the Structure of Matter" and "Wolfgang Pauli's Philosophical Outlook" in the same book. " 'faith in the central order' ": "Elementary Particles and Platonic Philosophy," *Physics and Beyond*, p. 247. And "First Encounter with the Atomic Concept," same volume.

See also, in Wigner, the whole section "Epistemology and Quantum Mechanics."

372   Einstein's Unified Field Theory; " 'all his abstract intuitions of reality' ": L. Barnett, *The Universe and Dr. Einstein*, p. 72.

Einstein wrote this bit of doggerel:

A thought that sometimes makes me hazy:
Am I—or are the others—crazy?

(in A. Koestler, *Act of Creation*, p. 134)

ACKNOWLEDGEMENTS

Three people believed this was a book when I thought of it as only an investigation, a sabbatical. Their support contributed to converting their belief into fact. They are: T. George Harris, Lynn Nesbit and James Silberman.

BIBLIOGRAPHY

Best-Written Book in the Bibliography
The Lives of a Cell, by Lewis Thomas

Don't be put off by such words as "prokaryocytes," "symbionts," "rhizobial" and "mitochondria," just to take samples from the fourth paragraph. You don't have to know them to get it.

Worst-Written Book in the Bibliography
Being and Time, by Martin Heidegger

Enormous Room for Improvement Dept.
All the books titled *Elements of Neurophysiology*
and all the books titled *The Mystics of Islam*

Most Surprising Essayist
Werner Heisenberg, *Physics and Philosophy*
and *Physics and Beyond*

Most Far-Out Autobiography
Memories, Dreams, Reflections, by C. G. Jung,
edited by Aniela Jaffe

Best Drug Book
Licit & Illicit Drugs,
edited by E. M. Brecher et al.

BIBLIOGRAPHY

Best Textbook for Bedside Reading
The Pharmaceutical Basis of Therapeutics,
edited by Louis S. Goodman and Alfred Gilman

You can look up all the pills prescribed for you, and if you can find the generic name, you can save money on prescriptions. Paragraphs in each section are very technical. You might need a chemistry translation, or Lehninger's *Biochemistry*—a classic textbook, but an expensive one.

Best Collections
The Nature of Human Consciousness,
edited by Robert E. Ornstein

Not only the best collection for this book, but the introductions are equally good.

Physiological Psychology,
edited by Richard F. Thompson

A *Scientific American* reader: nice graphics, somewhat abstract writing, and not all easy.

Best Brain Book
The Conscious Brain, by Steven Rose

Most Provocative
The Politics of Experience, by R. D. Laing

PERIODICALS*

Abrahams, V. C., et al., "Active Muscle Vasodilatation Produced by Stimulation of the Brain Stem: Its Significance in the Defense Reaction," *Journal of Physiology*, 154-491 (1960).

Alsop, Stewart, Column. *Newsweek* (March 11, 1974).

Anand, B. K., Chhina, G. S., and Singh, B. H., "Some Aspects of Electroencephalographic Studies in Yogis." *Journal of Electroencephalography and Clinical Neurophysiology*, 13:452–56 (1961).

——— et al., "Studies on Shri Remananda Yogi During His Stay in an Airtight Box." *Indian Journal of Medical Research*, 49:82–89 (1961).

Bagchi, B. K., and Wenger, M. A., "Electrophysical Correlations of Some Yoga Exercises." *Journal of Electroencephalography and Clinical Neurophysiology*, Suppl., 7:132–49 (1957).

Baker, A. A., and Thorpe, J. G., "Placebo Response." *AMA Archives of Neurology and Psychiatry*, 78:57 (1957).

Banquet, J. P., "EEG and Meditation." *Journal of Electroencephalography and Clinical Neurophysiology*, 33:449–55 (1972).

———, "Spectral Analysis of EEG and Meditation." *Journal of Electroencephalography and Clinical Neurophysiology*, 35:143–51 (1973).

Barber, T. X., "Physiological Effects of Hypnosis." *Psychological Bulletin*, 58:390–419 (1961).

Baynton, Barbara, Interview with James Prescott: "Touching." *Intellectual Digest*, 6–10 (March 1974).

* This section lists articles in journals, magazines and newspapers, in relation to the notes.

BIBLIOGRAPHY

Beary, J. F., and Benson, Herbert, "A Simple Psychophysiologic Technique Which Elicits the Hypometabolic Changes of the Relaxation Response." *Psychosomatic Medicine*, 36, 2:115–20 (March–April, 1974).

Benson, Herbert, Beary, John F., and Canol, Mark P., "The Relaxation Response." *Psychiatry*, 37 (February 1974).

————, Rosner, B. A., and Marzetta, B. R., "Decreased Systolic Blood Pressure in Hypertensive Subjects Who Practiced Meditation." *Journal of Clinical Investigtaion*, 52:82 (1973).

————, Rosner, B. A., Marzetta, B. R., and Klemchuk, H. M., "Decreased Blood-pressure in Pharmacologically Treated Hypertensive Patients Who Regularly Elicited the Relaxation Response." *Lancet* (February 23, 1974).

Blakemore, C., and Cooper, J. F., "Development of the Brain Depends on Visual Environment." *Nature*, 228:447–78 (1970).

Bogen, J. E. "The Other Side of the Brain." *Bulletin of L.A. Neurological Society*, I., 34:73–105(a); II., 34:135–62 (1969).

———— and Bogen, C. A., "III. The Other Side of the Brain." *Bulletin of L.A. Neurological Society*, 34:181–20 (1969).

———— and Gordon, H. W., "Musical Tests for Functional Lateralization with Intracarotid Amobarbital." *Nature*, 230, 5295:524–25 (April 23, 1971).

————, DeZine, R., Tenhouten, W. D., and Marsh, J. F., "The Other Side of the Brain, IV. The A/P Ration. *Bulletin of L.A. Neurological Society*, 37:49–61 (1972).

————, Gordon, H. W., and Sperry, R. W., "Absence of Deconnexion Syndrome in Two Patients with Partial Section of the Neocommissures." *Brain*, 94:327–36 (1971).

Bois, J. Samuel, "General Semantics and Zen." *ETC: A Review of General Semantics*, XVIII, 1 (April 1961).

Bradford, Robert H., "Torben the First: Free Spirit on the Tour." *Tennis* (September 1971).

Brain, W. Russell, "III. The Physiological Basis of Consciousness." *Brain*, LXXXI:426–55 (1958).

Bruner, Jerome, "On Perceptual Readiness." *Psychological Review*, 64:123–52 (1957).

Bruno, L. J. J., Hefferline, R. F., and Suslowitz, P. D., "Cross-modality Matching of Muscular Tension to Loudness." *Perception and Psychophysics* (1971).

Cadwallander, T. C., "Cessation of Visual Experience Under Prolonged Visual Stimulation." *American Psychologist* (abstract), 13:410 (1958).

Campbell, Colin, "Transcendence Is as American as Ralph Waldo Emerson." *Psychology Today*, 7, 11 (April 1974).

Cannon, Walter B., "The Emergency Function of the Adrenal Medulla in

Pain and the Major Emotions." *American Journal of Physiology*, 33:356 (1941).

Cheek, F., Newell, S., and Joffe, M., "Deception in the Illegal Drug Market." *Science*, 167:1276 (1970).

Cohen, W., "Spatial and Textural Characteristics of the Ganzfeld." *American Journal of Psychology*, 70:403–10 (1957).

Czikzentmihalyi, M., "Play and Intrinsic Rewards." *Journal of Humanistic Psychology* (in press).

Deikman, Arthur, "Deautomatization and the Mystic Experience." *Psychiatry*, 29, 4:324–28 (1966).

———, "Bimodal Consciousness." *Archives of General Psychiatry*, 25:481–89 (December 1971).

DiCara, L. V., and Miller, N. E., "Heart-rate Learning in the Non-curarized State, Transfer to the Curarized State, and Subsequent Retraining in the Non-curarized State." *Physiological Behavior*, 4:621–24(b) (1959).

——— and Miller, N. E., "Changes in Heart Rate Instrumentally Learned by Curarized Rats as Avoidance Responses." *Journal of Comparative and Physiological Psychology*, 65:8–12(a) (1968).

Dishotsky, N., Loughman, W., Mogar, R., and Lipscomb, W., "LSD and Genetic Damage." *Science*, 172:431–40 (1971).

Elwell-Sutton, L. P., "Sufism and Pseudo-Sufism." *Encounter*, XLIV, 5 (May 1975).

Engel, B. T., and Hansen, S. P., "Operant Conditioning of Heart Rate Slowing." *Psychophysiology*, 3:176–87 (1966).

Erikson, Erik H., "Stress." *Psychology Today*, 3, 4 (September 1969).

Evans, Frederick J., "Placebo Response: Relationship to Suggestibility and Hypnotizability." *Proceedings of the 77th Annual Convention, American Psychological Association*, 889–90 (1969).

———, "The Power of a Sugar Pill." *Psychology Today*, 7, 11 (April 1974).

Feldenkrais, M., "The Importance of Being Upright." *CIBA-GEIGY Journal*, 1.

———, "Mind and Body." Two lectures delivered at Copenhagen Congress of Functional Movement and Relaxation, Systematics.

Feldman, P. E., "The Personal Element in Psychiatric Research." *American Journal of Psychiatry*, 113:52 (1956).

Furst, C., "Automizing of Visual Attention." *Perception and Psychophysics*, 10, 2 (1971).

Galin, David E., and Ornstein, R. E. "Lateral Specialization of Cognitive Modes: An EEG Study." *Psychophysiology*, 9, 4 (1972).

Gazzaniga, M. S., Bogen, J. E., and Sperry, R. W., "Observations on Visual

Perception after the Disconnection of the Cerebral Hemispheres in Man." *Brain*, 88:221–36 (1965).

Gellhorn, E., "The Neurophysiological Basis of Anxiety." *Perspectives in Biology and Medicine*, 8:488 (1965).

Goleman, Daniel, "Meditation and Consciousness: An Asian Approach to Mental Health." *American Journal of Psychotherapy* (in press).

Gorton, Bernard E., "Physiology of Hypnosis." *Psychiatric Quarterly*, 23:317–43, 457–85 (1949).

Graden, J. F., "Anxiety or Caffeinism: A Diagnostic Dilemma." *American Journal of Psychiatry*, 131, 10 (October 1974).

Gray, Francine, "Blissing Out in Houston." *New York Review*, 36–43 (December 13, 1973).

———, "Parapsychology and Beyond." New York *Times Magazine*, 13ff. (August 11, 1974).

Green, E., and Green, A., "The Ins and Outs of Mind-body Energy." *Science Year, 1974*, Field Enterprises, Chicago, Illinois.

———, Green, A. M., and Walters, E. D., Sargent, J. D., and Meyer, R. G., Various papers on biofeedback. Especially papers dated September 7, 1971; April 5, 1973; May 10, 1973; March 9, 1972. The Menninger Foundation, Topeka, Kansas.

Gutmann, Mary C., and Benson, Herbert, "Interaction of Environmental Factors and Systemic Arterial Blood Pressure: A Review." *Medicine*, 50, 6 (1971).

Hara, T. J., et al. "Electroencephalographic Studies of the Homing Salmon." *Science*, 149 (1966).

Hirsch, H. V. B., and Spinelli, D. N., "Visual Experience Modifies Distribution of Horizontally and Vertically Oriented Receptive Fields in Cats." *Science*, 168:869–71 (1970).

——— and Spinelli, D. N., "Modification of the Distribution of Receptive Field Orientation in Cats by Selective Visual Exposure During Development." *Experimental Brain Research*, 13:509–27 (1971).

Hofmann, A., "Psychotomimetic Drugs. *Acta Physiol. Pharmac. Neerl.*, 8:240–58 (1959).

Kahn, Robert L., "Stress." *Psychology Today*, 3, 4 (September 1969).

Kasamatsu, Akira, and Hirai, Tomio, "An Electroencephalographic Study on the Zen Meditation (Zazen) Folio." *Psychiat. Neurol. Japonica*, 20:315–36 (1966).

Keen, Sam, "From Dolphins to LSD—A Conversation with John Lilly." *Psychology Today* (December 1971).

———, "The Sorcerer's Apprentice" (interview with Carlos Castaneda). *Psychology Today* (December 1972).

————, "We Have No Desire to Strengthen the Ego or Make It Happy" (conversation with Oscar Ichazo). *Psychology Today* (July 1973).

Kinsbourne, M., and Cook, J., "Generalized and Lateralized Effects of Concurrent Verbalization on a Unimanual Skill." *Quarterly Journal of Experimental Psychology*, 23:341–345 (1971).

Klein, Sheldon, "Zen Buddhism and General Semantics." *A Review of General Semantics*, XIV, 2 (Winter 1956–57).

Koenig, Peter, "Placebo Effect in Patent Medicine." *Psychology Today*, 7, 11 (April 1974).

Kondo, Akihisa, "Zen in Psychotherapy: The Virtue of Sitting." *Chicago Review*, 12, 2 (1958).

Kram, Mark, "The Not So Melancholy Dane." *Sports Illustrated* (April 7, 1969).

Lester, James T., "Stress." *Psychology Today*, 3, 4 (September 1969).

Lettvin, J. Y., Maturana, H. R., McCulloch, W. S., and Pitts, W. H., "What the Frog's Eye Tells the Frog's Brain." *Proceedings of the Institute of Radio Engineers*, 47:1940–51 (1959).

Levy, J. "Possible Basis for the Evolution of Lateral Specialization of the Human Brain." *Nature*, 224:614–15 (1969).

————, Trevarthen, C., and Sperry R. W., "Perception ou Bilateral Chimeric Figures Following Hemispheric Deconnexion." *Brain*, 95:61–78 (1972).

Levy-Agrest, J., and Sperry, R. W., "Differential Perceptual Capacities in Major and Minor Hemispheres." *Proceedings of National Academy of Sciences*, 61:1151 (1968).

Lilly, John C. "Mental Effects of Reduction of Ordinary Levels of Physical Stimuli on Intact Healthy Persons." *Psychiatric Research Reports*, 5:1–9 (1956).

Luparello, T., Leist, N., Lourie, C. R., and Sweet, I., "The Interaction of Psychologic Stimuli and Pharmacologic Agents on Airway Reactivity in Asthmatic Subjects." *Psychosomatic Medicine*, 32:509–21 (1970).

Luria, A. R., "The Functional Organization of the Brain." *Scientific American*, 222:66–79 (1970).

McGlashan, Thomas H., Evans, Fredick J., and Orne, Martin T., "The Nature of Hypnotic Analgesia and Placebo Response to Experimental Pain." *Psychosomatic Medicine*, 31, 3:227–46 (1969).

McQuade, Walter, "What Stress Can Do to You"; "Doing Something About Stress." *Fortune* (January 1972; May 1973).

Maturana, H. R., Lettvin, J. Y., McCulloch, W. S., and Pitts, W. H., "Anatomy and Physiology of Vision in the Frog." *Journal of General Physiology*, 43/2:129–75 (1960).

Melzack, R., "Why Acupuncture Works." *Psychology Today*, 7, 1:28–37 (June 1973).

——— and Wall, P., "Pain Mechanisms: A New Theory." *Science*, 150:971–79 (1965).

Miller, N. E., "Extending the Domain of Learning." *Science*, 162:671(a) (1966).

———, "From the Brain to Behavior." Invited lecture at XIIth Inter-American Congress of Psychology, Montevideo, Uruguay (March 30–April 6, 1969).

———, "Learning of Visceral and Glandular Responses." *Science*, 163:434–45 (1969).

——— and DiCara, L. V., "Instrumental Learning of Heart Rate Changes in Curarized Rats: Shaping and Specificity to Discriminative Stimulus." *Journal of Comparative and Physiological Psychology*, 65:1–7 (1968).

Olds, J., "Pleasure Centers in the Brain." *Scientific American*, 195:105–16 (1956).

Orme-Johnson, W., "Autonomic Stability and Transcendental Meditation." *Psychosomatic Medicine*, 35, 4:341–49 (July–August 1973).

Otis, Leon S., "If Well Integrated But Anxious, Try TM." *Psychology Today*, 7, 11 (April 1974).

Paskewitz, David A., and Orne, Martin T., "Visual Effects on Alpha Feedback Training." *Science*, 181 (July 27, 1973).

Pitts, Ferris N., "The Biochemistry of Anxiety." *Scientific American*, 220:12, 69–75 (February 1969).

Pribram, K. H., "The Neurophysiology of Remembering." *Scientific American*, 220:73–86 (1969).

Prince, R. H., "The Use of Rauwolfia for the Treatment of Psychoses by Nigerian Native Doctors." *American Journal of Psychiatry*, CXVII:147–49 (1960).

Puthoff, Harold, and Targ, Russell, "Physics, Entropy and Psychokinesis." Stanford Research Institute paper presented at Conference on Quantum Physics and Parapsychology, Geneva, Switzerland (August 26–27, 1974).

Radloff, Roland, and Helmreich, Robert, "Stress." *Psychology Today*, 3, 4 (September 1969).

Rao, H. V. A., Krisnaswamy, N., Narasimhaiya, R. L., Hoenis, J., and Govindaswamy, M. V., "Some Experiments on 'Yogis' in Controlled States." *Journal of All-India Institute of Mental Health* 1:49–106 (1958).

Rorvik, David M., "Jack Schwarz Feels No Pain." *Esquire*, 209 (December 1972).

Sargent, J. D., Green, E. E., and Walters, E. D., "Preliminary Reports on the Use of Autogenic Feedback Training in the Treatment of Migraine and Tension Headaches." *Psychosomatic Medicine* (1972).

Schwartz, G. E., "TM Relaxes Some People and Makes Them Feel Better." *Psychology Today*, 7, 11 (April 1974).

Bibliography

————, "Biofeedback: Self-Regulation and the Patterning of Physiological Processes." *American Scientist* (May 1975).

Selye, Hans, "Stress." *Psychology Today*, 3, 4:24 (September 1969).

Shapiro, A. K., "The Placebo Effect in the History of Medical Treatment: Implications for Psychiatry." *American Journal of Psychiatry*, CXVI:298–304 (1959).

————, "A Contribution to the History of the Placebo Effect." *Behavioral Science*, 5:109–35 (1960).

Smith, Adam, "Alumni Notes—Altered States U." *Psychology Today* (July 1973).

————, "Trying the Dance of Shiva." *Sports Illustrated* (August 13, 1973).

Sperry, R. W., "Neurology and the Mind-brain Problem." *American Scientist*, 40:291–312 (1952).

————, "Cerebral Organization and Behavior." *Science*, 133:1749 (1961).

————, "The Great Cerebral Commissure." *Scientific American*, 210:42 (1964).

————, "A Modified View of Consciousness." *Psychological Review*, 76:532–36 (1969).

————, "Memory Impairment Following Commissurotomy in Man." *Brain*, 97:263–72 (1974).

Spinelli, D. N., Hirsch, H. V. B., Phelps, R. W., and Metzler, J., "Visual Experience as a Determinant of the Response Characteristics of Cortical Receptive Fields in Cats." *Experimental Brain Research*, 15:289–304 (1972).

Sternbach, R. A., "The Effects of Instructional Sets on Autonomic Responsivity." *Psychophysiology*, I:67–72 (1964).

Suedfeld, P., "The Benefits of Boredom." *American Scientist*, 63:60 (1975).

Targ, Russell, and Puthoff, Harold, "Information Transmission Under Conditions of Sensory Shielding." *Nature*, 252, 5476:602–07 (October 18, 1974).

Tart, Charles, "A Psychologist's Experience with Transcendental Meditation." *Journal of Transpersonal Psychology*, 2 (1971).

Todd, J. H., "The Chemical Language of Fishes." *Scientific American*, 224 (5):98–108 (1971).

Walker, Evan Harris, "The Compleat Quantum Mechanical Anthropologist." Rhine Swanton Symposium, 73rd Annual American Anthropological Association Meeting, Mexico City (November 19–24, 1974)

Wallace, Robert K., "Physiological Effects of Transcendental Meditation." *Science*, 167:1751–54 (1970).

————, and Benson, Herbert, "The Physiology of Meditation." *Scientific American*, 220:85–90 (1972).

————, Benson, Herbert, and Wilson, Archie F., "A Wakeful Hypometabolic State." *American Journal of Physiology*, 221:795–99 (1971).

Warth, Mary Jo., "The Story of the Acid Profiteers." *The Village Voice*, 5 (August 22, 1974).

BIBLIOGRAPHY

Watts, Alan W., "Beat Zen, Square Zen, and Zen." *Chicago Review,* 12, 2 (1958).

Weiss, T., and Engel, B. T., "Operant Conditioning of Heart Rate in Patients with Premature Ventricular Contractions." *Psychosomatic Medicine,* 33: 301–21 (1971).

Wenger, M. A., and Bagchi, B. K., "Studies of Autonomic Functions in Practitioners of Yoga in India." *Behavioral Science,* 6:312–23 (1961).

Whatmore, George B., and Kohli, Daniel P., "Dysponesis: A Neurophysiologic Factor in Functional Disorders." *Behavioral Science,* 13, 2 (March 1968).

Wheeler, J., "The Universe as Home for Man." *Smithsonian and National Academy of Science* (April 25, 1973).

Wienpahl, Paul, "Zen and the Work of Wittgenstein." *Chicago Review,* 12, 2 (1958).

Wiesel, T. N., and Hubel, D. H., "Comparison of the Effects of Unilateral and Bilateral Eye Closure on Cortical Unit Responses in Kittens." *Journal of Neurophysiology,* 28:1029–40 (1965).

BOOKS*

Adam, G., *Interoception and Behavior*. Budapest, Akadémiai Kiadó, 1967.

Aaronson, B., and Osmond, H., eds., *Psychedelics: The Uses and Implications of Hallucinogenic Drugs*. Cambridge, Schenkman, 1971.

Abramson, H., ed., *The Uses of LSD in Psychotherapy and Alcoholism*. Indianapolis, Bobbs-Merrill, 1966.

Allen, J. P. B., and van Buren, P., eds., *Chomsky: Selected Readings*. Oxford University Press, 1971.

Assagioli, Roberto, *Psychosynthesis*. New York, Viking Compass, 1971.

Bailly, J. A., *Rapport des Commissaires par le Roi de l'Examen du Magnetisme Animal*. Paris, Imprimie Royal, 1784.

Barber, T. X., *Hypnosis: A Scientific Approach*. New York, Van Nostrand, Reinhold, 1969.

―――, *LSD, Marihuana, Yoga and Hypnosis*. Chicago, Aldine, 1970,

――― et al., eds., *Biofeedback and Self-Control 1970*. Chicago, Aldine, 1971.

―――, Spanos, N. P., and Chaves, J. F., *Hypnotism, Imagination and Human Potentialities*. New York, Pergamon Press, 1974.

Barnett, Lincoln, *The Universe and Dr. Einstein*. New York, Morrow, 1957.

Beckett, Samuel, *Molloy*, New York, Grove Press, 1955.

―――, *Waiting for Godot*. New York, Grove Press, 1954.

―――, *Proust*. New York, Grove Press, n.d.

Bennett, J. G., *Gurdjieff: Making of a New World*. New York, Harper & Row, 1973.

* These volumes back up the note references. Sometimes only a single chapter is relevant. Many of the books are technical, and the technical books are overrepresented.

BIBLIOGRAPHY

Bergin, A. E., and Garfield, S. L., eds., *Handbook of Psychotherapy and Behavior Change: Empirical Analysis*. New York, Wiley, 1971.

Birk, L., *Seminars in Psychiatry*. New York, Grune & Stratton, 1973.

Bonica, John J., ed., *Pain*. New York, Raven Press, 1973.

Brain, W. Russell, *Mind, Perception, and Science*. Oxford, Blackwell, 1951.

Brecher, E. M., et al., eds., *Licit & Illicit Drugs*. Boston, Little, Brown, 1972.

Brown, Barbara, *New Mind, New Body*. New York, Harper & Row, 1974.

Brownfield, C. A. *Isolation: Clinical and Experimental Approaches*. New York, Random House, 1965.

Bruner, Jerome. *On Knowing: Essays for the Left Hand*. Harvard University Press, 1962.

Buber, Martin, *Tales of the Hasidim: Early Masters*. New York, Schocken Books, 1973. (paper)

————, *Tales of the Hasidim: Later Masters*. New York, Schocken Books, 1974. (paper)

Campbell, Joseph, *The Hero with a Thousand Faces*. Bollingen/Princeton, 1968.

————, *The Mythic Image*. Bollingen/Princeton, 1975.

Cannon, W. B., *The Wisdom of the Body*. New York, Norton, 1939.

Castaneda, Carlos, *The Teachings of Don Juan: A Yaqui Way of Knowledge*. University of California Press, 1968.

————, *A Separate Reality*. New York, Simon & Schuster, 1971.

————, *Journey to Ixtlan*. New York, Simon & Schuster, 1972.

————, *Tales of Power*. New York, Simon & Schuster, 1974.

Chomsky, Noam, *Syntactic Structures*. The Hague, Mouton, 1957.

————, *Language and Mind*. New York, Harcourt, Brace & World, 1968.

————, *Aspects of the Theory of Syntax*. Cambridge, MIT Press, 1969.

Cohen, S. A., *The Beyond Within*. New York, Atheneum, 1967.

Coleman, J. E., *The Quiet Mind*. London, Rider & Co., 1971.

Conant, James, *On Understanding Science*. New York, New American Library, 1951.

Coopersmith, Stanley, ed., *Frontiers of Psychological Research*. San Francisco, W. H. Freeman, 1966.

DeBold, R. C., and Leaf, R. C., eds., *LSD, Man and Society*. Wesleyan University Press, 1967.

de Hartmann, T., *Our Life with Mr. Gurdjieff*. New York, Penguin Books, 1972.

Bibliography

Delgado, José M. R., *Physical Control of the Mind*. New York, Harper & Row, 1969.

De Ropp, Robert S., *Drugs and the Mind*. New York, Grove Press–Evergreen, 1957.

————, *The Master Game*. New York, Dell/Delta, 1968.

————, *The Church of the Earth*. New York, Delacorte, 1974.

Dimond, Stuart J., *The Double Brain*. Edinburgh, Churchill Livingstone, 1972.

———— and Beaumont, J. Graham, *Hemisphere Function in the Human Brain*. New York, Wiley, 1974.

Dobzhansky, T., *Mankind Evolving: The Evolution of the Human Species*. Yale University Press, 1962.

Dubos, R., *So Human an Animal*. New York, Scribner's, 1968.

Dworkin, Barry, *An Effort to Replicate Visceral Learning in the Curarized Rat*. New York, Rockefeller University Press, 1973.

Eccles, J. C., ed., *Brain and Conscious Experience*. New York, Springer-Verlag, 1966.

————, *Facing Reality*. New York, Springer-Verlag, 1970.

Esslin, Martin, *The Theatre of the Absurd*. Garden City, N.Y., Anchor Books, 1969.

Fagan, Joen, and Shepherd, Irma L., *Gestalt Therapy Now*. Cupertino, Calif., Science & Behavior Books, 1970.

Feldenkrais, M., *Awareness Through Movement*. New York, Harper & Row, 1972.

————, *Body and Mature Behavior*. New York, International Universities Press, 1949, 1973.

Frank, J. D., *Persuasion and Healing: A Comparative Study of Psychotherapy*. Baltimore, Johns Hopkins Press, 1961.

Freedman, A. M., Kaplan, H. I., and Sadock, B. J., eds., *Comprehensive Textbook of Psychiatry*, 2nd. ed. Baltimore, Williams & Wilkins, 1974.

Freedman, Meyer, and Rosenman, Ray, *Type A Behavior and Your Heart*. New York, Knopf, 1974.

French, Reginald, *The Way of the Pilgrim*. New York, Seabury Press, 1968.

Gardner, M., ed., *Great Essays in Science*. New York, Washington Square Press, 1963.

Gazzaniga, M. S., *The Bisected Brain*. New York, Appleton-Century-Crofts, 1970.

Globus, G. G., Maxwell, G., and Savodnik, I., *Mind and Brain: Philosophical and Scientific Approaches to the "World Knot."* New York, Plenum Press, 1974.

BIBLIOGRAPHY

Goodman, Louis S., and Gilman, Alfred, *The Pharmacological Basis of Therapeutics*, 4th ed. New York, Macmillan, 1970.

Gurdjieff, G. I., *Meetings with Remarkable Men*. New York, Dutton, 1963. (paper, 1969)

Hartmann, Ernest L., *The Functions of Sleep*. Yale University Press, 1973.

Heisenberg, Werner, *Physics and Philosophy*. New York, Harper Torchbook, 1962.

————, *Physics and Beyond*. New York, Harper Torchbook, 1971.

————, *Across the Frontiers*. New York, Harper Torchbook, 1974.

Held, Richard L., and Richards, Whitman, *Perception: Mechanisms and Models*. San Francisco, W. H. Freeman, 1972.

Herrigel, Eugen, *Zen in the Art of Archery*. New York, Vintage, 1971.

Hess, Walter R., *The Functional Organization of the Diencephelon*. New York, Grune & Stratton, 1957.

Hirai, Tomio, *The Psychophysiology of Zen*. Tokyo, Igaku Shoin, 1974.

Hoffer, A., and Osmund, H., *The Hallucinogens*. New York, Academic Press, 1967.

Huber, Jack, *Through an Eastern Window*. Boston, Houghton Mifflin, 1967.

Hulme, Kathryn, *Undiscovered Country*. Boston, Atlantic, Little Brown, 1966. (paper)

Huxley, Aldous, *The Doors of Perception*. New York, Harper Colophon, 1963.

Jacobson, Edmund, *Progressive Relaxation*. University of Chicago Press, 1938.

James, W., *Varieties of Religious Experience*. New York, New American Library,

Jonas, Gerald, *Visceral Learning*. New York, Viking, 1973.

Jung, C. G., *Memories, Dreams, Reflections*, Aniela Jaffe, ed. New York, Vintage Books, 1961.

Kamiya, J., et al., eds., *Biofeedback and Self-Control: A Reader*. Chicago, Aldine, 1971.

Kapleau, Philip, *The Three Pillars of Zen*. Boston, Beacon, 1967.

Koestler, Arthur, *Act of Creation*. New York, Dell, 1966.

————, *The Roots of Coincidence*. New York, Random House, 1972.

Kiev, A., ed., *Magic, Faith and Healing*. New York, Free Press, 1964.

Krishna, Gopi, *The Biological Basis of Religion and Genius*. New York, Harper & Row, 1971.

Krishnamurti, J., *Commentaries on Living: Third Series*. London, Victor Gollancz, 1962.

Kuhn, Thomas, *The Structure of Scientific Revolutions*. Phoenix Books, University of Chicago Press, 1967.

Bibliography

Laing, R. D., *The Politics of Experience*. New York, Ballantine, 1967.

Lefort, Rafael (pseud.), *The Teachers of Gurdjieff*. New York, Weiser, 1973.

Lehninger, A. L., *Biochemistry: The Molecular Basis of Cell Structure and Function*. New York, Worth, 1970.

Lewin, L., *Phantastica, Narcotic and Stimulating Drugs*. London, Routledge & Kegan Paul, 1931.

Lilly, John, *The Center of the Cyclone*. New York, Julian Press, 1972.

———, *Programming and Metaprogramming in the Human Biocomputer*, rev. New York, Julian Press, 1972.

Lindzey, G., Hall, C., and Thompson, R. F., *Psychology*. New York, Worth. 1975.

Luria, S. E., *Life . . . the Unfinished Experiment*. New York, Scribner's, 1973.

Luthe, W., ed., *Autogenic Therapy*, Vols. 1–5. New York, Grune & Stratton, 1967.

McGuigan, F. J., and Schoonover, R. A., eds., *The Psychophysiology of Thinking: Studies of Covert Processes*. New York, Academic Press, 1973.

Madow, Leo, and Snow, Laurence, *The Psychodynamic Implications of Physiological Studies on Sensory Deprivation*, Springfield, C. C. Thomas, 1970.

Maslow, Abraham, *Religions, Values, and Peak Experiences*. New York, Viking, 1970.

———, *The Farther Reaches of Human Nature*. New York, Viking, 1971.

Masters, John, *Bugles and a Tiger*. New York, Ballantine, 1969.

Masters, R. E., and Houston, Jean, *The Varieties of Psychedelic Experience*. New York, Dell/Delta, 1966.

Mehra, Jagdish, ed., *The Physicist's Conception of Nature*. Boston, D. Reidel, 1973.

Merton, Thomas, *Mystics and Zen Masters*. New York, Dell/Delta, 1967.

———, *Zen and the Birds of Appetite*. New York, New Directions, 1968.

Metzner, Ralph, ed., *The Ecstatic Adventure*. New York, Macmillan, 1968.

Miller, N. E., *Selected Papers*. Chicago, Aldine, 1971.

——— and Dworkin, B., *Biofeedback: Areas of Research and Application*. New York, Academic Press (in press).

——— et al., eds., *Biofeedback and Self Control, 1973*. Chicago, Aldine, 1974.

Milner, P. M., *Physiological Psychology*. New York, Holt, Rinehart & Winston, 1970.

Moss, Thelma, *The Probability of the Impossible*. New York, Hawthorn Books, 1975.

Mostofsky, D., ed., *Behavior Control and Modification of Physiological Activity*. New York, Appleton-Century-Crofts (in press).

BIBLIOGRAPHY

Mountcastle, V. B., ed., *Interhemispheric Relations and Cerebral Dominance.* Baltimore, Johns Hopkins Press, 1962.

Murphy, Gardner, and Murphy, Lois, eds., *Asian Psychology.* New York, Basic Books, 1968.

Murphy, Michael, *Golf in the Kingdom.* New York, Viking, 1972.

Naranjo, Claudio, and Ornstein, Robert, *On the Psychology of Meditation.* New York, Viking/Esalen, 1971.

Noone, Richard, *The Rape of the Dream People.* London, Hutchinson, 1972.

Obrist, P. A., et al., eds., *Cardiovascular Psychophysiology.* Chicago, Aldine, 1974.

Oppenheimer, J. Robert, *Science and the Common Understanding.* New York, Simon & Schuster, 1964.

Ornstein, Robert E., *On the Experience of Time.* Baltimore, Penguin, 1969.

———, *The Psychology of Consciousness.* San Francisco, W. H. Freeman, 1972.

———, ed., *The Nature of Human Consciousness.* San Francisco, W. H. Freeman, 1973.

Ouspensky, P. D., *In Search of the Miraculous.* New York, Harcourt, Brace, 1949.

Penfield, W., *The Excitable Cortex in Conscious Man.* Springfield, C. C. Thomas, 1958.

——— and Erickson, T. C., eds., *Epilepsy and Cerebral Localization.* Springfield, C. C. Thomas, 1941.

——— and Roberts, L., *Speech and Brain Mechanisms.* Princeton University Press, 1959.

Peters, Fritz, *Boyhood with Gurdjieff.* Baltimore, Penguin Books, 1972.

Pines, Maya, *The Brain Changers.* New York, Harcourt Brace, 1973.

Pribram, K. H., ed., *Mood, States and Mind.* Baltimore, Penguin, 1969.

———, *Languages of the Brain: Experimental Paradoxes and Principles in Neuropsychology.* Englewood Cliffs, N.J., Prentice-Hall, 1971.

Progoff, Ira, *The Cloud of Unknowing.* New York, Julian Press, 1969.

Rahula, Walpola, *What the Buddha Taught.* New York, Evergreen-Grove, 1974.

Ram Dass, *Be Here Now.* New Mexico, Lama Foundation, 1971.

———, *The Only Dance There Is.* New York, Doubleday/Anchor, 1974.

Reed, Graham, *The Psychology of Anomalous Experience.* New York, Houghton Mifflin Sentry Books, 1972.

Reps, Paul, ed., *Zen Flesh, Zen Bones.* New York, Doubleday/Anchor, n.d.

Rose, J., ed., *Progress of Cybernetics: Proceedings of the International Congress of the Cybernetics, London, 1969.* London, Gordon & Breach, 1970.

Bibliography

Rose, Steven, *The Conscious Brain*. New York, Knopf, 1973.

Roszak, T., *The Making of a Counter Culture*. New York, Doubleday, 1969.

————, *Where the Wasteland Ends: Politics and Transcendence in Post-Industrial Society*. New York, Doubleday, 1972.

Salinger, J. D., *Franny and Zooey*. New York, Bantam Books, 1972.

Satchidananda, Swami, *Integral Yoga—Hatha*. New York, Holt, Rinehart & Winston, 1970.

Schmitt, F. O., and Worden, F. G., eds., *The Neurosciences: Third Study Program*. Cambridge, MIT Press, 1973.

Scholem, Gershom, *Jewish Mysticism*, 7th ed. New York, Schocken Books, 1973.

Selye, Hans, *The Stress of Life*. New York, McGraw-Hill Paperback, 1956.

Shah, Idries, *The Pleasantries of the Incredible Mulla Nasrudin*. New York, Dutton Paperback, 1971.

————, *Wisdom of the Idiots*. New York, Dutton Paperback, 1971.

————, *The Dermis Probe*. New York, Dutton Paperback, 1971.

————, *The Sufis*. New York, Anchor Edition, 1971.

————, *Caravan of Dreams*. Baltimore, Penguin, 1974.

Shapiro, D. et al., eds., *Biofeedback and Self-Control, 1972*. Chicago, Aldine, 1973.

Sherrington, Charles, *Man on His Nature*. Cambridge University Press, 1940.

Smith, Grover, ed., *The Letters of Aldous Huxley*. New York, Harper & Row, 1969.

Smith, W. L., ed., *Drugs, Development and Cerebral Function*, Ch. 1. Springfield, C. C. Thomas, 1971.

———— and Kinsbourne, M., eds., *Hemisphere Disconnection and Cerebral Function*. Springfield, C. C. Thomas, 1972.

Solomon, Philip, et al., eds., *Sensory Deprivation: A Symposium Held at Harvard Medical School*. Harvard University Press, 1961.

Spielberger, C. D., ed., *Anxiety: Current Trends in Theory and Research*. New York, Academic Press, 1972.

Stephen, *Monday Night Class*. Seattle, The Book Publishing Company, n.d.

Sternbach, Richard A., *Principles of Psychophysiology*. New York, Academic Press, 1966.

Stewart, Kilton, *Pygmies and Dream Giants*. New York, Norton, 1954.

Stoyva, J., et al., eds., *Biofeedback and Self-Control, 1971*. Chicago, Aldine, 1972.

Tart, C., ed., *Altered States of Consciousness: A Book of Readings*. New York, Wiley, 1969.

Teeven, R. C. et al., *Readings for Introductory Psychology*, New York, Harcourt Brace, 1972.

Teyler, T. J., ed., *Altered States of Awareness: Readings from Scientific American*. San Francisco, W. H. Freeman, 1972.

Thomas, Lewis, *The Lives of a Cell*. New York, Viking, 1974.

Thompson, Richard F., *Physiological Psychology*. San Francisco, W. H. Freeman, 1972.

———, *Introduction to Physiological Psychology*. New York, Harper & Row, 1975.

Tinbergen, N., *The Study of Instinct*. Folcroft, Pa., Folcroft, 1951.

Torrey, E. Fuller, *The Mind Game*. New York, Bantam, 1973.

———, *The Death of Psychiatry*. Radnor, Pa., Chilton, 1974.

Trimingham, J. Spencer, *The Sufi Orders in Islam*. Oxford University Press, 1971.

Trungpa, Chogyam, *Cutting Through Spiritual Materialism*. Berkeley, Calif., Shambala Publications, 1973.

———, *Meditation in Action*. Berkeley, Calif., Shambala Publications, 1969.

———, *Born in Tibet*. New York, Harcourt Brace, 1968.

Updike, John, *Telephone Poles and Other Poems*. New York, 1963.

Von Bonin, G., *Some Papers on the Cerebral Cortex*. Springfield, C. C. Thomas, 1960.

Weil, Andrew, *The Natural Mind*. Boston, Houghton Mifflin, 1972.

White, Rhea A., and Dale, Lewis A., *Parapsychology: Sources of Information*. Scarecrow Press, The American Society for Psychical Research, Metuchen, N.J., 1973.

Widroe, Harvey, ed., *Human Behavior and Brain Function*. Springfield, C. C. Thomas, 1973.

Wigner, Eugene, *Symmetries and Reflections: Scientific Essays*. Cambridge, MIT Press, 1970.

Wilhelm, Richard, trans. C. F. Baynes, trans. *The I Ching or Book of Changes*, Princeton/Bollingen, 1967.

Wolstenholme, G. E. W., and Knight, Julie, eds., *The Pineal Gland*. Edinburgh, London, Churchill Livingstone, 1971.

Yates, Frances, *Giordano Bruno: The Hermetic Tradition*. New York, Vintage, 1969.

Zaehner, R. C., *Zen, Drugs and Mysticism*. New York, Vintage, 1972.

Zubeck, J. P., *Sensory Deprivation: Fifteen Years of Research*. New York, Appleton-Century-Crofts, 1969.

No author or editor: *Psychology Today* (textbook). Del Mar, Calif.: CRM Books, 1970.